GRAPHIC DESIGN HISTORY

Edited by
Steven Heller and Georgette Ballance

ALLWORTH PRESS
NEW YORK

05 04 03 02 01   5 4 3 2 1

Published by Allworth Press
An imprint of Allworth Communications
10 East 23rd Street, New York, NY 10010

Cover and book design by James Victore, New York, NY

Page composition by Sharp Des!gns, Lansing, MI

LIBRARY OF CONGRESS CATALOGING-IN-PUBLICATION DATA
Graphic design history / edited by Steven Heller and Georgette Balance.
p. cm.
Includes bibliographical references and index.
ISBN 1-58115-094-6
1. Commercial art—20th century—History. 2. Commercial artists—Biography.
I. Heller, Steven. II. Balance, Georgette.
NV998.4 .G667 2001
741.6'09'04—dc21
2001022588

Printed in Canada

Acknowledgments

The editors want to thank all the writers who allowed their essays to be republished in this anthology. Without their devotion to graphic design, and particularly its history, there would not be a chronicle. And thanks also to the publications from which we excerpted these essays, *PRINT, Graphis,* and *EYE* (as well as those publications that also publish essays on history that are not represented here, *CA, Design Issues, Baseline, Critique,* and *Step-By-Step*): without their collective support this field would be bereft of substantive historical data.

We further express deep gratitude to Philip B. Meggs, who launched the current graphic design history "movement" in the early 1980s with an NEA-funded series of lectures that brought design history to students and teachers. This series served as the basis for the first edition of his landmark book, *A History of Graphic Design* (now in its third edition). Without Meggs's contributions, we would have a much scantier history, and a much thinner book.

Thanks also to R. Roger Remington for initiating the first design history symposium at Rochester Institute of Technology, to Silas Rhodes and David Rhodes for supporting The School of Visual Arts "Modernism & Eclecticism: A History of Graphic Design" symposia for nine years, and to Ric Grefe for encouraging the AIGA's "Looking Closer" symposium, exploring criticism and history of graphic design.

Thanks to our collaborators at Allworth Press: Nicole Potter, editor; Jamie Kijowski, associate editor; Bob Porter, associate publisher; and, of course, Tad Crawford, publisher.

SH & GB

Table of Contents

3: Designed Lives

vii

Introduction

THE BEGINNING OF HISTORY
Steven Heller

Who are Massin, Merle Armitage, Georg Olden, and T. M. Cleland? What are *Fact, The Bald Soprano*, the NKF Catalog, and *For the Voice*? If these questions were asked on an exam, would you be stumped? If you were, would you know where to locate the answers? Do you understand that these answers relate to the history of your profession? Do you realize that graphic design even has a history?

Lest ignorance overshadow talent, graphic designers should be literate in graphic design history. Being able to design well is not always enough. Knowing the roots of design is necessary to avoid reinvention, no less inadvertent plagiarism. Although not all professionals are required to study the histories of their respective fields, many fields—and graphic design is certainly one of them—are built firmly upon historical foundations. Although graphic design history is routinely inserted as an afterthought or footnote in some histories of art and culture, it is a significant component of mass communication, from producing advertising to defining zeitgeist.

Granted, the word "history" sounds a bit musty, and designers, particularly young ones, are more interested in creating for the moment than learning about the past. Yet studying history should not be a chore.

When history is recorded with verve and presented with passion, it enlightens and nourishes. What is history if not a collection of narratives that comprise a legacy? What is a legacy if not a foundation on which to build and transform? Given the legacy of graphic design, it is clear that the intersection of applied and fine arts has enriched this field as well as the broader culture.

A compelling case has been made through recent conferences, magazine articles, and books, for the centrality of graphic design history in the education of all graphic designers. During this formative period in the digital age, when new media is altering traditional notions of graphic design practice, it is even more important that designers have the grounding provided by historical knowledge. Arguably, design history courses should continue throughout the undergraduate and graduate years, just like typography and computer skills, but this is often thwarted by small budgets and other priorities.

Philip B. Meggs and Richard Hollis each authored general history books—*A History of Graphic Design* and *Graphic Design: A Concise History*, respectively—which provide basic narratives that chart a continuum. Mildred Friedman's 1989 *Graphic Design in America: A Visual Language History* and Ellen Lupton's 1998 *Mixing Messages* offer supplementary commentaries on specific historical themes. Yet a well-rounded graphic design history program must consistently provide more in-depth analysis of an ever increasing subject range. Although it is useful to master the historical chronology, including where and when movements, schools, and styles, as well as pioneers, are found in time, this is but the armature around which more detailed research is presented. Graphic design history cannot be taught without the basic textbooks (and the pictures reproduced therein), but unexplored (and sometimes arcane) areas must be frequently introduced in order to enliven history.

History is only as engaging as the talents and skills of those who record it. The most potentially engrossing stories can be as dull as actuarial tables if historians rely on jargon. While jargon is a common shorthand for communicating to like-minded people, it can be stultifying and stupefying for the uninitiated. For graphic design history to be exhilarating—and particularly for students who would rather make design than read about others who preceded them—it must be presented in ways that underscore design's cultural resonance. A poster must not simply be a lesson in formal or theoretical practice, although this is indeed important, but rather a component of a larger context wherein it functions. A typeface should not be viewed only as an instrument for conveying words and sentences, but as representative of the particular period when it was created and the aesthetics of those who created it. A school like the Bauhaus, a movement like Constructivism, and a style like Psychedelia cannot be isolated from the societies (as well as the political milieus) in which they were founded. History must show that graphic design is not the product of a hermetically sealed environment.

Yet graphic design history does have its own heroes and villains, icons and eyesores, apart from other arts. While design historians must use cultural and political histories as backdrops, ultimately the stories they tell must be rooted in issues of design. The challenge is, therefore, to find pegs on which to hang design history so that it is relevant beyond the design ghetto. Many of the stories in this book are relevant outside of conventional graphic design areas of interest; in fact, some stories are possibly more significant outside the design universe. For example, the histories of *Avant Garde* and *Fact* (page 31), two smartly art-directed and editorially sophisticated political/cultural magazines that challenged current mores and taboos in ways that placed the publisher in jeopardy. The story is as much about these assaults on convention as it is about typography. Of course, other publishing stories, such as the origin of *Émigré* magazine (page 65), the evolution of *Fortune* (page 27) and the art direction of *Esquire* (page 51) are more about design, but can also be mined for insights into fashions, trends, and mores that affect the lives of everyone. Another example of cross-cultural interest is the story about Georg Olden (page 115), the first African-American graphic designer to work on the national stage as an art director for CBS television. It could have been written merely as a professional profile focusing on his best work, but as history it is more important to understand how Olden functioned within an all-white media corporation and the effects of racial prejudices on his career. While one can be color-blind with an analysis of his work, Olden's professional and creative lives are more compelling when seen through a sociocultural lens.

Preferences and prejudices determine how an historian presents a story. Some writers are solely interested in the facts of a professional life or commercial fashion or aesthetic movement. Some weave all kinds of details into a more inclusive, interconnected fabric. Other historians interpret the facts through an ideological filter—feminism, Marxism, consumerism, anticonsumerism, or are connoisseurs of certain objects in a fetishistic way. Others focus on the means and results of production as a way of exploring larger issues of design and its impact on society. And still others combine scholarship and journalism into an engaging hybrid. As an example, Georg Olden's life gave Julie Lasky an opportunity to investigate how one man had the strength to overcome racial prejudice, but at the same time become a victim of other forces that ruined his career. Lasky's research began as a journalistic pursuit that resulted in a historical document. But not every designer's biography is this dramatic. The profiles of Massin (page 167), Fortunato Depero (page 153), and Lester Beall (page 75) are more conventionally focused on their professional accomplishments, yet are no less important to design history. At this stage in the development of design history, all discoveries and approaches are requisite building blocks.

The essays in this book follow a variety of methodologies, yet each provides insight into the work or works while establishing relative significance in the world of design and cultural environment.

Graphic Design History is the first "reader" of the "graphic design history movement." Herein are various selected contributions to the collective literature, originally published in a variety of design periodicals, among them *PRINT, Communication Arts, EYE, Upper and Lower Case, Critique, Graphis,* and *Design Issues.* Yet the essays selected for inclusion suggest the catch-as-catch-can nature of graphic design history practice. There is no single wellspring, and despite invoking the term "movement," there is no central organization that encourages historical research.

As editors who also teach design history courses, we believe there is a need to create a bank of writing that has surfaced over the past decade or two. This book is an initial stab at making existing essays accessible. We have organized the material into the areas that are most frequently addressed, at least in magazines and journals. The overarching themes are theory and practice. The majority of the essays herein, however, deal with practice. We begin with essays that scrutinize how history is researched, taught, and written in "Legacy Considered." Then we segue to specific topics, including the history of magazines and periodicals, in "Between Covers," critical and professional profiles of practitioners in "Designed Lives," avant-gardes and their offshoots in "Avant-Gardes," and commercial cultures in "Mass Communications." We end the book with an epilogue, diverging from our essay format with an original interview with Louis Danziger, the founder, as it were, of the "movement," and the most influential teacher of graphic design history in the United States. In addition to his overview of the subject, we end with his own syllabus.

Over the past decade there has been more research, shedding increased light on graphic design. And as the literature grows, so does literacy. Nonetheless, despite the core history textbooks mentioned above, as well as a handful of supplementary books, graphic design history is currently in the formative developmental stage. New research must be encouraged, outlets must grow, funding must be available, and courses must be endemic to all design programs. Most importantly, young writers should be motivated to raise graphic design history from a parochial recounting to an invigorating drama that informs and inspires us all.

GRAPHIC DESIGN HISTORY

1. Legacy Considered

AMERICAN GRAPHIC DESIGN EXPRESSION:
THE EVOLUTION OF AMERICAN TYPOGRAPHY
Katherine McCoy

The debate continues—is graphic design an art, science, business, craft, or language? Graphic design in the United States has operated under multiple identities since its inception, with each of these identities dominant at one moment or another. And each may predominate from one project to the next in a designer's practice today. Often, graphic design is defined as a duality, combining two of these definitions, such as craft/language or business/art. This identity crisis is confirmed by the lack of agreement on a name for the field. Graphic design, visual communications, and visual design are all thoughtful names in current use. A variety of archaic terms persist, including commercial art, layout, and graphics design.

Unlike its venerable cousin, architecture, graphic design is a very new design expression, a phenomena of the last hundred years. A spontaneous response to the communication needs of the industrial revolution, graphic design was invented to sell the fruits of mass production to growing consumer societies in Europe and North America in the late nineteenth and early twentieth centuries. Rapidly expanding reproduction technologies provided the means for graphic design's participation in the vast economic, political, technological, and social changes of that era.

American graphic design's roots lie in European type-cutting and book-printing. This precursor to the profession was imported to early America as part of our European cultural inheritance. For literally centuries, from the invention of moveable type in the early Renaissance to the twentieth century, bookmaking, typesetting, and type design were an integrated craft and industry centered in publishing houses. This long tradition approached typography and book design as the visual presentation of verbal language, with a premium placed on clarity and legibility. Decisions in type design emphasized clarity rather than expression, relying on the words themselves for the expression of content. Typography was neutral to the message and made no attempt to be interpretive. Craft was highly valued and books developed increasing elegance and refinement as the years progressed, codifying this classical book approach into the standardized traditional text format that continues as the standard of book text today.

However artful the book design, the element of function relegated this activity to craft status rather than fine art. The predominance of text made this tradition largely a verbal language expression. Illustrational imagery was used sparingly in early books due to technical difficulty. When used, it represented literal phenomena and rarely mixed with the text or headline typography. Interpretive symbolic imagery was left to painting, or "high art." Through the centuries, painters have employed whole vocabularies of visual nonverbal symbols to convey meaning to their audiences, who were able to decode meaning through learned associations, the result of shared cultural experience.

It was not until the early twentieth century that meaning was embedded in visual typographic form. The early modern revolutionary artists of Futurism, Dada, Constructivism, and De Stijl turned their attention to text and visual communications as well as the more traditional areas of fine art, rejecting the traditional divisions between the fine arts, applied arts, and crafts. Functional expression was embraced as well as the "purer" self-expressive goals of high art—function was not viewed as the enemy of art. In particular, the Russian Constructivists retained their artists' identities even as they took on the role of public communicators in the Russian Revolution. The Bauhaus unified art, craft, and design in a coherent philosophy and sense of identity. Several early Modernists went on to execute some of the first serious "professional" graphic design, applying their early experiments to the pragmatic communications needs of manufacturing clients.

These revolutionaries explored new approaches to structuring language and imagery that were radical rejections of the classical text tradition. Their highly visual poetry used typographic forms and composition to interpret and extend the words' meaning. One does not have to read Italian to gain an appreciation of the Futurists' energetic celebrations of industry and political confrontation. Typography finally became an expressive visual language as well as a verbal one.

This visual/verbal dichotomy can be understood through a simple diagram that charts the process (in the Western humanist tradition) of the acquisition of meaning. Seeing and reading are two modes through which we traditionally think of receiving messages. Image and text are two carriers of those messages. Typically, we think of seeing as a visual process connected with images—we see the landscape, we see a painting. This process is intuitive, emotional, and simultaneous, experienced almost involuntarily. Upon encountering a vivid color photograph of a fire, a viewer might immediately sense fear and heat with little need to conceptualize. Or an image of a nude figure might stimulate sexual feelings instantly and involuntarily. Although associations gained through life experience influence this process, it is predominantly a direct experiential one, related to the philosophical theories of phenomenology.

On the other hand, the process of reading is typically connected with the verbal process of decoding text's written language signs—letters. To do this, one must know the code. One must have learned to read the particular language of the message. This process is cerebral, rational, deliberate, and linear. If one does not carefully link the proper sequence of signs, one cannot decode the message. Linguistics, structuralist philosophy, and post-Structuralism deal with these language dynamics.

In addition, there are two other linkages possible between seeing and reading and image and text. The early Modernists discovered that text can be seen as well as read, as the Futurists' experimental poetry proved. And images can be read. Neolithic cave painters at Lascaux knew this, as well as most painters until many Modernists rejected imagery in favor of abstraction. This process was reconfirmed by the Surrealists, by the emerging graphic designers of the 1930s and 1940s, by the New York school of advertising, and again by recent post-modern artists and photographers dealing with text/image relationships.

How an artist, designer, or craftsman defines oneself has much to do with one's use of these text/image processes. Nineteenth-century book designers/printers dealt largely with the reading of text, and aligned themselves with the literary field of language. Many early Modernists dealt with all four modes and saw themselves as integrated creators of communications balancing the identities of artist, designer, businessman, and craftsman.

American book designers/printers continued the European classical noninterpretive traditions with extremely literal presentations of both imagery and text. But with a public that was increasingly literate, the printer's activities broadened to include early manifestations of the mass media: political and commercial handbills in the late eighteenth century, and newspaper advertising, popular magazines, advertising cards, and posters in the late nineteenth century. These required headline-scaled typefaces. By the Victorian years, a great multiplicity of ornamental faces had been born and American wood type was developed as an inexpensive and accessible means of embellishment for popular communications. This much more decorative expression spoke with a louder voice than the subtlety of traditional books, making the reader's experience far more visual. Yet this larger scale of typography contained no coding in its visual form; the process remained one of reading text.

The late nineteenth century's early advertising, magazines, and posters stimulated a new and growing field of illustration. These illustrators rendered highly artful literal depictions of objects, scenes, and narratives with growing skill and rapidly evolving reproduction processes. But they employed little symbolism. And because they served the tainted world of commerce rather than practicing "serious" art, these first "commercial" artists were relegated to a class of servant, despite the large public following of many.

American graphic design was finally born out of two new factors. As the twentieth century got underway, an explosion of new reproduction technologies stimulated specialization, separating conception and form-giving from the technical production activities of typesetting and printing. Simultaneously the United States received its first European modernist émigrés, the migration reaching its height in the 1930s. These men understood design as a balanced process involving the powerful multiple modes of seeing and reading, and sensed the possibility of theory and method as guiding the creative process—the first rudimentary seeds of professionalism. These designers, including Bayer, Sutnar, Burtin, Moholy-Nagy, and Matter, brought with them Modernism's dual paths of ambiguity and objectivity. They shared an interest in ambiguity and the unconscious with new work in fine art, literature, and psychology. Interpretive typography and asymmetrical compositions seemed more appropriate in a new world where tradition was rapidly disappearing. Surrealism offered symbolic forms of conceptual communication that went beyond the power of the word.

On the other hand, these European designers believed that rationalism and objectivity were appropriate for a new world ordered by commerce and industry. They continued early Modernism's interest in abstraction and dynamic compositions. For the first time in the United States, they persuaded their clients to minimize copy into brief essential statements, rather than the text-heavy literal description favored in early American advertising.

Rudimentary ideas of systematic problem solving and design compositions were offered by Ladislav Sutnar and Andrew Kner. The role of designer was defined as a highly skilled interpreter of messages, a far more authoritative stance than the hired hand following the dictates of an autocratic client. Interpretation was central to the idea of communication. Systematic rationalism drew on science, while inventive compositions and symbolic interpretation related to art, balancing this identity between art, science, craft, and business.

These émigrés had a tremendous impact on a number of young American designers, such as Paul Rand and Bradbury Thompson. As they grew and matured in the 1950s, these men developed new approaches to composition, photography, and text/image relationships. Many of their discoveries formed the basis of the "big idea" method of conceptualizing design solutions which placed a premium on the flash of intuition and the individual designer's creativity—the Ah ha! method of problem solving. Centered in New York of the fifties and sixties, this individualistic process idealized the creative genius, symbolized by the maverick designer in his garret studio. (Ralph Caplan has critiqued designers for their willingness to play this role—what he calls the "exotic menial," the brilliant individual serving the needs of clients, but a servant nonetheless.)

The intuitive conceptual "big idea" method became a uniquely American visual communications expression, and was closely associated with the New York School of advertising of the 1950s and 1960s. Exemplified by Doyle Dane Bernbach's classic Volkswagen Beetle series, this advertising created intelligent and clever interplays between verbal and visual concepts. Short ironic conversational headlines were juxtaposed with provocative images, drawing on the lessons of Surrealism, and particularly Magritte. Unexpected combinations of images and/or contexts created ambiguity and surprise. This "picture is worth a thousand words" approach maximized the process of reading. Both text and image were to be decoded and read by the viewer, relying on semantic meaning with little interest in page structure or systematic organization. Unfortunately, many designers today associate this powerful approach with advertising's commercialism and fail to take advantage on the power of the conceptual image/copy concept method.

As this highly successful form of advertising began to dominate American visual communications, the first wave of Swiss design thinking and forms arrived on the American scene. First transmitted in the early 1960s through a few design magazines and books—Graphis and the "bibles" by Müller-Brockmann, Karl Gerstner, Armin Hofmann, and Emil Ruder—a few young American designers began to assimilate these ideas. Rudy DeHarak, the most notable of the American designers hungry for some structure, adopted the Swiss method on his own after seeing these influential examples in the design media. Then in the mid-1960s, several professional design offices began to practice these ideas to solve the needs of large corporate clients in Holland, England, Canada, and the United States. A number of corporations and institutions, including Container Corporation, Ciba-Geigy, Herman Miller, IBM, and Massachusetts Institute of Technology, adopted this method and aesthetic. Eventually U.S. corporate culture adopted "Swiss" graphic design as the ideal corporate style. What was originally very difficult to sell to business clients is very difficult to avoid today.

This graphic aesthetic and method was the second wave of European Modernism to influence the United States. Essentially different from the "big idea" approach, it is based on an assumption of modernist rational "method," a codified approach not so dependent on the individualistic inspiration and talent of the designer. This had a profoundly professionalizing influence in American graphic design, further replacing the commercial artist's servant image with one of a disciplined, educated professional. As this method influenced the field, graphic design began to split apart from advertising design, a major division that remains today.

This classic "Swiss" method prescribed an ordered process rather than the genius of inspiration, and promised far more dependable, however predictable, results. It assumed a rational systems process based on semiscientific analysis and problem solving. The ideal was the objective (dead serious) presentation of information, rather than the subjective expression of an attitude, emotion, or humor. "Swiss" was found to be more suitable for the corporation's demand for factual accuracy—the perfect style for an annual report—while the "big idea" was more suitable for advertising's persuasive goals. "Swiss" tended to rely on representational photography and minimalist typography, while the "big idea" was far more image-oriented, employing illustration and symbolic photography. "Swiss" graphic expression stressed the syntactic grammar of graphic design with structured grids and typographic relationships. This form of Modernism neglected some of early Modernism's discoveries with visually expressive typography and surrealistic imagery. For the most part, classic "Swiss" typography was meant to be read, and its imagery to be seen, only in the conventional modes.

Semiotics, the science of signs in visual language, was a theory explored in the late 1960s in Europe, especially at the Ulm school in Germany. This scientific approach to the analysis of meaning in communications was very compatible with the rationality of the "Swiss" method. Promising an alternative to intuitive design, semiotic theory began to inform some of the "Swiss" adherents in the United States. Although this difficult and complex theory was little understood, the "scientific" flavor reinforced that "objective" tone of "Swiss" design, and reinforced the idea that graphic design was more than a personal art form. Semiotics became the first codified theory of graphic design, a major step in the evolution to professionalism. As Massimo Vignelli has so often reminded us, theory as well as history and criticism are the essential trinity that distinguish a profession from a craft or trade.

The "big idea" originated in New York, an American synthesis. The visual symbolism owes some debts to Surrealism, but the copy concept verbal approach came from American wit and casual vernacular speech. Although "Swiss" found its first big growth in Chicago's heartland, introduced by Container Corporation and Unimark International, it is an essentially northern European, or Germanic, sensibility, expression, and paradigm. Its importation to Chicago repeated the route followed by many of the Bauhaus émigrés of the late 1930s—Mies, Bayer, and Moholy-Nagy.

This first wave of "Swiss" was strongly identified with the Swiss designers of Zurich—Müller-Brockmann and Gertsner—applying Bauhaus early modernist ideals. Their strict minimalist codified expression of functional messages could be described as Classic Modernism. No sooner than the Zurich Swiss became established in the United States, a second, more mannered form of "Swiss" developed that could be called Late Modernism.

Work from the Kunstgewerbeschule in Basel was far more experimental and complex, adding many "nonfunctional" design forms. Coming from a school where students and faculty had the luxury of time and experimentation, many rules were broken and the time was taken to develop the sensibility to a high level of aesthetic refinement and complexity. The irreverent Wolfgang Weingart rebelled against the Minimalism of his predecessor, Emil Ruder, in the late 1960s and initiated a body of work with his students that pushed early Modernism's constructivist experiments to their logical extremes. Enlarging on the earlier "Swiss" issues of structure and composition, he explored increasingly complex grids and typography in experimental compositions that became quite painterly. Yet the typographic play was mainly about the grammar of typography, and neglected semantic expression. This highly formal work was not very conceptual and has been criticized as merely decorative in the final analysis. Depending on one's critique, this movement could be labeled Baroque, Mannerist, or even decadent Modernism.

The Basel school's faculty and graduates began to come to the United States in the mid-1960s, with a real impact realized in the early 1970s when young American graphic designers "in the know" began to migrate to Basel for postgraduate training in graphic design. By the mid-1970s some of this complexity began to embellish basic American "Swiss" graphic design in the form of bars and rules and playful mixing of type sizes, weights, and faces in an essentially formalist agenda.

As classical "Swiss" discipline was gaining followers and even before Basel became an influence, Robert Venturi shook the U.S. cultural scene with his 1965 polemical treatise, *Complexity and Contradiction in Architecture*. Although most graphic designers remained unaware of his premises for many years—and many may not yet realize his profound influence—his challenges to modernist dogma sent shock waves rippling throughout the architecture and design world, stimulating new work that came to be called "post-Modern." His arguments in favor of historical pre-Modern architectural forms and crudely energetic commercial American vernaculars eventually contributed to a new phase of American graphic design.

The emergence of graphic design history in the 1970s dovetailed with Venturi's rediscovery of pre-Modern design. It was a definite sign of maturation when graphic design discovered that it had a history. Until then, graphic designers felt they were still inventing the discipline. The field seemed completely new, with no history, a premise supported by the Bauhaus modern ideal of constant newness. The first books and conference on design history provided a banquet of historical forms for designers. The results ranged from historical homage, appropriation, and quotation to eclecticism, imitation, and outright cannibalism.

But Pushpin Studios of the 1960s, a stream paralleling American "Swiss," already knew about the pleasures of history. This New York studio's popular eclectic celebrations revived, exploited, imitated, and occasionally parodied decades of design styles, but with an essential difference of intention from this new, more academic, "post-Modern" sensibility. Pushpin pursued a hedonistic "if it feels good, do it" free borrowing from history's nostalgia, essentially the same intention as the Victorian American eclecticism they so often imitated. post-Modernism's historicism was a more intellectualized, self-conscious critique on the meaning of history. Venturi, a professor as well as an architect, applied a semiotic analysis to historical and vernacular style, interpreting form as language invested with cultural meaning. Buildings were signs meant to be read by their audiences.

Popular-culture vernaculars, history, and the Basel school's mannerist Modernism came together in the mid-1970s to create a new, highly formal expression most often called "post-Modernism" or "New Wave" graphic design. Bored with the rigidity and minimalism of corporate American "Swiss," American designers, particularly certain educators associated with several of the better schools of graphic design, began to experiment. Working from a modernist "Swiss" foundation, they began to dissect, multiply, or ignore the grid and to explore new spatial compositions, introducing complexity and pattern, and frankly nonfunctional design elements. Hand-drawn gestures and vernacular bad taste were artfully introduced in highly aestheticized layered compositions. This phase could easily be labeled a baroque or decadent American Modernism rather than post-Modernism. The expression was still strongly linked with Modernism's interest in syntax and structural expressionism, although by now it had become personal hedonistic formal celebrations rather than impersonal disciplined presentations of functional information. The typography shared Basel's visual complexity and was mainly expressive of itself with little semantically encoded symbolic meaning. The use of American vernacular was also mainly formal, a borrowing of pop forms with little of Venturi's understanding of context or intention.

But it was a lot more fun than classical "Swiss," and "New Wave" quickly spread across the United States to become an accepted graphic style. Just as Modernism's classic "Swiss" was accepted, this too became accepted in the business arena and persists today in a wide variety of corporate applications. In fact, it is so accepted, one design historian, Philip B. Meggs, calls it the New Academy, as prescribed a method as the Beaux Arts school of nineteenth-century French architecture.

"New Wave"'s type of graphic post-Modernism is essentially formalist with a rather minor involvement with content—content being more a jumping-off point for graphic celebrations of style than the core of the matter. Certainly, the "big idea" school of earlier years was far more dedicated to the communication of content. In fine art, a more profound aspect of post-Modernism has emerged as a body of self-conscious critical theory and expression. In fact, in much postmodern art, photography, and music the central expression is a critique of our accumulated body of culture and symbol. Appropriation and pastiche recycle our experience in highly referential work that owes everything to what has gone before. All this has its roots in structuralist semiotics of the 1960s, as well as Venturi's ideas. Although semiotics never became a practical design method, it and Structuralism's successor, post-Structuralism, have recently provided a real method and expression in the visual arts and graphic design. Coming out of literary theory, visual phenomena are analyzed as language encoded for meaning. Meanings are deconstructed, exposing the dynamics of power and the manipulation of meaning.

Post-Structuralism and recent fine art have influenced a promising new direction that is more truly postmodern. Graphic design is analyzed in linguistic terminology as a visual language. The audience is approached as readers as well as viewers. In the best of this new design, content is again at center stage. Images are to be read and interpreted, as well as seen; typography is to be seen as well as read. M&Co.'s provocative narratives exploit the power of familiar clichés, vernacular typography, and close-knit text/image connections. Rick Valicenti's auditory typography speaks with a tone of voice and mixes image and letter in rebus-like "sentences." The connection of word and image is again as rich as the New York School's, but with a visual compositional interaction as well as a conceptual verbal one. The best new work draws on the formal lessons of Basel and "New Wave" while drawing on all four seeing/reading/text/image modes simultaneously in powerful visual/verbal conceptual expressions. There are layers of meaning as well as layers of form.

This work has an intellectual rigor, demanding more of the audience, but also rewarding the audience with more content and autonomy. The focus is on the audience to make individual interpretations in graphic design that "decenter" the message. Pieces are a provocation to consider a range of interpretations, based on deconstruction's contention that meaning is inherently unstable and that objectivity is an impossibility, a myth maintained to control the audience. Graphic designers have become dissatisfied with obedient delivery of the client's message. Influenced by recent fine art, many are taking the role of interpreter a giant step beyond the problem-solving tradition by authoring additional content and a self-conscious critique to the message, reviving roles associated with both art and literature. Gone are both the commercial artist's servant role and the Swiss designer's transparent neutrality. Wit, humor, and irony are reappearing in irreverent and sometimes self-deprecating pieces that often speak directly to the reader in the second person plural, often with multiple voices. Venturi's view of history and vernacular as symbolic languages is finally being explored. Stylistic forms are appropriated with a critical self-consciousness of their original content and context.

This new work is smart and cerebral, challenging its audience to slow down and read carefully in a world of fast-forward and instant replay, *USA Today* and sound bites. The emphasis is on audience interpretation and the construction of meaning, beyond raw data to the reception of messages. This direction seems aligned to our times and technology, as we enter an era of communications revolution and complex global pluralism. Desktop publishing is placing the production of low-end print communications in the hands of office workers and paraprofessionals. Even the simplest corporate report is now typeset and formatted, raising the visual expectations of our audiences. To distinguish highly informed graphic communications from the vast output of desktop publishing and Web design, a new demand for personal, interpretive, and eccentric design expressions is surfacing.

With this new interest in personal content, graphic design may once more turn toward the fine arts, but will be built on decades of progress in methodology, theory, and formal strategies. The multivalent character of graphic design continues to shift between opposing values. Is this fluidity an indicator of the field's persistent immaturity, or a confirmation of its relevance to a rapidly changing world? Oppositions—art/business, visual/verbal, European/American, scientific/intuitive—are graphic design's strength and richness.

Katherine McCoy is a Senior Lecturer at Illinois Institute of Technology's Institute of Design in Chicago, after co-chairing the Department of Design at Cranbrook Academy of Art for twenty-four years. A 1999 Medallist of the AIGA, she consults in graphic design and design marketing, writes on design criticism and history, and organizes continuing professional education programs through High Ground Tools and Strategies for Design.

Originally published in Design Quarterly 149, *MIT Press, Cambridge, Massachusetts, 1990.*

A HISTORY OF DESIGN, A HISTORY OF CONCERNS
Jorge Frascara

What did Herbert Bayer have in mind when he designed his "Universal" type in 1925?
What prompted Peter Behrens to conceive of a notion of integrated corporate image for
AEG around 1900? When did the concern for a need to know the public begin to appear in
the mind of designers?

As a practitioner today, I have an extensive panel of controls. I am interested in
knowing about: (1) the purpose of my client; (2) the content of the communication I have
to visualize; (3) the profile of the segment of the market the message is aimed at (this profile
can be broken down into finer and finer dimensions according to the complexity of the project. And we do not speak any longer about a "profile," but about clusters of profiles. These
profiles are based at least on social class, education, age, gender, value systems, systems of
beliefs, cognitive styles, emotional makeup, visual preferences, and daily habits); (4) the
media that are going to be used to convey the message; (5) the technical aspects that will
be involved in the production; (6) the economic aspects of the production and implementa-
tion of the message; (7) the ways in which the effectiveness of the message is going to be
measured; and (8) the ways in which the evaluation is going to be taken into account in
order to improve the design.

When did each one of these concerns come about? Miles Tinker, for instance, started
writing on legibility around 1925. When Adrian Frutiger was designing his Univers in the
early 1950s, he was riding on twenty-five years of legibility research. Herbert Spencer (the first
designer to carry on systematic research on the subject) published his *Visible Word* in 1968.
When Herbert Bayer did his Universal type, his attempt at producing letters based on geometry and simplicity defeated four hundred years of sensitive type design, from Claude
Garamond on. The 1920s, with the obsession for geometry and simplicity, generated a few
type monsters. We can see that different designers had different criteria in mind; and we can
also see that the history of design does not necessarily evolve along a line of constant improvement. It was also around the 1920s that the Gestalt psychologists began to publish their more
clearly formulated writings, providing designers with a new theory that created grounds for the
development of visual design criteria, reaching down, particularly, the field of type design, sig-
nage, and symbols. When Bayer designed his type, he did not know that a skilled reader jumps
from the beginning of a long word to the beginning of another long word aided by word sepa-
rations. These create tonal cues for peripheral vision to orient the reading task. He did not

know that creating an alphabet with letters of different tonal density upsets reading effectiveness. He did not know that the skilled reader uses the initial letter, word length and the ascenders/descenders profile to guess the word and jump to the next important one.

Something happened in World War II (and it didn't in World War I) that boosted the development of knowledge about human factors. Given that war machines had become more complex, they had to be designed aiming to facilitate the task of the user, so as to get the best out of the soldier. They also needed to be supported by instructional programs that could allow any soldier to replace an expert one in a matter of hours. The quality of instructional materials developed dramatically between 1939 and 1945.

The war was certainly a strong motivation for the improvement of the efficiency of production systems. I am not intending to say that the war was a good thing, but design is the child of the concept of efficiency. Cultures that do not care about efficiency do not have design as we understand it. As we understand it, to a great extent, design is connected to the facilitation of tasks, be it the design of a tool for personal use or a city's transportation system. The pressure for effectiveness in the use of material, energy, and personnel during World War II, pushed the development of everything that had to do with design, including, to a great extent, the then new terrain of ergonomics. In the visual design field, the notion of total identity became stronger. The Germans and the Allied Forces developed quite different styles in their propaganda: the Germans were rigid, the Allies quite informal.

Experimental psychology, cultural anthropology, and even sociology developed intensely at the time, and their research techniques affected the development of marketing analysis, the design of objects, the understanding of learning processes, and the knowledge of human behavior. Thus, while an advertisement from around 1900 would be centered on describing and praising the product, one from the 1950s would describe the product in connection with the pleasures that it would bring. And one from the 1990s would be focused on desirable experiences and try to connect them to the product.

When Lucio Costa and Oscar Niemeyer conceived Brasilia in the late 1950s, they were quite adamant about the notion of planning, but did not acknowledge the principle of self-organization, which was developed as a notion in the 1980s but crashed Brasilia's plan from day one. It was a plan with no room for human interaction, no flexibility, no spaces to absorb the effects of actual people living in the place. When the job was done in the mid-1960s, and the workers were asked to leave their temporary quarters so that those wooden facilities could be destroyed, they did not want to leave. The area for the government offices had no shops, cafés, or restaurants. Everything was separated. Very neat to see from a bird's view, but not very fit for humans to live and work in. The city of La Plata, in Argentina, instead, was designed in 1882–84, by a team led by Pedro Benoit, under the government of Dardo Rocha, in a gentle way. The designer did not attempt to create an architectural landmark that would be reported in specialist magazines. He added a measure of order to current building practices, ensuring that there would be enough green spaces, and created several diagonals across the grid to facilitate traffic flow.

What made Costa and Niemeyer work the way they did? Did they suffer from an excess of Modernism? I am intrigued by when and why certain concepts were added to the control panel of the designer, but also by when and why some others were forgotten.

The Bauhaus was an excellent school. But it was a culturally blind school. It was also intellectually empty. The notion of innovation it pursued was devoid of social responsibility and cultural sensitivity. They did not accept the value of other aesthetics or the different needs of different people. This lack of cultural sensitivity was part of their lack of awareness about the importance of content and context to design. They still believed in universal absolutes and were ready to steamroll any and every preference that departed from theirs.

The heritage of Bauhaus in the teaching of design is difficult to shake off. Still, most design schools have a "visual fundamentals" course at the beginning of their program. Is the visual, I wonder, the fundamental part of design? No question—it is important, but is it the motor of design? Certainly not. Design doesn't exist in order to produce visual things; design exists because there are needs to meet, tasks to undertake, goods to sell, people to train, objects of many sorts to help us live the way we want to. The visual and the physical are design's means to meet human needs, wishes, and desires. The visual is not the foundation of design. As soon as we look at design as a part of culture, as a part of the way in which human groups create their material world, then we realize the importance of content and context. How can one produce a good design for health education without knowing a bit about health, another bit about education, and a lot about the people one is intending to reach?

Of course, one should have a thorough knowledge of the tools of design, from conception to production, but in order for that knowledge to work, it has to be contextualized knowledge.

When did this come about? I would say in the 1960s. The 1960s were a time where political communications stopped being the exclusive domain of governments and political parties. A consciousness about the possibility for citizens' groups to become vocal in the public space created an awareness of the endless polyphony of human discourse, and uncovered the need to tailor messages to different clusters of people.

The Synchronic versus the Diachronic

Normally, writings about history of design center on the passing of time, and only a few deal with simultaneity; that is, with the connections between design phenomena and other things happening at the same time. There is no question that today the look of design is affected by the new technological possibilities. But it is also true that the philosophical concern for complexity and the critical-theory notion of the inescapability from subjectivity also affects it, as do globalization and a heavily biased market economy. The end of a century is always a time to look back, so we have now as many revivals as there were in 1900. I am therefore intrigued by the roots design has not only in design that came before, but also in the mindset of a given time, in a given place (the famous zeitgeist, "spirit of the time"). And across time we find similar phenomena, albeit with different appearances: the Eiffel Tower and *Apollo 11* are highly connected with each other in their attempt to demonstrate technological sophistication. The Fiat 500, the Vespa scooter, the hamburger, and the blue jeans all belong to the same value of utility, reliability, and no-nonsense product.

Making History, Making Sense

From our perspective, Herbert Bayer was not that different from William Morris. Both believed in the primacy of form over content, and in the importance of aesthetics to human life. Both believed that a society full of beauty was going to have a good effect on the morals and the life of individuals. They, however, stood for different value systems: Morris was enamored with a romantic past, and Bayer was enamored with a rational future. The contents were different, but the frames were similar.

Gèrard Paris-Clavel, instead, departs from both, in that he believes design has to be oriented at awakening social consciousness, has to be useful for the life of people, and, while being concerned with aesthetics, cannot be independent from content. While Bayer would find it fantastic to design for Container Corporation of America and *Harper's Bazaar,* and Morris would design Art Nouveau luxury furniture for the rich while believing he was helping the whole world, Paris-Clavel dedicates his work to help the dispossessed, educate the children, and support the workers—in general, to provide a voice to those who are not heard. This is different from Bayer and from Morris.

Innovation or Lifestyle?

There is another question: should the history of design be the history of obscure innovations that never saw the light (or saw very little of it), or should it be the history of design objects that had a strong impact on people? Of course, binary choices are dumb, but the point is that most histories of design have exclusively concentrated on the heroic invention of styles and almost none on the ways in which objects—useful objects and communicating objects— have affected the life of people. As an industrial object, the wood and lead pencil had a billion times more influence on our writing habits, and, therefore, on our life, than any locomotive designed by any design guru.

Another fetish of disproportionate dimension is the famous 1925 poster by Rodchenko that did not get printed until the 1950s. Nevertheless, it appears in many histories of design as a 1925 poster. Well, actually, it never existed as such. El Lissitzky's famous abstract book was not understood by anybody outside of his group of abstract friends. When he went back to Russia and started working, he had to give up his triangles and squares because nobody could understand the profound meaning he was intending. Kurt Schwitters was equally communicationally inept. His ads for Pelikan ink are the worst example of visual identity support one could ever fathom. They actually should be shown today as examples of bad design, not as the heroes that pushed the boundaries of the profession. True, one has to place them in their historical time, and accept that they were children of a despotic aesthetic movement. However, today's discussion of their contribution should be filtered by today's understanding of the practice of design and by today's control panel of the designer, and should evaluate anew the contribution made to the development of design by those that Herbert Spencer and so many others called Pioneers of Modern Design.

Four Kinds of Design

I could recognize four different kinds of design: design to support life, design to facilitate life, and design to improve life. And then, there is also inconsequential design.

Design to support life is the work directed at promoting and ensuring health and safety: industrial safety, traffic safety, and health education, for example. This kind of design is important, but it is not at the top of my scale. It is design that has to do with our biological life, that we share with all animals. Between a neurosurgeon and Michelangelo, I take Michelangelo any time. The first can help make things possible when they go wrong. The second represents the realization of something that is unique to being human.

Design to facilitate life is the task-oriented design; that is, design that helps us do things better, faster, more easily, and more efficiently. Instructional materials, sign systems, much furniture, and all tools are directed at that.

Lastly, there is design aimed at improving life: This is the design that focuses on human dimensions, such as spiritual qualities, cultural values, humor, pleasure, and, indeed, beauty and the awakening of consciousness. Good furniture, enjoyable books, and elegant solutions to difficult communication problems, are examples of that kind of design.

I am not suggesting here that a designed object would exclusively fall in either one or another category. An actual object could participate in two or three categories or could be restricted to one. Independent from the brief, a designer always has the possibility to introduce wit, beauty, and, in general, cultural value into any design project, no matter how pedestrian it can be.

Inconsequential design, in terms of the grand scheme of things, is the exclusively commercial design; that is, design oriented at supporting corporation A against corporation B. Indeed, this design is not inconsequential to the corporations, but its job does not affect society in one way or another. Whatever people choose to do with one corporation, they do not do with the other. It is useful in our market economy, because it affects the success of individual businesses and creates jobs for quite a few people, but, in essence, for the whole of society, nothing is lost and nothing is gained.

If we look at the history of design from this perspective, then one wonders why the locomotives designed by Raymond Loewy and Henry Dreyfuss should appear in so many history of design books. They were hardly visible in the human environment and their designers only added styling to a machine that was meant to do its job with one face or another. True, it apparently fed the American fantasy about how the future should look, but I would submit that cars had a far more visible presence and cultural impact on people than any locomotive could have ever dreamt of having.

Historically, design related to beauty has existed since the beginning of time. Closer to us, what William Morris intended to do in the 1870s was contribute to the beauty of daily life (as well as fostering the moral values he found in handcrafted objects).

The concern for facilitating tasks has been present since the first handmade useful object. The purposes of hitting the enemy or drinking water were apparently good motivations that inspired people to craft extensions of the human body in order to improve human performance and facilitate daily tasks.

When it comes to design aimed at supporting life, in communication design there are not many examples before the 1960s. Health and safety are absent from the communication design agenda until that time. We can find lots of posters promoting enrollment in the army but not much to ensure safety. The Vietnam War (different from World War II) unleashes for the first time a negative attitude about war; at the same time, environmentalism warns people about the quality of the air they breathe and the food they eat. A distrust about consumer products changes people's attitudes about the consumer culture and creates needs for communications that spread the new ideas about the social order. The political poster, not as the voice of political parties but as the voice of groups of ordinary citizens, appears in the 1960s.

The relevance of design—and different definitions of relevance—are recent questions. They emerge only in highly advanced societies that have arrived at a stage of context-sensitive self-consciousness. One can find moral imperatives in the past, but the concerns of the designer up until the 1960s were concentrated on aspects of the object. Moving the center of design from the products to the users of products and communications is a recent event. It is not my attempt to suggest that designers of the past were shortsighted and culturally insensitive. But I find it shortsighted and culturally insensitive to continue today to center design history on stylistic innovation. I would hope that today, instead of trying to keep on inventing style superheroes in design shows, it would be refreshing to pay attention to social and cultural relevance, to the effectiveness of design solutions, and to the contributions that design makes to its highest possible function: supporting and fostering the welfare of people.

Jorge Frascara teaches design at the University of Alberta and consults on traffic safety communications. He was President of Icograda, contributed to international standards for graphic symbols, and, among many other publications, he has written User-Centred Graphic Design *(Taylor and Francis, 1997) and has edited* Graphic Design, World Views *(Kodansha, 1990).*

My thanks to Dietmar Winkler for his opinions about the Bauhaus, and the ideas of content and context. To Bernd Meurer, for bringing to my attention the concept of self-organization. And to Clara Luzian, for factual information about the city of La Plata.

USSR
in construction

THE NINETEENTH YEAR
OF THE REVOLUTION

4-5

OGIZ – IZOGIZ • APRIL – MAY • 1936

2. Between Covers

<small>Construction Work</small>
Victor Margolin

Conceived in the spirit of the First Five-Year Plan, *USSR in Construction* was a propaganda magazine whose principal mission was to promote a favorable image of the Soviet Union abroad and at home. Published monthly between 1930 and 1940,* it is one of the most visually exciting magazines of the twentieth century, thanks to an expansive budget, lush rotogravure printing, inventive layouts and photomontages, and the use of die-cuts, gate-folds, and other experimental techniques.

With the formal adoption of the First Five-Year Plan in April 1929, the Soviet Union embarked upon an ambitious program of collectivizing its agricultural production and transforming itself into a major industrial power. Joseph Stalin, who had assumed Lenin's mantle of leadership in the Communist Party, had begun to shift the nation's political agenda from fomenting permanent revolution abroad to building a socialist state at home. This state came to be characterized by a strong centralized bureaucracy, an aggressive labor force under its control, and a powerful military to deter potential invaders.

USSR in Construction, founded on the initiative of the writer, Maxim Gorky, was envisioned as a publication that, in the words of the editors, would "reflect in photography the whole scope and variety of the construction work now going on in the USSR." Its format was probably influenced by the German bourgeois illustrated magazines of the early 1920s, *Berliner Illustrierte Zeitung* and *Münchner Illustrierte Presse,* as well as by their left-wing counterpart, the *Arbeiter Illustriert Zeitung.* Initially, *USSR in Construction* appeared in four separate editions: German, English, French, and Russian. In the late 1930s, a fifth edition in Spanish was added.

For more than a year, the magazine featured separate articles on a variety of state projects; then, the editors began to dedicate each number to a single theme. During the First Five-Year Plan, issues emphasized the huge industrial projects—electrosteel plants, textile mills, hydroelectric stations, coal mines, and canals—as well as the collectivization of agriculture. But as the 1930s progressed, the political objectives of *USSR in Construction* expanded to cover a broad range of themes that promulgated an image of national unity, heroic achievements, and collective well-being.

---

*It is possible that several issues were published in 1941, but I have found no catalog citations for them. The magazine resumed publication in 1949 as a general feature publication, after which it was reborn as *Soviet Union,* which is still published today.

Issues were devoted to the different republics and autonomous regions, expeditions to remote parts of the country, and the rise of rail and air travel. Some deal with raw materials, such as coal, gold, and timber, and others with themes of daily life—children, sports, and old age. Special political issues featured the Stalin Constitution, the election of the Supreme Soviet, and the occupation of Poland.

The editorial board, headed by editor-in-chief G. I. Piatakov, was a mixture of politicians and writers, including Maxim Gorky, then touted by the regime as the elder statesman of Soviet letters, and Mikhail Koltsov, one of the Soviet Union's best-known journalists.

Working under the editorial board, a production team that comprised writers, photographers, a designer or layout artist, and sometimes a special designer of charts and maps was assembled for each issue. Many of the Soviet Union's leading authors—Isaac Babel, Nikolai Fadeyev, Sergei Tretiakov, El Registan—planned and wrote text, working closely with teams of photojournalists that included Max Alpert, Semyon Fridland, Georgy Petrusov, Mikhael Prekhner, and Arkady Shaiket.

The most prominent designers were El Lissitzky, sometimes assisted by his wife, Sophie; Alexander Rodchenko; and Rodchenko's wife, Varvara Stepanova. Between them, they designed approximately twenty-five issues of the magazine. However, most of the issues were designed by N. Troshin, whose early layouts were relatively uninteresting, but who learned from the more experienced designers and created many inventive spreads over the years. Among the designers who worked occasionally for the magazine were Vladimir Favorsky, a woodcut artist and graphic arts instructor at the Vkhutemas, the national design school, and Salomon Telingater, who assisted Lissitzky with the All-Union Printing Trades Exhibition in 1927 and then became a successful book and magazine designer in his own right. Zoe Deineka, an artist strongly influenced by the Isotype statistics of Otto Neurath, did most of the maps and charts.

Initially, the editors seem to have had little understanding of what an art director or designer could contribute to the publication—the early issues were rarely more than sequences of pictures with explanatory texts. In the first years, the designer had a subordinate role and was credited only with the arrangement of photographs. The first cover, designed by O. Deineka, was simply a solid-colored page with a huge centered typographic logo. Even though some very strong pictorial covers would follow, the Deineka design was used regularly throughout the life of the magazine.

When John Heartfield arrived in Moscow for an extended stay in 1931, he was invited to design the layout and cover for an issue on the Soviet petroleum industry. Heartfield introduced a new dramatic title and strong images of oil rigs on both front and back covers and pushed for a fusion of photographs and text inside. But even after this forceful demonstration of what a designer could contribute to the magazine, the editors encouraged few graphic innovations until El Lissitzky designed his first issue on the Dnieper hydroelectric station and dam in 1933. Lissitzky was the first designer for *USSR in Construction* to be identified as an "artist." Before that, the terms "layout" or "composition" designated the designer's contribution. Lissitzky's extensive experience and growing reputation among government officials in the planning of exhibitions must have allowed him substantial leverage in defying his initial role on the magazine. He was the only Soviet graphic artist who grasped the radical changes in layout and typography that had been espoused by the promoters of the "New Typography" in Germany and, in fact, had had a major influence on this movement.

Both Heartfield and Lissitzky contributed something that had been missing from earlier issues: a sense of narrative. Lissitzky, in particular, had been preoccupied for years with the design of books, and brought to *USSR in Construction* an organic vision that resulted in dramatic integrated flows of images and words. For an issue on the Soviet Arctic done in 1933, he alternated detailed accounts of particular expeditions, including route maps, with spectacular photographs, spread over two pages, that function as more general metaphors for Soviet heroism through their depiction of, for example, a single figure surrounded by the snowy vastness of Arctic space.

Lissitzky was the strongest single influence on the art direction of the magazine. It was his work that demonstrated the way that text, images, charts, maps, and diagrams could be integrated into visual narratives that gave appropriate emphasis to each element in a presentation. Rodchenko and Stepanova were more oriented to the photograph itself, and while they designed exceptional issues on Kazakhstan, Soviet parachutists, and the Soviet timber industry, their narratives did not have the broad historical sweep that Lissitzky's conferred. Troshin also remained oriented to the visual arrangements within the spreads rather than to the additional graphic devices that could have produced a richer narrative structure.

The magazine's initial format included a title page with a large photograph and a masthead whose typography changed frequently in the early years. In fact, the editors never did establish a set of typographic rules. Generally, typography was subordinated to the photographs. In many issues, a sans-serif face in a small point size was used. Texts were printed entirely in blocks of uppercase type with little indentation. While some of the issues improved on this format, the general lack of typographic sophistication in the magazine reflected the underdevelopment of the Soviet printing industry as well as the paucity of training in typography, particularly the manipulation of Western alphabets.

More than compensating for the typographic limitations was the theatrical display of photographs, which evolved gradually. The magazine measured 11½" by 16½", resulting in enormous spreads. In addition, the art director experimented with foldout pages that occasionally yielded huge horizontal photomontages. Rodchenko and Stepanova designed a sequence for a 1935 issue on the aforementioned Soviet parachutists in which a square of paper was folded several times to produce a series of images that the reader discovered during successive unfolding. The final image was of Stalin amid hundreds of parachutists drifting down to earth. On several occasions, the spreads folded out to become four-sheet posters.

Photographs were printed by rotogravure. Frequently, the pictures were retouched, and sometimes drawn elements were substituted for photographic ones within the image. Initially, pictures were printed in sepia, but after several years the editors began to experiment with different colored inks and eventually printed the images in a spectrum of colors that included blue, green, red, and purple. Sometimes these colors varied from page to page and occasionally different colors were used for specific sections of the same page. Only rarely did the editors attempt four-color printing. The striking effects of the single tints, however, provided more visual drama than would have been achieved through sequences of four-color photographs.

Gradually, *USSR in Construction* evolved a style of visual rhetoric that shared the characteristics of Socialist Realism as defined by Maxim Gorky, Communist Party official Andrei Zhdanov, and others at the All-Union Congress of Soviet Writers in 1934. Here, Gorky introduced the concept of "romantic realism," which he defined as a blend of how things were and how they could be.

Although Socialist Realism's artistic conventions were clearly defined for painting, sculpture, and literature in the 1930s, its aesthetics were more difficult to apply to photo-journalism and graphic design. Hence both photo-reporters and designers were able to find space for experimentation in *USSR in Construction*. For Lissitzky, however, the regime's growing rhetoric of pomp and ceremony prompted the development of a new style of "epic narrative" that was, in fact, a sophisticated application of Socialist Realism's tenets to magazine layout.

This was particularly evident in the special album on the Soviet Constitution that he designed with the assistance of his wife in 1937. Incorporating four issues, the album was marked by heraldic emblems, banners, and other regalia that gave dignity and nobility to the theme. As the narrative shifted thematically within the issue, so did Lissitzky's layouts, moving from highly emotional adulation of Stalin to sober presentations of industrial statistics. Although the album represents the aims of the Socialist Realism, it is a project of high quality, unlike many Soviet paintings, sculptures, and novels of this period.

Nonetheless, the Constitution album pointed up two issues of content the *USSR in Construction* had to deal with in the late 1930s: the growing cult of Stalin, which imposed increasing obligations on the editors to pay homage to the leader in visual form as well as in the text, and the frequent dissonance between the magazine's optimistic rhetoric, which presented all aspects of Soviet life positively, and the oppressive nature of particular events and policies. (This dissonance was reflected in the magazine's staff; by 1937, most of the original members of the editorial board had disappeared from the masthead.)

In the years between 1935 and 1939, while the major show trials and purges took place in the Soviet Union, *USSR in Construction* continued to present a view of Soviet society intended to convince fellow travelers and sympathizers abroad that the country remained a paradise in the making. Soviet citizens were shown to be capable of Herculean tasks in the factories as well as on the farms. They always expressed immense joy in being part of a heroic social experiment that was claimed to vastly exceed the hopes and capabilities of all other nations of the world.

Despite its self-conscious creation of an optimistic national image, *USSR in Construction* was the Soviet Union's most extensive visual record of everyday life. During its eleven years of publication prior to World War II, one could find photographs of new factories, housing projects in remote republics, recent consumer goods, smiling Stakhanovite workers, automobile assembly lines, recreation facilities, and the visages of all the diverse ethnic groups that constituted the Soviet Union.

From a design point of view, the magazine is sheer visual pleasure. But its political charge to celebrate the Stalin regime, even as the Soviet leader increasingly engaged in dubious and destructive social practices, makes it impossible for one to appreciate this work solely on aesthetic grounds.

Our response to the magazine is complicated by the fact that we are accustomed to regarding art produced under repressive regimes as compromised and mediocre. What the magazine therefore challenges us to do is probe the relationship between its appearance and its intentions rather than simply enjoy it uncritically. And this is a challenge that might well be applied to our understanding of all graphic design.

———————————————————

Victor Margolin is associate professor of art at the University of Illinois, Chicago. He is editor of Design Discourse: History, Theory, Criticism.

———————————————————

Originally published in PRINT, *May/June 1994. © 1994 Victor Margolin.*

WHEELS OF FORTUNE
William Owen

Fortune was launched at a time when the conventional magazine had no systematic type style and the role of the designer, if there was a designer at all, was confined to the application of decorative vignettes and ornate type. *Fortune*, however, was no follower of convention. The first issue of February 1930 included a design manifesto, probably by the magazine's first art editor, Thomas M. Cleland, which began with a statement of rationalist intent: "The design of *Fortune* is based upon its function of presenting a clear and readable text profusely illustrated with pictures, mostly photographic, in a form ample and agreeable to the eye." There followed a discussion of typography, proportions, paper, and printing methods, all of which had been selected with the intention of going "beyond the technical limitations of most periodicals" and combined to give a generosity of presentation "which shall be in accord with the best principles of fine bookmaking."

Fortune was aimed at America's business elite. Launched as the Depression hit its deepest trough, the monthly celebration of the power of U.S. capital was a brazen gamble on the part of its impresario publisher, Henry Luce. Self-confidence bordering on arrogance, however, was to be the magazine's hallmark, manifest in its great size (11½" × 14"), in the weight of its 200-plus pages, on a heavy, uncoated stock specially chosen to take the saturated color printing, and in its high cover price ("One Dollar a Copy," set proudly in 24pt on the masthead). Luce promised that his magazine would be "as beautiful a magazine as exists in the United States. If possible the undisputed most beautiful." In its early years, *Fortune* certainly exemplified the best in U.S. craft typography, exploring the limits of the possible applications of traditional type structures to magazine design.

Cleland's format conveyed an impression of tastefully restrained abundance: a protestant aesthetic of beauty in economy. A simple two or three column grid, using only three gradations of type size for heads, standfirst, and body copy, was surrounded by wide margins. The design's sole concession to decoration was the *trompe l'œil* border around the titlepiece, fudge, and cover illustration. Inside, the gravure-printed color photographs and illustrations were framed by a 4pt solid black border, a radical departure from the elaborate photographic vignettes of commercial magazine design. Color was used at its best in the pictorial maps and diagrams which illustrated the key information and documentary features. Type was in Baskerville, printed by letterpress and deeply impressed into the page.

Like F. W. Goudy and W. A. Dwiggins, Cleland belonged to the generation of

American typographers schooled in the classical Roman tradition. His choice of Baskerville, the most precisely cut of the eighteenth-century transitional fonts, was a clear indication of his aesthetic sensibility. Baskerville, he wrote, was "free from archaisms and familiar to modern eyes yet had none of the condensation and 'meanness' of later faces." For Cleland, the face had a classical yet technocratic grandeur which could reconcile the pretensions of U.S. big business with the practical occupation of making money.

Fortune's art editor for most of the 1930s was Eleanor Treacy, who gradually eroded the monumental symmetry of Cleland's design to create a more fluid visual dynamic. Treacy commissioned magnificent industrial photography from a new wave of photojournalists influenced by the style and content of constructivist photography. Among the most prolific and accomplished were Walker Evans and *Fortune*'s full-time photographic editor, Margaret Bourke-White.

Treacy's successor, Francis (Hank) Brennan, arrived in 1938 from Condé Nast, where he had worked with M. F. Agha, the Russo-Turkish art director who had introduced elements of the new typography to *Vanity Fair* and *Vogue*. Brennan complained that Cleland's bookish format "could not easily accommodate such devices as bleed pages, asymmetrical layouts, the growing use of charts and diagrams." He stripped the ornate border from the cover and with new art director Peter Piening he introduced a harder-edged, less formal design for the March 1942 issue. For the next three years almost the whole of *Fortune*'s content was devoted to the war effort. Stencil faces, News Gothic and Futura italics, together with a renewed emphasis on charts, diagrams, and maps, gave visual expression to the performance of the "working front."

Through its intensively researched editorial, *Fortune* became an encyclopedia of science, industry, and cultural and political life. It was the design, which set a new standard in the communication of complex information, that established its purpose. After 1941 the magazine led corporate America's embrace of European modernism, employing the talents of German, Dutch, French, and Italian émigrés to create a remarkable synthesis of visual and literary journalism. Abstract conceptual covers and illustrations were commissioned from Fernand Léger, Hans J. Barschel, Edmund Lewandowski, Herbert Matter, and Ladislav Sutnar. Herbert Bayer produced a series of diagrams to explain complex scientific subjects, which he called "patterns for intelligent visualization" but which Brennan referred to simply as "functional graphics, designed as integral parts of a given story."

Piening took sole responsibility for art direction in 1943 and was succeeded in late 1945 by fellow German Will Burtin. Burtin had served a traditional print apprenticeship before attending the Cologne Werkschule, where he was introduced to the new typography. At *Fortune*, however, he rejected narrow functionalism for an approach in which "individual job requirements led quite naturally to their own visual expression." As he was to describe it in *Graphis* in 1949: "I attempted to prove my contention that the character of a material and its interpretation, illustration, text, technical data, type character, size, page units, colors, and shapes, are part of one integrated entity." But this process, he explained, "asked for a measure of discipline difficult to define. If followed sternly it resulted in rigid, mechanical design . . . instinct and creative urge put to work at the proper place seemed to be most necessary implements."

Burtin's solutions to the problems of communicating complex data combined visual clarity with high drama. Drawing on a knowledge of montage and photograms and on the superb technical draftsmanship of the *Fortune* art department, together with designers of the caliber of Bayer, Gyorgy Kepes, and Lester Beall, he created both flat and three-dimensional flowcharts, tables, maps, and exploded diagrams notable for their use of simple formal elements and color. This was *Fortune*'s richest period of graphic experiment, though not its most commercially successful.

The emphasis in U.S. business had undergone a subtle transformation immediately after the war, with a shift in interest from industrial power to management and marketing finesse, and the rise of highly conservative corporatism. In 1948 Burtin's design was deemed more suitable for a look-through than a reading magazine, and Luce criticized the editorial content as insufficiently staunch in its backing of "the American enterprise system."

A substantial redesign was begun in 1949 by the Dutch designer Leo Lionni, assisted by Walter Allner, a graduate of the Dessau Bauhaus who was to become art editor from 1962 to 1974. The new format was introduced in September 1951 and was to remain substantially unchanged until 1969. Its ordered type and modular arrangement of pictures was in clinical contrast to Burtin's exuberance. However, Lionni's restraint was better suited to *Fortune*'s new emphasis on the management profile and corporate review, and on readability.

Fortune's wheel had come full circle, and in a preface to the September 1951 issue entitled "The Function of Form," Lionni echoed Cleland's initial message: "Though the functions of magazines, and consequently their forms, are as variable as their titles, the first function of any magazine is to get itself read." Lionni aimed to avoid the kind of false modernity that is sometimes accomplished by graphic tricks" intending the design to "be functional rather than merely looking functional." Thus, he spurned sans serifs and chose instead Bodoni Italic for heads and Century Expanded for body text. The visual dynamic was primarily symmetrical and the editorial structure was reorganized to present a clear beginning (news and reviews), middle (features), and end (roundup). In summary, *Fortune* became more like a conventional magazine, although until its remaking as a small-format title in 1972, it retained much of its grandeur, its immense graphic sophistication, and its intellectual ambition.

For over forty years *Fortune* easily maintained its stature as *the* great American magazine. Given the massive resources and talent that went into its making, resources of a magnitude today commanded only by television producers, it is unlikely that its visual and journalistic achievements can—in print—ever be repeated.

William Owen, the author of Modern Magazine Design *(Rizzoli), has worked as a journalist, designer, and magazine consultant.*

Originally published in EYE, *February 1991*

1,189 Psychiatrists Say Goldwater Is Psychologically Unfit To Be President!

VOLUME ONE, ISSUE FIVE $1.25

TWO MAGAZINES OF THE TURBULENT '60S: A '90S PERSPECTIVE
Philip B. Meggs

Magazines rise, then fall; they thrive when they fill the needs and interests of audiences and/or advertisers; they decline and cease publication when the audience grows tired, editors lose touch, or times change. Only rarely does a publishing venture stop because the editor is thrown into prison by the U.S. government for violating obscenity laws; yet this is precisely what ended the collaborative efforts of editor/publisher Ralph Ginzburg and designer Herb Lubalin. In the magazines they produced, Ginzburg and Lubalin squarely faced controversial issues in American culture. Their wide-ranging content—exposés, investigative reports, and visual portfolios—encompassed politics, controversial art, scientific theories defying accepted dogma, and human sexuality.

During the 1960s, the United States was in the midst of a social and sexual revolution characterized by openness in dialogue and conduct. This new freedom followed the buttoned-up, repressive 1950s, when novels such as *Lady Chatterley's Lover* were banned for having sexually oriented themes; postal inspectors ferreted out "obscene" material from the mails; and congressional committees searched for communists and communist sympathizers. Writers and performers were routinely blacklisted for their political beliefs.

As various movements in the 1960s gained momentum—free speech, women's liberation, civil rights, Vietnam War protest—Ginzburg's magazines responded to, and helped define, the changes taking place in America. He pressed against the limits of press freedom by going beyond the accepted boundaries, challenging both the government and conventional standards.

In the ongoing American political struggle between conservatives and liberals, the 1960s saw the liberal agenda advance on many fronts. A liberal was defined by his or her support for civil rights for minorities, women's liberation, government programs such as Head Start and Food Stamps to help people living in poverty, and environmental protection. Ginzburg and Lubalin embraced these causes and values, and their work often reflected a liberal viewpoint. Lubalin's design approach frequently projected urgency and immediacy, especially when controversial issues were the subject.

Specifically because he admired this design approach, Ginzburg asked Herb Lubalin to design his magazines. Lubalin was an extraordinary art director who emerged as one of the original voices in 1960s American graphic design. After spending most of the fifties and early sixties as creative director of Sudler and Hennessey, a pharmaceutical advertising agency, Lubalin established a series of design partnerships. He was a generalist. In addition to art-directing Ginzburg's magazines, he redesigned the faltering *Saturday Evening Post* twice and produced a steady stream of packaging, logos, typefaces, book formats, book jackets, and advertising campaigns. He might be called a baroque constructivist, for he had the soul of a constructivist and the heart of a Victorian. He could be functional, modernist, decorative, nostalgic, and historical within the covers of a single magazine issue. Reviving nineteenth-century vernacular typography, he compressed it into the chunky asymmetrical rectangles of contemporary design.

Perhaps more than any other 1960s designer, Lubalin understood and creatively exploited the new freedom of phototype for spatial compression, manipulation, and overlapping; he used the new techniques, not just for formal manipulation, but for communicative and expressive results.

Fact, a bimonthly, premiered in January/February 1964 and lasted until July/August 1967. The masthead on the first issue proclaimed: "This magazine is dedicated to the proposition that a great magazine, in its quest for truth, will dare to defy not only Convention, not only Big Business, not only the Church and the State, but also—if necessary—its readers." Circulation soared to 185,000 by 1965, ultimately climbing to 250,000 before the magazine's demise.

One version of *Fact*'s birth was provided in 1967 by its managing editor, Warren Boroson, who wrote, "According to a few rumors that have been floating around, Fact Magazine was bankrolled at a meeting between Adam Clayton Powell, Jimmy Hoffa, Tim Leary, Elizabeth Taylor and Fu Manchu in an LSD session at THRUSH headquarters in Passaic, New Jersey."

A more reliable account comes from Ralph Ginzburg. The U.S. Postal Service, at the time a guardian of American culture and censor of all materials sent through the mail, socked Ginzburg with a twenty-eight-count indictment in May 1963 for mailing obscene material, including his *Eros* magazine, the "journal of love" that shook American prudishness to its foundations. Although the next issue of *Eros* was already at the printers, Ginzburg yielded to his lawyer's advice to suspend publication and "stay as far away from sex as possible." *Eros* and Ginzburg's trial and conviction were discussed in an earlier *PRINT* article (May/June 1991, pp. 49–57). During the seven years between Ginzburg's indictment and imprisonment, he edited and published *Fact*, then *Avant Garde*.

At the time Ginzburg suspended publication of *Eros*, he had a suite of offices near the New York Public Library, a highly motivated professional staff, and a large contingent of subscribers wondering when their next issue of *Eros* would arrive. He decided to launch a new magazine to fill the void, characterizing it as "a hell-raising, muckraking magazine of dissent that would try to improve society by bringing to the fore data that was not generally known."

Ginzburg saw *Fact*'s role as that of "antidote to the timidity and corruption of the American press." He believed, as did many other Americans of the time, that the public was not getting the whole story on issues ranging from the Vietnam War to government corruption and environmental problems. For example, after a college student at a large Washington antiwar rally allegedly immolated himself on the Pentagon lawn to protest the Vietnam War, the television networks and major newspapers reported that a small fire of undetermined origin had been quickly extinguished by the authorities. The health and sexual conduct of celebrities and political figures were treated with great discretion (in contrast to the current mania to tell all).

In conscious opposition to sanitized information, *Fact* provided an outlet for controversial writers who wanted to speak out against corrupt politicians, race hatred, police brutality, or insurance fraud, but who often could not get their material published in the establishment press. Its contributors included such eminences as historian Arnold Toynbee, Bertrand Russell, and Dr. Benjamin Spock. For readers, *Fact* provided an alternative to what many considered the pap of 1960s American mass media. Later, managing editor Warren Boroson wrote, "Most American magazines, emulating the *Reader's Digest,* wallow in sugar and everything nice; *Fact* has had the spice almost all to itself."

Though a self-proclaimed outlet for muckrakers, *Fact* rejected the scruffy homemade look of the underground press as well as the screaming typography of sensationalist tabloids. Rather, it was clothed in exquisite serif typography set off by outstanding illustration. It sported a perfect bound 8½" by 11" format printed in black ink on uncoated paper, and was wrapped in a luxuriant, glossy cover stock. *Fact* was produced on a tight budget, so Lubalin developed an economical programmed system consisting of an 18-point Times Roman Bold headline centered at the top of the page, with the author's name below it. An interval of white space separated these from the two columns of 10/12 Times Roman text, which began under a 24-point subhead. Each article began on a right-hand page facing a full-page illustration.

Each issue contained about ten articles, and several titles were often clustered under the *Fact* logo on the covers. Letters to the editor were used as "fillers" at the end of articles. Faced with a fee limitation for illustration, Lubalin commissioned one artist to illustrate all of the articles in each issue; thus, each issue showcased an artist's talents and made this "group rate" for drawings more attractive than if the budget had been divided among ten artists. The illustrations were conceptual and emblematic, capturing and often commenting upon the subject.

Fact's editorial content and design approach can be observed in the May/June 1967 issue. Illustrated throughout by Etienne Delessert's biting visual interpretations of the articles, this issue was selected for reproduction here because it is one of the most provocative in overall editorial and graphic content.

The cover features a two-faced portrait of George Romney, former Michigan governor who was a candidate for the Republican presidential nomination. The lead article deals with Romney's views as a Mormon; thus Delessert showed him with Mormon founder Joseph Smith. The commercial savvy of popular author Jacqueline Susann is conveyed as her head emerges from a typewriter whose keys are all dollar signs. Illustrators selected to work on an issue were given wide creative latitude; here, Delessert montages film with illustration for an article by a woman who was arrested by the Los Angeles Police Department vice squad for sexual acts with her husband and collages a newspaper with illustration for an article about the alternative paper *The East Village Other.* Other articles include an exposé of the diet industry and Americans' obsessive fear of all things Communist.

One of Ginzburg's frequent editorial techniques was to survey the powerful, rich, and famous on controversial topics; the May/June 1967 issue includes a survey of twenty-eight prominent Americans on pornography. (Billy Graham and Ronald Reagan were both asked to participate, but did not respond.)

The demise of *Fact* resulted from a lawsuit by Barry Goldwater, who ran against Lyndon Johnson in the 1964 presidential election. When Goldwater raised the possibility of using nuclear weapons in Vietnam, Ginzburg recalls thinking, "This guy is a complete nut!" *Fact* subsequently polled members of the American Medical Association who listed their specialty as psychiatry and asked their opinions of Goldwater's mental state. *Fact* published what Ginzburg calls "a perfectly accurate sampling of the opinions received" from the psychiatrists who responded. Goldwater sued *Fact* for $2 million, and after a legal struggle lasting several years was awarded $75,000, which swelled to $90,000 when lawyers' fees were added. This put *Fact* out of business.

The Goldwater piece provoked a storm of controversy. One view upheld the right of the press to make no-holds-barred disclosures about political-office seekers (*Fact* had published allegations that Goldwater suffered two mental breakdowns); the opposing position maintained that public figures had certain rights of privacy. Psychiatrists who responded to *Fact*'s survey were accused of unprofessional behavior, i.e., making an evaluation of an individual's mental state without ever having conducted an interview.

Just as *Fact* rose from the ashes of *Eros*, *Avant Garde* appeared just six months after *Fact* folded, in January 1968. Despite its short life span, *Fact* had been an editorial success, garnering a healthy subscriber base and winning many awards for its distinguished and influential design. But Ginzburg—longing for the qualities of *Eros*—wanted to launch a very lavish and sensuous magazine of art and politics. He sensed the need for a magazine not for mass consumption, but for people ahead of their time, a "rarefied, even elitist audience" whose interests and tastes were not being catered to. For the third time, Ginzburg asked Herb Lubalin to art-direct one of his magazines.

The development of a logo for *Avant Garde* was a protracted affair. Ginzburg wanted one that would dramatically express the advanced, the innovative, the creative. Initially, Lubalin submitted a series of sketches that did not satisfy Ginzburg's sense of "avant-garde." One was modeled on the Coca-Cola logo; another proclaimed "avant-garde" in imitation Hebrew letters. Finally, Lubalin came up with a solution to Ginzburg's liking. Because the title contained awkward letterform combinations that created difficult spacing problems, Lubalin devised a typographic design of tightly interlocking capital ligatures. After his logo received a positive response, he yielded to the urging of the design community for a typeface based on his capital-ligature scheme. In 1970, ITC Avant Garde was released by International Typeface Corporation. It quickly became one of the most widely used type families of the '70s and remains a typographic staple today.

At that time, phototypesetting was rapidly diverting the typesetting market from metal type. Avant Garde was released with a wide range of capital ligatures and alternate characters that were made possible by the increased spatial flexibility of phototype. Lubalin later expressed regret for releasing these characters because, though Avant Garde was designed to make difficult letter combinations fit together better, the alternate characters were widely abused in poorly designed type treatments.

Avant Garde magazine was reviewed in Magazines for Libraries, a reference book to guide librarians in their magazine selections. Wrote Bill Katz, the reviewer, "Ralph Ginzburg's venture is a cross between his successful Fact magazine and Eros, although the first issue owes more to the former than to Eros. Such articles as 'What Makes Nixon Run' and 'The Hate Mail of Captain Levy' are well enough written, but straight from Fact. The photography is excellent, but not overly consequential. The overall impression is one of a Madison Avenue whiz kid serving up bohemia for suburbia."

My impressions as a subscriber were much kinder and gentler than Katz's assessment; in fact, I was downright ecstatic when the first issue—in all its generous 11" × 14" dimensions—arrived in the mail. Here was Fact's muckraking mated with Eros's sensuousness, outfitted in some of Lubalin's finest editorial designs.

Richard Lindner's exotic blend of Pop Art and Cubism graced the first cover. Avant Garde covers were typically emblematic, single images that made a strong visual statement. No type appeared except the logo, in contrast to today's magazine cover photographs, tortured and defaced by a dozen garish screaming headlines.

Avant Garde covers often included works from portfolios reproduced inside. Cover art and accompanying portfolios ran toward the bizarre, the fantastic, and the erotic—see pop artist Tom Wesselman's Seascape #17 cover for issue 5. Art with Freudian overtones was favored, such as George Tooker's "magic realism" painting for issue 7; it became a symbolic icon of its era.

Avant Garde's political coverage was feisty, openly liberal, and honored no sacred cows. An editorial feature called "Dial-a-Hawk" provided readers with telephone numbers of major political and military figures. The list included right-wing newspaper columnist Patrick J. Buchanan—then a special assistant to President Nixon—who in 1992 sought the Republican presidential nomination.

Political activism coexisted with avant-garde popular culture. A feature titled "Andy's Girls" profiled the "stars" who achieved their fifteen minutes of fame in Andy Warhol's underground films. Ginzburg's editorial technique of asking many people to provide their opinions on a controversial subject gained a visual counterpart when Avant Garde invited nineteen artists to redesign the dollar bill. Some dollar designs, including one by Leonard Baskin, were judged to be mediocre and were not reproduced.

Radical politics, art, and currency design were accompanied by some of the most radical typographic design of the era. Unlike most magazines, which were printed on web presses on cheap, lightweight coated stock, Avant Garde was printed in signatures using a variety of papers. Fairly long articles were printed in two colors on newsprint and interspersed with full-color portfolios on coated stock.

In the premiere issue, a full-color portfolio of Lindner's work printed on coated paper was followed by a lengthy article about American pilots slaughtering Vietnamese civilians for sport. "The Hate Mail of Captain Levy," illustrated by Brad Holland, presented five pages of letters received by Dr. Howard Levy, a dermatologist court-martialed and impris-

Art Center College

oned for three years after refusing to teach Green Berets how to use medicine as a political weapon in Vietnam. A photo essay, "Galahad's Pad," presented photographer Julio Mitchel's journalistic essay of life in a Manhattan hippie commune made famous by thirty police raids within a period of six months.

The second issue published a twelve-page portfolio of Bert Stern's photographs of Marilyn Monroe, printed in six colors using Day-Glo inks in the silk-screen process. Stern was the last photographer to photograph Monroe, in an extended and rather uninhibited session that took place on June 21, 1962, at the Bel Air Hotel in Hollywood. Manipulation of photographic images by photomechanical techniques was very popular in the late 1960s, and Stern experimented along those lines with his Monroe images. The portfolio was followed by the tallest, longest headline I had ever seen in a magazine. Over five inches tall and running over the seven-page length of the article, nineteenth-century woodtype pounded out the lengthy title of a feature about the editor of *The East Village Other*.

The sense of scale, texture, and imagery found in *Avant Garde*'s pages was remarkable. See, for example, Jim Spanfeller's intricate linear drawing layered with a huge red fingerprint for Karl Menninger's article about criminal justice. Lubalin freely departed from conventions of editorial design, creating a livelier visual pace than in most magazines. A double-page Simms Taback drawing of Einstein and Freud introduces their correspondence about the nature of war—an image bracketed by vertical headline type on each side, with the entire spread devoid of text type.

Avant Garde became a major influence on typographic design; within its pages Lubalin explored type with a ceaseless, restless energy. For example, I am unaware of seeing full-page typographic titles before *Avant Garde*, a technique that has lately been used with great success by Fred Woodward at *Rolling Stone*. Lubalin saw letterforms as entities, or beings; in the opening spread for a feature on the rock group The Fugs, the *i*'s in the copy on the right "embody" the band members, shown in a photo by Peter Hujar on the left.

Lubalin's obsession with asymmetrical geometric composition of type is seen in a back-cover announcement for an antiwar poster competition. The competition received over two thousand entries from twenty-four countries. Winning entries included a meticulous line image by illustrator James Grashow and a blatant typographic collaboration between Billy Apple and Robert Coburn.

Avant Garde mastered the photographic essay. Years later, referring to his collaboration with Lubalin on *Eros*, Ginzburg would describe their partnership in this way: "Lubalin and I worked together like Siamese twins. It was a rare and remarkable relationship. Although I was somewhat able as a photographer, I had no experience or training as a graphic designer. Herb brought a graphic impact. I never tried to overrule him, and almost never disagreed with him."

One day, Alwyn Scott Turner dropped off at the *Avant Garde* offices a portfolio of two thousand of his fifty thousand photographs of Americans and suggested that an issue be devoted to the best of them. Ginzburg and Lubalin thought it was a remarkable idea, so they produced *Avant Garde 13* as a sixty-eight-page image portfolio of Turner's work. Each image was centered on a page. Acute sensitivity was shown in pairing images for each double-page spread.

In any discussion of *Avant Garde,* complex issues surrounding sexual content inevitably surface. During the 1960s, erotic images were seen by many people as a celebration of human sexuality, not pornography. The 1960s threw off the chains of fear and timidity common to the fifties; but attitudes change so much from decade to decade that some materials found in *Avant Garde* and *Fact* might not be published in the climate of the 1990s. *Avant Garde* published a photographic portfolio by Thomas Weir entitled "The Virgin Forest." Weir's photographs of nude young girls posing in the woods were presented as a manifestation of sexual liberation; today, this would be totally unacceptable in light of serious concerns about child exploitation, molestation, and abuse. Sexual imagery in graphic art is under attack these days from both left and right. A resolution by the Southern Baptist convention in June 1991 called for the annihilation of the National Endowment for the Arts because photographs exhibited or made with grant funds were considered erotic or sacrilegious. Feminists attack sexual imagery as a degrading objectification of women. The AIDS epidemic has caused many people to fear sexuality, as in the era before the advent of the birth control pill.

Avant Garde reproduced the Horn/Griner photography studio's 1969 calendar, depicting infamous historical events, in its entirety. The calendar was distributed to two thousand ad agencies, editorial art directors, and other purchasers of photography. Each month featured a different bare-breasted female, attesting to the male dominance of the graphic design and advertising professions during the late sixties. Given that a majority of graphic designers and art directors are now female, I seriously doubt that the Horn/Griner calendar would be as well received today.

In terms of sexual imagery, *Avant Garde* was not above a bit of celebrity sensationalism, publishing a portfolio of John Lennon's erotic lithographs. Lennon was a much better songwriter than lithographer. Fortunately for *Avant Garde* readers, his lithographs were Lubalinized—that is, transformed by Lubalin's masterly skill for enhancing art and photography through inspired placement, scale, and contrast.

A special issue presented a portfolio of Pablo Picasso's erotic engravings, an aspect of his work somehow overlooked by art magazines and the museum establishment. The cover afforded Lubalin an opportunity to try out his newly released Avant Garde typeface. In the layout of the Picasso issue, however, Lubalin freely departed from Picasso's intention, overprinted etchings on bright yellow or blue pages, reversing etchings from a bleed black page, printing them in pale colored inks, and surrounding them with frames of violet or green. One wonders about the possible conflict between Lubalin's stunning page design and the integrity of Picasso's original images.

The final feature in the final issue of *Avant Garde* was "Belle Lettres: A Photo-Alphabet." Five Dutch designers, Ed van der Elsken, Anna Beeke, Pieter Brattinga, Anthon Beeke, and Geert Kooiman, posed a dozen nude models on the floor of an Amsterdam gymnasium to create an illustrated alphabet. Shortly after its publication, Ralph Ginzburg went to jail, and *Avant Garde* ceased publication, leaving a quarter of a million disappointed subscribers.

In 1972, Bill Katz published a revised edition of *Magazines for Libraries.* Again reviewing *Avant Garde,* he wrote: "After five years this pseudo little-art-political magazine continues to stagger on. [Apparently Katz was unaware that *Avant Garde* had folded after its summer 1971 issue.] A hodgepodge of colored plates, poetry, fiction, and various degrees of 'shock material,' it seems to never have established any definite character or reason for existence. It is no better—indeed, now seems worse than the first time it was analyzed here. Libraries can avoid without missing anything." I believe the content, imagery, and design of *Avant Garde* stood as its own best defense against Katz's attack.

Avant Garde captured the sensibilities and passions of the turbulent 1960s in a manner unlike that of any other magazine. From a '90s perspective, it not only represents its time and creators, but also reflects an openness and optimism amounting to innocence that is almost quaint. Mainly, it remains a monument to Herb Lubalin's singular brilliance as a graphic designer.

Lubalin, who died in 1981, had a legendary reputation for being a man of very few words. When asked about his taciturn nature, Ginzburg explained, "Herb spoke with his pencil."

Philip B. Meggs is School of the Arts Research Professor at the Virginia Commonwealth University School of the Arts. He is the author of A History of Graphic Design *(currently in its third edition),* Typographic Design: Form and Communication, *and* Revivial of the Fittest: Digital Versions of Classic Typefaces.

Originally published in PRINT, *March/April 1994*

POST–*SATURDAY EVENING POST*: MAGAZINE DESIGN AND ITS DIS-CONTENTS
Ellen Lupton

It has become common in recent years to bemoan the passing of the "Golden Age" of the American magazine, the slipping into oblivion or disrepair of *Esquire, Fortune, Harper's Bazaar, Holiday, McCall's, Playboy, Show*, and other publications that assumed a legendary stature in the 1950s and '60s. Technology often takes the blame: Magazines must compete in an era pervaded by television, a medium in which pictures predominate over words and programming is deliberately paced to accommodate the rhythmic intrusion of advertising. The "information explosion" has saturated the sponge of America's leisure time, encouraging more aggressive bids for readers' attention. In their struggle for survival, many magazines have shortened their articles and broken them up with more photographs, sidebars, pullout quotes, information graphics, boxed stories, and, of course, ads, which have found a home in the once-sacred "editorial well" of numerous publications, from *Mademoiselle* to *Esquire*.

While a conventional book is a continuous stream of characters mastered by a single writer, a magazine is a texture produced by editors, designers, advertisers, and readers, as well as authors. The magazine is a kind of paradigm for the post-Modern literary text: Features such as discontinuity, equivocality, ambitious visual effects, and the free mixture of high and low cultural references are being heralded by critics as hallmarks of a new voice in literature which rejects the monumentality, elitism, and formal autonomy of the modernist work of art. Yet the magazine, which emerged as a mass medium in the nineteenth century alongside the novel and the newspaper, has always incorporated, in varying manners and degrees, these principles of heterogeneity.

A periodical that weathered almost 150 years of magazine history but failed to survive the social and economic stresses of the '60s was the *Saturday Evening Post*. Founded in 1821, the *Post* was a model for the mass-circulation magazine. An advocate for the emerging consumer economy, it accepted advertising from its inception, and enjoyed a healthy circulation, which had reached 90,000 by the advent of the Civil War. Beginning at the turn of the twentieth century, its covers and pages became a showplace for American illustrators. The sentimental realism of Norman Rockwell, who created 321 *Post* covers during his career, exemplified the magazine's romantic and normative vision of middle-class, Midwestern, Anglo-Saxon America.

The *Saturday Evening Post* occupies a curious place within the "Golden Age" of magazine design, epitomized by the urbane cosmopolitanism of *Esquire* and *Harper's Bazaar*.

The *Post* never really made it to the Golden Age, and its 1961 redesign was a bid for survival in a changing marketplace. Executive editor Robert Fuoss blamed television for some of his problems: "We are competing with television and many other things for people's leisure time. So we wanted to produce a livelier, a great magazine."[1] The *Post*'s biggest competition was not just television, however, but other magazines, which were appealing to a younger and more culturally varied audience. In addition to toning down the magazine's overt Republicanism, Fuoss and art editor Kenneth Stuart hired sophisticated designers and photographers, including Saul Bass, Art Kane, and Herb Lubalin, to create dramatic opening pages for features and fiction pieces.

Despite its changed design strategy, the *Post* continued to struggle throughout the '60s, and opted for a second redesign in 1968. Once again, Herb Lubalin was called in for advice, but his new logo failed to save the magazine, which folded in February 1969. One strategy pursued by the *Post* was to terminate half of its subscriptions, limiting its readership to addresses with high-income zip codes. The magazine hoped to lower its ad rates while offering advertisers a more attractive demographic profile. As a column in the *New Yorker* commented sarcastically, the *Post* was punishing "the inconsiderate and economically unviable person who buys magazines and newspapers for the information and entertainment he can get out of them, without ever considering that he has an obligation to buy the many lovely products advertised in their pages."[2]

This unforgivable act of cynicism heralded a growing tendency to tilt a magazine's delicate balance of power in favor of advertising. According to Sam Antupit, who was art director of *Esquire* during the 1960s and who has continued since then to have a quiet influence on magazine design, the difference between the Golden Age and the "Ersatz Age" of today lies in this shift in the roles of editorial and advertising. While the best publications of the '60s were thought of as self-contained entities *supported by* advertising revenues, today more magazines are conceived as marketing tools deployed *in the service of* advertising. "Instead of being produced for an audience," says Antupit, "magazines are now made for a market, a collection of shopping baskets." *Esquire,* for example, has become a service magazine instructing its readers on how and what to buy, but not how to think.

Yet Antupit recalls that even publishers in the so-called Golden Age had to battle against the interests of ad departments. Women's service magazines such as *McCall's* were the first to succumb, perhaps because of advertising's traditional focus on women as the primary purchasers of branded consumer goods. "The Golden Age is a myth," says Antupit. "Magazines then had the same problems they have now. The problems simply have gotten worse: aggressive ad departments, editors who aren't visually oriented, and publishers who are the product of business schools. These people are only concerned with content when it threatens—or even can be perceived as threatening—ad revenues."

Today, a major source of competition for many magazines continues to be other magazines. As *New York Times* advertising reporter Randall Rothenberg pointed out, increased magazine profits during the 1980s emboldened publishers to launch numerous new titles, which are now forced to compete with each other for a limited supply of advertising revenues—advertisers cannot afford to buy all the open space in an infinitely expanding frontier of periodicals. Rothenberg advised magazines to market themselves to advertisers not as an alternative to television, but as a supplement to it, suggesting that print and broadcast media have become a seamless surface of interchangeable messages rather than materially distinct entities. The medium, perhaps, is no longer the message.[3]

Walter Bernard, who in 1968 helped initiate the influential style of *New York* magazine with Milton Glaser and publisher Clay Felker, states that the economic squeeze on the magazine industry during the last few years has put increasing pressure on art directors to make magazines profitable. Bernard explains, "Editors have decided that we're in a Visual Age. So when a magazine begins to fail, they think it's time to redesign. A huge burden of expectation is invested in the art director." At its most rigorous, a redesign strategy sets out to visually express an altered editorial attitude—see, for example, Sam Antupit's 1985 redesign of *Harper's*, which accompanied editor Lewis Lapham's new concept of the magazine as an analytical collage of cultural artifacts. More superficially, format changes are effected to satisfy the shifting tastes of a maturing readership or to put forward a freshly powdered face for soliciting prospective advertisers (thus the continual identity shifts of the magazine *Self* in the late 1980s).

As early as 1959, Herb Lubalin credited TV with forcing attention to the relationship between word and image in print advertising. In the 1960s, media prophet Marshall McLuhan heralded the rise of a progressively visual culture and the fall of the "Gutenberg Galaxy." McLuhan's invocation of TV as the democratic genie of the age echoed the technological optimism of the 1920s constructivist avant-garde. László Moholy-Nagy and El Lissitzky embraced the image as a supplement to and even replacement for the word, and they were especially entranced by mechanically transmitted pictures—photographic, lithographic, and telegraphic. Today, remarks on the rapid replacement of words with images are commonplace, whether inflected with tones of pleasure or disappointment.

A 1989 essay by design critic Joseph Giovannini mourns the lost integrity of the text in contemporary magazines, which he blames on "competition from television, the VCR, and other nonprint media," resulting in "aggressively designed pages that freely mix and cut words, photographs, and graphic devices, creating a page of design rather than a page of text."[4] Meanwhile, some of the young designers responsible for such "pages of design" reject the aesthetic moralism of their antitechnological elders and herald television as a source of legitimate—and unavoidable—inspiration.

But is the word really disappearing? While images indeed have gained leverage in the conduct of public and private life, words nonetheless continue to proliferate. Early arguments against the introduction of sound into motion pictures—such as the claim that film is an inherently silent, visual medium whose artistic integrity would be violated by sound—seem hopelessly antiquated in the face of the contemporary medium. Today's cinema depends on clever dialogue and soundtrack sales, as well as sophisticated visual effects, to colonize the senses. The word, whether written or spoken, has the alchemical power to transform the meaning and usefulness of an image. Silent television is an untenable commodity, and so is a magazine without captions.

As design historian Philip B. Meggs has pointed out, magazines remain powerful *because* they incorporate the written word, not in spite of it; typography is still the preferred medium for complex information.[5] Many of the devices that Giovannini claims have spoiled the traditional unity of the text are nonetheless *textual* in nature, if not strictly *verbal*. A look at contemporary magazines reveals that the picture has not, in fact, replaced the word, but rather that words have become more material, more embodied, more pictorial. While sophisticated illustration was a hallmark of 1970s art direction (recall the *New York* magazine of Walter Bernard and Milton Glaser), art direction of the 1980s was marked by a fascination with typography.

Spy magazine has exemplified—and parodied—the recent fuss over type, serving as a witty commentary on the literary and graphic conventions of magazines. The flashy information graphics incorporated by news publications in the 1970s and '80s—see, for example, Walter Bernard's 1977 makeover of *Time*—perform in *Spy* as ironic satires of journalistic seriousness. Stephen Doyle, whose firm Drenttel Doyle Partners designed *Spy*'s original format in 1986, recalls, "We let the magazine use its own body parts to point to itself." In the early issues, elaborate maps of Manhattan offered data about gangster life (from executions to leisure spots) or the commercial zones of Manhattan (from the Meat Packing District to the Cheap, Ugly Clothing for the Whole Family District). Under the art direction of Alexander Isley, the absurd fastidiousness of these maps became a finely tuned language of information graphics, which married a taste for the ridiculous with a profoundly archival sensibility. Isley's graphs, tables, diagrams, and flowcharts have been copied in numerous other magazines.

A related spirit of typographic preciousness inflects the current graphic styles of *Spy, Rolling Stone, Premiere, Entertainment Weekly, GQ, Egg,* and others, suggesting that designers are finding texts as materially engaging as pictures. A common device, perhaps inspired by *Spy,* is to treat images as if they were type, injecting icons and tiny photographs into bodies of copy. The current immersion in the typographic specificity of the printed page—more typefaces and type sizes, more drop caps and pullout quotes, more heads and subheads—indicates a renewed *writerliness* in magazine design, a general détente between graphic designers and the printed word. Roger Black comments, "Art directors used to be frustrated illustrators and photographers. Now they're frustrated writers and editors."

A designer might use typographic devices to make copy more readable (or skimmable), to build a clear structure for a disparate collection of texts and pictures, or to diverge from the one-way path of a conventional literary document. News magazines such as *Time, Newsweek,* and *U.S. News and World Report* include full course stories as well as bite-size info-chunks for the impatient reader. Theatrically disjunctive typography is common in women's fashion magazines, whose editorial material consists largely of short elliptical passages, their length and language equivalent to that of advertising copy. A magazine such as *Vogue* is essentially a portfolio of deluxe ads whose sophistication has surpassed that of the editorial matter framing it.

While TV has been the world's most conspicuous medium since the 1950s, for designers working in the 1980s and 1990s, the personal computer has had an even more direct impact. The magazine and digital type-foundry *Emigre* is a forum for the neo-avant-garde designers Zuzana Licko and Rudy VanderLans, who have tried to gorge a new graphic identity for the word which embodies the technological soul for the small but mighty Macintosh. For designers who prefer traditional letterforms, microcomputers have made it generally cheaper and easier to produce a magazine and have encouraged the use of run-arounds, drop caps, curved lines of type, and other devices.

Two magazines produced entirely on "desktop publishing" equipment are *Entertainment Weekly* and *Smart,* neither of which looks overtly hi-tech—no mannered stair-stepping or futuristic fonts. Yet the computer's impact is far from negligible. Michael Grossman, design director of Time-Warner's infant product *Entertainment Weekly,* says microcomputers have enabled his staff to routinely perform technical acrobatics prohibited by conventional production methods. Technology also has given the public, through animated television graphics, "a new visual slang, a new tolerance and appetite for typographic variety."

Roger Black, design director and part owner of *Smart,* says the computer is encouraging people to introduce new magazines; he sees the designer-entrepreneur as one possible trend of the 1990s and beyond. *Smart's* art director, Rhonda Rubinstein, groups computer-aided publishing in two camps: "On the one hand, there's *Emigre* with an esthetic that makes the use of the computer conspicuous, and on the other hand there are the more classical publications, like *Smart,* that view the computer as an expedient tool and methodology with no inherent esthetic." The computer is changing the *institution* of magazine publishing—its cost (cheaper), its bureaucracy (smaller), its subject matter (more specialized), and its market (more focused).

The graphic mores of fashion, celebrity, and entertainment periodicals are, for obvious reasons, more permissive than those of news, political, and literary journals. It is these magazines—*Interview, L.A. Style, Premiere, Rolling Stone*—which beckon young designers with the promise of glamour. Walter Bernard explains, "Serious magazines like *Time* and *Newsweek* need an infusion now of young talents, but designers embarking on careers in art direction aren't attracted to the discipline and conservatism demanded by their huge circulation and objective, reportorial tone."

Yet Bernard's own 1977 redesign of *Time*—with its illustrative information graphics and bright, large photographs—reveals the subtle influence of his earlier *New York* magazine, whose look was directed at a young, ultra-urban, style-conscious audience and came to influence regional magazines across the country. *New York* was what Bernard and Rochelle Udell, associate editorial director of Condé Nast, call a "feeder publication," a relatively low-circulation magazine that is picked up by young designers and comes to influence the mainstream of publishing. "Feeder" magazines in the 1980s included *Spy, Emigre, The Face,* and *Metropolis.*

In an interview, Michael Grossman frankly discussed the delicate customs governing the grammar of a given publication and the designer's relative lack of freedom within them. A magazine's code of propriety results from the expectations of readers, editors, and advertisers, the current imagery of magazines, and the art director's own inclinations toward conformity or innovation. Describing his work at *Entertainment Weekly,* which promotes itself as a critical guide to the mass media, Grossman explains that the magazine has deliberately absorbed some of the graphic devices of the contemporary culture press (*Premiere, Rolling Stone, Spy*) and of the entertainment industries more generally (movies, television, album covers). His goal was to translate these sources into a readable, user-friendly language viable for a mass-circulation weekly. Grossman explains, "Visually, I know I can get away with more than *Time* or *Newsweek* can, but less than *Rolling Stone*. We've positioned our-selves at the edge of the mainstream. We're not *People* magazine or *TV Guide,* but we're not avant-garde either." Grossman is more interested in inventing a unique graphic style.

Among the culture magazines, *Rolling Stone* has played a particularly influential role during its more than twenty years of publication. Its original format, designed by Robert Kingsbury in the late '60s, introduced elegance and order into the chaotic look of the under-ground press movement.[6] Kingsbury's distinctive "Scotch rules," borrowed from nineteenth-century typography, remain part of the magazine's subtly neo-Victorian image today. Several influential art directors have spent time at *Rolling Stone,* including Mike Salisbury, Roger Black, and, currently, Fred Woodward.

While Woodward's thoughtfully eclectic typography and active involvement in the editorial process have brought him much-deserved respect from other art directors, *Rolling Stone* epitomizes the glut of advertising in contemporary periodicals. For example, the five-page cover story of the June 1990 issue is interrupted by three full pages of ads and a twelve-page, detachable "advertorial" for All Star, an athletic-shoe manufacturer. Ads which imitate the look of editorial matter date back to at least the 1920s in American publishing, when many product pitches masqueraded as factual journalistic reports. Now such ads com-monly encase a body of information which is literally editorial—for example, All Star's "Summer Music Guide." The advertiser thus becomes a publisher, commissioning its own designers and writers, exercising full veto power, and in essence creating its own separate, removable publication within the magazine.

For Walter Bernard, the softening of the distinction between advertising and edito-rial is exemplified by the rise of the multipage fashion ad. During the 1980s, campaigns for Gap, Guess, Benetton, and Ralph Lauren were able to colonize more than a dozen consecu-tive pages in magazines, claiming territory not only in fashion periodicals but in others, ranging from *Vanity Fair* to the *New York Times Magazine.* Such ads enjoy a continuity rarely afforded to editorial matter; like detachable advertorials, they construct an autono-mous, self-enclosed world inside a publication.

A few magazines have decided to eliminate advertising altogether. As of June 1990, *Ms* magazine went ad-free, changing its name to *Ms: The World of Women.* During the 1980s, this formerly semiradical feminist journal degenerated into little more than a career woman's service magazine, losing its political edge. Despite its concessions to the era's mainstream val-ues, the magazine failed to be an economic success. A complete redesign by Sam Antupit accompanies the repositioning of *Ms,* which now depends on subscriptions for support.

The ad-free strategy of *Ms* is not likely to become a sweeping trend in publishing. Most designers, editors, and publishers will continue to contend with the fragile aesthetic and economic line between advertising and editorial. Magazines have historically depended on the sale of ad space, but they must preserve their own voices to maintain credibility before readers. Without such credibility, even advertisers will be scared away. When the pur-suit of profit outweighs the expression of an editorial viewpoint, journalism's traditional functions—to inform, persuade, and entertain—are overwhelmed.

It is amusing to speculate about the Magazine of the Future. Will it be distributed on cable television? Will it be modified for the unique purchasing patterns of each viewer?

Will it consist entirely of ads? Will it be wholly owned by Rupert Murdoch? But for graphic designers, the most important question is this: Will it have an art director?

One of the lasting legacies of the Golden Age is the preeminence of the art director, a powerful figure whose name ranks respectably high on the masthead of major magazines. Will that figure still be needed in the smaller, more narrowly focused publications encouraged by cheaper magazine production? Speaking of the future of publishing, Roger Black suggests that the designers who will survive the coming decades will be those able to meet the challenges of technology. These challenges are not simply aesthetic—perhaps the most innovative thing about *Emigre* will turn out to be, in the long run, not the magazine's computer-vernacular style but Rudy VanderLans's decision to turn the roles of publisher, editor, designer, chief reporter, production manager, and director of marketing into a single job description.

Black feels that the "yuppie clutter" which dominated magazine design in the 1980s is being replaced by a new concern for simplicity. "We are experiencing a revival of the sixties," says Black. "Helvetica and grids instead of torn paper and ransom-note typography." He thinks that this move backward toward functionalism is important preparation for the future, when designers will be called on—if they are prepared—to guide readers/viewers through texts whose structure is not yet known. Today's problem of how to make a familiar medium look new could be replaced by how to make a new medium look familiar.

Black would also like to see designers become more active in publishing itself, as he has done in the recent launch of *Smart*. Roger Black, Inc., consults with clients not only on design but also on editing and fact-checking; by linking his studio with a publisher, as he plans to do soon, Black hopes his firm will help initiate new magazines. Microcomputers, by simplifying design and production, are reversing the trend toward specialization. The number of staff positions required to run a magazine is shrinking, while the number of magazines is swelling. Black comments, "The publishing industry will need more and more people—but fewer *untalented* people." And those people may be expected to play a greater role in conceiving, structuring, and editing the *content* of publications.

I was surprised that many of the art directors I spoke with, including Roger Black, Michael Grossman, Terry Koppel, and Rhonda Rubinstein, said their work was tending toward greater simplicity rather than complexity. "Layering" was one of the buzzwords of the '80s, signaling the replacement of functionalism with a postmodern love for irony, ambiguity, and equivocation. With the Green consumer politics which launched the nineties, the term "layering" now evokes the multiple skins of paper and polystyrene encasing microwaveable dinners. Perhaps the refined typographic detailing which marked magazine design in the 1980s has laid the ground for a more word-conscious, writerly design ethos in the years to come.

Ellen Lupton is adjunct curator of contemporary design at Cooper-Hewitt, National Design Museum, Smithsonian Institute in New York. She is chair of the graphic design department at Maryland Institute, College of Art in Baltimore She is the author of numerous books, including Design Writing Research: Writing on Graphic Design, *coauthored with J. Abbott Miller.*

Originally published in PRINT, *November/December 1990*

Notes

1. *Business Week*, 19 August 1961.
2. *The New Yorker*, 20 July 1968.
3. Randall Rothenberg, "Improving Magazines' Prospects," *New York Times*, 13 June 1990, p. D9.
4. Joseph Giovannini, "A Zero Degree of Graphics," in *Graphic Design in America: A Visual Language History* (Minneapolis: Walker Art Center; New York: Harry N. Abrams, 1989), pp. 200–213.
5. Philip B. Meggs, "Time vs. Newsweek: Coping and Competing in the Age of CNN," *PRINT* 42, no. 5 (September/October 1988): 98–104.
6. Steven Heller, "The Underground Revisited," *PRINT* 39, no. 2 (March/April 1985): 35–43.

APRIL 1968
PRICE $1

Esquire

THE MAGAZINE FOR MEN

The Passion of Muhammad Ali

ESQUIRE AND ITS ART DIRECTORS: A SURVIVOR'S TALE
Steven Heller

In revoking *Esquire*'s second-class mailing privileges, the Postmaster General of the United States charged that the magazine was obscene, its content not "information of a public character." Although this sounds like the kind of detour around the First Amendment Senator Jesse Helms might try, the action was actually taken in 1943 against a ten-year-old magazine whose reputation for taboo-breaking was more accidental than deliberate. Publisher David Smart never intended for *Esquire* to be revolutionary when he founded the magazine in 1933. Rather, he envisioned a deluxe men's companion of literature, fashion, art, and girls. It was the last—specifically, the sultry "pinups" painted by Alberto Varga, creator of the Varga Girl—that prompted official action. *Esquire* appealed the case all the way to the Supreme Court, which in 1946 ruled that the Postmaster General had no discretion to withhold any privileges simply because the magazine failed to live up to some vague standard of public morality. Justice William O. Douglas wrote that such an act would be "a power of censorship abhorrent to our traditions."

This wasn't the last time *Esquire* would ignite controversy or challenge taste. Indeed, for almost six decades, *Esquire* has been an American publishing institution without equal in the realms of art, literature, and, sometimes, politics. Alternately a trendsetter and bellwether, it has at times rocked the foundation of propriety, challenged cultural traditions, and itself been shaken by the pressures of public opinion. For these reasons, *Esquire*, more than any other periodical in American history, deserves serious examination of those aspects that have made it unique: its astute editors, esteemed contributors, and numerous incarnations. A multifaceted analysis would fill a hefty book, however, so for this special issue of *PRINT*, I've decided to focus on one very integral, but often ignored, dimension of *Esquire*'s publishing history: its art directors and their impact on the magazine's development.

When *PRINT* celebrated *Esquire* for the first time, in 1958, it was one of the most editorially stimulating and visually exciting monthlies around. Though ostensibly a "men's magazine," each issue transcended that narrow definition owing to premier fiction and nonfiction by critically acclaimed authors, new work by important (or soon to become important) photographers and artists, and light features on contemporary style and fashion that both reported current trends and set their own standards. It was also irreverent—even downright sacrilegious at times. *Esquire* was a magazine in the original sense—a *storehouse* of information and entertainment without equal. And it remained that way through its most fertile period, from the mid-1950s until the early 1970s, after which its loyal constituency began to falter.

The March/April 1958 article, titled "Henry Wolf, Strategic Designer: Proof That Better Design and Better Business Can Go Hand in Hand," is a portfolio of Wolf's alluring pages and spreads and a validation that *Esquire* had graphically come of age. Even though the publication had been around since 1933, and had employed Paul Rand to design some of its features between 1935 and 1940, Wolf's tenure marked an exemplary marriage of sophisticated content and intelligent design. The article suggests that *Esquire*'s young art director was someone to be reckoned with. In the 1950s, art directors were not nearly as peripatetic as they are today, so when *PRINT* published this piece, it was not merely reporting on a hot property, but documenting the work of a practitioner whom its editors believed had staying power. (Ironically, shortly after the feature was published, Wolf ended his six years with *Esquire* and moved on to be art director of *Harper's Bazaar*.)

Wolf was hired as "graphics editor" of *Esquire* in 1952, five months after he joined the promotion art department as a junior designer. He was twenty-six, one of the youngest design stewards at any national magazine. Not only his age but his sudden elevation from the chorus line to a leading role on the masthead was the stuff of publishing industry legend. Arnold Gingrich, *Esquire*'s founding editor, who set the tone of the magazine in the 1930s by spicing high literature with a touch of salaciousness, had returned to the company after resolving a disagreement with publisher David Smart that had forced the former's temporary retirement. After Gingrich left in the early 1940s, *Esquire* took a nosedive, becoming essentially a girlie magazine with some mediocre fiction and fashion sections. Its layout was tawdry, replete with crass novelty lettering and sentimental *Cosmopolitan*-style illustration. When Gingrich returned, he sought to cure its most superficial ills by replacing then art director George Samerjan with a bright new talent.

Wolf recounts the decisive event: "In the fall of '52, the top editors met to discuss how terrible the magazine looked and how they would like to make a change. Apparently, some promotion pieces that I had designed were lying on the table. Gingrich asked his editors, 'Why can't the damn magazine look like these things?' Nobody said a word. Then Arnold, in his direct way, asked, 'Who the hell did these?' Someone said, 'We've got this young Viennese kid downstairs who does good work very fast.'" Wolf was immediately called up from the "slave ship" to the executive offices to meet Gingrich, who asked him to design a special eighteen-page section on Italian design. "I was shocked," recalls Wolf. "I said, 'I can't do that because Samerjan designs the spreads and assigns the art.' I asked Arnold how I was going to get the photographs. He said he had them and that I should take them home, do the section over the weekend, and bring it back on Monday. Again I balked. 'But where do I get the photostats?' He told me to be resourceful. With that, I did the piece, and Gingrich was very pleased. He asked if I would like to design the entire magazine. I said, 'Not me. I'm the lowest guy in the bullpen.'" But Gingrich was intent, and the next week Samerjan was gone Soviet-style—without a trace. And to co-art-direct with Wolf, Gingrich hired the former art director of *Flair*.

Since Wolf's style was more refined and ultimately at odds with that of his veteran colleague, he realized that two chief art directors for *Esquire* would be chaotic. He suggested that Gingrich make a change. "It could be him or me," continues Wolf. "But two heads were neither necessary nor productive. This happened on a Thursday afternoon. During the weekend, I was certain I had ruined my life. On Monday, I came in and my colleague was gone! I didn't know whether he was sick or what. Next thing I knew, someone was moving my things into his corner office." Wolf had just turned twenty-seven, and this was the opportunity of a lifetime. "It took a year or two to get the magazine the way I liked," he says. But eventually he redesigned the cover to reflect his own taste for conceptual photography (shot by Dan Wynn and Ben Somoroff); assigned Ed Benguiat, who was in the bullpen, to streamline the rather horsey *Esquire* masthead into a distinctive logotype; imposed restraint on the interior typography; and developed a stable of expressive illustrators, including Tom Allen, Robert Weaver, Tomi Ungerer, Rudy DeHarak, and R. O. Blechman. "Still," he laments, "I couldn't get rid of the girlie gatefold for some time because Gingrich didn't want to lose that part of his audience."

Gingrich's tastes molded *Esquire* and influenced the young Wolf. Once in a televised interview, newsman Edward R. Murrow asked Gingrich how he decided what went into the magazine. "I do a magazine I'd like to get in the mail," replied the dapper man-about-town, on whom the "Eskie" image was apparently modeled. "I like fishing, I like cars, I like some girls." He also appreciated what his editors and art director liked and gave Wolf as many as eight pages in each issue to present whatever he wanted. Wolf exulted over this atmosphere of trust and creative growth. He recalls showing Gingrich a painting by the young Robert Weaver for the first time. "Arnold said, 'I don't like it, but I am fifty-five and you are twenty-nine, so let's run it and see what happens.'" This scenario was repeated countless times.

By 1957, Wolf was finally given the title art director and could do essentially whatever he wanted. He holds Gingrich responsible for this freedom and the loyalty it inspired. "To me, Arnold was the quintessential Great American," recalls Wolf. "I smoked Camels because he smoked Camels. I wore black knit ties because he wore them. But more important, the magazine *was* Arnold. I didn't do the work for money [not until two years after Wolf was put in charge was his salary increased from $125 to $250 a week], but to make Arnold happy. He was my Medici, my mentor." This fact did not go unnoticed among the top *Esquire* editors, Clay Felker, Ralph Ginzburg, and Harold Hayes, all of whom gave Wolf a wide berth.

In the late 1950s, *Esquire* was not just a collection of random stories and features but an entity with a massive "editorial sandwich," or well. Some vestiges of the past remained during Wolf's tenure, such as the girlie pics and gag cartoons, but the editorial mix had changed considerably. This was due in part to the concerns of its star editors. Ginzburg, who would go on to found *Eros* and spend time in jail for violating obscenity laws, was, not surprisingly, interested in issues of censorship. And Felker brought in stories like "The New Bohemia," which dealt with the contemporary social milieu. Wolf's interests in high and low culture were manifested in exciting photo shoots by some of America's up-and-coming image-makers. Indeed, all writers and artists wanted to be showcased in *Esquire*. "To have Ben Shahn and Richard Lindner do cartoons and illustrations for $75 and $150 was amazing," says Wolf. But even this hotbed had to cool down sometime. A change came when Wolf was offered the job of his former teacher Alexey Brodovitch at *Harper's Bazaar*. "I didn't want to leave Arnold," he recalls with palpable regret, "but I was made a terrific monetary offer, and Arnold said, 'If it doesn't work out, you can always come back.'"

Wolf left in 1958 and did not return (except briefly some years later to do the type for the fortieth-anniversary issue). He was replaced by his assistant, a young cartoonist and writer, Robert Benton, who later became an Academy Award–winning film director. Benton was art director during what has been described as a period of "fun anarchy." Gingrich was loosening control, and Harold Hayes and Clay Felker were in a face-off for the editorship. For most of Benton's tenure, no one was really in charge, allowing him freedom that otherwise might have been impossible. Benton is credited by many of those with whom he worked for bringing editorial illustration to its next conceptual stage. Robert Andrew Parker, for instance, walked in off the street with his series of "Imaginary War" paintings, which Benton rushed into print. Milton Glaser recalls that he was a terrific collaborator with the likes of Harvey Schmidt and Gloria Steinem. Glaser also notes that "Benton was wonderfully inventive and funny and gave a very special stamp to the magazine during this period. It differed from Henry's *Esquire* not in terms of design but on the literary side. He had great ideas for stories that he and [writer] David Newman [later his movie collaborator] were always generating. To a large extent, they formed the backbone of *Esquire*'s character at that time." Benton and Newman's most lasting contribution was *Esquire*'s "Dubious Achievement Awards." Each year, the "Dubies" laid waste to pompous, hypocritical, and scandalous public figures with biting wit and needle-sharp truth that sometimes bordered on libel.

In 1963, Harold Hayes won the hard-fought editorship of *Esquire*. A year later, Benton left to begin his movie career, and David November was brought in to "do the mechanicals for Harold," as one former staff member put it. Hayes, though an insightful editor, was doing the art direction—and doing it poorly. The magazine was beginning to slide downhill again, when Sam Antupit was introduced to him.

Antupit had previously been Wolf's assistant at *Harper's Bazaar* and *Show*. He was working at Push Pin Studios when outgoing editor Clay Felker, whom he knew casually, asked if he would like to be art director of *Esquire*. "I didn't know Hayes, but *Esquire* was a plum," he recalls. As the story goes, Felker put a note in Hayes's typewriter the next morning telling him to call Antupit and hire him. "Clay really had a great feeling for *Esquire*, even though he was on the way out," Antupit relates. "And he knew that the magazine was kind of bumbling around at that time. It wasn't really a magazine, but rather looked as though it was composed of whatever was ready by deadline." Antupit took the job with the proviso that he be formally called "art director" (in consolidating power, Hayes had been loath to give away that title), and that he have full control of the visual content. The single exception to this was an agreement that George Lois, whose agency, Papert Koenig Lois, was doing benchmark advertising, would conceive and design the covers. "It didn't bother me that George was doing the covers because there was so much else to do, anyway," explains Antupit. "And Harold made a really good point about why it was a smart decision politically. You see, every editor felt that his or her articles were the best in the magazine and that they should be featured on the cover. Hayes said testily that it was up to him to decide which was the most important, but he couldn't do that without alienating his editors.

So here was the perfect thing. An outsider read all the manuscripts and picked the one that he wanted to illustrate. Sometimes he didn't pick Harold's lead. The Andy Warhol soup can thing was not the main feature, but it was one of the best covers George ever did."

If any icons of American graphic design are worth preserving, George Lois's *Esquire* covers from the mid-1960s to the very early 1970s are. Most were collaborations with photographer Carl Fischer that took an average of three days to produce; they are considered among the most powerful propaganda imagery in any medium and certainly the most memorable magazine covers ever. Harnessing the technique of photomanipulation, Lois and Fischer produced images equal in acerbity and acuity to those of the pioneer German photomontagist John Heartfield. Eclipsed by the image, however, the usually brilliant cover lines are often overlooked. Hayes and Lois worked on them together. As Antupit recalls, "Half the sentence would be said by one, and then the other would interrupt and finish it. It was a great working relationship."

Antupit was one of the wittiest art directors around, but he resolved not to goose up the content (as he is credited with doing), but to reformat *Esquire*, giving it a framework in which he could best show his own concepts. He standardized all the column widths and made room for illustration. "They had had David Levine doing postage-stamp spots, as if he was some little old man from the Bureau of Printing and Engraving," he says. "So I opened up the columns for art and started a gray pace going to fight the ads." In fact, the primary goal was to *distinguish* editorial from advertising. Under Wolf, there had been a "very elegant pace"; the ads in his *Esquire* really fit hand in glove with the editorial. "But after that," continues Antupit, "the ads got to be really shouting, screaming stuff, and the fashion ones were awful—not just tasteless and colorless, but stupid and gross. I tried to set up a little matrix so that every time there was an ad, you were already into what you were reading. And the runover continued around the ad."

Esquire was still blessed with an editorial well, despite attempts by the advertising department to interrupt it. Antupit used it shrewdly, too, by creating the most cinematic pacing allowed by page-turning. "To establish a rhythm right away, I tried to do a really tight first article that was cohesively designed from the first to sixth pages. Then, near the end of the book, came the fashion, so that you could end on something much brighter than the crummy ads back there." *Esquire* had earned a reputation as a "reading magazine," but curiously, one of the difficulties for the reader was the absence of subheads in masses of elegant, though gray, type. "Harold thought subheads were crutches for readers who had good legs," explains Antupit. Another of Antupit's strengths was conceptual art. "I really worked closely with illustrators and photographers so that there was never a decorative piece of art." He also succeeded in limiting the cartoons to one that occupied a full page and a number of smaller cartoons in the front matter. "That was not entirely my doing," he admits. "The old *Esquire* cartoonists were actually dying off."

Antupit's goal, to let a reader open the magazine anywhere and know that it was *Esquire*, was accomplished both with typography and illustration. The type was understated by today's standards, but playful. Antupit consistently used new illustrators (including one student per issue) because "the same few old hands were used to excess by most national magazines, thus creating a visual sameness." But there was a fine line between the look of

Esquire and that of other magazines. "I really felt uncomfortable about being given pages to fill," he says about a responsibility bestowed on him by Hayes. "Every so often, I would have a terrific portfolio, but I didn't want to show something that was too ethereal compared to what the rest of the magazine was doing." One of Antupit's proudest accomplishments was a story on the building of the Verrazano Narrows Bridge linking Brooklyn to Staten Island, with dramatic photographs by Bruce Davidson. The photo-essay had been so strong that Gay Talese was assigned to write an accompanying text. "The feature started out being twelve pages, but that was too much," Antupit says. "To have all photography and no text wasn't *Esquire*. It was *Life* or *Look*."

During the late '60s, *Esquire* covered the social and political revolutions of the era. While many of its covers announced stories about political folly and changing mores, its sardonic parodies, Dubious Achievement Awards, and campus supplements underscored a commitment to a new generation of "New Left" constituents. For a while, Harold Hayes even seemed to trade *Esquire*'s male focus for a more ecumenical stance. But contrary to appearances, Hayes was no radical. As Antupit says, "Harold would get a lot of his ideas from *Time* magazine. Here we're all going to openings and talking with writers and getting cut by the leading edge, and Harold's reading *Time*. He was never a flaming activist." To counter his southern provincialism, Hayes, a native North Carolinian, placed his trust in his top-notch editors and art directors. Antupit notes that he also "had an absolute genius for putting the wrong writer with the right idea—I mean, sending Jean Genet and Samuel Beckett to the 1968 Democratic Convention in Chicago was brilliant. I think Harold just wanted to keep everybody off balance."

Esquire was also at the top of its form in the late '60s because Hayes ignored demographics and other marketing pseudosciences. Antupit remembers that the ad department once suggested that Hayes include a few editorial pages on vodka so they could sell more vodka ads. "He refused, saying, 'If you got off your fat asses and went to more agencies, you could get more advertising.' He didn't succumb to that trade-off garbage one bit." Editorially, he also made instinctively right decisions. For a typical Antupit assignment, the fashion photographer Hiro, who had never worked in journalism before, was sent to cover Martin Luther King's funeral. He returned with three photographs, the best one showing mourners sitting on tombstones, awaiting the arrival of King's cortege. Antupit decided to pitch Hayes on running it as a double spread with inset text. In characteristic Hayes fashion, the editor bellowed, "Inset it? You asshole! Make it a double spread and start the text on the next page." Hayes earned Antupit's respect, and in return he got exemplary work. "My loyalty was to Harold," he said, "because I had never run across anybody like him."

After staying at *Esquire* for five years (1964–69), Antupit decided to open a studio with Richard Hess. "Your style becomes your rut," he freely admits. "And the *Esquire* style became my rut. I was looking at everything in terms of, 'How can I twist it a little?' because that was our way. When that approach became stale, I knew it was time to leave." Antupit wanted to hire Dugald Stermer, the activist art director of *Ramparts* magazine, to replace him. But Hayes preferred two men who became known as the French Connection: Jean-Paul Goude and Jean Lagarrigue. Antupit had originally used them for their wildly conceptual illustrations; they knew little about type or magazine design. But Hayes apparently liked their quirky ideas. More important, he was attracted by the fact that no other American magazine was using their talents. While Goude and Lagarrigue did the conceptual work, Bob Daniels, the former art director of *Atlanta* magazine, was hired to do basic art direction.

About a year after the triumvirate took over, a young British illustrator named Richard Weigand ambled into the *Esquire* offices looking for freelance work. He was interviewed by Goude, who told him, "We're looking for somebody who can help us, since we're not as secure about doing type as we are about doing illustration." Weigand was ostensibly hired for a pasteup job, but while Daniels administered the "good features," he ended up art-directing the rest. Gradually, the editors also assigned "the more complicated stuff" to him. But this ad hoc art direction was not really working out, and Hayes knew it. When Daniels left in 1971, the same year that *Esquire*'s format shrank from *Life*-size to *Time*-size, Weigand was asked to "fill in." "I wasn't made art director," he recalls. "I was just told to do the magazine." Lagarrigue had gone back to France and could not get a return visa, and Goude was languishing in his absence. Gradually, Weigand and Goude started working together. Weigand recalls with mild amusement, "After about a year, Hayes grudgingly said, 'I suppose you'd better be the art director.' Actually, what's funny is that at the time, I tried to get others to take the job and nobody wanted it."

The early 1970s were not a good time for *Esquire*. Both its size and constituency had dwindled. Its hot themes were cooling. The unrest on campus was ostensibly over, the Vietnam war was coming to an end, and Richard Nixon was about to be Watergated out of office. Lifestyle was looming as a dark cloud on the cultural horizon, and the old magazines were finding it hard to adjust. *Esquire* had returned to something of its macho, Hemingway-inspired ethos, but was still floundering. Moreover, *New York* magazine and the *National Lampoon* were shaving off different sets of younger readers from *Esquire*'s potential audience. Hayes was uncertain in what direction the magazine should go, which might have accounted for his demand that Weigand and Goude present at least five viable features at every editorial meeting. "The magazine was not too editorially healthy, although there was still some great writing," recalls Weigand. "Consequently, they had lots of pages open, so we produced a lot of features." Goude's ideas were always about what Weigand calls "social esthetics." "He believed in integration of the races as well as classic American values—which I, too, liked, as a European. That's why we tried to influence fashion. But *Esquire*'s fashion editors were producing crappy post–flower power stuff. We couldn't find examples of what we thought Americans should look like, so we made up our own stuff." And Hayes gave them free rein, when he was convinced that the ideas were good.

Weigand admits that more time was spent on the conceptual than the typographic aspects of *Esquire*; and though the quality of visual features was certainly high, the layout was a bit anarchic. Another factor in the typographic malaise was Hayes's constant fiddling with heads until closing time, which made it difficult to do any type finessing. But Weigand was committed to making *Esquire* the best magazine he could because, like Antupit, he thought Hayes "was the best editor I ever worked for." Hayes ran *Esquire* like a boot camp. "He could be a bit of a bastard," says Weigand, "but I got so used to it that it took me a long time to get used to other editors who were indecisive."

In 1973, a brief news item appeared in the *New York Times*: "Harold T. P. Hayes, the editor and assistant publisher of *Esquire*, has quit because of a disagreement about titles," says the publisher, Arnold Gingrich." Hayes, then forty-seven, had been groomed to be publisher upon Gingrich's mandatory retirement at seventy, but he had insisted on keeping the editorship of the magazine, which ran counter to company policy. With Hayes gone, George Lois, who had continued to do covers through the Antupit, Goude, and Weigand tenures, resigned. Don Erickson, who had been managing editor, was appointed editor. Though skilled and intelligent, he did not, according to Weigand, possess Hayes's editorial savvy and acuity.

"I sort of dismissed myself," says Weigand about the outcome of his unhappy working relationship with Erickson. Goude stayed on, but he was in turn unhappy without Weigand there. For a little while after Lois left, Weigand and Goude had designed the covers. But Erickson brought in Onofrio Paccione to continue independent covers in the Lois tradition. They were not as effective, probably owing more to editorial misdirection than to any lack of ability on Paccione's part.

Bob Ciano, who had previously brought intelligent design to *Opera News* and *Redbook* magazines, was hired as art director in 1976 and lasted about a year. *Esquire* had lost its footing, but since it was trading on its reputation, it continued to have a certain cachet. Ciano believes *Esquire* "had gotten soft. It had lost the sense of what was happening outside." The editors knew a change was needed. "But they wanted to make it the 'old' *Esquire*, whatever that might have been. I think that in many ways, it *was* the old *Esquire*, but the old *Esquire* wasn't as pertinent then as when Hayes was editor—times had changed."

Ciano was brought in to revitalize the look, and the first thing he did was to make the type simpler and more playful. "It was all over the lot," he says. "We went back to using Baskerville and other very classical typefaces." The layouts were also toned down from the previous incarnation, but more important, the visual content was beefed up. "I let photography and illustration really carry the look of the magazine," says Ciano modestly about some noticeable improvements, including a disturbingly sardonic fashion piece titled "Bums." For this, Ciano took four homeless men who lived outside his apartment building and photographed them as "makeovers," with new clothes and coifs. "I also got the editors to write more provocative headlines for all pieces." He had support in this area, since Erickson had inherited or hired what Ciano describes as "a scary group of editors," including Gordon Lish (a brilliant fiction editor), Nora Ephron, Jeffrey Norman, and Harry Stein. "I think the magazine became much better during this period, but it was not succeeding on a business level," continues Ciano. "We were turning out good issues, yet we weren't making an impact on the newsstand." In fact, *Esquire* never really did well on the newsstand, relying much more on subscriptions.

After a few months, Ciano says, "The magazine started to get a look. It wasn't the kind of aggressive look that came later. It was driven by the content rather than the other way around." *Esquire* was changing, but not fast enough for the business side. Erickson was moved upstairs to an office "with an oak desk and tea set," where he assumed a more managerial role, and Lee Eisenberg, a brash young editor, was promoted. Eisenberg had the singular distinction of being the only editor of a national magazine who was under thirty years old. Perhaps management thought that he would return a youthful relevance to *Esquire*.

"The problem," Ciano says, "was much more fundamental. *Esquire* had lost its hotness among media buyers. The aura was gone, and I don't think that had much to do with what actually appeared on the pages."

Within a few months of his appointment, Eisenberg imbued *Esquire* with a "service" bent. Stories like "Unbeatable Summer Buys," "How to Cut Off Your Jeans and Get the Legs Even," and "Scared When You Throw a Party?" were the cover lines on the "Hot Summer Issue" of 1976. In an apparent nod to the Lois tradition, he also went outside to have *Esquire's* covers conceived and designed, hiring the former art directors of *National Lampoon,* Michael Gross and David Kaestle, who were then partners in Pellegrini, Kaestle, and Gross, Inc. Eisenberg wanted to confer on *Esquire* some of the *Lampoon's* irreverence, but the *Lampoon* was a very special humor publication, not a men's magazine with cultural aspirations. The first covers were well-composed photographic still lifes of objects and human forms illustrating important articles. Though handsome, they suggested the magazine's inherent confusion and failed to attract a substantial number of readers. Next, Gross and Kaestle were told to use celebrities on the cover, and overnight, *Esquire* became a yuppie version of *People,* or what one critic called "a men's magazine for women." In another decisive move, Ciano was fired. "With any change in editor," Ciano explains, "the art director becomes vulnerable. Eisenberg and I just did not get on. We were on different wavelengths."

Since Kaestle and Gross were already working on *Esquire's* covers, Eisenberg invited them to redesign and art-direct the interior. One of the more radical moves they soon instituted was to virtually eliminate illustration from the magazine. Kaestle says he preferred conceptual photography because so much illustration—basically by the same few illustrators—was appearing in other publications. Emphasis on photography gave *Esquire* its visual distinction. But Ciano notes that sometimes "strained photographic solutions were used when an illustration would have been more appropriate." Eventually, Michael Gross became sole art director. After one or two issues, however, Eisenberg was replaced by Byron Dobell, who had been Hayes's assistant. And Dobell rehired Sam Antupit, now the veteran designer of over fifty magazines and proprietor of Antupit & Others. He reluctantly took the assignment on a freelance basis because, as he says, "*Esquire* had deteriorated into a second-rate college humor magazine."

Antupit started from scratch and reclaimed the job of doing the covers. But, he says, "as Hayes predicted, every editor lobbied for his or her own article being featured, and it was a mess." Moreover, the editorial meetings had deteriorated. "Articles would get assigned without the rest of the staff knowing about it. It was hard to brainstorm ideas. I guess I was just used to Harold's kind of democracy." Antupit helped nurse the dying *Esquire* for eight months.

Aware of the problems and seeing no happy future, John Smart (the late founder's brother), sold the company to Associated Newspapers Ltd. in London, which handed editorial control over to Clay Felker. After leaving *Esquire* in 1963, Felker had founded *New York* magazine, but had recently lost it to Rupert Murdoch and was looking for a property in which to revive his journalistic passions. This new acquisition allowed him the opportunity to reinvent *Esquire.* Not surprisingly, he brought in his former *New York* magazine partner and design director, Milton Glaser, with whom he shared fond memories of the old *Esquire.*

Felker's familiarity with the "New Journalism," a fiction/essay/reportage hybrid made popular by the likes of Tom Wolfe, came from his days at *Esquire*. Moreover, he wanted to bring a new relevance to the magazine.

It was under Felker and Glaser that the most radical, and probably most disastrous, changes were instituted. "Shortly after taking over," Glaser relates, "Clay decided he really wanted to produce a magazine that was more on the news. As you know, *Esquire* always had excruciatingly long lead time—four, five, sometimes six months—partly because of press configurations. Clay was uncomfortable with this rhythm; he had experience doing a weekly, which sharpened his instincts and smell about news. He basically thought that by producing a magazine that came out more frequently—using this very odd hybrid frequency of the fortnightly, which is neither a weekly nor a monthly—we could make a more timely publication." Glaser changed the logo (and essentially the name) to "*Esquire Fortnightly*," replaced the booklike perfect binding with saddle stitching, and overhauled the interior to look, not surprisingly, like *New York* magazine. "It was a disastrous decision," he admits, "really strategically and economically incorrect." Indeed, the common complaint was that readers couldn't finish one issue before another was in their hands.

In reinventing *Esquire*, Felker took an unavoidable step. The magazine was faltering because its past was irrelevant to a new generation of readers and its present was unresponsive to older readers. Short of euthanasia, a radical makeover was the only editorial course. But the perceived equity in *Esquire*'s name was not enough to offset the industry's perception that it was a dinosaur. "I think we could have taken two courses," says Glaser in retrospect. "One was to go with history and try to rearticulate the magazine. The other was to use it as a launching pad for a totally different kind of proposition. Either would have been acceptable. And I think if we had produced a lively, energetic, fresh new thing, we could have succeeded, even though we might have lost the historical edge." But, as Glaser also admits, neither Felker nor he had a clear enough idea of what they wanted *Esquire* to be. "One thing was certain," he says without hesitation, "people around the country didn't want *Esquire* to be another version of *New York*."

By 1978, *Esquire* had lost $5 million, forcing Felker and Glaser to trade in their equity to Associated Magazines for a monetary transfusion. Despite attempts to streamline the circulation and attract new advertisers, *Esquire* was once again on the block—and at a good price, too. In April 1979, Phillip Moffitt, 32, the editor and chief executive officer of 13-30 Corporation, a Knoxville-based media company, and Christopher Whittle, 31, the publisher and chairman, agreed to buy 80 percent of *Esquire* for around $3 million, as well as accept its debts. Shortly thereafter, Robert Priest, a talented young British designer who had been art director for a Canadian Sunday newspaper supplement, *Weekend*, was hired to art-direct yet another new *Esquire*.

Unlike Felker, Moffitt and Whittle had a clear idea of who their audience should be—male baby boomers who had yet to be tapped by a commercial magazine. Priest explains that his mandate was to develop an identity that, unlike Glaser's tentative approach, would appeal to "men who were not necessarily macho anymore, but who had feelings. Men were being handled with dignity. The new subtitle, 'Man at His Best,' really signified that men were important figures in the community. With that, the reader was established. And I tried to make a design that was masculine. It was important that the identity be put on paper."

One of the easiest ways to return *Esquire* to something of a "friend and companion" was to go back to the monthly frequency, perfect binding, and old (or, at most, modified) original logo. Like several of his predecessors, Priest believed that magazines are defined by their art; he decided to make *Esquire* more international in this respect by using artists and photographers from Europe and Canada who had not saturated the American market. "I've always been a designer who considers the overall look of a magazine more important than the individual story," he says. "I am not really a content-driven magazine designer like Fred Woodward or Bob Best." Priest built a framework based on the precise use of a single dominant typeface, Century Schoolbook. Even more unusual was his use of large pull-quotes, initial caps, and long headlines with emphasized words or letters, which would eventually become a standard; many other magazine art directors began to borrow and steal. Priest not only returned the magazine to visual accessibility, he developed a powerful identity, too. But *Esquire* was also at its most "aggressively visual" during Priest's tenure, because it was intentionally competing with other media—like TV and films. "There was more competition for the reader's attention than ever before," says Priest. "It had to be different."

Priest allows that good chemistry existed during his tenure. The staff was astute, and Lee Eisenberg, who was back again as a senior editor, "was full of good ideas and very funny, and probably the only one from the old regime whom Moffitt was comfortable with because they were the same age." But most important for Priest, Moffitt was the guy who said yes or no in the end. "Of course, I got along very well with the other editors," he says, "but at the end of the day, I discussed the package with Moffitt." At that time, collaboration between Moffitt and Whittle was healthy for the magazine, which after only a year had moved into the black. While Priest deserves credit for a portion of its success, Whittle's marketing strategy helped *Esquire* reemerge. Moreover, Moffitt's idea to have special issues on themes such as "Men Who Made It" and "The Powers That Be" once again made *Esquire* incomparable for charting its generation's accomplishments.

After four years of good work, Priest decided to take on new challenges as design director for *Newsweek*. Replacing him was *Esquire*'s third female art director, April Silver. (The first two, Rochelle Udell and Margery Peters, each held that title briefly under Milton Glaser's design direction.) Says Priest about his former associate, "She was much quirkier than me, and in a way I can see the femininity in her work. She was brilliant. Her visual ideas were very kooky. And her ideas for photographs were spectacular." Silver left after about a year when she was invited to do the dummies for *New York Woman*, edited by *Esquire* editor Betsy Carter and published under Moffitt's auspices.

Around this time, trouble was brewing between the two principals of the 13-30 Corporation. Unable to resolve their differences, they split up, and *Esquire* was sold to the Hearst Corporation. Lee Eisenberg was eventually named editor-in-chief, and one of his first decisions was to hire Wendall Harrington as design director. Sadly, the resuscitated *Esquire* fell into a state of visual mediocrity. Apparently, Eisenberg felt that Priest's typography interfered with, rather than enhanced, the reading experience, and wanted something less aggressive. But Harrington was untutored in magazine design, and she banished Priest and Silver's legacy in favor of a look that mimicked other magazines. Harrington stayed about a year before Rip Georges was hired away from Regardie's to replace her as art director.

A former art director of *Wet* and *L.A. Style,* Georges practiced a stunning decorative approach to design. Whether he could handle a magazine of content was a big question. But an even bigger one was whether *Esquire* had actually revived its past literary, satiric, and reporting traditions. Judging from the pre-Georges issues, the magazine was again in a state of flux, with some excellent pieces sandwiched between the fluff of the "what, me worry?" generation. Yet with Georges directing design, and Eisenberg apparently more secure in his editorial stance, *Esquire* returned to some of its historical irreverence, while continuing to maintain its new baby-boom persona. Recently, it even ignited some of that old-time controversy. Angered by the June 1990 issue on the American Wife, which featured such articles as "Your Wife: An Owner's Manual" and "The Last Housewife in America" (complete with photograph of the "endangered species" scrubbing a toilet bowl), Tammy Bruce, president of the Los Angeles chapter of the National Organization of Women, called for a boycott of the magazine.

A few years ago, *Esquire* also increased its physical proportions, not to *Life*-size, but to an imposing squarish shape that helped the design considerably. While Georges did not give the magazine a Priest-like typographic distinction, his was elegant and vivacious typography. Rather than stress identity, as Priest had done, Georges designed stories individually, based on content; his aim was to make *Esquire*'s look the sum of its parts. A recent article on the girls (now in their forties and fifties) who inspired classic rock lyrics suggested a return to the magazine's recipe for surprise, while an anthology of quotes from men and women on Warren Beatty's sexuality looked as though it were designed for a downtown Manhattan culture tabloid. Although *Esquire* was awarded the 1990 National Magazine Award for design, Georges admitted recently that "I never got the magazine that was in my head down on paper." Unfortunately, he never will, since after an almost two-year stay, he moved on to Condé Nast briefly to be art director of its new publication, *Allure,* then took over the art direction of *Mirabella.* His replacement at *Esquire* is Terry Koppel, known for his quirky typography, raucous design, and offbeat sense of humor.

Koppel says that even though he had been warned not to accept the job at *Esquire,* he took an immediate liking to Eisenberg and sympathized with his goal to bring the magazine—with its heritage intact—into the context of the nineties. "Despite the usual peccadillos of editors," he says, "Eisenberg has been an extraordinary collaborator." Indeed, Koppel has been given much the same mandate as his early predecessors to come up with regular visual features. He speculates that the synergy between Eisenberg and himself allows for greater art-directorial latitude than was allotted to those who immediately preceded him. Already, Koppel has begun to "go back in time, but not mimic the past." In doing so, he wants to "evoke the spirit and controversy *Esquire* had in the sixties, but define it as clearly a magazine for today." He has achieved this in part with a string of attention-getting covers unlike anything *Esquire,* or anyone else for that matter, has recently done. A striking image of Jack Nicholson (taken from his role in *The Shining*) that illustrates *Esquire*'s series on American rebels transcends the rather clichéd personality covers so common to contemporary lifestyle and hero-worship magazines. Koppel explains that his are "not like Lois's great conceptual covers," but they have the same end in "forcing readers to pick up the magazine."

"I have no preconceived notions," he insists. "I'm just trying to be as outrageous as I can be with a million-circulation magazine—that is, until the numbers come in." Though he jokes about sticking his neck out, he is in a position to take risks: "*Esquire* has around seven hundred thousand subscribers, which means it's insulated from vacillations on the newsstand." So far, his efforts have been praised by *Esquire*'s management, but Eisenberg, his most fervent supporter, recently surprised the publishing industry when he resigned his editorship to start up an English version of *Esquire*. (Koppel will design the prototype.) In an unexpected appointment, Terry McDonnell, editor of *Smart*, was named the new editor. As only the seventh top editor in *Esquire*'s six decades, his effect on the content and design will be closely monitored.

Writing in the *Antioch Review* in the 1980s, maybe with *Esquire* in mind, Clay Felker said that certain magazines exist for specific moments in time, and after their time is over, they should be laid to rest peacefully. At any point in its almost sixty years of editorial and art-directorial ups and downs, should *Esquire* have been laid to rest? And, if so, when? Even though Henry Wolf believes that Harold Hayes "did the last good work on *Esquire*," he says nostalgically, "I think *Esquire* should have gone out with Arnold. It would have been the right thing . . ." Sam Antupit equivocates: "It shouldn't have died, but it should have gone from the big size to the current size without the *Time*-size in between." Robert Priest also argues for the magazine's continued viability, but says, "I find the attitude toward women a little disturbing today."

Despite *Esquire*'s rocky history, it is a venerable institution, boasting more lives than a cat, and it has purred, screeched, and whined throughout its multiple incarnations. Whether it succeeds or fails, each editor and art director will try to reinvent it in his or her own image. One thing certain is that though critics look nostalgically to *Esquire*'s past for their model, the magazine's legacy and readers demand that it remain, as always, a magazine for the present.

Steven Heller, a senior art director of the New York Times, *is the author/editor of over eighty books on graphic design, illustration, and satiric art. He is co-chair of the MFA/Design program of the School of Visual Arts.*

Originally published in PRINT, *November/December 1990*

ÉMIGRÉ

THE MAGAZINE THAT IGNORES BOUNDARIES

MARC ALEXANDRE SUSAN

A.K.A. MAXUSAN

WILLIAM CONE

VLADIMIR NABOKOV

PETER PLATE

LEWIS MACADAMS

JACK KEROUAC

ZUZANA LICKO

TOM BONAURO

LORD BYRON

HANS SLUGA

DIANE BEST

PIET MONDRIAAN

LEV NUSSBERG

ANDREI TOLUZAKOV

BERT VAN DER MEIJ

JOHN HERSEY

ALICE POLESKY

CARLOS LLERENA AGUIRRE

SCOTT WILLIAMS

ROBOT DOG

KRISTINE McKENNA

CAPTAIN BEEFHEART

ANNE TELFORD

KAREN M. McDONALD

ARTHUR RIMBAUD

TOM CLARK

RUDY VANDERLANS

LEONID LAMM

PRICE FIVE$

KICKING UP A LITTLE DUST
Michael Dooley

Ding ding. *Ding* ding.

It *had* been a bright, quiet Sunday morning in October, but now the door's electric eye chimes are being triggered. Except no one is coming in. Rudy VanderLans looks out through the glass of the door to his studio, a stark white windowless bunker in a rapidly gentrifying industrial section of Berkeley, California, and sees scraps of paper debris tossed madly about by a big wind. "Strange weather," he distractedly comments.

He then gets back to the work at hand.

But every now and again, *ding* ding, *ding* ding.

At high noon, VanderLans goes outside to investigate. He stares at the sky, which has turned completely *black*, except for the sun, a blazing golden disk that cuts through the smoke. The scene resembles nothing so much as the die-cut cover of *Emigre* #8, minus the logo.

He goes back into the studio, drags out the portable television, and hooks it up. "There must be *something* on the TV." *Click, click, click.*

A fire has broken out in the Oakland hills, and it's spreading. VanderLans calls his wife, type designer Zuzana Licko. Yes, she can see it from their home near UC Berkeley. No, they don't appear to be in serious danger at this point.

But VanderLans can't concentrate. The electricity is going crazy. *Ding* ding. The reports grow more ominous. The blaze will eventually claim several lives and hundreds of homes.

He drives home to Licko. They need to be prepared to start from scratch. They pack their valuables into the car. Clothes. Books. Passports.

Passports.

Back before the fire, before *Emigre* established itself as a highly influential and controversial showcase and forum for experimental design, back before some critics lauded it as innovative, inspirational, and embodying our cultural *zeitgeist* and others derided it as illegible, self-indulgent, and just plain ugly, way back in 1983 when VanderLans was assembling the first issue, he used his fingerprint, from his passport, as cover art. His resources were meager, so he used what was on hand. Photocopied resizings of typewriter type. Clip art. Torn paper. Halftones shot by friends. He and the two other Dutch immigrants who founded the magazine had hardly any knowledge of publishing and distribution. They simply wanted to promote the artistic and literary projects that they and their acquaintances were producing.

Issue number one was subtitled "a magazine for exiles," a reference to the artist-as-outsider. After that, it was "the magazine that ignores boundaries." Fingerprints and suitcases and airplanes and globes were recurring motifs. Much of the subject matter dealt with traveling and being international citizens. There was a heavy emphasis on how exposure to various countries and different cultures generates inspiration.

The America VanderLans discovered when he arrived in 1981 inspired him to embark on a personal journey of discovery. *Emigre* was to be his vehicle. Its nonlinear, free-floating hierarchy of visual and verbal information that sprawled and overlapped all over its poster-sized pages was a world beyond the rigid strictures of his modernist design education. "I had been so brainwashed about designing according to a grid that I wanted to make *Emigre* look a lot more spontaneous," he explains. "My only grid was going to be the four crop marks. And in California, anything goes. You could do whatever you wanted. People were always very encouraging. There was no finger-pointing, saying 'this was not the way it was supposed to be done.' That did not exist here. At least I didn't see it. And that might have to do with the ignorance you feel when you go to another country. You don't see many things. And that's sometimes in itself very liberating."

VanderLans first became aware of America's potential to help him travel beyond, in his words, "the dead end of Swiss Modernism" when he was still an aspiring illustrator at Holland's Royal Academy of Fine Art in the Hague and saw the work of a designer across the ocean. "Milton Glaser inspired me tremendously. It looked like he was a pure illustrator who taught himself how to be a graphic designer as well. I had been taught design functions around typography, whereas Milton Glaser's work was based around illustration. It was very expressive. And he could make that type of design function perfectly within society. People were excited about it and had fun with it and enjoyed it. And it was functioning at many levels. His posters were up in art museums. It was art, and it was also graphic design. And that touched something way deep inside me and I thought, *jeez*, if that is possible then a *lot* is possible."

Glaser's designs were the travel brochures that began to stir VanderLans's desire to explore new ground, and the ten issues of the eponymous magazine of Rotterdam design group Hard Werken were his maps. Published between 1979 and 1982, *Hard Werken* was a portfolio of the group's radical concepts doubling as an arts publication. They ran downbeat fiction and poetry and articles about art, film, and underground music. They arranged idiosyncratic photos and illustrations and typewriter text in anarchistic collages over a large-page format. They painted directly onto the mechanical boards. They allowed for mystery and ambiguity in their designs. In short, they served as a guide for the early *Emigre*s.

It was only after VanderLans came to the United States that he became involved with the work of his native countrymen. He remembers being attracted by their interdisciplinary talents. "These people were very much like Milton Glaser in the sense that they were not schooled as Modernist designers. Actually, most of them were fine artists. They had no knowledge of design. It was all self-taught. Their work was based on illustration and photography and their type was self-invented, and it was all just so incredibly vibrant, so uninhibited. They were designing magazines, they were designing book covers, they could do house styles and corporate identities in a very different way. But it worked. And people bought it."

But people weren't buying *Emigre*. Not for the first couple of years, anyway. After a few issues, the other founders left for financially greener territories, and VanderLans became the sole publisher and editor as well as art director. With the second issue, Licko began contributing her fonts, whose architectural construction provided a rational counterpoint to VanderLans's grid-resistant layouts. Their bedroom piled up with undistributed copies. Yet they continued to pursue their labor of love at a time when other Bay Area designers were making their fortunes by providing the yuppie market with decorative designs in pretty pinks and beiges.

Their perseverance eventually paid off. With the worldwide distribution of the seventy-plus, and growing, number of fonts created by Licko and a handful of other designers, *Emigre* has become the mainstay of their business enterprise. Its print run is a mere seven thousand, up from the five hundred of a decade ago. Its advertising is only for its own products. The fact that it makes a profit is attributable to VanderLans's continued belief in low-budget production values. "I am often disgusted with the waste that exists within graphic design. So much money is spent on the printing of materials the world can do so easily without." Despite the impression conveyed by feature articles about *Emigre* that tend to focus on select full-color examples, the typical issue strives to make the most of inexpensive monochromatic printing.

Economy, as well as inventiveness, is also the hallmark of *Emigre*'s music label, which VanderLans recently created with company profits. He has released nine CDs so far, with categories ranging from hip-hop to industrial to folk pop to '60s West Coast music. As with the designers featured in *Emigre*, the only criterion for the selection of bands is the personal taste of Rudy VanderLans. So far, press reviews have been very favorable, and one band, Basehead, has already gone on to sign an eight-record deal with a larger label.

VanderLans figures his label needs more focus if it hopes to repeat the success of the magazine. *Emigre* became a viable commodity only after its contents became more clearly defined. This change began to take place around six years ago, when he found himself talking with friends about design topics and ideas not found in established publications. "*PRINT* was doing all their stories about Michael Vanderbyl and Eastern European design, which is all very valid and very good," he says. "There is no other magazine that does a better job. But I also felt there were other things going on in design and nobody was paying attention. Actually, if anyone paid attention to this work, it was to criticize it as bad or ugly or ungrounded or stupid or naïve. I thought it was the most exciting thing happening.

"So I felt maybe there was a little bit of a niche there, to show the work of young graphic designers who had some radical ideas that the mainstream didn't exactly appreciate or understand or believe, people who were kicking up a little dust in the world of graphic design."

The dust-kickers included teachers and students from Cranbrook and Cal Arts who specialize in designing in ways that aren't supposed to work according to conventional standards. People like Ed Fella, whose vernacular style has earned him the reprobation of anti-designer. People like Jeffery Keedy, who, when asked by VanderLans why he doesn't design pretty typefaces, responded, "Well, it's been done, let's face it." *Emigre* has reprinted an essay by Dutch design dust-kicker Piet Schreuders in which he explains why "the profession of graphic design is criminal and really ought not to exist at all." It also has published an article by pixel-kicking computer design nerds Erik van Blokland and Just van Rossum in which they discuss the merits of creating a computer font virus that will "slowly transform Helvetica into something much more desirable."

Appropriately enough, *Emigre*'s design is as extreme as its editorial stance. Although much is made of "the *Emigre* look," in truth, the format varies from issue to issue. It has ranged from an intricate weaving of text and graphics that challenges conventions of legibility to a stark simplicity, typical of recent issues. This is, again, in contrast to *PRINT*, which VanderLans considers poorly designed, finding its covers to be nothing more than clever visual concepts and its department head designs to be much less than typographically elegant.

As fellow Bay Area designer Chuck Byrne points out, "*PRINT*'s attitude is that the layout of the magazine should be neutral because it presents design. Rudy's attitude is exactly the opposite. Why does it have to look like the time before? The *subject matter* is different from the time before. The *people being covered* are different. To redesign the magazine every time would make the traditional editor or publisher hysterical. Well, Rudy just has this ongoing design problem that he goes about solving with each issue. Or he turns it over to someone else who is absolutely crazed."

Byrne discounts complaints that the layouts are often indecipherable. "Rudy doesn't design the way he does just to be radical. He has gotten extraordinarily good at making the type a sophisticated extension of the content of the story. Those pages are very well crafted. There is an organic relationship between the presentation of the word and its actual meaning. The only people who have tremendous problems reading *Emigre* are graphic designers, who have been trained to make type clear. The rest of the world doesn't live in that purist atmosphere. It doesn't know it's not supposed to read *Emigre*. Younger people look at it the same way they look at other magazines, because magazines are changing."

VanderLans simply stands by his philosophy that people read best what they read most. "If people read 'ugly' against-the-rules typography every day, they will eventually get used to it and be able to read it without any problems. It's just a matter of giving it to them again and again and again."

Because he has taken such aggressive stances and published such inflammatory material, many consider Rudy VanderLans to be some kind of punk. So people expecting to meet the Sid Vicious of the design world are taken aback when they are first confronted by a charming, soft-spoken, wholesome-looking fellow with clear bright eyes and an easy smile.

VanderLans *is Emigre*. He may not agree with some ideas expressed in his magazine, or, when he relinquishes editorial control to other designers, he may even find some layouts hideous. Nevertheless, his fingerprints are deeply embedded in every issue, so much so that *Emigre* is often accused of being self-indulgent—which he readily admits it is.

"*Emigre* is a *tremendously* self-indulgent magazine. It *should* be that. The one thing Zuzana and I have always done with all our work is to try to please ourselves, first and foremost. And then if people out there are also going to like it, that's just really great. But we have never believed in the idea of marketing, never believed in the idea that if we do *this* combined with *that*, then *those* people will like it. Marketing only looks into what people already like. Well, we *know* that. It's *boring*. We're interested in finding out what people *could* like in terms of what they haven't seen yet, or heard yet. Which is a more difficult route to go, but it's much more exciting for us."

As for the incendiary nature of the articles, "I know what we're doing is not always considered proper according to the mainstream. But it's not our intention to be provocative only. We really hope to contribute to how people look at graphic design. We are interested in people who have something very intelligent to say, who are very sincere, and who are really passionate about their work. And it just so happens that oftentimes some consider what we publish to be provocative or obnoxious or vulgar or whatever. But that is not why we go to these people. That is not why we show their work.

"It's very easy to shock people. There's nothing to it, especially in America. We could just try to make nude photographs of every graphic designer we like and put them into center spreads."

April Greiman, whose computer-generated self-portrait for *Design Quarterly* showed her to be no stranger to full frontal nudity herself, has been a longtime fan, not only of *Emigre*'s visuals, but of its adversarial stances. "Why *not* put out some startling articles saying 'let's create a virus to destroy Helvetica'? I heard Herb Lubalin say Helvetica was the most destructive face that was ever invented, it was just the total downfall of good typography. And that was twenty years ago. He said the biggest tragedy to typography is the invention of Helvetica because you can't make any mistakes. It just kind of numbs you out. It's so perfect, it's dead, stillborn. Personally, I think it would be great to put out a virus to put it to sleep."

Not surprisingly, *Emigre*'s assaults on Modernism have incurred the wrath of several members of the established design community, who deride it as a visual abomination. Living legend Massimo Vignelli was particularly vituperative in a *PRINT* "Oppositions" debate [September/October 1991 issue] in which he accused *Emigre* of being an irresponsible aberration of culture. When the debate was published, VanderLans was asked if he had spilled a cup of hot coffee in Vignelli's lap.

In fact, VanderLans has never met or even talked with Vignelli. And although he is less than flattering about Vignelli's fashions, which he describes as resembling prison clothes, he has always admired his design work. "Massimo Vignelli is someone who was held up very high in art school in Holland," he says. "I remember so well when he came out with the New York City subway sign system. That was the big thing in the mid- and late '70s in Holland, working on corporate identities and sign systems. And everybody looked at that as an example."

As for the criticism, "For all I care, Massimo Vignelli can hate *Emigre*. Esthetically. But then to go on and say it's bad for culture as a whole, that really hurts. Because how, then, do we go about making culture? By just copying Massimo Vignelli? Or is it maybe possible to create our own ways of expression?

"The problem I have is when people talk about our work as *wrong*, as if there was never any place for it anywhere. I believe *that* is wrong. I think for too long, Modernist designers have figured *everything* should be treated in this cold, rationalist way and that's *stupid*. It's naïve, it's childlike.

"I know there are areas within design where there should not be any kind of mistake about legibility at all, like highway sign systems. Anything we've learned about legibility, we should apply there. People have a split-second to read a highway sign. You cannot put in any personality or anything like that. But there are so many projects in this world that could be done in very *irrational, illegible* ways, without any problem. There are punk magazines to be designed. Are you going to use Jan Tschichold's three rules of typography for that? That's silly! That doesn't make sense.

"To me it looks like the world of young designers, what they are thinking and what they are feeling, is passing Massimo Vignelli by. All I hope is when I'm his age, I'm not going to be that bitter and close-minded."

Byrne detects a more personal agenda at work. "Part of the reason established designers don't like *Emigre* has to do with a turf imperative. Massimo believes Rudy is threatening his predominance in his field because of his following. Massimo and all those Modernists were revolutionary, but now when it comes time to change what they changed, they are proving to be the biggest fucking crybabies you've ever seen. They're just worse than the people they tried to change before."

Greiman, who views *Emigre* as part of technology's expansion of the paradigms of culture as well as the parameters of readability, perceives an even deeper issue. "The International Style was based on a simple set of values, and we're living in an age of enormous complexity. The tools that we have are much more complex and allow more levels of information. *Emigre* is one example, and a very good example, of a different kind of reading, a textural, emotional reading. And that's probably something that whole generation of Modernists just doesn't even begin to understand.

"I think the reason Vignelli would be outraged is that whole International Style represents a dinosaur that is definitely wagging its tail for the last time. Major capitalism and so-called democracy and all this corporate money that supported design so it had to have one look, one voice, one color, one typeface, all that neutral Swiss greedy stuff, that world is crumbling. We're in a different time. The power structures, the big-bucks people telling people at the bottom of the pyramid what kind of information they could have and when they can have it, is now being totally blown apart by the information revolution and by being truly able to network. There can now be a participatory, interactive kind of information flow."

Besides having captured the spirit of an emerging technological democracy, VanderLans and Licko have also blazed a trail for others in the creation of their own fonts and designs. The computer provided the tool for designers to work with text in ways previously unimaginable, and *Emigre* provided the permission. As with punk music, the potential for freedom implicit within its pages has energized and empowered many others to take rule-defying risks. Byrne notes how "people saw an openness that had not been available before in Modernist design and they started to get really excited about it. Every issue seemed like a revolution. And that turning away from a strict discipline of the way things *should* be organized continues to have a dramatic impact on design."

VanderLans considers the abandoning of restraints and the receptivity to continual change as a fundamental distinction between his contemporaries and Vignelli's. "Back then, all those designers wrote books with guidelines on how design *has to be done*. None of the people in *Emigre* have this idea that rules should be laid down, particular rules like fifty-two characters on a line, twelve words in a line. I think those times are gone. We now see graphic designers much more as pluralists. And I think that's very healthy. That's true creativity, for them to work in many different ways according to the type of project given to them. And they will be very wild and incredibly brilliant."

Marc Treib, a designer-writer who was VanderLans's advisor at UC Berkeley's graduate program during the early 1980s, holds him in high esteem. "Rudy's work is pure research as in research-and-development, and it will be regarded in twenty years the same way we look at Constructivist photography." But Treib takes issue with some of VanderLans's emulators, those who confuse syntax with semantics at the expense of their clients. "I disagree with people who simply think if they make the design more complex it will have a more complex meaning. If they're designing writing on Baudrillard or Derrida or one of the fashionable people, they want something that represents deconstruction, but of course what they're doing is making it harder and harder to figure out what the hell's going on in the text, which is difficult enough. It's like getting a book that is already underlined, and if you have some idiot who is marking phrases that are unimportant in terms of your reading of the book, it's something you have to overcome to get back to the original message."

Still, there are several venues in which a spastic jumble of text, typography, and layout accommodates and appeals to the fits-and-starts reading habits of an audience plugged into the *click, click, click* of Macintosh computers and MTV. VanderLans admires the courage of mass-circulation youth-oriented magazines like *Beach Culture* that have incorporated structural as well as stylistic devices from *Emigre* into their editorial makeup. "You can't change magazine design by finding yet another way to use a pull-quote or to insert a drop cap. You're going to change it by writing differently, by setting up the structure of your article entirely differently." And, as if in an echo of the seminal punk rock band MC5's exhortation to "kick out the jams," VanderLans exclaims, *Throw out the headlines!*"

He regrets that *Beach Culture* was not a commercial success. "Eventually, such magazines will make it, but there have to be people who continually work like that to have the mainstream accept it."

VanderLans has definitely established his place in mainstream culture. Styles that inflamed designers when they appeared in *Emigre* are now ubiquitous, disseminated, and assimilated throughout the spectrum of print and electronic media. Licko's fonts, initially scorned and ridiculed as ugly, are now so established that other type foundries are knocking them off. Aspiring designers constantly show up with their portfolios, often without calling. *Ding* ding. *Ding* ding.

But their newfound status offers no protection from the brickbats of critics. Even as their work continues to be pilloried as deviant, it is now disdained for being too commonplace. Two designers, in separate articles from a recent issue of *PRINT,* stated that they deliberately avoid using the fonts because of their identification with the magazine. Many others believe *Emigre* and its fonts have had their day in the sun and should move aside for the next hot new trend to set the design world aflame.

Byrne disagrees with this evaluation. "The best editorial concept I've seen in the last decade is the *Emigre* issue called 'Heritage.' It was absolutely fucking brilliant! There were these incredible interviews, the layouts were incredible, but there was also this great idea of 'let's go back to Switzerland twenty years later and take the pulse, the blood pressure, run a set of X-rays and see what's going on here.' And Rudy continues to come up with very sophisticated ideas, very advanced and perceptive themes for the magazine."

Greiman, who has appeared in *Emigre* herself, concurs. She believes it will continue to fill a void, at least in her own reading habits. "I just find people are stuck on style wars. That's why I don't read the middle-America design mags. I think they're boring. *PRINT*, *CA*, *Graphis*, they're so superficial. It's just really slick printing and beautiful photos of well-printed items. And it's a waste of my time. It puts me to sleep."

Although *Emigre* is hardly in danger of becoming an oversize *PRINT*, VanderLans concedes the difficulty of continuing to travel along the cutting edge. Yet he maintains a steadfast optimism and determination to retain his resident alien status in the design world. He even looks forward to new challenges to his turf. "I can still get excited over people who are doing things very different from how I do them, because I'm very interested in why they're doing it differently. And as long as I find those people for whom design is still this wide-open area, I'll continue to publish."

British graphic designer Nick Bell easily qualifies as one of those people. A recent *Emigre* devoted to briefs he created as an instructor for the London College of Printing included an insert of random slashes on butcher paper. Accompanying text explains that this is an example of a typeface he created called Psycho. If not taken literally as yet another punk skewering of the carcasses of design establishment dinosaurs, Bell's gesture can be viewed as a jab at *Emigre* itself, taking its assaults on Helvetica and legibility to their absurdist conclusion.

VanderLans calmly explains that "there has never been a five-year or ten-year business plan for *Emigre*. I think I would stop publishing it when I myself get bored with it. But if I'm going to bore other people, then that's really too bad. The bottom line is, if I can't make a living off it, then I'll stop doing it. Right now, Zuzana and I keep selling more magazines, we keep selling more typefaces, we continue to sell more records. So there must be people out there who enjoy what we're doing."

In fact, the operation has expanded to the point that it could no longer be contained within the bunker. Last May, VanderLans and Licko emigrated to Sacramento. Their new office-warehouse has plenty of room for expansion. It also has a view through the windows of a tree-lined street in a peaceful, pleasant residential neighborhood just a short stroll from their new house.

VanderLans was contemplating such a move last October, as he stared at the sun asserting itself against the black, threatening sky. Since they make all their income through mail order, they could run the office from anywhere in the United States. And so, the publisher of the magazine that ignores boundaries was "seriously thinking of moving up north, but still in California. California is too nice."

And anything goes.

Michael Dooley is a Los Angeles–based creative director, educator, and writer. His articles have appeared in PRINT, *the* AIGA Journal, Emigre, *and* Interiors.

Originally published in PRINT, *September/October 1992*

1958

*The automobile industry
has given more people
more jobs
than the last two wars
put together.*

P. L. Smith, M. D.,
Yardley, Pa.

3. Designed Lives

LESTER BEALL: A CREATIVE GENIUS OF THE SIMPLE TRUTH
R. Roger Remington

Creativity speaks to the heart of the process of graphic design. What were the creative forces that allowed Lester Beall to produce consistently great art and design over the span of a forty-four-year career? Over this span of time, Beall produced solutions to design problems that were fresh and innovative. He studied the dynamic visual form of the European avant-garde, synthesized parts into his own aesthetic, and formed graphic design applications for business and industry that were appropriate, bold, and imaginative. In his mature years he led the way with creative and comprehensive packaging and corporate identity programs that met the needs of his clients. Along the way in his work, manner, and style, Beall proved to American business that the graphic designer was a professional that could creatively solve problems and at the same time deal with pragmatic issues of marketing and budget. The qualities and values that led to Beall's effectiveness are timeless and provide contemporary practitioners with an historical reference base upon which to evaluate present standards.

Beall felt that the designer "must work with one goal in mind—to integrate the elements in such a manner that they will combine to produce a result that will convey not merely a static commercial message, but an emotional reaction as well. If we can produce the kind of art which harnesses the power of the human instinct for that harmony of form, beauty, and cleanness that seems inevitable when you see it . . . then I think we may be doing a job for our clients." For Beall that creativity was present at every stage of the design process. He said, "The designer's role in the development, application, and protection of the trademark may be described as pre-creative, creative, and post-creative."

Born in Kansas City, Missouri, in 1905, Beall's early childhood years were spent in St. Louis and Chicago. He was educated at Chicago's Lane Technical School and graduated from the University of Chicago. He began his design career in 1927. By 1935 Beall had decided to move to New York and in late September of that year had opened a studio/office in his apartment in Tudor City on Manhattan's east side. While maintaining the office in New York, he moved to Wilton, Connecticut, where he established his home and studio in a rural setting. He was to remain in Wilton until 1950. Many of the significant works from this period were done in this location. Through the 1930s and 1940s, Beall produced innovative and highly regarded work for clients including the *Chicago Tribune*, Sterling Engraving, The Art Directors Club of New York, Hiram Walker, Abbott Laboratories, and *Time* magazine. Of particular interest was his work for the Crowell

Publishing Company, which produced *Collier's* magazine. The promotional covers "Will There Be War?" and "Hitler's Nightmare" are powerful designs which distill messages of the time. In these works he utilizes angled elements, iconic arrows, silhouetted photographs, and dynamic shapes, all of which captures the essence of his personal style of the late 1930s. Also of interest in this period are the remarkable poster series for the United States Government's Rural Electrification Administration. In all Beall designed three series of posters between 1937 and 1941 with the simple goals of increasing the number of rural Americans who would electrify their homes and increasing public awareness of the benefits of electricity. His poster for the ill-fated "Freedom Pavilion" at the 1939 World's Fair was another dynamic example of this time in which he used what he called "thrust and counter-thrust" of design elements.

During the 1950s and '60s Beall's design office expanded both in its staff and scope, adding associate designers and mounting full-scale corporate identification campaigns for large companies such as Caterpillar Tractor, Connecticut General Life Insurance Company, The New York Hilton, and Merrill Lynch, Fenner Pierce and Smith, Inc. His identity program for International Paper Company from 1960 was his most extensive identity program and is noteworthy for the graphics standards manual, one of the first to be so fully articulated.

Beall maintained, throughout his life, a core of sources which stimulated his perception, creativity, and methods of making art and design. He was a highly visual person with a great need to express himself. Always first and at the center of his ways of working were his form experimentation in the drawing and painting of the human figure. He was always at work in his studio, whether it was creating design, art, or photography. His wife, Dorothy Miller Beall, characterized her husband as "first of all an artist, not only because of a vital and important talent, but because of an emotional spiritual quality, a very special attitude." His daughter Joanna remembers this fine art expression as "a major part of his thinking." Beall, in his memoirs, confirms this by recalling that "all through my life as a designer, I have spent considerable time developing myself as an artist. I am constantly drawing, with particular emphasis on the figure, which I find fascinating though difficult in terms of evolving something that is not completely abstract but certainly not literal or realistic."

Photography also was a lifelong interest to Beall and an important part of his creative process. He experimented with photography and photographic processes almost from the beginning of his career in design in Chicago. Cameras, a photographic studio, and a darkroom were always necessary for his visual experiments. In the 1930s he had seen the experimental photographic work of the European avant-garde designers such as Herbert Bayer, El Lissitzky, and László Moholy-Nagy. Beall would experiment regularly with photograms, and with straight photography both in and out of the studio. Even today, many of Beall's photographic images remain unusual and innovative visual experiments. Beall carried his camera with him on all his travels. These images formed an image bank from which he drew inspiration for his lectures. Others found their way into direct graphic design application for his clients such as in the cover for *ORS*, a journal for health services professionals. A more complex photographic technique is used on the cover of *What's New*, a house organ of Abbott Laboratories. This image from 1939 shows a complex integration of photographic and graphic elements, set in a scale which juxtaposes the size relationships of foreground and background.

The psychologist Erich Fromm said, "Education for creativity is nothing short of education for living." Beall's creative activities were powerfully influenced, enhanced, and supported by the working environments that he established to support them. Whether he was working from his office near the Loop in Chicago, an office in a New York skyscraper or from the pastoral setting in Connecticut, Beall was sensitive to the importance of the space around him and how this could influence his creativity. In 1968 he wrote: "By living and working in the country I felt I could enjoy a more integrated life, and although I still need the periodic stimulation of New York City, the opportunity and creative activity in an area of both beauty and tranquility seemed to me to far exceed anything that a studio and residence in New York might offer—the way a man lives is essential to the work he produces. The two cannot be separated. If I could condense into a single idea the thinking we are trying to do here at Dumbarton Farm, it would be to achieve, through organic and integrated design, that power of inevitability . . . This has for a long time been an effort to work out a way of living for me and my family—and for the people who work with me. It gives me more time at home. It surrounds me with atmosphere I feel is pretty essential to good creativity." With Beall it was not so much that he had his studio in the country, but that he had a way of life built around the country, part of which involved having his studio there at his elbow.

As with other pioneers of his era, Beall believed that the designer cannot work in a vacuum. He remarked, "all experience in fields directly or indirectly related to design must be absorbed and stored up, to provide the inspirational source that guides, nourishes and enriches the idea-flow of the designer." Beall's own interests in other art forms provided further stimulus to his immense curiosity and creativity. Dorothy Beall wrote that Lester "believed that anyone interested in design must necessarily be interested in other fields of expression—the theater, ballet, photography, painting, literature, as well as music, for from any of these the alert designer can at times obtain not only ideas related to his advertising problem, but genuine inspiration." His books and periodicals were another great source of inspiration for Beall. He collected books and periodicals seriously from the beginning of his design career in Chicago. By the Sixties, Beall had accumulated a major personal collection of publications on creative forms such as art, design, photography, and architecture. He also collected seminal magazines such as *Cahiers d'Art* and rare volumes such as the famous *Bauhausbucher*. Music was another important ingredient of Beall's creative environments. He was very familiar with jazz, having grown up with it in Chicago. While working in his studio there in the mid-1920s, he would often listen to live broadcasts on radio. Throughout his life, he would surround himself with music, be it jazz or the classical compositions of Europeans such as Stravinsky, Prokofiev, and Shostakovich.

Beall, in 1963, when writing about what he saw as the qualifications of a designer, listed "an understanding wife." Throughout their life together, from the earliest days of struggle in Chicago to the golden years at Dumbarton Farm, Dorothy Miller Beall was by his side, relating to his friends and clients. She participated as she could to realize her husband's work, career, and life. She said, "I have always felt very close to my husband's career, having been a part of it from the very beginning." Together, Dorothy and Lester built living environments for themselves and their family which were rich with collected folk art, antiques, and Americana, as well as contemporary works. Beall said, "A lot of wives take a dim view of their husbands coming home for lunch. Dorothy actually looks forward to my coming home; perhaps even too much so. I enjoy getting over to the house, being surrounded by the things in my home." In remembering the beginning of Beall's career, Dorothy recalled: "It was a time of discovering the interdependence of painting, sculpture, and the technique of modern industry and of the underlying unity of all creative work." For many years after Beall's death, Dorothy preserved the artifacts of his career, sustained his name in the design press with articles, and was continually supportive to inquiring students or researchers.

Beall was a major synthesizer of the ideas of European avant-garde artists and designers into the mainstream of design for American business. An associate, Fred Hauck, with whom he had shared a studio in Chicago and New York, was probably the major vehicle through which Beall received those exciting ideas from Europe. Hauck, who had lived and painted in Paris and had gone to Hans Hofman's school in Munich, returned to Chicago and shared with Beall an enthusiasm for the European artists and designers, especially the Bauhaus. Hauck showed Beall valued copies of the Bauhaus books and publications of the avant-garde which he had brought back with him. This interest, as well as such publications as *Arts et Metier Graphiques* and *Gebrauschgraphik*, helped Beall consolidate his own thinking away from a limiting vision of design as ordinary middle-American commercial illustration and toward a new, dynamic, and progressive form of graphic communication.

Beall earned great respect from his clients and staff. Bob Pliskin recalled that Beall "was a good man to work for. He had the gift of enthusiasm and he knew how to communicate it. He gave us freedom and guidance too. His studio was a happy, stimulating place where work was fun and clocks did not exist. And Beall could teach. He taught us to spurn symmetry, which he called an easy out . . . a static response to a dynamic world. He taught us that the solution to a design problem must come from the problem. That form must follow function." About Beall's graphic design imagery of the 1940s, Plisken wrote, "You couldn't miss Beall's work. It riveted you . . . held your attention . . . and planted an idea in your head. He was a skillful typographic designer and he liked working with type and typographic symbols. He loved arrows. Loved them and used them in nearly everything he did. It was a natural symbolism for him because the arrow was and is the simplest, most direct way to move the eye from one spot to another."

The recognition of Lester Beall's pioneering efforts has been slow in coming. It is fitting that his importance to design is now to be acknowledged again by the American Institute of Graphic Arts. Looking back, however, he was consistently commended for the excellence of this work. As early as 1937, Beall was given the first one-man exhibit of graphic design at the Museum of Modern Art in New York. Then, in 1942, Beall's greatness was acknowledged as he accompanied a distinguished group of colleagues—namely, Dr. Agha, Alexey Brodovitch, A. M. Cassandre, Bob Gage, William Golden, and Paul Rand— in an ADG exhibit, "A Half Century on the Greatest Artists of the Modern Media." August Freundlich remarked in the brochure, "These are men who have bridged the gap between art and commerce. Although we fully recognize their success within their commercial regions, it is their success as creative artists, as creative thinkers, as innovators, as inventors that concerns us." It took the New York Art Directors Club until four years after Beall's death in 1969 to vote him into their prestigious Hall of Fame in 1973. At that time Bob Plisken, who worked for Beall in the early 1940s, spoke on his behalf: "In my opinion, Beall did more than anyone to make graphic design in America a distinct and respected profession." Lorraine Wild, in her writing on American design history, has characterized Beall as a leader of those designers from the 1930s to the 1950s whose work has a "quality of openness and accessibility. It is evidence of all the energy spent trying to make a real contribution to the common good and the environment. The stakes were clear—a new profession was formed." Another distinguished design historian, Ann Ferebee, knew Beall personally and is steadfast in referring to his formative work as "the conscience of American design." Philip B. Meggs, in his *History of Graphic Design*, credits Beall with "almost single-handedly launching the Modern movement in American design." The excellence of Beall's life and work has made him into a near mythic figure who, even a quarter of a century after his death, still dazzles the imagination of many students and professionals alike.

"The quality of any man's life has got to be a full measure of that man's personal commitment to excellence. . . ." Beall would have felt good about these words spoken by Vince Lombardi, because competition and commitment were the ways in which he was able to achieve brilliance in his professional career in design. Beall said, "When a designer designs a beautiful product he has unveiled a simple truth. In short, this product of his creativeness communicates a simple message—a message that will outlast the product's function or salability. The designer, furthermore, can then be said to have contributed something of value to his culture." So it is entirely appropriate that Lester Beall's legacy to the profession of graphic design is now honored; his was surely a "lifetime achievement."

R. Roger Remington is Professor of Graphic Design at Rochester Institute of Technology. His work in design history has involved archiving the major American pioneers of Modernism, interpreting this history in two books as well as conferences, and developing innovative courses in graphic design history at RIT.

Originally published in the AIGA Rochester Newsletter, *1995*

On Merle Armitage: The Impresario of Book Design
Roy R. Behrens

In the early 1940s, shortly after the novelist Henry Miller had moved back to the United States from Paris, he concluded that a noncommercial artist in America "has as much chance for survival as a sewer rat."

Refusing to borrow or to hire out for "stultifying work," he sent out a letter inviting support from the readers of *The New Republic,* requesting, among other things, "old clothes, shirts, socks, etc. I am 5 feet 8 inches tall, weigh 150 pounds, 15½ neck, 38 chest, 32 waist, hat and shoes both size 7 to 7½. Love corduroys."

The appeal worked and a number of curious mailings arrived, one of which contained a complete tuxedo. "What'll I ever do with this?" Miller asked a friend, then used it to dress up a scarecrow that sat for a generation on the picket fence in front of his Partington Ridge house in Big Sur, California.

Among the other gifts was a cash contribution from Merle Armitage, a civil engineer, set designer, concert promoter, gourmet, art collector, author, and book designer. Armitage was also living in California, and soon after, when he visited Miller's home for the first time, he described his profession as that of an "impresario."

"But I have heard that you were a writer?" replied Miller. "If the truth were known," Armitage explained, "I write books so that I will be able to design them." In fact, Armitage had designed nearly two dozen books by that time, many of which he had also written.

But Miller was incredulous: "Does a book have to be designed?" he asked. "A book is a book, and I don't see how you can do much about it."

Born in 1893 on a farm eleven miles from Mason City, Iowa, Merle Armitage's inclination toward design, engineering, and problem-solving can be traced back to his childhood. His paternal grandfather had been a friend of J. I. Case, an important pioneer in the development of steam-driven farm machinery; and a few miles east of the Armitage home was Charles City, site of the invention of the first gasoline-powered farm tractor.

One day as the young Armitage and his father were helping a neighboring farmer named Wright with the repair of a windmill, a messenger rode up on horseback and handed the man a telegram. "He passed it around," Armitage remembered, "and my father read it aloud. It said: 'We flew today at Kitty Hawk' and it was signed Orville and Wilbur." Armitage was just as impressed by the immediacy of the telegram as by its message: "The two were equally exciting to me: to fly through the air, to send a message over the wire. Both left me absolutely enslaved to things mechanical."

His father, according to Armitage, was a dreamer who should never have become a businessman. Nevertheless, "he had great vision," and, at a time when steers ranged free to feed on grass, he made a fortune (which he later lost in a market crash) on the innovation of corn-fed beef. "Finding that corn grew luxuriantly in the new land," recalled Armitage, his father "conceived the idea that purchasing range cattle and feeding them all the corn they could eat for two months would produce new flavor."

It was by his father's influence that he became intensely interested in farm implements, steam locomotives, and automobiles, and in engineering and inventing. At the same time, it was his mother (a schoolteacher) who encouraged his artistic abilities by the choice of the pictures she hung in their home, by the brazen act of painting the front door a bright Chinese red (thus creating "a neighborhood sensation"), and by reinforcing his early attempts at drawing.

His mother's parents, the Jacobs, lived in Mason City, described by Armitage as "a sweet Iowa town of tree-shaded streets and friendly people," the town that was later immortalized as River City in *The Music Man* by Meredith Willson. (It was also the hometown of Bil Baird, the puppeteer.) Today, across the street from Willson's birthplace is the Charles H. MacNider Museum, a majestic Victorian-era mansion that was built by an Armitage family friend, who was also the owner of the First National Bank.

When Armitage was still a teenager, it was a rivalry between MacNider and another Mason City banker that resulted in the hiring of a young Chicago-based architect named Frank Lloyd Wright (no relation to the Wright brothers, apparently) to design a new bank, offices, and an adjoining hotel for the City National Bank (which remains and may soon be completely restored). Within the next decade, Wright—until he was discredited by eloping with a client's wife—Walter Burley Griffin, William Drummond, and other gifted young architects designed innovative Prairie Style houses within a planned community, so that Armitage's little hometown is now widely known as the site of a marvelous cluster of gem-like early modern homes.

The ancestors of both Wright and Armitage had settled in Wisconsin, from which the latter had then moved to northern Iowa. Wright was commissioned to design the City National Bank in 1908 through the efforts of J. E. Markeley, a friend and Mason City businessman whose two daughters were students of Wright's aunt at her Hillside School, in Spring Green, Wisconsin, which was housed in buildings that Wright had designed. By the time the Mason City hotel project began, Armitage was fifteen years old, and he and his family had already moved to a cattle ranch near Lawrence, Kansas, and then to Texas.

In one of his autobiographies, Armitage refers to the architect's son, Frank Lloyd Wright Jr. (known as Lloyd), as "an old friend." In 1923, when the American press reported, incorrectly, that the Wright's Imperial Hotel in Tokyo had been devastated by an earthquake, Armitage (in his capacity as a publicist) was recruited by the architect to help to set the record straight. They remained what Armitage described as "casual friends" for many years, dining together for the last time in New York in 1953. Wright died in 1959.

Art, design, advertising, and mechanical engineering: In Armitage's young imagination, these allied yet differing interests combined in the form of a breathtaking automobile, the Packard.

It was his childhood fascination with this motor vehicle, he recalled in 1945, "[which satisfied] esthetic as well as utilitarian demands," that led him to start a collection of Packard advertising material, publications that, like the machine they advertised, "reflected advanced design and a kind of artistic integrity. Brochures of other makes of that time usually contained retouched half-tone illustrations, hard and unlovely as those in heavy-hardware catalogs. Packard used distinguished line drawings, excellent typography, and hand lettering which would be acceptable today."

He was also influenced by the "sleek and smart" styling of the passenger trains on the Santa Fe Railway (known then as the Kansas City, Mexico and Orient Railroad Company), which he noticed as early as 1902, when he and his father drove to Lawrence. "The literature and advertising of the Santa Fe," he remembered, "even its world-renowned symbol (of Aztec origin) suggest discernment, and a sophistication seldom associated with a railroad." Having never attended college, Armitage said it was the corporate image and advertising publications of Packard and the Santa Fe Railway, "together with the scant treasures of our library, [that] were in a very personal sense my substitutes for college and university—my first contacts with esthetic appreciation and the cosmopolitan amenities of life."

Given Armitage's childhood influences, it is fitting that his first two jobs, beginning at age seventeen, were as a civil engineer in Texas, apparently connected with the Santa Fe Railway, and then as a graphic designer in the advertising department of the Packard Motor Car Company in Detroit. He remained in these positions for less than a year, and soon after decided that he should become a theater set designer, a move that eventually led to a lucrative thirty-year career as a concert impresario.

Armitage is mostly remembered today as an extraordinary book designer who was also the art director of *Look* magazine (1949–1954), an art collector (Dürer, Rembrandt, Goya, Gauguin, Cézanne, Van Gogh, Picasso, Marin, Klee, and Kandinsky), and a past president of the American Institute of Graphic Arts (1950–1951). But during the first fifty years of his life (as he explained to Henry Miller), he earned an ample income as the promoter and manager of dancers, opera singers, and opera and ballet companies. Among his illustrious clients were Anna Pavlova, Yvette Guilbert, Feodor Chaliapin, Amelita Galli-Curci, Mary Garden, Rosa Ponselle, and the Diaghilev Ballet.

He was also the cofounder and general manager of the Los Angeles Grand Opera Association, a board member of the Los Angeles Symphony Orchestra, and manager of the Philharmonic Auditorium of Los Angeles. He knew and authored books about some of the finest artists of the century, among them Igor Stravinsky, Martha Graham, George Gershwin, Pablo Picasso, Rockwell Kent, and Edward Weston.

Armitage's success as an impresario, as noted by Jay Satterfield, was due in part to his willingness to promote "highbrow" performances by using "lowbrow" advertising ploys, including false scandals and erotic suggestion. At the time, announcements of concerts were usually made quietly through restrained, tasteful notices, in contrast to slapstick, flamboyant affairs like the circus. Armitage's innovation was to stake out a middle ground: By promoting cultural events in much the same way that automobiles and railways were advertised, he believed that a much wider audience might "be led to realize that the arts, and their enjoyment, were reasonably normal activities needing to be classified neither with afternoon tea nor epileptic fits."

As time went on, he explained, "I became more and more convinced that posters, advertisements in newspapers and magazines, as well as thousands of announcements and circulars used by a concert manager, must reflect the quality of the performer not only in the text, but more important, in the design. Soon I found myself laying out every piece of printing concerned with my concerts, opera or ballet seasons."

It was this same philosophy that prompted him to become a book designer, resulting from his decision to use phenomenal books to promote artists whom he admired—not just concert performers, but visual artists, composers, and writers as well. Determined "to work only with publishers who would give me a free hand in design," he not only often wrote or edited his own books; in many cases, he was also the publisher.

Of the more than two dozen volumes that Armitage both authored and designed are *Rockwell Kent* (Knopf, 1932), *So-Called Modern Art* (Weyhe, 1939), *United States Navy* (Longmans, 1940), *Notes on Modern Printing* (Rudge, 1945), *Rendezvous with the Book* (McKibbin, 1949), *Railroads of America* (Little Brown, 1952), *George Gershwin: Man and Legend* (Duell, Sloan and Pearce, 1958), and two autobiographies, *Accent on America* (Weyhe, 1939) and *Accent on Life* (Iowa State University Press, 1965). In addition, he designed more than forty other books, which he either edited or wrote essays for, and over sixty others by other authors. In the books of his own writings—his autobiographies, for example, or those in which he talks about the design of books—portions of the narrative are often recycled, if somewhat revised and reshuffled, so that their enduring significance is more as adventures in daring design than as freshly written texts.

When Armitage was four years old, Frank Lloyd Wright had collaborated with one of his clients on an "artist's book" about aesthetics, the soul, and domestic architecture, titled *The House Beautiful* (Auvergne Press, 1897). The text was derived from a popular talk by a nationally known Unitarian minister, William C. Gannett. Wright designed the book, while his client, William H. Winslow, set the type and hand-printed an edition of ninety copies in the basement of his new home, only twenty of which now survive.

Thirty-five years later, Wright wrote and designed a second extraordinary volume, titled *An Autobiography*. The first edition was published in 1932 by Longmans, Green and Company, based in London and New York; the second, which came out in 1943, by Duell, Sloan and Pearce in New York. Both editions are much sought after by admirers of book design, largely because of the boldness with which Wright treats the section openings as continuous spreads, not just single facing fields that happen to be juxtaposed. Perhaps the most stirring example is the magnificent title spread for "Book Two–Work." Wright approached book designing with the same "organic form" philosophy that governed his architecture, with the result, as a critic declared at the time, that the design of his autobiography "compares in brilliance and originality with his buildings."

As Richard Hendel pointed out in *On Book Design*, "Designers are to books what architects are to buildings." Merle Armitage designed his first book in 1929, and, in subsequent years, he designed at least nine books for Longmans, and thirteen, including several of his best known titles, for Duell, Sloan and Pearce, the publishers who were responsible for Wright's autobiography. In light of their contacts, one wonders to what degree Armitage, the *enfant terrible* of book design, was inspired by the work of Wright, the bad boy of architecture, and vice versa. While Armitage admired Wright's architecture, he also liked to make it known that "on the prairies, and long before Frank Lloyd Wright became an influence, the Santa Fe [Railway] had constructed its stations on a horizontal motif."

One wonders too to what extent Wright and Armitage were influenced by W. A. Dwiggins's *Layout in Advertising* (1928) or his celebrated interpretations of Robert Louis Stevenson's *The Strange Case of Dr. Jeckyll and Mr. Hyde* (Knopf, 1929) and H. G. Wells's *The Time Machine* (Random House, 1931). Anyone who cared about book design in those days, wrote Armitage, "was aware of the Nonesuch and the Golden Cockerel Presses and the work of Eric Gill, Francis Meynell, Stanley Morison, and others in England." He himself collected the books of Bruce Rogers, "perhaps the greatest designer of them all," and "had long admired the distinguished work of such Americans as W. A. Dwiggins, with its Oriental influence."

In Dwiggins's layout for *The Power of Print–and Men* (Mergenthaler, 1936), there is a geometric sweep and some use of the tactics that Armitage called "my inventions" that "stirred violent criticism" and caused him, in certain circles, to be reviled as "the destroyer of book tradition, the bad boy of typography, the usurper of the placid pools of bookmaking": "i.e., use of the endsheets, double-page title pages, large readable type, generous margins, etc." Other notable aspects of Armitage's books, as Hendel has said, are "his cinematic treatment of the opening pages" and his "exuberant typography."

Armitage was just as direct and outspoken as Wright, and if he was despised or avoided (George Macy called him "that bull-in-our-china-shop"), it surely was partly because of the tone with which he communicated. He was, as described by a close friend, Robert M. Purcell, "a mercurial man in the truest sense. He was like quicksilver, and no thumb could hold him down. He was quick to joy, quick to anger, quick to create. He, like most of us, liked appreciation of what he did, and was quick to take umbrage if he was crossed, although he was a good resounding arguer and would take his lumps if he lost a point, or bellow with laughter when he won."

In photographs, Armitage is a big man with a huge head and broad smile, who often wore a cowboy hat and string tie, a person who would not be popular now in an age of political correctness and disingenuous double-talk. According to Purcell, "He had a mammoth lust for food, and the build to prove it; he liked hearty food, no nincompoop lemon Jell-O salad with shreds of lettuce for him. He lusted after art, art that dominated and spoke out, no pastels and chalk for him. A lust for good music, not a tinkling piano and chaminade, but Wagner, Brahms, Beethoven, Bach, and among the neo-Moderns, Satie, Ravel, and Stravinsky. A lust for good conversation, and in no way detouring away from a hearty argument with rolling thunderous opinions."

He must have been literally lustful as well. He used up four marriages, the last one ending sadly in an annulment, after no more than two months. A few years later, when Armitage was close to eighty years old and living alone on his Manzanita Ranch near Yucca Valley, California, his friend Purcell "happened to comment on having seen him with a very nice looking widow of about forty, four decades his junior. He said, 'Oh, yes. She comes out to the ranch and services me.' I had never heard that term in that context. It came probably from his Iowa farm youth where his father covered cows in order to breed tremendous herds and became one of the first major feeders, in Iowa, where feeding now is a bigger business than breeding."

Frank Lloyd Wright was short and slim, and it must have been more than amusing to see the large figure of Armitage, looking even larger by comparison, at the feet of the elephantine ego that lived in the undersized physical corpus of the self-described "world's greatest architect." At their last luncheon together, Wright complained to Armitage that some people believed that his school at Taliesin West produced only "little Frank Lloyd Wrights." "But just remember this, young man," he said to Armitage, "there are no little Frank Lloyd Wrights."

Nor was there anything puny about Merle Armitage. His was a boisterous ego that lived in a spacious body, a bombastic tree of a figure that fell from a fatal stroke on March 15, 1975. Years earlier, the always impish Wright poked fun at the expansiveness of Armitage—both physical and social—when he gave him a signed photographic portrait by Yosef Karsh. It is inscribed, "To Merle, the Armitage," and dated February 30, a day, of course, that doesn't exist.

Author's note: Among the sources for this essay were the entry on "Merle Armitage" in The National Cyclopedia of American Biography *(New York: James T. White & Co., 1952); the Armitage entry by Richard Hendel in J. A. Garraty and M. C. Carnes, eds.,* American National Biography *(NY: Oxford University Press, 1999); Jay Satterfield, "Merle Armitage: Accent on Taste," in* Books at Iowa *(Iowa City: University of Iowa, April 1996); Robert M. Purcell,* Merle Armitage Was Here! A Retrospective of a Twentieth Century Renaissance Man *(Morongo Valley, Calif.: Sagebrush Press, 1981); and various writings by Armitage, particularly* Notes on Modern Printing *(New York: Rudge, 1945), and his autobiographies,* Accent on America *(New York: Weyhe, 1939) and* Accent on Life *(Ames: Iowa State University Press, 1965).*

Roy R. Behrens teaches graphic design and design history at the University of Northern Iowa, edits Ballast Quarterly Review, *and regularly contributes to* PRINT, Leonardo, Gestalt Theory, *and the* North American Review.

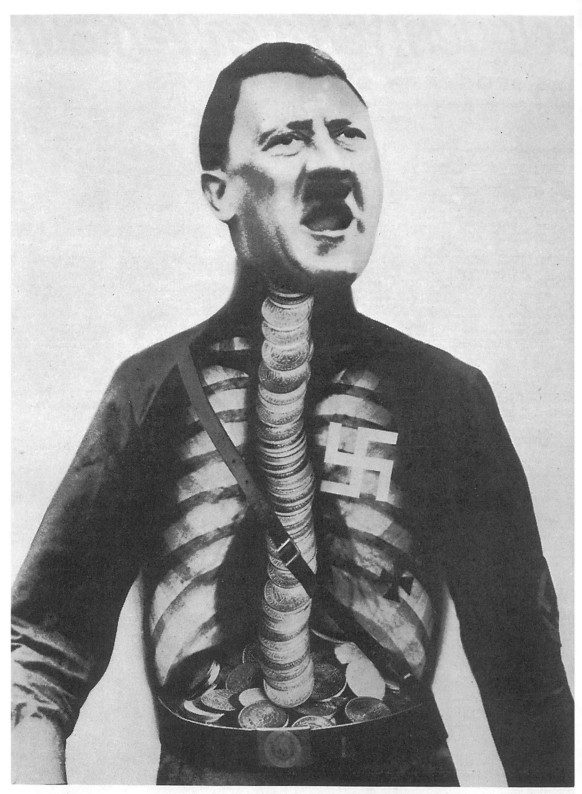

ADOLF, DER ÜBERMENSCH: Schluckt Gold und redet Blech

HEARTFIELD IN CONTEXT
Maud Lavin

John Heartfield (1891–1968), the German photomontagist known as an artist and a political propagandist for Left, peace, and anti-Nazi causes, has been canonized only recently in the unofficial pantheon of modern artists. Although he was honored in the former East Germany during his lifetime, full recognition in Western Europe and the United States was slow to come during the Cold War years. Broad public discussion of Heartfield's Dada and later twenties' work was initiated by museum exhibitions: the 1977 *Berlin Tendenzen der Zwanziger Jahre* (Tendencies of the Twenties) and the 1978 *Dada and Surrealism Reviewed,* curated by Dawn Ades at the Hayward Gallery. Gradually, during the eighties, Western art-world interest in Heartfield's Weimar photomontages increased because so many contemporary artists had turned to media-based work; Heartfield's Leftist politics were made palatable by foregrounding his crucial anti-Nazi propaganda in publications and exhibitions. Then, in 1991, the Akademie der Künste zu Berlin, together with two other German museums, organized a major retrospective which traveled for four years to museums in Germany, England, Ireland, Scotland, and the United States, including the Museum of Modern Art in New York, accompanied by a massive, 342-page catalog published by Abrams. As impressively detailed as the catalog was, the museum installations, at least in New York and Los Angeles where I saw the exhibition, gave visitors almost no historical context for Heartfield's art, not even defining the figures lampooned in his political caricatures. The montages were primarily shown as sanctified originals. Heartfield's art canonization, however, can be problematic when it threatens to upstage the history of the montagist's politics and mass-media involvement.

Though Heartfield himself showed his work on occasion in art contexts—initially, in the Berlin Dada exhibitions of 1919–20—he presented his photomontages mainly through newspapers, book jackets, and posters. He designed the photomontages to function within the contexts of photo layouts and news stories of which they were an integral part. Heartfield first began showing his work publicly through the independent Malik publishing house in 1916. Immediately after World War I, he also participated in the Berlin Dada group; from about 1918 to 1922 he was a cosignatory of the Dada manifestoes, a contributor to Dada periodicals, and an associate of Grosz, Richard Huelsenbeck, Hannah Höch, and Raoul Hausmann. The continuity between Heartfield's Malik work, his Dada production, and his later newspaper photomontages is his commitment to disseminating cultural and political criticism through periodicals and other formats.

So, rather than fetishizing Heartfield's individual iconic images, I want to focus here on the Malik publishing house in Berlin, where he designed book jackets, layout, and typography from 1916 to 1932, and on the *Arbeiter Illustriete Zeitung* (*AIZ*: Workers' Illustrated Newspaper), Berlin's popular communist newspaper, to which he contributed covers and photomontages from 1929 to 1933. (Heartfield continued to work for both institutions from 1933 to 1938 when they operated in exile in Prague due to their opposition to the Nazis.)

To very different degrees, two smaller shows featuring Heartfield's work and organized before the 1991–94 blockbuster employed a contextual approach and are worth revisiting: a Peace Museum, Chicago exhibition of Heartfield's photomontages made for the newspaper *AIZ*, presented in both published and poster form, which was curated by Viktoria Hertling; and a show at Goethe House in New York of books, periodicals, and portfolios produced by the publishing house Malik Verlag, in which both Heartfield and Grosz were well represented. Organized by James Fraser and Steve Heller, this was the first exhibition of the Malik Verlag in the United States.[1]

Malik was an educational and propagandistic organization begun in 1916 by Heartfield, his brother Wieland Herzfelde, and their friend, George Grosz. Heartfield, then a painter, and his poet brother turned away from traditional art practices and founded Malik in order to establish their pacifist stance against the war. Since government censorship disallowed founding new periodicals, Herzfelde took over the almost-defunct *Neue Jugend*, then a student periodical, and began to publish Grosz's satirical antiwar portfolios. In 1918, the November Revolution swept the Socialist Party into power with massive popular support, but Leftist artists and intellectuals were alienated by its earlier support of the war as well as by its hiring of the right-wing vigilante Freikorps to bloodily suppress opponents. Herzfelde, Heartfield, and Grosz joined the German Communist Party (KPD) in late 1918; thereafter, the Malik publishing house served communist goals but was not an official organ of the party.

As Malik's graphic designer, Heartfield grabbed attention with his disruptive design for its periodicals and bold, emblematic images for its book jackets. During his early Malik years, Dada aesthetics informed his work, as in his almost anarchic typography for *Neue Jugend*. Heartfield's book jackets were composed in a no less direct way, with posterlike montages of simple photographs and symbols—a design practice which reflected Herzfelde's policy of accessibility (a policy that even influenced the large typeface of Malik's book series).

Neue Jugend (1916–17), a pacifist literary periodical with an initial circulation of about thirty thousand, included contributions from Grosz, writer Else Lasker-Schueler, literary critic and activist Gustav Landauer, and others, and was the first of a series of proto-Dada and Dada political periodicals published by Malik. As each periodical was banned for its criticisms of the government, it would be replaced by another with a new name but essentially the same contributors. Unlike Dada movements in other cities, Berlin Dada was a politically engaged movement, and Heartfield and Grosz did not differentiate their Dada work from their Malik production.[2] As one of their contributions to the 1920 International Dada Fair, for example, they submitted the weekly issues of *Neue Jugend* from May and June 1917.

Two years after *Neue Jugend* was banned in 1919, Malik published an issue of 7,600 copies of an antimilitary Dadaist periodical entitled *Jedermann sein eigner Fussball* (Every Man His Own Soccer Ball). Heartfield's cover photomontage—of an array of Weimar government leaders, including General Hindenburg and President Ebert, as if posed for a beauty contest—is a satire on the layout of conservative periodicals; it is of historical importance as the first published political use of photomontage.[3] The issue also contained a Grosz drawing critical of the German Protestant church, an antimilitary article by Mynona, and an antipatriotic poem by Walter Mehring. (Mynona—Salomon Freidlander—was primarily a fiction writer, and Mehring primarily a poet, in the Berlin Dada group). Anticipating the government's confiscation of the issue, the editorial staff marched on February 15, 1919, through Berlin neighborhoods accompanied by a frock-coated musical band. The entire issue was sold out in a few hours.[4]

Other marketing strategies, though less sensational, were equally effective. Of primary importance to Herzfelde was to offer Leftist material to workers at a low price while still producing attractive enough books to compete with mainstream publications. Malik sold Grosz portfolios in signed and unsigned editions, inviting the bourgeoisie, the target of Grosz's satire, to finance its dissemination to the working class.[5]

From 1920 to 1926, Herzfelde also published seven series of more populist books: Little Revolutionary Library, Collection of Revolutionary Works for the Stage, Red Novel Series, Below and Above, The Fairy Tales of the Poor (children's books), Science and Society, and the Malik Library Series. This last included translations of Upton Sinclair and Maxim Gorky; a book of essays by Grosz and Herzfelde, *Art Is in Danger,* and a journalistic account by Fritz Slang of the 1905 sailors' uprising in Odessa, illustrated by stills from Eisenstein's *Battleship Potemkin*—a range designed to appeal to a wide audience. In 1922, introducing the Kleine Revoltionäre Bibliothek of eleven titles (including Zinoviev's biography of Lenin, theoretical tracts by Georg Lukács and Kurt Wittfogel and Grosz's *Face of the Ruling Class* graphics portfolio), Herzfelde explained his rationale for producing such series: "This collection publishes documents, biographies, theoretical materials, all of which are designed to stimulate and develop revolutionary awareness and zeal. It should give the individual lacking time for extensive study the opportunity to increase his knowledge of the class struggle and to enlarge his revolutionary horizon."[6]

A 1923 Malik prospectus advertised four editions of Grosz's *Ecce Homo* ranging in price from 16 to 700 marks. The same ad announced paperback and hardcover editions of Lukács's *Political Essays* at 3.3 and 7 marks and four differently priced bindings of Sinclair's *Man nennt mich Zimmerman* (*I Am Called Zimmerman*). By 1927 Malik could attract 100,000 buyers of Sinclair's *Petroleum* and 120,000 of Domela's *Der Falsche Prinz* (*The False Prince*).

The principal designer of Malik book jackets, Heartfield created emblematic compositions and wraparound images, as in the cover for Sinclair's *Der Sumpf,* 1924 (translated as "The Swamp," apparently because "The Jungle" suggested a boy's book). Though some of his designs incorporated Grosz drawings, most relied on contemporary photographs—news photos, publicity images, staged photos—possibly to underline the topical relevance of the books, and most of the designs were black and white with red accents. Heartfield's cover for the 1924 Malik yearbook *Platz! dem Arbeiter* (*Place of the Workers*), a collection of political statements by Kurt Tucholsky, Rosa Luxemburg, Wittfogel, and others, consisted of four rows of news photographs of revolutionary scenes. In its initiation of newsreel film footage, this format suggested both contemporaneity and political activism, as did the Marxian headlinelike banners that appear above and below the photos: "Philosophers Have Always Interpreted the World Differently. What Matters Is to Change It;" and "The Dominant Ideas of an Era Are Always the Ideas of the Dominant Class."

Just as an understanding of Malik Verlag as a propaganda system is essential to a reading of Heartfield's Malik designs, so, too, I consider it crucial to see his photomontages for *AIZ*, a communist photonewspaper, in context. Though the Peace Museum exhibition when I saw it at SUNY Westbury was small—limited to some forty photomontages, most produced for *AIZ,* with a few additional posters and book jackets—it managed to relate the images well to contemporaneous political events. However, the show lacked any display of whole issues of *AIZ* or of a Heartfield montage in the context of its customary two-page spread. Unlike the Goethe House show, which focused on Malik as a disseminating institution, the installation at Westbury did not provide enough information about *AIZ*—or about Heartfield's role in selling the newspaper.

AIZ was in existence, in one form or another, from 1921 to 1938, and was issued weekly after 1926. Although not the official press of the party, it was the leading communist newspaper in the Weimar Socialist Republic, an era when disillusionment with the corrupt judicial system and police brutality of the Weimar government as well as enthusiasm for the Soviet revolution caused the German Communist Party to function as a viable minority party in Germany. However, *AIZ* differed from the Russian party line in its vehement opposition to the Nazis when they began to rise in power in the late twenties.

AIZ's contents and coverage were aimed at the working class (a 1929 self-administered survey showed that its readership consisted of 42 percent skilled laborers and 33 percent unskilled). Heartfield produced photomontages for *AIZ* at roughly a monthly rate beginning in 1919. During that time the paper's circulation grew from 350,000 readers to 500,000 in 1931. Even at its peak, most readers bought copies on the newsstand, so there was great pressure on the cover image to sell the paper. This is one reason why many of Heartfield's *AIZ* covers—such as "The Meaning of the Hitler Salute: Motto: Millions Stand Behind Me!" (*AIZ*, Oct. 16, 1932), the famous photomontage of a saluting Hitler being paid off by a colossal figure of a capitalist—have a direct, posterlike character.

Heartfield's post-1924 "contemporary history photomontages" (as he termed them) were most often based on photojournalism taken from his own archive, one built from newspaper clippings and material found at picture agencies. At other times, Heartfield staged his own photographs but remained within photojournalistic formats.

To open up an issue of *AIZ* is to realize how embedded the meaning of Heartfield's work is in its mass-media framework. For example, "Adolf, the Superman: Swallows Gold and Spouts Junk" (*AIZ*, July 17, 1932), another well-known image which superimposes a news photo of Hitler speaking at a rally with photos of a skeletal rib cage, a belt, a pile of coins and a swastika, does indeed, as the exhibition notes, "portray Hitler as the spokesman of German capitalism." But it is precisely this alliance that is spelled out in the narrative, photographic layout of the newspaper as a whole. The cover of the July 17, 1932 *AIZ* presents two half-page portraits of men: one in Nazi uniform is identified as the wealthy Prince August Wilhelm of Prussia; the other, an unknown worker named Paul Michel whose leg was lost in an accident, is labeled "A Civilian Cripple Since 1910." The reader is told that this worker's welfare payments were reduced by Nazi legislation, and the headline asks if two members of such different social classes can support the same Nazi regime: "Prince and Worker in One Party?"

On page one of the same issue runs a half-page news photo of a workers' demonstration in Detroit being brutally dispersed by police, with a caption that alludes to the contradiction posed by the cover image: "Never can the party of princes and millionaires interest the workers." Nazism is here aligned textually with capitalism and police brutality to workers. The connection is pushed further; below the photograph of the demonstration are three smaller photos documenting confrontations between Nazi members and workers. Opposite this is the full-page Heartfield photomontage of Hitler "swallowing gold and spouting junk."

Though famous as an independent iconic image, this photomontage depends on its position within the photojournalistic narrative fully to convey its import—that Hitler and the Nazis are fed by specifically capitalist funding. (In the same issue is a story on the financiers who, according to *AIZ*'s claim, contributed to Hitler, such as Fritz Thyssen.) In its similarities to the straight photograph of a "news event," the Heartfield photomontage assumes a documentary truth-value; yet in its differences, it suggests a political reality that is obscured by conventional media representations and party rhetoric. The Heartfield image thus exists in a dialogue with the photojournalism that surrounds it, raising questions of verism, manipulation, and belief.

Heartfield's contribution to political photomontage—some would say his creation of that practice—is that his images direct a rereading of commercial mass media as well as function as strong political polemics.[7] A good example of this critique is Heartfield's photograph of a head swathed in newspapers, "Those Who Read Bourgeois Newspapers Will Become Blind and Deaf" (*AIZ*, Feb. 9, 1930), which *AIZ* used to illustrate a story on the deceptive practices of the Catholic and bourgeois press. Page one shows two almost identical photographs—one straight, the other retouched—of a German woman painter, Keimer-Dinkelbuehler, sitting in front of her easel at the Vatican where she has been commissioned to paint the Pope's portrait. In the manipulated image, the *AIZ* caption explains, her skirt has been lengthened by the bourgeois press to cover her legs. The suggestion is that if such an image is falsified, no photograph, no truth, is safe from manipulation. Opposite the two photos, on page two, is the full-page Heartfield photograph of the anonymous head smothered in newspapers. The newspapers are mainstream socialist ones; the object of Heartfield's ridicule is the opposition and its manipulation of reality. Though it retains a degree of photographic verism, Heartfield's photograph is obviously staged. Here, then, he uses artifice to expose the falsely "true" appearances of conventional photojournalism.

At times, Heartfield goes to great lengths to remind his viewers that his photomontages are mostly constructed of bits of unaltered photojournalism. In "Goering: The Executioner of the Third Reich" (*AIZ*, Sept. 14, 1933), Heartfield identifies Nazi minister Hermann Goering with the Reichstag fire, an act of arson which the Nazis laid on a communist conspiracy and used as an excuse to outlaw the party and jail its leaders. In the pho-tomontage, Goering, wearing a bloodied Nazi uniform and holding an ax, looms in the fore-ground, with the burning Reichstag in the background. His face is contorted in an expression between a bellow and a snarl, and the accompanying text, which labels Goering as the real arsonist, concludes: "Photomontage by John Heartfield. The face of Goering is taken from an original photograph and was not retouched." In effect, this is a directive to read the photographic fragments as indexical, bearing a one-to-one relationship with reality.

Heartfield's brother Wieland often collaborated with him on the written text, and they frequently used direct statements from the mass media—or ones that sounded as if they were quotations. For example, in "Hurrah Die Butter ist all!" (Hurrah the Butter is Gone!; [*AIZ*, Dec. 19, 1935]), Heartfield constructed an image of a family happily complying with the government slogan, "Guns Instead of Butter," by eating iron. Under the caption is added this Goering statement justifying the government's rearmament program during a decline in the nation's standard of living: "Iron has always made a country strong; butter and lard have at most made the people fat." The quote, from a speech given by Goering in Hamburg, is typical of a media excerpt appropriated and/or adapted by the Herzfelde brothers to expose the cruel reality under the rhetoric.

In fragmenting and recomposing media excerpts, Heartfield commented on media constructions of reality—a critique that began during his Dada period and continued after-ward. Heartfield invoked the verism connoted by photojournalistic fragments in creating his illusions, and thus his photomontages imply a more "truly" seen event; they seem to reveal the absurdities inherent in the real. Visually, this can amount to exposing the unseen aspects of a situation as in the montaged X-ray view of Hitler swallowing capitalist gold. What is significant is that the illusionism of Heartfield's *AIZ* work both depends on and refutes the so-called "truth" of photojournalism. Further, the meaning of Heartfield's *AIZ* pages is determined by the text and images that accompany them, and, in a larger sense, by the ide-ology of *AIZ* as a disseminating institution.

Such a contextual reading continues to be urgent today in considering Heartfield's impact on contemporary artists—like Krzysztof Wodiczko with his locally based, largely art-world-advertised installations and Stephen Kroninger with his montage caricatures for mass-market magazines and newspapers—and a reminder that there exists more than a formal and political kinship. For these contemporary artists, too, their distribution and marketing sys-tems powerfully mediate their work's reception.

This essay is excerpted from Maud Lavin's forthcoming book, Clean, New World: Cultural Politics and Graphic Design, *to be published by the MIT Press. An earlier version appeared in* Art in America *in February 1985. The author of a monograph on the Berlin Dada artist Hannah Höch* Cut with the Kitchen Knife *(New Haven: Yale University Press) and coauthor of* Montage and Modern Life *(MIT, Cambridge).*

Maud Lavin is the author of a monograph on the Berlin Dada artist Hannah Höch, Cut with the Kitchen Knife *(Yale UP) and coauthor of* Montage and Modern Life *(MIT). She teaches art history and cultural criticism at the School of the Art Institute of Chicago.*

Notes

1. *John Heartfield Photomontages 1919–1959* was curated by Viktoria Hertling for the Peace Museum, Chicago, and the Malik Verlag exhibition by James Fraser and Steve Heller. A catalog was published for the Malik exhibition, *The Malik Verlag 1916–1947* (New York: Goethe House, 1984).

2. In a general sense, all Dada art can be considered political in that it addresses issues of language and representation. Berlin Dada, however, was the one Dada group overtly involved in political struggle, specifically societal events during and after the Weimar revolution.

3. Dawn Ades, *Photomontage* (New York: Pantheon, 1976), p. 11.

4. On the basis of this *Jedermann* issue, charges were brought against Herzfelde as the editor and Mehring as a writer for "seeking to bring the Reichswehr into contempt and distributing indecent publications." Although neither was jailed at the time, Herzfelde was later imprisoned without a hearing from March 7–20, 1919, along with many other communists following a general strike in Berlin. Malik's history is marked by a series of major censorship trials instigated by the Weimar government, the most well known being George Grosz's 1928–30 trial for blasphemy. This case centered around Malik's publication of Grosz's drawing depicting Christ in a gas mask. Called "Shut Up and Do Your Duty," the drawing protested the fate of men forced into the military, particularly those of the soldiers who had been drafted and died in World War I. The case went through several trials and retrials, creating judicial, theological, and even legislative controversies. In the end, Grosz and Herzfelde as his publisher were acquitted, but the drawings were confiscated and printing blocks destroyed, reflecting the confused state of justice in the Weimar Republic. See Beth Irwin Lewis, *George Grosz: Art and Politics in the Weimar Republic* (Madison: University of Wisconsin Press, 1971), pp. 70–71, 74, 221–225.

5. Grosz portfolios of prints and/or drawings published by Malik include: *Kleine Grosz-Mappe* (Small Grosz Portfolio), 1917; *Erste Grosz-Mappe*, 1917; *Gott mit uns*, 1920; *Ecce Homo*, 1923; and *Hintergrund* (Background), 1928.

6. Wieland Herzfelde as quoted in *The Malik Verlag, 1916–1947* (New York: Goethe House, 1984), p. 36.

7. This involvement of the viewer in decoding mass media images recalls Walter Benjamin's admiration for Heartfield in his 1934 essay, "The Author as Producer," in which Benjamin calls for a particular kind of political art: "The best political tendency is wrong if it does not demonstrate the attitude with which it is to be followed. . . . What matters, therefore, is the exemplary character of production, which is able first to induce other producers to produce, and second to put an improved apparatus at their disposal. And this apparatus is better the more consumers it is able to turn into producers—that is, readers or spectators into collaborators." Walter Benjamin, "The Author as Producer," in *Reflections*, ed. Peter Demetz, trans. Edmund Jephcott (New York: Harcourt Brace Jovanovich, Inc., 1978), p. 233.

Behrens=Fraktur

5 Cicero   Nr. 81

Franz Schubert

Initialen zur Behrens=Fraktur

3 Cicero   Nr. 82   Nr. 86   24 Cicero   Nr. 87

A B C D E   A W

3 Cicero   Nr. 83

A B C D E

6 Cicero   Nr. 84

A B C

6 Cicero   Nr. 85

A B C

Korpus Behrens=Fraktur   Durchschossen

Der Rabe bemerkte, daß der Adler ganze dreißig Tage über seinen Eiern brütete. Und
daher kommt es, ohne Zweifel, sprach er, daß die Jungen des Adlers so allsehend und
stark werden. Gut! das will ich auch tun. Und seitdem brütet der Rabe wirklich ganze
dreißig Tage über seinen Eiern; aber noch hat er nichts, als elende Raben ausgebrütet

18

PETER BEHRENS: DESIGN'S MAN OF THE CENTURY?
Philip B. Meggs

Being in the right place at the right time, according to conventional wisdom, is often critical to significant accomplishment. As the career of the German artist, designer, and architect Peter Behrens (1868–1940) unfolded, fate put him in the "right place" several times with significant results. In graphic design, Behrens recognized the need for new typographic forms to express a new era, and he conceived and directed the first unified corporate identity program. His influence on product design was so significant that he has been called "the first industrial designer." His major buildings include a 1909 factory whose structure and glass curtain walls influenced the direction of architecture. The roster of architects who launched their careers as Behrens's apprentices include such titans as Walter Gropius, Ludwig Mies van der Rohe, Le Corbusier, and Adolf Meyer.

At the beginning of the century, Behrens contributed to design curriculum reform by developing new approaches to introductory visual education. As a theoretician, Behrens's articles and speeches often crystallized and focused important issues about design in an industrial society, suggesting new directions. Behrens advocated functionalism, truth to materials, and standards of uniformity. Given the scope of Behrens's contribution, it might be argued that he occupies a position in twentieth-century design somewhat similar to the positions of Cézanne and Picasso in painting: Behrens was a catalytic innovator whose work altered the course of design in this century.

Behrens was orphaned at age fourteen and received a substantial inheritance from his father's estate, which provided ongoing economic independence. He chose art for his career and studies in his native Hamburg. Social realism became the focus of his early paintings which depicted poor people and the industrial landscape. In 1892, Behrens was a founder of the Munich Secession, an organization formed by artists who, excited by new developments such as Impressionism and post-Impressionism, broke with the academic tradition. In Munich, a renaissance in German arts, crafts, and design was emerging. In 1897, Behrens gave up painting for applied art and embraced the 1890s Art Nouveau movement, called *Jugendstil* (Youth Style) in Germany after the new magazine *Jugend* (Youth), whose pages were filled with Art Nouveau designs and illustrations. Behrens began to make large multicolored woodcuts inspired by French Art Nouveau and Japanese prints, and he became a frequent contributor of illustrations and decorative designs to *Jugend* and *Pan* magazines. New printing and manufacturing techniques and the excitement of Art Nouveau were creating tremendous interest in the applied arts, and many artists embraced graphic and product design. Behrens's close friend Otto Eckmann abandoned painting for design and illustration and, in November 1894, auctioned all his paintings. His letter to the auctioneer bid his paintings a "cordial farewell" and concluded, "may we never meet again."

In 1900, the Grand Duke of Hessen, who sought to "fuse art and life together," established a new artists' colony in Darmstadt, hoping to encourage both cultural development and economic growth in light manufacturing such as furniture and ceramics. The seven participating artists, including Behrens and Vienna Secession architect Joseph Maria Olbrich, all had experience in the applied arts. Each artist was granted land to build a house, and Behrens designed his own house and all its furnishings, from furniture to cutlery and china.

A sense of urgency existed in the German art and design community. A new century was at hand, and the need to create new forms for a new era weighed heavily upon artists. Typographic reform was one of Behrens's major interests and he struggled unsuccessfully for a time to develop a new typeface with a conservative type founder. Then he came into contact with 32-year-old Dr. Karl Klingspor, of the Klingspor Foundry, who agreed to manufacture and release Behrens's first typeface, Behrensschrift, in 1901. The Klingspor Foundry was the first German typefoundry to commission new fonts from artists, and it achieved international prominence when it released Otto Eckmann's 1900 Eckmannschrift, which created a sensation. Drawn with a brush instead of a pen, Eckmannschrift was a conscious attempt to revitalize typography by combining medieval and Roman attributes with those of Japanese prints.

In contrast to Eckmann's gestural vitality, Behrensschrift was an attempt to reduce any "poetic flourish" which would mark the forms as the work of an individual hand and thereby reduce their universal character. Behrensschrift looks very calligraphic to the late-twentieth-century eye viewing this typeface more than sixty years after Paul Renner designed his geometrically constructed Futura. However, ornate Art Nouveau forms dominated new typeface design in the early 1900s, and Behrens's typeface looks very standardized relative to the typographic fashion of the time. Behrensschrift was an attempt not only to innovate a new typographic image for the new century but to create a uniquely German type. Behrens combined the heavy, dense feeling of black letter with the letter proportions of Roman inscriptions, while standardizing letterform construction. Horizontals and verticals are emphasized and diagonals are completely eliminated and replaced by curved strokes in letters such as *W* and *V*. Some typographic authorities were outraged by Behrensschrift, but with its feather-stroke serifs and clarity—compared to the dense black-letter typefaces then in use in Germany—Behrensschrift was a resounding success for both book and job-printing typography.

In the promotional booklet for Behrensschrift, Behrens compared reading text type to "watching a bird's flight or the gallop of a horse. Both seem graceful and pleasing, but the viewer does not observe details of their form or movement. Only the rhythm of the lines is seen by the viewer, and the same is true of a typeface."

German art critics of the period were interested in the relationship of forms in art and design to social, technological, and cultural conditions. Behrens was deeply concerned about these issues and believed that, after architecture, typography provided "the most characteristic picture of a period, and the strongest testimonial of the spiritual progress [and] development of a people." Another attempt to express the spirit of the new era occurred in 1900 when Behrens set his twenty-five-page booklet, "Celebrations of Life and Art . . ." in sans-serif type. German typographic historian Hans Loubier suggested in the 1920s that this document might contain the first use of sans-serif type as running book text. All-capital sans-serif type is used in an unprecedented way on the title and dedication pages. The popularity of sans-serif types in the twentieth century vindicated Behrens's experiment.

In 1903, Behrens moved to Düsseldorf to become director of the Düsseldorf School of Arts and Crafts. Innovative preparatory courses preceded study in specific disciplines such as architectural, graphic, or interior design. Behrens's purpose was to go "back to the fundamental intellectual principles of all form-creating work," allowing "the principles of form-making to be rooted in the artistically spontaneous, in the inner laws of perception, rather than directly in the mechanical aspects of the work." Students drew and painted natural forms in different media, then made analytical studies to explore linear movement, pattern, and geometric structure. These introductory courses were precursors of the preliminary course at the Bauhaus, where two of Behrens's former apprentices, Gropius and Mies van der Rohe, served as directors.

A dramatic transformation occurred in Behrens's work in 1904 after the Dutch architect J. L. M. Lauweriks joined the Düsseldorf faculty. Lauweriks was fascinated by geometric form and had developed an approach to teaching design based on geometric composition. His grids began with a square inscribed with a circle and the numerous permutations made possible by subdividing and duplicating this basic structure. The geometric patterns thus developed could be used to determine proportions, dimensions, and spatial divisions in the design of everything from chairs to buildings to posters. Behrens's application of this theory proved catalytic in pushing twentieth-century architecture and design toward rational geometry as an underlying system for visual organization. His work from this period reveals the tentative beginnings of constructivism in graphic design, wherein realistic or even stylized depictions are replaced by an architectural and geometric structure. Often, Behrens used square formats, but more frequently, he used rectangles in ratios such a 1 square wide to 1.5 or 2 squares tall.

The major event in Behrens's career occurred in 1907, when Emil Rathenau, director of the Allgemeine Elektricitäts Gesellschaft (AEG), appointed him artistic adviser for the company. Rathenau had purchased European manufacturing rights to Thomas A. Edison's patents in 1883, and AEG had grown into one of the world's largest manufacturing concerns. A visionary industrialist, Rathenau sensed the need for a unified visual character for AEG products, environments, and communications. In 1907, the electrical industry was synonymous with high technology: Electric teakettles were as advanced as computers and videocassette recorders are today. As design adviser to the concern, Behrens began to focus intensely upon the design needs of industry, with design responsibility ranging from large buildings to stationery.

Otto Eckmann had been a designer and consultant for AEG, but he died of tuberculosis in 1902 at age 37. Behrens executed several graphic designs for AEG in 1906; then, in 1907, was commissioned to design an important AEG pavilion for the 1908 German Shipbuilding Exhibition.

The year 1907 also marked the founding in Munich of the Deutscher Werkbund (German Association of Craftsmen), which advocated "a marriage of art with technology." Behrens played a major role in this first organization created to inspire good design in manufactured goods and architecture. The group's leaders, including Hermann Muthesius, Henry van de Velde, and Behrens, were influenced by William Morris and the English Arts and Crafts Movement, but with significant differences. While Morris was repelled by the products of the machine age and advocated a return to medieval craftsmanship in romantic protest against the industrial revolution, the Werkbund embraced new technology and advocated design as a way to give form and meaning to all machine-made things, including machine-made buildings.

With visionary zeal, Werkbund members advanced a philosophy of *Gesamkultur*, a new universal culture existing in a totally reformed man-made environment. Design was seen as the engine which could propel society forward to achieve *Gesamkultur*. Soon after it formed, the Werkbund split into two factions. One, headed by Muthesius, argued for the maximum use of mechanical manufacturing and standardization of design for industrial efficiency. Its adherents believed that form should be determined solely by function and wanted to eliminate all ornament. The other faction, led by van de Velde, argued for the primacy of individual artistic expression. A design philosophy is merely an idle vision until someone creates artifacts which make it a real force in the world. Thus, Werkbund members consciously sought a new design language to realize their goals. Behrens's work for AEG became an early manifestation of Werkbund ideals.

Behrens's work for AEG represents a synthesis of two seemingly contradictory concepts: neoclassicism and *Sachlichkeit* (loosely translated, "commonsense objectivity"). His neoclassicism grew from a careful study of the art and design of ancient Greece and Rome. Rather than merely copying the stylistic aspects of this work, he found a new formal language of harmony and proportion to achieve a unity of the parts with the whole. *Sachlichkeit* was a pragmatic emphasis upon technology, manufacturing processes, and function. Artistic conceits and questions of style were subordinate to purpose. In concert, these two concepts guided Behrens in his quest for forms to achieve *Gesamkultur*.

The AEG graphic identity program made consistent use of three linchpin elements present in corporate identity programs as the genre evolved a half century later: a logo, a typeface, and consistent layout of elements following standardized formats. Behrens designed a typeface for AEG's exclusive use to bring unity to its printed materials. At a time when graphic design in Germany was dominated by traditional black letter and decorative Victorian and Art Nouveau styles, Behrens designed a Roman-style letterform inspired by classical Roman inscriptions. Initially, this was not available in type, so display type on all AEG printed graphics was handlettered. In 1908, a typeset variation named Behrens-Antiqua was released by Klingspor Foundry, first for the exclusive use of AEG, then later, for general use. Behrens had three important goals in designing this new type: It differentiated AEG communications from all other printed matter; its forms were universal rather than individualized by the touch of an artist's hand; and it strove for a monumental character which could evoke positive connotations of quality and performance. Behrens-Antiqua possessed the solemn, monumental quality of Roman letterforms, tempered by the rhythm of the serifs. The ornaments were inspired by ancient Roman brasswork, whose geometric properties satisfied Behrens's belief that geometry could make ornamentation universal and impersonal.

In 1908, he designed the hexagonal AEG trademark. This pictographic honeycomb design containing the firm's initials signifies mathematical order while functioning as a visual metaphor that relates the complexity and organization of a twentieth-century corporation to a beehive. Geometrical spatial divisions based on Lauweriks's grid structures are one unifying graphic theme of Behrens's AEG publication designs.

The use of various graphic devices gave AEG materials a consistent appearance. In addition to modular divisions of space using Lauweriks's grid, these included: framing the pace by a medium-weight rule; central placement of static elements; exclusive use of Behrens-Antiqua type; use of analogous colors, often two or three sequential colors on the color wheel; and simple, objective photographs and drawings with subjects isolated from their environments.

Industrial products designed by Behrens ranged from electric household products such as teakettles and fans to streetlamps and electric motors. He brought the formal eye of the painter and the structural approach and professional ethics of the architect to product design. The combination of visual form, working method, and functional concern in his work for AEG products enabled him to produce a body of work which has led to his being proclaimed the "first industrial designer." An innovative use of standardization is seen in the design of AEG teakettles with interchangeable parts: three basic kettle forms, two lids, two handles, and two bases. Three materials were used: brass, copperplate, and nickelplate; and three finishes: smooth, hammered, or rippled. All these elements were available to assemble three sizes of teakettles, and all the kettles used the same heating elements and plugs. This system of interchangeable components made it possible to configure eighty-one different teakettles, though only thirty were actually brought to market.

Beginning in early 1907, Behrens designed a series of AEG arc lamps that produced intense light by means of passing an electrical current between two carbon electrodes. These were 300 times brighter, used less energy, and were safer than the gaslamps of the time. Because the carbon rods had to be replaced every eight to twenty hours, Behrens designed convenient exterior clips for dismantling them quickly. Their forms and proportions suggest Lauweriks's grid, while the overall shapes evoke the harmonious design and graceful curves of Greek vases. The arc lamps were widely used in factories, railway stations, and public buildings.

Behrens believed neutrality and standardization were appropriate in product designs created for machine manufacture. By designing streetlamps and teakettles using simple forms shorn of decoration, Behrens stripped connotations of social class and wealth from these products. His work pointed toward a new sensibility about design, which matured in the 1920s. This rational approach decreed the need for form to emerge from function rather than being an added embellishment.

Between 1909 and 1912, Behrens directed the design for the AEG factory complex in Berlin. The Turbine Hall, designed by Behrens in collaboration with structural engineer Karl Bernhard, is one of the most influential buildings of the early twentieth century. A vast open space is formed by twenty-two giant girder frames enclosing an interior space 401 feet long and 49 feet high. In addition to the roof and glass walls, these girder frames support two traveling gantry cranes, each with a 50-ton lifting capacity for moving giant turbines under construction. The huge window areas are "curtain walls" floating in the space. The massive concrete columns at the corners are non-load-bearing. Except for the identifying logo and name on the end of the roof, there is neither ornament nor embellishment. The structure and proportions of functional elements are designed to convey the aesthetic of the building. Its appearance suggests a massive industrial factory engineered for the assembly of giant steam turbines. This major architectural design by Behrens—with its exposed exterior steel girders along the sides, glass curtain walls, and form determined by function—became a prototype for future design evolution. Behrens's philosophy and the usual studio shop talk were surely a wellspring of ideas for his apprentices of this period: Gropius, Mies van der Rohe, Le Corbusier, and Meyer.

At the 1914 Werkbund annual conference, the debate between Muthesius's rationalism and standardization versus van de Velde's expressionism was soundly determined in favor of the Muthesius approach. Up until this 1914 meeting, Behrens played a key role among designers who rejected the ornament of both historicism and Art Nouveau design and advocated a spartan approach, stripped of decoration. The austere orthodoxy of the International Style was the evolutionary extension of these beliefs.

Behrens began to accept architectural commissions from other clients in 1911; graphic and product design occupied less of his time. In 1914, Behrens's contract with AEG was terminated, although he continued to work from time to time on AEG projects. Until his death in 1940, Behrens's design practice centered upon architecture. His buildings were often massive and ranged from expressionism immediately after World War I to modernist works in the late 1920s and early 1930s whose geometric simplicity and white stucco walls reflected the influence of Gropius and Mies.

One may ask why Behrens has not been more widely recognized or even lionized for his importance to twentieth-century design. Perhaps the answer is yet another fact in the devastating impact of Adolf Hitler upon the century. Hitler's rise to power during the 1930s caused many of Europe's leading modern artists and designers to join the flight of scientific and cultural leaders from the continent to the United States. When Gropius and Mies arrived here, they established architectural and educational programs that transformed American architecture. However, the aging Behrens remained in Germany. During his final years, he struggled to come to terms with the New Order and even signed correspondence, "Heil Hitler." Ironically, he was shunned by some longtime associates for his efforts to adapt even as he was being investigated and attacked by the Nazis for his artistic and political background and prior association with Communists and Jews, including Albert Einstein.

During the late 1930s, Hitler's architect, Albert Speer, planned the transformation of Berlin into an imperial city of the Third Reich, designed in a monumental Empire Style. One of the buildings planned for the grand boulevard stretching from a proposed Arch of Triumph to a domed Great Hall was a new administrative building for AEG to be designed by Behrens. Nazi cultural watchdogs were outraged "that this forerunner of architectural radicalism should be allowed to win immortality on 'the Fuehrer's avenue.'" Hitler backed Speer in his decision to use Behrens, quelling the opposition. The design for the AEG building was completed in October 1939, but it was never executed, as the grand scheme for Berlin became an early casualty of World War II.

Behrens had been plagued with heart trouble since his mid-thirties, and he died of a heart attack on February 27, 1940, at age 72. Neither the design professions nor the newspapers took much notice of his passing.

The neglect of Behrens's pivotal role in twentieth-century design, at least in the United States and England, may relate to factors other than the taint of his accommodation with Nazism. Perhaps his drift away from Modernism in the later 1930s fueled the failure to fully recognize his earlier importance. Over the past half century, the legacies of Hitler and Stalin have warped our perceptions of the human condition. But as the walls of the past crumble and a new era of international culture hopefully emerges, perhaps one small result will be a greater acknowledgment of Peter Behrens's impact upon design in this century.

Originally published in PRINT, *March/April 1991*

Lucian Bernhard: The Master Who Couldn't Draw Straight

Steven Heller

The Priester Match poster is a benchmark of modern graphic design. Although its subject is mundane, its composition is so stark and its colors so startling that it seizes the eye in an instant. If I so much as think of a match—wooden or paper—I immediately conjure up the name and image of Priester, even though the poster is almost nine decades old. Of course, the aim of all good advertising is to make the mundane memorable. However, before 1905, when the Priester Match poster first appeared on Berlin hoardings, most advertising posters were wordy and ornate. Its persuasive simplicity was something new. Moreover, no one had ever heard of its creator, Lucian Bernhard, who was just eighteen years old. A doctor's son from Stuttgart, Germany, he had left home to seek his fortune as a poster artist in Berlin, and, thanks to this one poster, in short order influenced an entire genre of advertising.

Many know about Bernhard's important early work from looking through poster books. Remarkably often the most striking examples—those that excel in terms of graphic simplicity and strength—are his. Lucian Bernhard was not only an innovative posterist, but also a prolific trademark, package, alphabet, textile, furniture, and interior designer. He worked in Berlin during the century's first two decades, and subsequently in New York, where he developed some of the most recognizable American business advertising and trademarks for clients like Amoco, Cat's Paw, and Ex-Lax, as well as thirty-five popular display typefaces, including Bernhard Gothic. But who was this BERN HARD whose two-tiered signature reads for the uninitiated as two names? And what influenced him to make imagery that was so distinct from that of his contemporaries? The answers are not easy to come by—Bernhard deliberately invented many of his early biographical accounts. His son Karl Bernhard admits that "Lucian," as he calls him, enjoyed toying with the details of his life, rewriting and retelling his stories differently depending on his audience or mood. Bernhard believed that whatever really happened in his youth had little relevance in judging his adult life and work. Nevertheless, through conversations with his children, Karl, Manfred, and Ruth, and with various now deceased friends, including Fritz Eichenberg, Aaron Burns, and Cipe Pineles, I have managed, over time, to sew together some of the biographical threads.

One story has Bernhard growing up in Stuttgart, where at an early age he fell in love with drawing and became fascinated with letters. In this account, he was always at odds with his physician father, who wanted him to follow a career in medicine. Unwilling to bend to his father's wishes, Lucian, when still a teenager, ran away to Munich and never returned.

However, another account has him living a happy and contented childhood with his parents. Even his sons tell conflicting tales.

What is known is that Bernhard's formative years coincided with the explosion of Art Nouveau in France and Jugendstil in Germany. In Munich, the popular satiric journals *Simplicissimus* and *Jugend* were publishing the most acerbic and original cartoons in Germany, and they exerted an influence on all German graphic art. Apparently, as a youth, Bernhard visited Munich's Glaspalast, where he saw a major exhibition of European Art Nouveau applied arts, including the wildly colorful cabaret and theatrical posters of Jules Chéret, Henri Toulouse-Lautrec, and Alphonse Mucha. Also on view were maquettes for the uniquely economical advertising posters of the famed Beggerstaffs (the Britons James Pryde and William Nicholson). The latter pieces were to have a strong effect on the young Lucian's own poster making. In later years, Bernhard recalled to his son Karl his sense of "walking drunk with color" throughout this exhibit.

So inspired was he, in fact, that (according to another biographical account) when he returned to his parents' drab Wilhelmine-styled home, burdened by its excessive nineteenth-century Imperial appointments, he took the opportunity of his parents' chance absence to repaint every wall and stick of furniture with the new, modern colors he had just seen. Upon returning, his father was so outraged by this act of defilement that he ordered his son, then age seventeen, to leave the house forever, literally disowning him—or so the story goes.

Berlin is where Bernhard decided to pursue a career. It was also where, by his own Dickensian account, he was penniless and forced to sleep in sewer pipes stored above ground—where he had to beg for his food or even steal it. But there are other, less dire descriptions of his early days in Berlin. One, related by a close Bernhard friend, has him writing poetry and selling it on the street to earn a living. Another has him working as a messenger for a publishing house. Karl tells a story of Bernhard running errands for a local political caricaturist in exchange for work space in his studio. It is this unnamed caricaturist who encouraged Bernhard to enter his first poster contest.

Poster competitions were regularly sponsored by Berlin business establishments as a way of identifying new talent for the expanding advertising industry. The one sponsored by Priester Match Company was judged by some of the leading promoters of the burgeoning poster movement. The sum of 200 marks (then about $50) went to the winner. More important, the poster was printed. Bernhard jumped at the opportunity, and with precious little time to produce his entry, he made some instinctive design decisions which had stunning repercussions.

First, he decided to use a brown/maroon background—an unusual color choice since posters of the time featured either black or primary colors—on which he rendered an ashtray and a pair of matches. Seeing that the ashtray needed some other graphic element to balance the composition, he added a cigar. Logically, from the cigar came smoke, and from the smoke came—what else but a few scantily clad Jugendstil dancing girls? The ashtray needed grounding, so he placed it on a checkered tablecloth. At the top of the poster in black letters he handlettered the word "Priester." Proud of his finish, he showed it to his caricaturist friend, who congratulated him on the wonderful cigar poster. Bernhard immediately saw his error, and proceeded to, one might say, deconstruct the image by painting out the cigar, then the smoke, then the dancing girls, then the ashtray, then the tablecloth—leaving only the red matches with yellow tips and the brand name Priester.

He met the deadline—barely. But the judges, finding his entry too odd, threw it into the trash bin, where it would have remained had not the most important judge, who arrived late, taken the situation in hand. He was Ernst Growald, sales manager for the Hollerbaum and Schmidt lithography firm, widely known as Berlin's leading printer of advertising posters and a protoadvertising agency. Growald was a man of vision who understood the role of advertising in Germany's expanding economy. He also had taste, and not finding any noteworthy entries on the table, turned his eye to the poster in the trash bin. He pulled it out, hung it on the wall, and reportedly exclaimed: "This is my first prize! This is genius!" At eighteen years old, Bernhard won the contest—and gained a long-term benefactor. With Growald as his agent and broker, he never again wanted for paying jobs.

Bernhard used the Priester poster as a model for all other work and capitalized on its success. Though his subsequent posters were good—often gorgeous—he never really achieved the impact of the Priester work. He did, however, produce countless images for a wide range of German (and later foreign) products. By the time he was nineteen, he had become so sought after that he was compelled to open his own studio on the Budapest-strasse, where he eventually hired additional artists. Within ten years, he had an elegant new studio on the Lützowuferstrasse, which grew to employ around thirty artists and assistants.

Bernhard's success rested on his inventing a new style of poster art known as the *Sachplakat*, or object poster, in which all but the most necessary visual and copy elements— i.e., an unambiguous image with its trade name—were excluded. Even more impressive is that, in 1920, this untrained high school dropout was made the first professor of poster art at the Berlin School of Arts and Crafts.

The first decade of the twentieth century was significant for Bernhard and German arts and crafts because a marriage between art and industry was being promoted through organizations like the Deutsche Werkbund, and celebrated at frequent industrial expositions. As the broad avenues and boulevards of cities began teeming with automobiles and buses, these densely traversed areas became hubs of advertising, with posters adapting not just to the clutter of hoardings but to the pace of the street. Bold, reductive graphic imagery was necessary to capture viewer attention. Bernhard's *Sachplakat* epitomized this new form, which also included images of unusually bright yet aesthetically pleasing color. Text was kept to a minimum. Growald encouraged others to work in this mode, and formed a loosely knit "school" known as the Berliner Plakat.

As a charter member—indeed, its foremost innovator—Bernhard was involved with many of the movement's exponents and supporters, including Dr. Hans Sachs, a Berlin dentist, and Rudolf Bleistein, a lace merchant, who founded the Friends of the Poster Club in 1913.

Bernhard designed this organization's logo and text typeface and was cofounder of its journal, *Das Plakat*, a 1916 issue of which was devoted almost entirely to his work. Bernhard's prominence in the movement reflected his acute awareness that industry required radical forms of graphic publicity, and that the designer was in a unique position to influence those with the power to bring these forms about. At the time, throughout the industrial world, new national corporations were beginning to replace smaller businesses, and thus had a need for distinct, unified identities. Peter Behrens, the father of corporate identification, set the standard with his integrated design systems for the German electric company AEG. Bernhard, not tied to any one company, understood that graphic unity would benefit all industry.

Bernhard developed intimate friendships and congenial working relationships with many of Germany's most important businessmen. It was his practice of working directly with owners or directors of companies that fostered noteworthy programs for clients like Bosch automotive parts, Adler Typewriter, Manoli Cigarettes, and Henkell Champagne. But Bernhard didn't just work for fellow countrymen who were his friends; Growald put him on a nonstop schedule that involved making posters for a number of foreign concerns, including shoe and coffee companies in pre-Soviet Russia.

While his posters from this period bear a stylistic imprint, Bernhard by no means performed as a one-man band. He routinely gave credit to the craftsmen at the printing shop who made the final drawings and interpreted his color requirements from large maquettes.

In addition to creating memorable imagery, Bernhard made inroads in typography. Before World War I, a powerful reform movement in lettering began to challenge the medievalism that had dominated German typography since Gutenberg. Behrens, Rudolf Koch, and Otto Eckmann led the way, and Bernhard, who had designed his own version of the spiky German blackletter, Fraktur, was an eager member. In 1910, the formidable Berthold Type Foundry issued a "block" letter that looked suspiciously like Bernhard's own poster lettering. This forced Bernhard to complete and promote his own alphabets in order to protect his inventions. His first typeface, a bookface called Antiqua, was released by the Flinsch Foundry in Frankfurt in 1913. He promised more, but World War I put a temporary halt to his output.

With the start of hostilities, Bernhard was drafted into the army. However, this incurable rebel did not conform easily to the military regimen. For example, rather than accept a government-issued uniform, he designed his own and had his tailor—who was also Kaiser Wilhelm's tailor—manufacture the garment. Though Bernhard was a lowly private, his uniform was styled like an officer's. He also refused to travel to the front on the standard crowded troop train, but rather, booked his own passage on a comfortable sleeper reserved exclusively for officers.

Bernhard would have remained at the front for the duration of the war had it not been for his company commander, who in civilian life had also been involved in the graphic arts and knew and admired Bernhard's work. He insisted that Bernhard take a home-guard assignment making posters in support of the war effort. Bernhard spent the rest of his military service safely out of the line of fire. After the war, and during the economic turmoil that followed, this same admirer hired Bernhard to design emergency currency, which, owing to the extraordinary inflation rate, was revalued daily.

With the war lost and Germany in the throes of economic and political upheaval, Bernhard, who was avowedly apolitical, accepted an invitation to visit the United States for an unspecified period. It was 1922 and the invitation came from Roy Latham, who ran a lithography firm in Long Island City, New York. He proposed that Bernhard speak before various art directors associations in New York and elsewhere about advertising and logo design. Despite his poor knowledge of English, Bernhard accepted. It was Latham's intention that Bernhard be shuttled around the country to promote his own work and perhaps persuade American art directors to consider modern design as an alternative to the overly rendered, often saccharine painted illustration that constituted much of American practice. Sadly, the tour never got off the ground. American advertising was ruled by the copywriter, who was little interested in Bernhard and what he represented. Moreover, advertisers viewed Bernhard's efforts as *too* modern, even while the Bauhaus was causing a stir with its truly radical experimentation, which made Bernhard's work look conservative by comparison. Bernhard later said that he was fascinated that the youngest and, from his European vantage point, seemingly the most progressive, Western nation was so intent on preserving old styles.

Despite his disappointing U.S. reception, Bernhard became infatuated with New York City—particularly, one learns, with its women. He decided to stay on for another six months, which turned into a full-time residency, as he forsook his adopted Berlin, flourishing studio, and family.[1] In one respect, his move to New York was opportune, for he hated being the boss of a large studio. Apparently, even at the height of his Berlin success, with thirty employees working from nine to five, Bernhard would keep aloof from everyone and lock himself in his office/sanctum, which was also his second apartment (complete with shower), emerging only after dark when all the workers had left. It was therefore no emotional wrench for him to leave the studio, which he now placed in the hands of his manager and partner, Fritz Rosen, with whom he had cosigned many posters.

In the early 1920s, visas were not needed to enter the United States, so Bernhard traveled freely between Berlin and New York as business demanded. In New York, he worked with one assistant out of his apartment.

To introduce him once again to American poster users, Roy Latham arranged that Bernhard be given an exhibition at the New York Art Center (and later at the Composing Room's influential Gallery 303), which was well attended and favorably covered in the press. Nevertheless, commissions were slow to arrive. During his first few years in New York, Bernhard was hired on occasion by advertising agencies to render sketches for ad campaigns, but most of these were rejected. Although his German style was not appreciated, he refused to cater to American tastes. So for five years, until around 1927, he engaged in his other German vocations and worked exclusively on interior and furniture design for wealthy Manhattan clients.

Bernhard eventually lived, worked, and taught design students on East 86th Street in Manhattan. Karl indicates that he was not a very patient teacher; however, we have it on the authority of Fritz Eichenberg, the book illustrator and wood engraver, that he was "a good man." Eichenberg recalled that, as a perfect stranger, he was generously taken under Bernhard's wing after emigrating from Nazi Germany. He also reported that Bernhard always had pretty female models around the apartment. "When I would knock on the door," said Eichenberg, "invariably a lovely waif would open it while another modeled for Lucian's painting or scrubbed him in the bathtub."

During the late 1920s, Bernhard helped found, with the financial backing of a prosperous immigrant furrier named Weiner, the first international design consortium, called Contempora. It was based on the Vienna Werkstätte's notion of the "complete work of art," whereby useful products designed by artists could be sold at reasonable prices to the middle class, and at the same time improve the visual environment. The contributors were a quirky mix: former Jugendstil cartoonist-turned-furniture-designer Bruno Paul in Munich; fashion designer Paul Poiret in Paris; illustrator Rockwell Kent in New York; and architect Erich Mendelson in Vienna. They produced everything from graphics to textiles, fashion accessories to furniture. Contempora even produced a line of chairs for Grand Rapids Furniture Company. But despite a reasonable amount of publicity, Contempora failed, a casualty of the Great Depression.

With all of his forward-looking activities, one might assume that Bernhard was sympathetic to the precepts of the modern movement. In truth, he wasn't. According to Karl, his father liked to say he was a doer, not a theorist or ideologue. His work, though well reasoned and carefully designed, was based not on systems but instinct. He apparently disapproved of the Bauhaus and any form of instruction that made too much (or too little) of the advertising process. If Bernhard had a philosophy at all, it might be found in his words: "You see with your eyes, not with your brain. What you do with your hands should express the physical process and should never be mechanical."

Sometime during the late 1920s, Bernhard was introduced to a Baltimore advertising agent named Joe Katz, who, like Growald in Berlin, had vision, taste, and high hopes that Bernhard could have an impact on American advertising. This was before the era of communications departments and perceptual marketing specialists, and so the same advertising agent who bought space in newspapers and magazines also acted as a hands-on creative consultant. Katz convinced many of his clients that Bernhard could offer a fresh look to old products. In the meantime, Bernhard had developed a new style, which, though rooted in the German idiom of simplicity, was decidedly less elegant than his European work—more hard-sell, hence more acceptable, to American clients.

The first important account arranged by Katz was REM cough syrup. Bernhard was introduced to Walter Hollander, president of REM, who commissioned him to produce a series of subway and bus car cards as well as twenty-four-sheet billboards. The billboard was the American equivalent of the European poster, and a formidable advertising tool. Bernhard used it to make REM a household word, turning out one billboard a month for the next twenty years. In this work, the lush purples and forest greens that characterized his German style were replaced by stark primary colors, more in keeping with the perceptual requirements imposed by the highway and urban street than with aesthetic verities.

His process is worth noting. Bernhard usually conceived the ideas himself. Some were typographic, while others involved a combination of word and image. With some, he would render only a comp; with others, he would do the finished piece. His assistant for many years, Ted Sandler (who after a decade or so became a designer for William Golden at CBS), would also render finished art. Sandler's finishes were usually slicker and more painterly than Bernhard's. In 1932, Bernhard's son Karl (followed, a year later, by another son, Manfred) came to New York from Germany and worked as an assistant in his studio. As a form of on-the-job training, Karl finished many of the billboards and ads.

Katz had succeeded in procuring steady assignments from Amoco Gas, then privately owned by Jacob Blaustein, who also took a personal interest in Bernhard's design. Beginning in the late '20s and continuing for twenty years, Bernhard produced one twenty-four-sheet poster a month for Amoco. Because advertising was still a copywriter's game, many of these posters were dominated by lettering, often one word or a short slogan accompanying the logo. Indeed, most of the ideas took Bernhard less than an hour to sketch and the finish was done by Sandler or Karl. Another harmonious relationship grew between Bernhard and the president of Ex-Lax. What began as a simple job to design the company's matchbooks ended up as a long-term commission to create its new trademark, packaging, and the interior design of its Brooklyn factory and administrative offices. Other regular accounts included Radio City Music Hall, Marlboro Shirts, the Theater Guild, Westinghouse, and Cat's Paw, the logo for which is now considered a vernacular treasure.

Bernhard could never draw straight lines. Yet he never used ruling pens, either. He did, however, exploit this weakness as a strength. Though most of his original alphabets were eventually redrawn, cut, and polished by other craftspeople using the proper drafting tools, not one of his letterforms is perfectly geometric. Bernhard insisted that "the eye does not see precise straight lines or circles." Even Bernhard Gothic, designed for ATF to compete with Paul Renner's Futura (which Bernhard disliked because of its geometric precision), gets perceptibly fatter toward the middle of the *I* or *L*. Type historian Helmut Lehmann-Haupt reported in *American Artist* that "Bernhard is interested in streamlining the Gothic. And seeks the means to overcome the rigidity prescribed by the prophets of the machine age."

In Germany, Bernhard had developed typefaces for the Flinsch and Bauer typefoundries, including a transitional bold brush script. He designed his first elegant script, Bernhard Kursive, in 1922 while traveling to New York on a steamship. In 1928, he joined forces with American Type Foundry, for whom he produced his family of gothics, which owed more to the personal style of Koch's Kabel than to Futura. Until he arrived in the United States, Bernhard had developed only one text face, Bernhard Antiqua, which was used for the text in *Das Plakat*. He believed that sans-serif type should not be used for text, although Bernhard Gothic and others soon became popular text faces. He once wrote: "There is no doubt that the best type for continuous reading is the one in which schoolbooks, novels and newspapers are printed, Garamond, Jenson or Goudy Old Style." But understanding that display faces were subject to whims of fashion, he was happy to clutter the market with new advertising faces. He referred to his bold gothics as perfect for hardware ads, and his cursives as ideal perfume scripts.

After the war, Bernhard turned his attention away from graphic design and focused almost exclusively on painting. Since the 1930s he had painted rather mundane portraits of beautiful women, asserting that this was his true art. The switch in emphasis came about because the business was changing; design decisions were no longer being made by the founders of companies but by committees and middle-level art directors. Bernhard soon discovered that art directors were bringing in specialists to do portions of campaigns or identities, and since he was accustomed to doing the entire job, he was unwilling to adjust to the limitations that specialization imposed. He once said, "If I am going to be forced to specialize, I will do it with painting." Increasingly, Bernhard's sons saw to the studio's daily operations and continued to turn out packaging and advertising into the early 1960s.

Bernhard did, however, have two significant postwar projects—or passions. One was a phonetic alphabet called Fonotype. Eight years in the developmental stage, it was designed to simplify the English language so that foreigners could learn it quickly. The other project was Magnettype, a pre-photolettering method of producing a photographic type layout. The idea was to put newly designed Bernhard display faces in negative form on magnetic panels; these would be arranged on a magnetic board in any configuration and then shot as a photograph. The result, of course, would be a positive print. But as Karl admitted, "Like 99 percent of all inventions, the concept was reasonable but the process quite flawed. Qualitatively it was not very good, and the fact that photolettering came into being within a year of this product made Magnettype obsolete. But even more important, most of our clients wanted the classical typefaces, Bodoni, Garamond, and Jenson, rather than our new display faces." The project was eventually dropped.

Curiously, toward the end of Bernhard's life—he died in 1972—the old master, then in his eighties, decided to return to graphic design. He received a few random jobs, but his comeback was stifled not by physical or mental disability but by a new generation of art directors who had no idea who he was. All they could see when Karl dutifully brought around the portfolio was a lot of dated-looking work. Also, though he was extraordinarily prolific and left behind some significant artifacts, Bernhard was never quite as inventive as when he was eighteen and inadvertently created that paradigm of economical design, the Priester Match poster.

Originally published in PRINT, *March/April 1993.*

Note

1. Bernhard was married twice. His first marriage (date unknown) produced one daughter, Ruth (born 1905), and ended in divorce. His second marriage, which took place around 1911, produced four children, Leah Margaret (deceased), Karl, Manfred, and Eugene Alexander. These children emigrated to the United States in the early 1930s and lived with their father until 1939, when their mother joined them. Although Bernhard remained married to his second wife until her death, the couple did not live together in the United States.

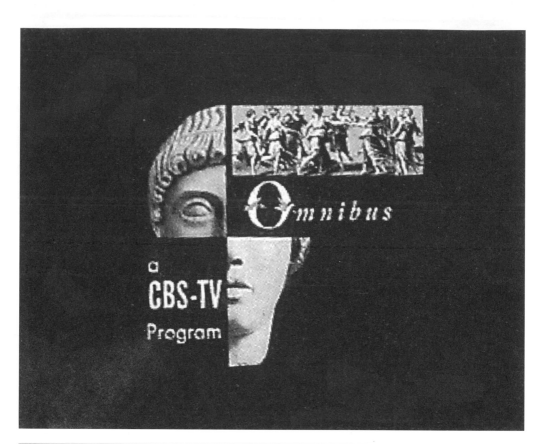

THE SEARCH FOR GEORG OLDEN
Julie Lasky

Oddly, it was a detective with the Los Angeles Police Department who offered us the first hard fact about Georg Olden—the date of his death.

Until that moment, almost everything we knew about the former CBS art director and advertising executive seemed shaky. Reference books gave the year of his birth as 1920, and 1921. His first name popped up on databases with and without the final *e*. Independent sources reported that he was the uncredited designer of the CBS Eye logo, while other sources independently spluttered at that heresy. We had heard of his involvement in a racial discrimination suit against McCann-Erickson, the advertising agency where he worked in the 1960s, but McCann's legal office claimed they could tell us nothing but the address of his home in Westchester. William Kunstler, the lawyer and human rights advocate whom the press reported as representing Olden in his lawsuit, didn't remember him.

He was said to be brilliant and mediocre—warm, congenial, aloof. He hated and took pride in his racial identity. He died a suicide, a homicide, on the East Coast, no, the West.

Olden, one of a handful of black men to have executive status in the 1950s, and perhaps the only black designer ever to be classified as elite, was clearly a casualty of something. His life pitched so high and dropped so fast that it appears more mythic than real. In myths, the most elaborate sequence of tragic events can be blamed on a single cause, and those who knew Georg Olden seem to attribute everything—success or failure, depending on the type and degree of their attachment—to his color. Yet few things seem more complex that the job of pinning Georg Olden down. Judging from their recollections, his associates never had a clear fix on him, and the picture is even more staticky almost a generation after his death. If Olden is not better known today, the fault lies partly in his failure to reveal himself. And yet given the precarious role of being a black man in a field that had only recently admitted ethnic whites to positions of power, it's no wonder that Olden remained unknowable. In a sense, the deceptive security of that world, followed by its sudden withdrawal, was mythic if read as the parable of the promises and disappointments of the civil rights era.

"To call Olden the Michael Jordan or Colin Powell of communication arts does not give him his full due," observes Lowell Thompson, a Chicago designer who recently founded a hotline to raise the profiles of minority talent in advertising. "Both Jordan and

Powell achieved their superstar status in times and places much more open to black American participation: post–Jackie Robinson sports and the post-Truman military. Olden was a *wunderkind* at a time when there were probably more African-Americans hanging from dogwood trees in Mississippi than hanging around water coolers in the offices of all the corporations in our country."

Today, Olden is remembered by his peers but seems to elude contemporary history books. The neglect infuriates Michele Y. Washington, a Chicago designer who regularly gives a slide presentation and is preparing a book on black graphic artists. "If you go back and read Phil Meggs's *History of Graphic Design*, the section on CBS only talks about Bill Golden and Lou Dorfsman," Washington points out. "It doesn't even mention television graphics. And yet, you can easily find Olden's work in any Art Directors Club annual. He was a pioneer. He was classified by [the Japanese magazine] *Idea* as one of the top fifteen designers in the United States. He was considered the dean of TV graphics. *I* call him, sarcastically, the Invisible Man."

Many of the people interviewed for this story responded warmly when they heard his name. "Ah," they would say, nodding (or so we imagined) over the telephone. "Whatever happened to Georg?" We told them he was shot to death in what police described as a "common law dispute" in his home in Hollywood, California, on February 25, 1975. But the essence of their question remained unanswered. In the process of trying to understand what happened to Georg, not merely what became of him, we spoke to dozens of acquaintances, family members, and friends, searched through several databases, and came up with more than a few hard facts.

He was born Georg Elliott Olden on November 13, 1920, in Birmingham, Alabama, to the Reverend James Clarence Olden, a Baptist minister, and Sylvia Ward Olden, a singer and music teacher. His sister, the distinguished opera coach Sylvia Olden Lee, 76, relates that in the middle of the night before his birth, their mother was awakened by sirens and, looking out her window, saw an unnatural glow. She ran out to enjoy the spectacle of flames engulfing a granary, sending kernels bursting into the sky like popcorn. "After she came home, she couldn't go back to sleep because of labor pains," Mrs. Lee recalls. "Georg was born at 8 A.M."

Their father's father, also called George, was a slave on a plantation in northern Kentucky who escaped across the Ohio River when the Civil War began and eventually joined the Union army. After gaining his freedom, he adopted the name of his master, Oldham, but changed the spelling. (The site of the plantation, near Louisville, appears on contemporary maps as a polygon called Oldham County.) This grandfather married the daughter of a Baptist minister and became a minister himself, producing a third clerical generation with James, Georg's father.

Georg's mother came from New Orleans. A photograph on a dresser in Sylvia Lee's Philadelphia home shows a woman with hair swept up in the Edwardian style and light skin inherited from her Irish mother. She has a vivid, contemporary beauty, reminding us that not one person whom we interviewed about Georg Olden failed to comment on his looks. "The literature on Mr. Olden's achievements and the responsive attitude of those who have worked with him cannot prepare you for your first meeting with him," wrote Nina

Blanchard in a 1965 profile for *Elegant,* a black-culture periodical. "First of all, he is awesomely handsome, extremely male, and very polite, all of which can be momentarily unsettling for a woman attempting to conduct a serious interview."

Two years before Georg was born, his father was offered the pulpit of a Congregational church in Birmingham and moved his family from Meridian, Mississippi. Months after Georg's birth, the family moved again, to Washington, D.C., where James became minister of the Plymouth Congregational Church.

"Daddy's greatest contribution to this earth was that he was born with his dukes up. He kept fighting," recalls Sylvia Lee, who remembers the Ku Klux Klan shooting through the front window of his Birmingham church. "Every day, he went down to Congress to persuade the government to think in terms of the brotherhood of men and to live up to the Constitution."

In 1933, James left his family, and, after years of working as an itinerant minister and civil rights activist, returned to his father's homeland, Kentucky. The year after his departure, Georg entered Dunbar High School in Washington, D.C. Dr. Lawrence Graves, alumni director for the school, which was segregated by law when Olden attended, remembers the class of 1938 as a model for younger students like himself. The jazz pianist Billy Taylor was a member, and another classmate became a vice president of American Express. Olden "was a kind guy; he wasn't a conformist," says Bernice Jeter Elam, who remembers him from art class. "Cartoons were his main source of pleasure. He was always doing them, while we were painting scenes or a still life. If I remember correctly, he was a lot of fun. He was a good-looking young man, good features. I wouldn't say he was romantic to a girl who thought that you ought to be on time or conform to what a lot of the other guys were doing, but you recognized that he was talented and thought he was a bohemian artist."

A symptom of Olden's nonconformity was that he didn't graduate with his classmates. He drew cartoons for *Flash,* a black biweekly illustrated magazine where he also worked as art director at the age of sixteen. His other passion was swimming. He competed in the sport, winning several trophies. But while he was pursuing these activities, he failed most of his academic subjects. According to Sylvia Lee, their mother arranged for Georg to make up the credits the next year. And when he announced his ambition to go to Pratt Institute in New York after graduation, she refused, saying, "Wouldn't it be foolish to put money in your further education when you flunked out when it was free?"

Although his mother wanted him to attend Howard University, he enrolled in Virginia State, a public college close to home. Arthur Young lived down the hall from him, and relates that "Chuck"—this was a nickname Olden apparently brought to college with him and its origins remain obscure—"would take art classes and drew cartoons for the *Virginia Statesman.* He had a thriving wit and sense of humor and could see the funny side of any situation. He liked to drink beer—or anything else that would pour. He was generally well liked on campus."

Sylvia Lee recalls that Olden grew more disciplined and productive in college. By 1941, he was about to make the dean's list and "even his room was straight." That was the year of America's entry into World War II. Soon after the Japanese bombed Pearl Harbor, Olden dropped out and went to work as a graphic designer for the Office of Strategic

Services in Washington, the wartime intelligence division that was a forerunner of the CIA. According to an unidentified newspaper clipping from 1952, he received this job after he was commissioned by then Secretary of the Interior Harold Ickes to design a series of petroleum conservation posters for national distribution.

The OSS brought Olden into an elite group of designers and offered him a comfortable place to contribute to the war effort without actually enlisting. Sylvia Lee remembers visiting him at his workplace. Posted on the wall, next to designs bearing messages like "Keep 'Em Flying" and "Dim the Lights," was an electric blue plaque that urged his employers to "Keep Olden here." Meanwhile, as reported in a 1947 profile published in *Opportunity* magazine, a black quarterly, he designed posters, working with a crew that included "Jo Mielziner, Broadway scenic designer; John Cosgrave, *Fortune* magazine cover designer; Will Burton [*sic*], Art Director for Fortune; Eero Saarinen, world-famous architect; Sam Berman, internationally known caricaturist; Oliver Lundquist and Donal McLaughlin, industrial designers; and William Arthur Smith, illustrator for *Cosmopolitan* magazine.

"What greater opportunity would Georg Olden want than to be associated with the men and women of the caliber he found in the Office of Strategic Services! In the first place, he never wanted to specialize in any particular branch of art. He had a burning desire to be well-rounded, capable of attacking any kind of presentation problem. In the unusual, challenging situation he found in the OSS, he was able to acquire a full working knowledge of each of his coworkers' specialties. The bustling creative environment of [OSS director] General Donovan's office produced a new Georg Olden. He became armed with confidence and mature skills."

Olden's recent marriage might also have contributed to his maturity. At twenty, he became engaged to Courtenaye Macbeth, a divorced twenty-three-year-old model and actress with two children. Sylvia Lee was Olden's guardian after the death of their mother in 1939, and she was horrified by the thought of a woman with "two baby children taking on a *third* child, *my brother*." She refused to give her consent, forcing Olden to wait until his twenty-first birthday, on November 13, 1941, for a legal union. He and Courtenaye were married a little more than a month later, on Christmas day, two weeks after Pearl Harbor. His sister refused to attend the small church ceremony.

While he continued working for the OSS over the next several years, Olden earned some success as a cartoonist. He drew combat-related cartoons for the "Servicemen's Edition" of the *National CIO News* and published a few pieces centering on domestic themes for the *New Yorker* and *Esquire*. A copy of the *New Yorker* cartoon reproduced in the December 9, 1944 issue is found among other effects of his estate, framed under glass. Revealing a hostility toward advertising one might not have expected from a future ad executive, it shows a radio announcer barking into a microphone, "'Insist on Pasfo! Remember that when you drop the first letter and interchange the next two, simultaneously substituting an "e" for the final "o," it spells "SAFE." Yes, Pasfo is the safe way to counteract the annoying discomfort that so often accompanies the common head cold.'"

Curiously, Olden dropped the final *e* from his own first name around this time and signed his cartoons "Georg" with angular—almost childlike—letterforms. "You have to do something to attract the attention of the magazine editors," he explained in a 1963 article in *Advertising Age,* failing to consider, perhaps, that this Scandinavian spelling, along with his rendering of Caucasian cartoon figures, served as much as a blind to racial identity as it did a vehicle to recognition. Magazine editors, who probably would have assumed they were dealing with a white man in any event, might well have believed Olden was Nordic.

Olden's attitude toward his race was one of the most ambiguous aspects of his life. He was a member of the National Urban League and in the 1950s designed the organization's symbol, a black equal sign in a circle. And yet colleagues describe a man who, in his speech, bearing, grooming, and, some say, air of aloofness and snobbery, was "whiter than a lot of white people." Such comments were rarely made for attribution because the speakers, white or black, didn't want to appear hostile or envious. In their hesitancy to open up, however, one realizes what kind of lose-lose situation Olden occupied. He was in no position to trumpet racial pride in the pre–civil rights era; nor, one suspects, would he have wanted to. ("Acceptance is a matter of talent," a 1963 *Ebony* article quotes him as saying. "In my work I've never felt like a Negro. Maybe I've been lucky.") But all the custom-tailored suits in the world couldn't admit him into the white communities that hired him, either. By omitting the *e* in cartoons he sent to unmet editors of posh magazines, Olden might in fact have found a way to spell "SAFE" while unconsciously recognizing—as the Pasfo cartoon suggests—that the alteration was contrived. George Lois, the eminent art director who began his career at CBS at the time Olden was there, recalls teasing him about his name: "I would say, 'Georg, you're one letter away from greatness.'"

In 1945, Olden became involved with the San Francisco conference that marked the founding of the United Nations. A 1953 biographical note written for the Urban League, probably by Olden himself, relates that "When the United Nations held its founding conference . . . Mr. Olden was selected by the then Secretary of State, the Hon. Edward R. Stettinius, to work with the International Secretariat as a graphic designer on the strength of his reputation with OSS." In the *Opportunity* magazine profile, Olden is said to have "designed numerous types of presentation records, maps, elaborate organizational charts, and sketches of various [United Nations Organization] scenes."

Olden's move to CBS took place soon afterward. In the summer of 1945, Sylvia Lee, then living in New York with her husband, violinist and conductor Everett Lee, remembers Georg stopping off for a visit on his way to a holiday in New England. He was unemployed, but cheerfully shrugged off questions about job prospects. When pressed again, he blithely announced, "Well, if I don't get anything, I always have this," and pulled a letter out of his pocket from a CBS executive inviting him to work in the new TV division.

Once again, *Opportunity* fills in the details: "His assignment to CBS came when, after V-J Day, Colonel Lawrence W. Lowman, head of the Communications Branch of OSS, returned to his civilian status as Vice-President of CBS in charge of television. He asked Hu Barton [Olden's OSS supervisor] to send him a man who had a full grasp of the whole range of commercial art techniques. Barton immediately recommended Olden."

The fairy tale rhetoric is justified. Other African-American men were coming out of a segregated military to take jobs that offered little hope for advancement. Olden found himself working for one of the most enlightened corporations of the pre–civil rights era.

Indeed, one of his colleagues at CBS in the late '40s was Frederic Morrow, who left the company's public relations department in 1952 to serve as a liaison between the black community and Eisenhower's presidential campaign and, after being rudely awakened to the apartheid of the American South, became the first black special assistant ever to work in the White House. "Olden seems to have miraculously bypassed all the usual problems of rising through the corporate ranks by using a tried-and-true method usually reserved for the white and well-born," observes Lowell Thompson. "He started at the top at the very beginning of an industry."

Television was quite rudimentary in those days. Broadcasting quality was poor—the period was dubbed the "sit-and-squint era." Indeed, only about 16,000 TV sets existed in the entire country when Olden joined CBS, according to *Ebony*. At first, he was a one-man operation who handled six shows a week, but by 1951 the medium, and Olden's responsibilities, had grown dramatically. A newspaper clipping reports that he had a staff of "five artists, two letterers, two typesetters and a production foreman," and worked on over fifty shows a week. Two years later, according to the Urban League biography, his staff numbered fourteen, "with duties extending into the advertising and promotional spheres in addition to the now sixty shows a week." In 1957, Olden described the challenges of his job in a publication put out by the Art Directors Club of New York: "The medium is incapable of really differentiating between subtleties of tonal and color contrast because, for one thing, the average home receiver is almost never 'perfectly' tuned. Speed is of the essence in the design and execution of much of the art for television. . . . Often all art for a show is designed and finished on a few days' notice; for news programs, it is usually just a matter of hours."

Thanks in part to Olden's example, the new medium was seen as a source of black employment. "Handful Able to Break in Technical End of TV" was the headline of a 1950 article published in *Ebony* which observes that "because television is still in the try-and-hope-it-works stage, a great many Negro performers stand excellent chances of making the grade as regular TV employees." The article goes on to commend Olden as a "top-ranking Negro technician in video."

Four years later, another article in *Ebony* trumpeted, "CBS Leads All TV Networks in Hiring of Skilled Negroes." One hundred fifty African-Americans were reported to be on the payroll of the network "as supervisors, technicians, musicians, and clerical workers," with Georg Olden again featured as the first and most impressive example. Among the other black employees interviewed were a film control operator, a scene painter, a print machine operator, a program handler, a script reader, a press representative, and a wardrobe mistress. The great jazz bassist Milt Hinton is identified as one of three black musicians working on the "Robert Q. Lewis Show," appreciated here for its color-blind hiring policies.

Ebony's early optimism about the role TV could play in career opportunities for African-Americans had been misplaced, however. It was a tribute to both CBS's liberalism and Georg Olden's survival skills that he was among the "less than 200 of the estimated 72,400 full-time television employees in the nation" who were black, according to the 1954 *Ebony* article. Television had not offered the hoped-for job opportunities, yet Olden was thriving. While William Golden and his design staff handled print promotion and advertising for the CBS network division, and Lou Dorfsman—later Golden's successor—did the equivalent for CBS radio, Georg Olden supervised the creation of on-air promotion, titles drawn on 4-by-5 cards and flashed in front of the camera. Clippings supplied by his widow indicate that he also helped create the vote-tallying graphics for the 1952 presidential contest between Adlai E. Stevenson and Dwight D. Eisenhower, the first national election returns to be televised. This paragraph, from the *New York Times*'s morning-after coverage on November 7, 1952, was circled, presumably by Olden:

> Columbia's greatest advantage [over the other networks] was the ease with which a viewer could follow the constantly changing figures. There were forty-eight individual panels, on which were recorded the tallies from the different states. Each panel was shown in close-up and the figures practically filled the screen. Similarly, large panels were used for the total popular and electoral votes. The visual effect was excellent.

Olden was undoubtedly the first person to design news graphics for CBS, and he drew or commissioned title sequences for almost all of the network's prime-time programs, which is to say, for much of what constitutes the golden age of television: *Ed Sullivan, Burns and Allen, Face the Nation, Lassie, Gunsmoke, The Late Show*. The reference book *250 Years of Afro-American Art: An Annotated Bibliography* cites 108 appearances of his work in *Graphis* and Art Directors Club annuals between 1951 and 1960. In control of the most powerful communications medium of his day, he spread the distinctive style of 1950s print graphics, hiring artists such as David Stone Martin, Ed Benguiat, and Alex Steinweiss to work on titles and promos.

George Lois recalls that his favorite Olden graphic was for *Private Secretary*. Bob Gill designed the title of this situation comedy exactly as an incompetent clerical worker might have drummed it out on a manual typewriter—with *x*'ed-out spelling errors and unaligned letters. To the end of his life, Olden kept the CBS press release announcing that he had won a 1956 New York Art Directors Club medal for this work. The memo is signed "Nice going and congratulations—FS," a personal note of appreciation from CBS's president, Frank Stanton. Stanton, for his part, still has some of the original on-air promo cards. "There's no better way to testify to the quality of Olden's work," he said recently.

Olden's position and reputation at the network have given rise to a rumor that he, not William Golden, designed the CBS Eye symbol in 1951. And, indeed, several people interviewed for this article brought up the rumor spontaneously and vigorously.

Lowell Thompson, who has done his own research on Olden, makes the case that if the Eye were designed for on-air promotion, Olden should have handled the job. Thompson also refers to an anecdote published in a recent biography of CBS chairman William Paley that relates that Bill Golden grew bored with the symbol a year after it was designed and suggested to Stanton that they replace it. "Would a confident, proud author of as strong a symbol as the CBS Eye want to kill it?" Thompson asked in a personal communication. "At best Golden seems guilty of amazing fickleness. At worst, could his suggestion have had anything to do with his knowledge that he was not the father? And another tidbit for thought: Could the Eye have been the work of both men?" There are historical reasons why Olden might have participated in the development of the Eye and been denied credit, Thompson concludes. Color has often barred the achievements of African-Americans from being recognized, and Olden's color might have made him vulnerable to exploitation.

Thompson is correct in assuming that the symbol was originally designed for on-air use: In an article for *PRINT* titled "My Eye," published in 1959, shortly before his death, Golden himself describes the first application: "It was originally conceived as a symbol in motion. It consisted of several concentric 'eyes.' The camera dollied in to reveal the 'pupil' as an iris diaphragm shutter which clicked open to show the network identification and clicked shut.

"To guard against possible monotony, three other versions were prepared. One was essentially [a] still photo with moving clouds, and the other two I've forgotten. . . . Currently the iris diaphragm appears more frequently and it now opens on a photo of coming attractions, clicks again, and reveals a program title. *The title is not designed by us*." (May/June 1959, our italics).

In support of Thompson's hypothesis, Golden never states that he created the symbol. Several paragraphs later, he remarks that the logo evolved "when CBS established the Radio and Television Networks as two separate divisions. The two networks were urged to do everything possible to create their own identities." He recalls submitting "three identifications to a dozen or so people who attended the original viewing. I can't report that any of them—including the 'eye'—were received with uncontrollable enthusiasm by the group."

However, Golden's statement that the promotional title containing the symbol was "not designed by us" suggests that he or his immediate staff conceived the Eye and passed it to Olden or one of his subordinates for video application. This idea fits not only what we learned about Golden through interviews with his colleagues and contemporaries—including Herman Aronson, CBS's former director of production; George Lois; Alex Steinweiss; Saul Bass; and Golden's protégé and successor, Lou Dorfsman—but also what we know about Olden's history at the network.

All design professionals understand that an art director may receive full credit for work done as part of a collaboration. Yet Olden was not a junior designer in Golden's department. He headed his own staff in another section—indeed, another CBS building. This suggests that although Golden was professionally Olden's superior, his hogging credit for any collaboration would have bordered on a breach of ethics, not to mention a breach of Golden's reputation for generosity. As the annuals show, Olden was recognized throughout his career at CBS; and it seems unlikely that he would have been denied credit for the Eye when his contributions to the network were written up everywhere from in-house press releases to the *New York Times*. Certainly, Golden's willingness to jettison the symbol (an anecdote he himself relates in the 1959 *PRINT* article) suggests that the Eye did not have the stature when it was created that it would acquire over time. And the similarity of Golden's and Olden's names makes it easy to understand why this particular rumor would be perpetuated. If there's a final word in this matter, we believe it ought to belong to Lou Dorfsman and Frank Stanton. Dorfsman dismisses the rumor as absurd, and Stanton states, "To the best of my knowledge, Olden had nothing to do with the [development of the] Eye. That was something I followed very closely in lots of meetings with Bill. Olden's name never came up in connection with any of it."

(Parenthetically, the most complete description of the Eye's origin comes from George Lois, who claims that the symbol was in fact a joint effort, but one between Bill Golden and Kurt Weihs, a designer in Golden's department. Here's how Lois tells it: "Bill had to do a logo, and he and Kurt were fooling around with different ideas. Somehow, Bill saw a Shaker genealogy chart with very beautiful calligraphy—this was happening not too long after the WPA projects, when there was a tremendous rebirth of folk arts in America. Way at the top was something that if you looked at it today, you would say, 'That's the CBS Eye.' It symbolized God. The proportions were kind of awkward but basically it had the black outside shape of the Eye; it was just drawn badly. Bill thought it was a striking graphic and showed it to Kurt; and in half an hour or an hour, Kurt had redrawn it. He walked it in to Bill, and Bill took it up to Stanton, and Stanton said, 'I like it,' and that was it. Kurt was the designer and Bill was the creative director.")

In 1960, Olden left CBS. He had worked for the company fifteen years and built up an impressive résumé. That year, too, he had taken a government-sponsored trip to the Far East to teach television techniques. Sylvia Lee has a picture of him posing with a group of Buddhist monks in an unidentifiable Asian country and reveals that Olden, who had been losing his hair, was inspired by the monks to shave his head. Press accounts from this point on liken his appearance to Yul Brynner's, though the more frequent comparison is Harry Belafonte.

Olden's stated reason for leaving CBS for a job as a television group art director at BBDO in New York was that he wanted to "work on cigarets, beer and automobiles, and realized that only at an ad agency could this be done." (*Advertising Age*, May 6, 1963). Sylvia Lee recalls that Georg talked about moving into advertising a few years before he actually did so, and that her husband, Everett, counseled him to remain at CBS, reasoning that advertising agencies come and go but TV was here to stay.

Nineteen-sixty, the year he moved to BBDO, is when *Ebony* magazine caught up with him once again and published a five-page profile called "The Man at the Window." Leading off with a half-page photograph of Olden silhouetted against the eponymous aperture, the article points out that only "top-flight" executives have windowed offices on Madison Avenue. Summed up by his association with the ultimate status symbol, Olden is described as "an artist, a dreamer, a designer, a thinker and a huckster." And here we are treated to a glimpse of his lifestyle. Whereas the press had previously given his addresses as the unfashionable Bronx, and then Queens, he is pictured here with Courtenaye in a $70,000 house in White Plains—a prestigious suburb in Westchester County—set on four acres with a swimming pool, badminton court, miniature playground, kennels, and private stream.

Three years later, he was hired as a vice president by the second largest agency in the world, McCann-Erickson, and made a member of the Professional Advisory Council (PAC), a think tank conceived by McCann's chairman of the board, Paul Foley. As described by Martin Fox in a 1965 *PRINT* article about McCann's parent company, Interpublic, the members of PAC were part of a "creative task force" encouraged to roam from campaign to campaign, supplying whatever marketing or creative skills they could offer rather than focusing their efforts on a single product. Much of the exploratory nature of PAC involved new methods of research. For instance, Fox describes Olden's work on a campaign for Tums as the "most offbeat" of four produced by the council, "yet it was the one that proved most effective when subjected to persuasion testing techniques." For this spot, Olden drew a whimsical line figure in his familiar cartoon style, whose belly is the site of volcanic activity. A bottle and roll of Tums are displayed, and the final image is a serene seascape. Olden also worked on campaigns for *Encyclopedia Britannica* and Belvedere cigarettes.

In 1963, Olden was asked by the U.S. Postal Service to design a five-cent stamp commemorating the centenary of the Emancipation Proclamation. He was the first African-American to have such a commission—a fact documented in *Jet* magazine as historic. His solution—a broken chain—has the economy of much of his CBS work, and seems to have been accomplished with the same kind of efficiency. In a tearsheet from an unidentified design magazine, he boasts that he showed the post office nothing but the finished art, much to the distress of the National Archives, which requires federal artists to turn over all sketches and notes. As a result of the commission, he was invited to the White House. Sylvia's daughter, Eve Lee, an actress and German-language scholar in Los Angeles, remembers seeing a photo of him posing with John F. Kennedy and Secretary of State Dean Rusk in the Oval Office. "He labeled the picture 'Me,' 'Jack,' and 'Dean' and drew arrows," she laughs, "as if we didn't know who those people were." In April 1964, he was one of seven men invited to a dinner chaired by Adlai Stevenson, then U.S. representative at the United Nations, to honor "Negroes prominent in the economic world."

By 1970, Olden had won seven Clio awards for his commercials. In fact, he designed the Clio itself, when the award evolved out of the American Television Commercial Festival. In 1967, he received an advertising prize at the Cannes film festival, and he designed another postage stamp, this one commemorating Voice of America. He had split up with Courtenaye in this period and married Terri Phillips Baker, a singer, in 1966. Two years later, his son, Georg Olden, Jr., was born.

Olden was a role model for young black designers, recalls Dorothy E. Hayes, cocurator of the unprecedented exhibition *Black Artists in Graphic Communication.* Opening on January 9, 1970, at Gallery 303 of the Composing Room, a New York type house that showcased innovative design work, the exhibit featured projects by forty-nine African-American visual artists, including the painter Romare Bearden, photographer and filmmaker Gordon Parks, founding Pushpin member Reynold Ruffins, and illustrators Leo and Diane Dillon. Herb Lubalin and Tom Carnase designed the installation. Olden, one of the event's advisors, contributed a reel with seventeen commercials, and showed up everywhere in the extensive press coverage. It would be his last appearance as the handsome, self-possessed business leader posing with starlets hired for the occasion.

In August 1970, Olden was laid off from McCann. The ostensible reason was economic—a recession—but Olden, who seems not to have experienced a day's unemployment since that carefree journey to New England 25 years before, was devastated by what he clearly saw as a betrayal. After decades of honoring every code of conduct and lifestyle embraced by the white community and serving as an inspiration and role model for African-Americans, he was being treated as a disposable commodity. He believed that the real reason for his dismissal was McCann's reluctance to promote him to the top executive ranks; if you couldn't move up in advertising, he told the press, the only place to move was out. He filed charges of racial discrimination with the Equal Employment Opportunity Commission and the New York State Division of Human Rights. And perhaps the ultimate indignity was that, as a result of investigating his complaint, the EEOC found that McCann did engage in discriminatory practices by underrepresenting "Negroes" and "Spanish-surnamed Americans" in the agency's 410-member staff (*New York Times,* July 25, 1972). However, neither that agency nor the Division of Human Rights found malfeasance in McCann's dismissal of Olden because at least twenty other employees "of professional stature" had been laid off at the same time, some of whom had earned larger salaries, and only one of whom besides Olden was black. (The press didn't state that in laying off two black employees, the agency had dismissed 22 percent of its African-American staff.) Moreover, Olden had never requested a transfer from PAC to central administration, a fact that weakened his argument that McCann was afraid to offer a high executive position to a black man (*Advertising Age,* February 15, 1971).

Olden refused to accept the commission's findings. His sense of betrayal was so acute that, as printed in the February 8, 1971 issue of *Advertising Age,* he implied that the Division of Human Rights's investigator was in collusion with McCann. The article quotes him as saying that he had "received information from 'extremely reliable sources' that McCann was 'prepared to spend $1,000,000, if necessary, to fight me and that I could not win, let alone hold out to the end in a lengthy and costly litigation against such resources.'" Asked about these "extremely reliable sources," Sylvia Lee explained that Olden told her he had overheard a phone conversation in which Paul Foley himself vowed to spend a million dollars to get rid of him. In an affidavit to the Division of Human Rights, Foley responded that Olden "was hired because he is a superb talent in contemporary graphics and art direction. . . . We hired him and paid him a substantial salary [$40,000] to use these great talents to enhance the effectiveness of advertising persuasion in the TV commercial form. We did not expect Georg to be an advertising strategist, writer or conceptualizer. He did not disappoint us (*Advertising Age,* February 15, 1971)."

Olden turned to the Center for Constitutional Rights for representation and was put in touch with William Kunstler. The *New York Times* of January 8, 1973 announced his filing of a class action suit against McCann in U.S. District Court for the Southern District of New York "on his own behalf and on behalf of other black persons similarly situated."

Wondering what the climate was like for African-Americans at McCann in Olden's day, especially the seven black employees who remained after he was dismissed, we called Billy Davis, a music producer who headed the agency's music department for eighteen years beginning in 1969. Davis came to McCann shortly before Olden left and recalls hearing about the lawsuit in the hallways, though he never met Olden. Nor did he experience discrimination; he says, "Never, not for one minute. Certainly not from the management that was in place at that time. Of course, I would be looking for it."

John Morning, a New York–based graphic designer who began his career in a division that handled sales promotion at McCann a few years before Olden arrived, knew him, as many designers did, by reputation. Asked about his own treatment at the agency, Morning said, "I did not find it difficult, particularly. Quite frankly, no black people worked there to speak of." About Olden's insistence that he was forced out of what was essentially a dead-end job, Morning observes, "I had more the impression that the [PAC] he was part of sort of fell apart of its own weight. The idea that, here, there was a think tank with some of the best minds at McCann was part of the agency's marketing approach. I think, after a while, they found it wasn't really paying off and decided to do away with it. I suspect that's why Olden got canned. I would be skeptical about the Division of Human Rights being able to do anything about it. They didn't have much teeth; I don't believe they were nearly as effective then as they became later. I don't think they would have given an agency as big as [McCann's parent company] Interpublic a bad time. Remember, in its time, Interpublic was comparable to what Saatchi & Saatchi is today."

Upon leaving McCann in 1970, Olden took a job as vice president of marketing and advertising at the newly founded Off-Track Betting (OTB) Corporation. Richard Dangler, a senior vice president at OTB, remembers him as "an intelligent and forceful individual" who worked at the company for about a year and a half and had a hand in designing the OTB logo.

This was the job he said he liked best, Eve Lee recalls, though Dangler describes a hectic environment and twenty-two–hour workdays: "We had to immediately put a computer system and marketing plan in, and build what came to be 150 branch offices within three years—that's 50 offices a year."

Dangler couldn't or wouldn't say why Olden left OTB after less than two years. The *New York Times* reported on July 25, 1972 that Olden was "putting together his own company." When we next picked up his trail, he was in Southern California, in the final phase of his life, and at the point when he acted as his own best chronicler.

> 5131 DeLongpre Avenue, Hollywood
> June 8, 1973
>
> Dear Abijah [his pet name for his sister, borrowed from the "Li'l Abner" comic strip]:
>   Done sold Tara as any fool kin plainly see.
>   Done moved to the coas as any fool kin plainly see.
>   Done found me a pad which is groovy and has pool in case I decides to go in
> training agin just to beat Mark Spitz's ass. . . .

His letters are signed with yet another name, "jij," in imitation of the way his father pronounced "George." The signature resembles three lowercase *i*'s of slightly different lengths, like three candles burning unevenly.

It was his older brother, James Clarence Olden, Jr., who responded to this letter, sending a copy to Sylvia Lee. (An attached note suggests that the siblings felt less confident about Georg's well-being than the following would lead one to believe):

> Sunday, June 17, 1973
> Detroit, Michigan
>
> Bretheren,
>   I was pleasantly surprised by your communiqué of June 8th.

Under the circumstances I can well understand the unloading of the White Plains pad. I just hope you came out O.K. financially, but being aware of your having been ensnared with former broads, I doubt it.

As to your new plans—directing and so forth—if I can in any way judge your future by your past activities, you'll be O.K. To elaborate: If any one ever had a guardian angel to always arrange your landing on your feet instead of your up-to-now unscathed ass, you have. . . .

Olden had been left by his second wife and was living in Hollywood with a girl-friend he called Maya. Her real name, according to records released by the Los Angeles district attorney, was Irene Mikolajczyk. She was a white woman, born in Germany, twenty-eight years old. At this point, Olden's ambitions had been fulfilled to the extent that he had directed one episode of the TV series *Mod Squad*. How he broke into television, and why his directing career didn't appear to extend beyond that single experience, is still unknown.

On October 22, 1973 Georg wrote to Sylvia about the McCann lawsuit. The diction he affected in correspondence to his family—one doubts his business colleagues ever saw this side of him—is thicker, more harshly jocular, and desperate sounding than in previous letters. The suit is still going on, he relates. He has heard of a janitor in Michigan whose efforts to get promoted were blocked, netting him $4 million in a lawsuit filed against his employer, the Detroit Edison Company. "Since I was a bigger nigger than he was I ought to get 8," Olden cracks. "In fack I used to be a big nigger but I just happened to fall on hard times. But frankly speaking you know me and you know I don't give a [word obliterated]." He goes on to taunt, half-affectionately, half-bitterly, his brother-in-law, Everett Lee, for having light skin that allowed him to pass.

Olden was shot to death by Maya on January 25, 1975, days before his class action suit was scheduled to go to trial in New York. Court records indicate that four bullets were fired from a .357 Magnum, with two live rounds left in the chamber. The transcripts of the hearing, if any existed, would have been destroyed ten years after the incident, according to a reporter of the Municipal Court of Los Angeles. However, information gleaned from existing records indicates that Maya was arrested on one count of murder and pleaded not guilty. Although prosecutors requested $25,000 bail, she was released on $1,000. And her decision to waive trial by jury and plead her case directly to the judge indicates that she had a strong case, probably self-defense. In fact, the relationship had been violent, sources close to Olden say. Maya was acquitted on May 14, 1975.

Although he had earned the equivalent of a six-figure salary at McCann, Georg Olden's life ended in poverty. His widow found stacks of rejection slips for the novels he had hoped to publish and cartoons he had tried to syndicate. She learned that he had been spending what little money remained buying copies of *Who's Who*, which would continue to sum up his accomplishments for several years after his terrible demise. The entry in the last two editions (both published posthumously) concludes with this statement:

As the first black American to achieve an executive position with a major corporation, my goal was the same as that of Jackie Robinson in baseball: to achieve maximum success and recognition by my peers, the industry and the public, thereby hopefully expanding acceptance of, and opportunities for, future black executives in American business.

It's a strange, sad feeling to hear the voice of the dead man rise above the list of impersonal facts and articulate his goals, almost as if he could still fulfill them.

Editor's Note: PRINT *is indebted to Michele Y. Washington and Lowell Thompson for help in researching this article and wishes them all success in future investigations into Georg Olden's life and work.*

Thanks also to Eve M. Kahn, Michael Dooley, and Ian Jones for additional research.

We are grateful to the many people who shared memories or gathered information related to Olden. In addition to those mentioned in the article are Grace Darby of the New Yorker; *Tuan-Sue Kao and the staff of the United Nations library; Lorraine Martin and her classmates at Dunbar High School; Marty Rubinstein and Kristina Slavik of CBS; Dorothy E. Hayes; Tobias Moss; Peter Palazzo; Christopher Rudge of Interpublic; Trisha McAlmond; and Detective Buck Henry of the LAPD.*

Finally, this article could not have been written without the generous cooperation and support of Sylvia Olden Lee, Eve Lee, Terri Baker Weiss, and Georg Olden, Jr.

Julie Lasky is editor-in-chief of Interiors *magazine in New York.*

Originally published in PRINT, *March/April 1994*

Labor

NUMBER OF PEOPLE
EMPLOYED
1909
14,250
1914
21,599
1918
49,118
1924
100,000

1924

1918

1914

1909

GENERAL MOTORS

BUICK · CADILLAC · CHEVROLET · OAKLAND · OLDSMOBILE · GMC TRUCKS

AN EMINENT PREMODERNIST: THE CURIOUS CASE OF T. M. CLELAND
Philip B. Meggs

If one casually asked at a 1920s New York Art Directors Club or AIGA meeting, "Who are the leading graphic artists working in America today?" T. M. (for Thomas Maitland) Cleland would probably be on each person's shortlist. His vast output included typefaces, books, magazines, advertisements, decorative borders, ornaments, and illustrations. His clients included the Metropolitan Museum, Strathmore, Westvaco, General Motors, Cadillac, and *McClure's* magazine. He designed the original formats for *Fortune* and *Newsweek*. Morris Benton collaborated with Cleland on American Type Founders' 1917 Garamond revival. Cleland designed its extensive collection of ornaments and borders; these designs sparked an international mania for French Renaissance graphics during the first half of the century and made Cleland's name a household word in the graphic arts. Yet today, Cleland is virtually forgotten.

Along with book designer Bruce Rogers and typeface designer Frederic Goudy, Cleland belonged to a small group of practitioners who had emerged at the turn of the century, after William Morris led the late-nineteenth-century English Arts and Crafts movement in a campaign to rediscover and appropriate design forms from the past. Morris's American disciples quickly settled on sixteenth-century ornament and artifact as their model. They steered American graphic design toward a comfortably traditional approach, rooted in Italian and French Renaissance design as well as *its* resource, the design arts of ancient Rome. Rome was the model for the American Republic; Roman monuments, architecture, and alphabets had captivated American designers from Thomas Jefferson onward.

After World War I, the modern movements in art and design romped across Europe, irrevocably changing the continental landscape with cubist-inspired posters and constructivist-derived buildings. Curiously, the United States was virtually untouched by the revolution until the 1930s. Architects, graphic artists, clients, and the public all retreated to the haven of established forms and ideals.

Neither a visionary nor an innovator, Cleland achieved graphic excellence by seeking sound traditions and high standards. He remained a designer of his time, expressing the values and views of early-twentieth-century America. The modus operandi of this primarily self-taught artist was not the modernist quest for novelty and originality, but emulation—replicating the forms and sensibilities of the past. This proved to be exactly what America wanted during this period.

In 1929, when Cleland was at the height of his powers, Pynson Printers published an elegant, oversized book of his work called *The Decorative Work of T. M. Cleland: A Record and Review*. Its biographical essay, by Alfred E. Hamill, is our major source of information about Cleland. He was born in 1880, in Brooklyn, to a mother raised in western New York and a physician father reared in Scotland and rural Massachusetts. When he was six months old, the family moved to Manhattan, then moved several more times, joining the northward residential migration occurring in Manhattan during the century's last years. Cleland attended a succession of New York City public schools and was apparently a mediocre student who spent his time making toy theaters and occasionally copying illustrations from magazines.

To escape his boredom with school, Cleland, at the age of fifteen, persuaded his parents to let him leave his nearly completed "grammar school" program and enter art school. Years later, he would whimsically claim that he had wanted to become an artist "because he was naturally lazy and looked upon the free and 'easy' manner of drawing of certain masters as a facile means of getting on in the world and having a good time at small expense of exertion." He attended the Artist-Artisan Institute, and once again proved to be a mediocre student, spending much of his time at the vaudeville theater across the street from the school. His instructors considered him unpromising, and one frankly told him he was wasting his time in art school.

One day, Cleland watched an older student make a painstaking ornamental drawing in pen-and-ink for reproduction in a magazine. The "facile action of the pen, the blackness of the ink, the crisp precision of the lines, held him spellbound." He was amazed to learn that this decorative drawing was a commissioned assignment and would be reproduced in the magazine by a photomechanical process for plating and printing. That very evening, Cleland began work on decorative motifs such as acanthus forms and scrolls. The older student encouraged Cleland to develop his decorative work and submit it to American Bookmaker, a trade publication that often reproduced work by young artists.

Cleland later recalled working frantically on drawings of initial letters, and having them accepted by American Bookmaker. The thrill of seeing these designs reproduced with his name under them in a magazine inspired the heretofore lackluster and unmotivated student to develop his abilities as a decorative graphic artist. Shortly thereafter, he actually sold a drawing—an ornamental border printed in red ink on yellow paper that appeared on the cover of a modest sports magazine—for five dollars. This was more money than the 1890s teenager had ever had in his life. Cleland was developing an obsession with ornamental drawing: this passion and unwavering willingness to invest tremendous hours to achieve perfection became the springboard that propelled him into the mainstream of early-twentieth-century graphic arts.

At sixteen, the would-be artist left school to begin his professional career. The five dollars were invested in a book, *The Decorative Illustration of Books* by Walter Crane, that he had seen in the window of Macmillan's lower Fifth Avenue store. This book provided Cleland with a direct link to William Morris and his Kelmscott Press, as well as to historical graphics. Cleland was energized by an awareness that, in the distant past, printing had been an art form and that Morris and his followers were boldly making it so again. In this country, Will Bradley's beautifully designed publications provided a model of excellence from someone who worked with commissions from business and industry; Cleland later credited Bradley as a major catalyst.

Though lacking in any knowledge of printing, Cleland designed a brochure with illustrations and ornaments and took it to the only printer he knew, a friend of the family. Over the next few years, Cleland worked with this printer, whose shop was located in a third floor loft. The modest assortment of type and two job presses aided by the tutelage of a "pressman of the old school who rarely descended into a state of sobriety for more than four days a week, but whose knowledge of his craft was second only to his mastery of profanity," enabled the young artist to learn all aspects of the graphic arts. Cleland regarded his work from this period as being "mostly sorry and unpromising stuff," but these early experiences laid the groundwork for the quality and craftsmanship of his mature work.

One afternoon, Cleland was gazing at a copy of Morris's Kelmscott Chaucer in a window at Scribner's bookstore, when a young member of Scribner's staff, Lewis Hatch, came to the door and invited Cleland inside to look more closely. Hatch became a mentor of sorts who introduced Cleland to wonderfully designed and illustrated books, arranged modest commissions for lettering and binding designs, and finally helped him secure a position as a designer with the Caslon Press.

When the Caslon Press folded, Cleland acquired a small foot-powered press and some fonts and launched his own printing shop from a room he constructed in his father's basement. He managed to produce two small books along with small job printing projects. His work caught the notice of printing enthusiasts in Boston, who persuaded him to move his operation there and launch the Cornhill Press. However, promised capital was not forthcoming, and the press struggled for a year before finally failing. This was a dark time for Cleland. The only benefit of the disastrous Boston adventure was his friendship with the renowned printer Daniel B. Updike, who contributed to the younger man's growing fund of knowledge and provided periodic commissions.

Although Cleland was now a man in his twenties, he was forced by economic circumstances to move back into his father's Manhattan house. Then, in early 1904, he received a commission from the Bruce Type Foundry to design a typeface. The resulting face, Della Robbia, was inspired by inscriptional lettering on decorative sculptures by the famed Della Robbia family, active as sculptors during the Italian Renaissance. (Years later, Cleland complained about the widespread use of his youthful attempt at typeface design, which, he felt, fell far short of acceptable standards.)

Della Robbia was designed during a period when Cleland was shedding a Gothic heaviness in his work; now, he moved toward forms inspired by the Italian and French Renaissance. The slender commission received for Della Robbia was used to pay for his first trip abroad, in the spring of 1904. Two months spent traveling in Italy, absorbing that country's architecture, painting, and decorative arts, formed the visual vocabulary that would characterize his mature work. For typographic inspiration, he made rubbings from stone inscriptions wherever he went.

By coincidence, a young woman he had met and become friendly with on the steamer to Italy was also a passenger on his return voyage; the following year they were married.

Facing new economic responsibilities and still smarting from the failure of his Cornhill Press, Cleland abandoned printing and focused on graphic design and illustration. A position as art editor of *McClure's* magazine from 1906 until 1908 enabled him to stabilize his finances. *McClure's* was one of America's finest magazines; its fiction and essays by Jack London and Rudyard Kipling were illustrated by the top artists of the day, including Howard Pyle, N. C. Wyeth, and Jessie Wilcox Smith. Character studies and social criticism, on such topics as the plight of the poor and the problems of a manufacturing town oppressed by a railroad monopoly, were accompanied by halftone photographs.

At *McClure's*, Cleland struggled with the problem of ornamental designs framing halftones on coated paper, using them as a transitional element between type and image. He realized that printing, like other art forms, had an essential character; this was compromised by the coated paper and presswork required by the grainy halftones of the day. Fine line ornaments and frames lost value and color. Cleland developed a fine line technique for achieving tonal effects not unlike traditional copperplate engraving. This solution became wildly popular.

Many magazines of the time displayed thin, bastard Bodoni lettering centered over columns of type; Cleland innovated with ornate borders centered over stately Roman titles. Magazines and newspapers across America aped the appearance of Cleland's work without always understanding the design problems he was attempting to solve.

Cleland's 1914 cover for the Hotel Claridge wine list caught the attention of John A. Kingman, head of advertising for the luxury car manufacturer Locomobile Company of America. Kingman retained him to create Locomobile's graphics. Cleland proceeded to apply French Renaissance elegance to luxury automobile catalog and advertising design. His typographic ads have a crisply neoclassical look with their Bodoni types, sparse spatial organizations, and taut ornaments and borders. This work became the prototype for American advertising during the 1910s.

Unhappy with the quality of printing and typesetting from his suppliers, Cleland established his own printing facilities for producing Locomobile graphics. Then, when America entered World War I, he left the business to go into military service.

Upon returning to civilian life, Cleland spent a difficult year trying to rebuild his business. An opportunity to write, illustrate, typeset, and print a book, *The Grammar of Color*, helped him recover and even expand his printing facilities. This magnificent oversized book for the Strathmore Paper Company explained through a series of foldout pages the effective use of colored inks on colored paper. Cleland clearly learned a great deal from this project: the use of colored papers and printing inks, as well as unusual color combinations, became a hallmark of his work. Indeed, his explorations of color in printing were strikingly modern in contrast to his traditional typography, imagery, and layout.

After the book was published in 1921, Cleland felt torn between the demands of printing and design. He realized he had to either jettison his ambitions to be a printer and focus exclusively on design, or expand his printing involvement and facilities. His decision to abandon printing was difficult, but after he resolved once again to quit, he never went back to it. Cleland also began to develop his painting skills, and illustration became a major part of his work.

During the 1920s, big business moved to the forefront of American life, as profits, advertising, and consumer credit lifted the nation toward unprecedented prosperity. A 1921 magazine article by Edward E. Purinton proclaimed, "Among the nations of the earth today America stands for one idea: *Business*." "Industry will finally be the savior of the community," it concluded. By creating jobs and ending idleness, business, Purinton believed, could solve the decade's "decadence of morality and increase in crime." Campaigning for the presidency in 1928, Herbert Hoover advocated "rugged individualism" and wrote, "Big business is producing in America what the Socialists held up as their goal: food, shelter, and clothing for all." In this heady pro-business atmosphere, Cleland provided American industry with an apt graphic expression. His renowned border designs framed advertisements for Locomobile, Cadillac, and Marmon cars with an aura of luxury. They projected an ambiance of tradition and permanence, authority and wealth. Architects created a similar idiom by cladding banks, financial institutions, and corporate offices in imposing granite exteriors, with pediments and columns.

The 1929 stock market crash and subsequent Depression changed everything: Cleland's golden quarter-century ended around his fiftieth birthday. It seems fitting that the lavish book—five years in preparation and production—about Cleland's work was published in 1929 as well. The following year, Henry R. Luce hired Cleland as art director of his new business monthly, *Fortune*. Cleland established a remarkable cover format, using three of four colors of opaque ink printed on Strathmore's luxurious colored cover stock. Even though Cleland served as art editor for only three issues, his format and cover vision were maintained during *Fortune*'s first decade.

As the Depression deepened and modernist design made inroads during the 1930s, Cleland's romanticism seemed quaint and dated. He continued to be active, but became a traditionalist mainstay in the graphic arts field rather than the pacesetter he had been in the 1910s and '20s.

In February 1940, Cleland delivered an address (later published) to the AIGA in New York entitled "Harsh Words." It was a stunning denunciation of Modernism, which he called "a disturbing Babel of undigested ideas and indigestible objectives." He believed its "poison is aggravated in the case of printing and typography, by the fact that of all the arts, it is, by its very nature and purpose, the most conventional. If it is an art at all, it is an art to serve another art. . . . It is not the business of type and printing to show off, and when, as it now so frequently does, it engages in exhibitionistic antics of its own, it is just a bad servant." The new typography "seems to be new as the neu in neurosis from which it largely derives," he said. Advertising designers were criticized for putting type on cockeyed angles, and photographs that bled off the page on two edges were denounced for competing with "the three dimensional things in the room" because they lacked a frame. He dismissed sans serif type as "simplification for simpletons," adding, "these are block letters for blockheads." He sadly concluded, "The order of the day, it seems, is disorder." If these protests strike us as ultraconservative and narrow-minded a half century later, we must remember the context of Cleland's time.

Cleland continued to secure ample assignments, notably for book illustration, well into old age. His stamina was revealed in a September 19, 1955 letter to Dr. Robert L.

Leslie, proprietor of a renowned Manhattan type shop, the Composing Room. Cleland thanked Leslie for honoring him with a seventy-fifth birthday party. "[My] present condition of all work and no play is making a more than ordinarily dull boy of me. . . . I work from 14 to 16 hours a day, seven days a week, hence letters must be written after midnight."

A well-known designer of the 1940s and '50s, Clarence Hornung, now ninety-four years old, remembers Cleland as a meticulous artist who frequently made numerous revisions. After recalling that Cleland often tore up completed work, then redid it, Hornung suggests that the reason for Cleland's long hours was his intense dedication.

Cleland died on November 9, 1964, at age eighty-four. He survived his wife by about twenty years; the couple did not have children. People who knew him remember his aristocratic bearing, his cultivated tastes, and his pride at being self-educated. He circulated in an affluent country-club set and may have even been, according to Hornung, "a bit of a snob . . . in fact, quite a bit of a snob."

One wonders why his contemporaries Bruce Rogers and Frederic Goudy are venerated today, while Cleland, whose work was actually more widely published and influential during the first three decades of the century, is so little known. Perhaps the answer is that Cleland's work was more commercial: It is easier to admire Rogers's monumental Oxford Lectern Bible or Goudy Old Style than Cleland's Cadillac ads. Nonetheless, Cleland deserves to be remembered and appreciated, for more than anyone else, he set the standard and direction for American advertising and editorial design in the opening years of this century.

Originally published in PRINT, *March/April 1995*

H. N. WERKMAN: THE OUTSIDER
Alston W. Purvis

Since Hendrik Nicolaas Werkman's death in 1945 at the hands of the German occupation forces, his contributions to graphic design have remained a matter of controversy. To some people, myself included, he is a hero and an innovator of free typographic expression; others consider him only an interesting and ephemeral anomaly in the history of graphic design. And some traditional typographers, even in his own country, view his revolutionary creations with outright hostility and derision. One of my former colleagues from the Royal Academy at The Hague, a type and book designer, was actually astounded to learn that I had devoted an entire chapter to Werkman in my book, *Dutch Graphic Design, 1918–1945*. "Who was this Werkman?" he demanded. "He might have been a war hero, but he was not a typographer nor was he a designer. An amateur painter? What was he?"

Werkman can best be described as a design maverick. Although he was well aware of developments in De Stijl, Dadaism, Constructivism, and Futurism, he never joined these movements, and unlike proponents of De Stijl, he never intended to remake society. He abjured all canons and did not try to introduce new ones; he fits into no convenient drawer of modern graphic design history. Except for a thirteen-year interval before 1923, he was never a conventional typographer, and although he was a skillful commercial printer, he was never committed to the craft of printing for its own sake.

To his supporters, his graphics—in a country known for its innovative and audacious approach to design—radiate a transcendence that takes them into an almost mystical realm and makes them immediately recognizable. Characteristic of his work are playfulness, experimentation, innocence, boldness, intensity, freedom, and unwavering optimism. He was prepared to use any means necessary to achieve the results he desired.

The son of a veterinarian, Werkman was born in the Dutch province of Groningen in 1882, the same year as James Joyce. Both men developed outside of the European cultural mainstream: One would revolutionize typography and the other would transform the novel. Werkman's first serious employment was as a type sorter or printer's devil. He then decided to become a journalist and began writing articles for two provincial newspapers; later, he helped set type for one of the papers as well. He also considered his early attempts at photography important enough to print on a toy press a business card reading: "H. N. Werkman Amateur-Fotograaf Groningen."

After giving up journalism, which he referred to as five years of "dog's work," he was hired in 1907 as foreman for a local printer, and within a year he was able to set up his own printing establishment in the city of Groningen. The firm prospered, and by 1917 he had become one of the most successful printers in that part of the Netherlands. There was little to distinguish his printing from that of similar firms, however, and his early typography gives no hint of his later work.

Werkman's prosperity gave him the leisure to paint, a hobby he had wanted to pursue since the age of fourteen, when he had been inspired by a Van Gogh exhibition, and in 1920 he joined the Groningen art circle, De Ploeg. From October 1921 until March 1922, he published a monthly art magazine called *Blad voor Kunst* (*Magazine for Art*), which presented work by other De Ploeg members as well as Werkman's own thoughts on art. For the last number of this journal, Werkman designed an abstract cover—a woodcut in red, yellow, and blue that was influenced by a Groningen exhibition of work by the De Stijl artists Theo van Doesburg, Vilmos Huszár, and Bart van der Leck. It offered the first clue to the evolution of his future work.

Werkman's printing company failed in 1923, largely because of his indifference to what seemed to him the dismal art of making money. Willem Sandberg, graphic designer and director of the Stedelijk Museum in Amsterdam after World War II, referred to Werkman as someone for whom anything utilitarian was totally beyond comprehension. He moved the remnants of the business to an attic workshop in a canal warehouse. Although he was able to earn a meager living from commissions such as wedding and birth announcements, invitations, brochures, stationery, bookplates, and posters, the new endeavor never flourished. Ironically, though, misfortune engendered a new sense of independence. As one of his friends remarked, "Werkman's art is the result of unemployment." At the age of forty-one, his world abruptly became one of color, type, and form, with the poetic side of his nature taking precedence over all else. Even his commercial pieces reflect this predilection.

The initial expression of Werkman's new direction was an intriguing and mysterious pamphlet that his friends in Groningen found in their mailboxes on September 12, 1923. Commencing with the slogan, "GRONINGEN BERLIN PARIS MOSCOW 1923—Beginning of a Violet season," it announced an avant-garde publication bearing the cryptic title *The Next Call*, and declared the birth of a new era in the arts. "It must be attested and affirmed," the pamphlet stated. "Art is everywhere." At that time, Berlin, Park, and Moscow were all centers of progressive art movements, and by adding Groningen to the list, Werkman proclaimed the beginning of an art movement in that city, too.

The Next Call would be a nine-part series appearing at irregular intervals from 1923 until 1926. Except for two numbers printed on single foldout sheets, each issue consisted of eight pages, including the front and back covers, and was printed on inexpensive paper in editions never exceeding forty copies. In spite of Werkman's ever-precarious finances, his friends and correspondents received the publication free of charge.

The first issue of *The Next Call* was mailed on September 22. In large, crude uppercase sans-serif letters, it set forth an axiom that would evince Werkman's life philosophy:

EEN RIL DOORKLIEFT [A Chill Permeates]
HET LIJF DAT VREEST [The Body that Fears]
DE VRIJHEID VAN DE GEEST [The Freedom of the Spirit]

The cover is a typographic arrangement combining two lowercase *r*'s and a larger lowercase *e* with the impression of a lock plate removed from the side of a door, giving the lock plate a new identity as an uppercase *E*. Werkman had now begun to merge conventional printing with a special technique in which the paper was placed faceup on the bed of the handpress. This permitted him to freely adjust and modify previously inked design elements, making each print distinctive. This process could be repeated indefinitely with an unlimited number of shapes and colors.

The second number of *The Next Call* appeared the following month, again with the lock plate as a design component on the cover. On the inside spreads, playful human figures are assembled from pieces of type. On the back page, "Paris" is printed above "BOULEVARD" and then covered over with a piece of paper, showing that Werkman's printed pieces were constantly being modified. All copies of *The Next Call* display subtle dissimilarities. The printing seems intentionally uneven, the letterspacing erratic, and the inking inconsistent.

After the mundane third issue, *The Next Call 4*, which appeared in the beginning of 1924, is a welcome change. The typography is more experimental and is filled with movement, tension, humor, ambiguity, and rhythm. Both the cover and back page are grids of numbers. Bold contrasts of type style, direction, and size produce arrangements that seem to have miraculously fallen into place by chance. On the second and third pages, Lenin's death on January 21, 1924 is solemnly observed by two columns of type assembled from *O*s and *M*s. Lined up, they resemble soldiers escorting a casket. Again, perhaps, a pun comes into play, as *oom* in Dutch means "uncle."

The fifth issue came out in June, and with it the lock plate makes its last appearance. The typography is even livelier as pages alternate between text and image. On page 2, Werkman used nearly every typeface in his collection yet managed to attain a semblance of balance.

The sixth issue of *The Next Call* was mailed on November 1, 1924. Fragments from printed pieces, such as *Life* magazine, are pasted on the tops of both the front and back of the folded sheet, increasing the distinctiveness of the copies and making them individual collages. The title of the typographic assembly, "Plattegrond van de Kunst en Omstreken" (Map of Art and Environs) comes from the remark of a friend who said as he watched Werkman building the composition, "It looks like a map of art and its perimeters." The text on the back page states that "*The Next Call* sustains international communication with editors of numerous avant-garde publications and subscribes to: *Het Overzicht*, F. Berckelaers and Jozef Peeters, Antwerp. *De Stijl*, Theo van Doesburg, Leiden. *Mécano*, I. K. Bonset, Paris. *Merz*, Kurt Schwitters and El Lissitzky, Hanover. *La Zone*, A. Cernik, Bruno Julianov, Belgrade. *Zenith*, L. Mitzitch, Belgrade. *Blok*, H. Stazewski and others, Warsaw. *Disk*, K. Teige, Prague, and many others." Werkman, at that time, was unaware that Bonset was one of the pseudonyms for the wily Van Doesburg.

The seventh issue, also printed on a single sheet, appeared in February 1925. There were two versions of the cover, one having a vertical and horizontal arrangement and another a diagonal composition made up of rules, type, and large em spaces.

The eighth number, dated September 1925, suggests industrial development with typographic constructions depicting machinery. The composition on page 2 resembles a forklift and the one on the back page a truck. An ambiguous and cynical "credit" and "debit" list jokingly refers to the dour state of Werkman's financial affairs.

The Next Call served a number of important functions. It provided Werkman with a means to distribute his various manifestoes on art; it served as a forum for the exploration and exhibition of his experimental typography; and it kept him in touch with the international avant-garde. Perhaps the most important objective of *The Next Call*, however, was to jolt De Ploeg out of apathy. Werkman had become increasingly disillusioned with the conservative views of some of his De Ploeg colleagues, and he expected the publication to deliver a clearly defined challenge to their complacency. From the beginning, though, his efforts did little to impress his fellow artists, most of whom reacted with perplexity, scorn, and curiosity rather than empathy. In spite of some begrudging admiration for his creativity, they found his work too progressive and obscure.

The Next Call came to rest in November 1926 with the ninth issue—typographically the most serene. Type forms seem to meander freely through space in the rhythmical center spread on pages 4 and 5, but Werkman's melancholy text suggests both the end of the series and his own disillusionment:

> struggling is useless
> struggling is not useless
> not struggling is useless
> not struggling is not useless
> useless struggling is useless
> useless struggling is not useless
> not useless struggling is useless
> not useless struggling is not useless

It closes with the following wistful poem, also by Werkman:

> *once when the earth*
> *was still not round*
> once when
> art was still *not* art
> once when the ant
> was not yet diligent
> *once* when he
> was still *young*
> *once* when she
> *was* still small

From 1923 until the end of his life, Werkman continued to earn a sparse living as a commercial printer, and except for a few visits to Amsterdam and a trip to Cologne and Paris in 1929, he remained in the semi-isolation of Groningen in the northeastern corner of the Netherlands. But he never abandoned his explorations of more creative typography and printing projects.

While publishing *The Next Call*, Werkman produced larger monotypes using similar printing methods. In 1923, he printed the first of over six hundred *druksels*, a derivative of the Dutch word *drukken,* meaning "to print." By applying different thicknesses, impressions, and viscosities of ink, he was able to create elaborate patterns of tone and depth, and by using coarse papers, he exploited assorted textures that emanate through the layers of ink. He later explained his technique in a letter to a friend: "I use an old hand press for my prints; so the impression is done vertically, and the impression can be regulated instinctively. Sometimes you have to press hard, sometimes very lightly, sometimes one half of the block is heavily inked, the other half sparsely. Also, by printing the first layer of ink on another sheet of paper you then get a paler shade, which is used for the definitive version. Sometimes a single print goes under the press fifty times."

Werkman's *druksels* could be called printed collages, and in this way they are analogous to what Kurt Schwitters, Raoul Hausmann, and others were doing in Germany during approximately the same period, when Russian Constructivism, Futurism, De Stijl, Cubism, Dadaism, and Surrealism freed typographical elements from their utilitarian and logical functions. His *druksels*, though, do not fit into any particular category and represent, in effect, a new medium.

In Werkman's hands, the basic letterpress was pushed beyond previously known possibilities. Every subtlety played a part—the unique oddities of wood grains, scratches on damaged or heavily used pieces of type, the thickness of ink, disparate methods of inking, and diverse paper textures. Werkman had become entranced with the printing process itself and often thought of his materials as animate beings. "There is paper so beautiful that one only wants to caress it and otherwise leave it unblemished," he said. He was not concerned with the design of typefaces in themselves and used whatever happened to be available in his type drawers, including rules and the reverse sides of wooden types. Details were of secondary importance.

Although Werkman's approach to typography was essentially "nonfunctional," there is a similarity between his approach and that of Piet Zwart. Both used type as collage, and although Werkman was less influenced by De Stijl than Zwart was, he emphasized the qualities inherent in printing elements and flirted with the constructivist belief that art should reflect the nature of its material. In addition to the *druksels*, Werkman produced in 1926 and 1927 a number of typographic drawings created on the typewriter. These were called *tiksels*, a play on the Dutch word *tikken*, meaning "to type."

With a few lapses, the years following the last issue of *The Next Call* were productive ones for Werkman. His work, while never relinquishing any of its natural, almost primitive, intensity, became more refined. In 1929, he began to use the ink roller as a drawing and painting instrument, applying it directly to the paper. At the same time, he began to employ a simple stamping technique in which elements such as pieces of wood type were inked individually and pressed onto the paper, and in 1934, he started using stencils as well. He also modified type elements by partially covering them with bits of paper. He named the new stencil series of *druksels* "Hot Printing" after Hot Jazz.

Werkman's pieces were often affected by adverse economic conditions that forced him to print on wrapping paper. Also, as he sometimes had to rely on a limited supply of inks, it is possible to date some of the *druksels* by their colors.

Among the work he produced during this period were compositions done in 1931 that have some of the same sense of balance, movement, and innocence of Alexander Calder's mobiles, and a series called the "Proclamatie" posters. These were circulated in 1932 as manifestoes in an attempt to inaugurate a new version of *The Next Call*, but the project never got beyond the initial stages. Werkman's 1933 poster for *De Rekenmachine* (*The Adding Machine*), an expressionist play by Elmer Rice, cleverly represents a calculator constructed out of typographic material. The ten-part series of bookplate designs made for "M.C.v.L." in 1934 are built out of type and printing "furniture." *Preludium*, a booklet printed as a futile protest against attempts by some De Ploeg members to accept twelve new artists whom Werkman considered bourgeois, was published in September 1938.

Between 1926 and 1945, Werkman produced nine calendars, which reflect his other experimental typography. In 1939, he began to incorporate illustrations into the calendars, an addition that anticipates his subsequent wartime design.

Werkman never sought abstraction for its own sake, and his vision remained essentially pictorial. Although his work is interlaced with poetry, he did not use words phonetically as did Schwitters, Van Doesburg, and Paul van Ostaijen. Instead, his typography and message enrich one another.

Both expressive and reflective, Werkman's compositions are consistently inventive, direct, and playful, often relying on the intervention of chance. A virtuoso of serendipity, he relished the steered accident and discovered his configurations through the printing procedure itself. Layout and design did not precede the typesetting and printing processes; rather, the three were fused into one creative procedure. No previous typographic guidelines applied, and each situation provoked its own resolution, or, as Werkman later wrote, "the subject proclaims itself and is never sought." In the manner of poetry, much is inferred, and the viewer/reader is often required to provide the interpretation. Werkman once commented that secluded paths are the most beautiful; he lived in his own private world. He was the dreamer, the pundit of the unforeseen, the loner and outsider of Dutch graphic design, and by 1940, he had redefined the symbolic significance of letterforms.

Werkman's phenomenal and influential role in avant-garde typography would reach a climactic and tragic end with his clandestine publications during the German occupation. Most notable was *De Blauwe Schuit* (*The Blue Barge*), the magnificent culmination of the innovative typographic experiments he had begun in the early '20s with *The Next Call*. Standing apart from other underground printing of the time, *De Blauwe Schuit* followed its own course, and Werkman was one of the few who used design as a political tool against the occupation. The forty issues of this publication consisted of booklets in various formats ranging in size from four to fifty pages. Printed on whatever was available, they were inexpensively produced and were distributed only to a small circle of insiders.

The most interesting issues of *De Blauwe Schuit* were the two folios of Hassidic legends produced in 1942 and in December 1943. Werkman had been introduced to the world of Hassidic Judaism by the Protestant minister F. R. A. Henkels, one of the founders of this publishing venture. Each folio was printed in an edition of twenty and consisted of ten illustrations and texts by the renowned Jewish writer Martin Buber. Because Werkman used the stencil and ink roller technique, each illustration was an original print. This publishing bravado, however, led to his imprisonment and death.

Werkman was arrested in Groningen by the SS on March 13, 1945. One month later, he was executed with ten others at the nearby town of Bakkeveen, only two days before the Canadian army liberated Groningen.

Author's Note: This article is dedicated to Jan van Loenen Martinet (1913–1993), whose generosity in sharing his extensive Werkman archives and knowledge made it possible.

Alston Purvis is Associate Professor, chairman of the Graphic Design Deparetment, and Director of the Visual Arts Division at Boston University. He taught for ten years at the Royal Academy for Fine Arts in The Hague, Netherlands and is the author of Dutch Graphic Design, 1918–1945 *(Van Nostrand Reinhold, New York, 1992).*

Originally published in PRINT, *May/June 1995.*

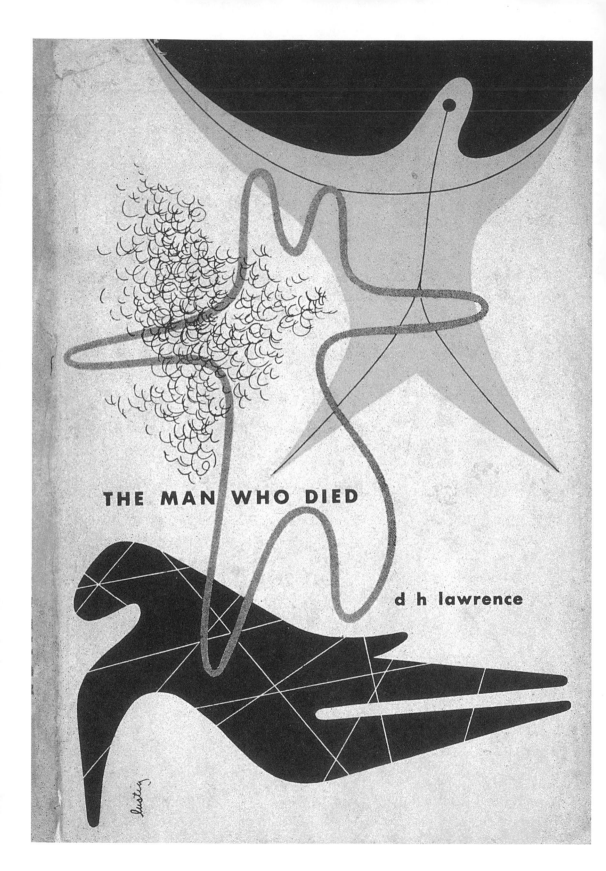

THE MAN WHO DIED

d h lawrence

The history of graphic design is replete with paradigmatic works—as opposed to merely interesting artifacts—that define the various design disciplines and are at the same time works of art. For a design to be so placed, it must overcome the vicissitudes of fashion and be accepted as an integral part of the visual language. Such is Alvin Lustig's 1953 paperback cover for *Lorca: 3 Tragedies*. A masterpiece of symbolic acuity, compositional strength, and typographic ingenuity, it forms the basis of many contemporary book jackets and covers.

The current preference among American book-jacket designers for fragmented images, minimal typography, and rebus-like compositions must be traced directly to Lustig's stark black-and-white cover for *Lorca* (which is still in print)—a grid of five symbolic photographs tied together through poetic disharmony. This and other distinctive, though lesser known, covers for the New Directions publishing house transformed an otherwise realistic medium—the photograph—into a tool for abstraction through the employment of reticulated negatives, photograms, and setups. New Directions publisher James Laughlin hired Lustig in the early 1940s and gave him the latitude to experiment with covers for the New Directions nonmainstream list, which featured authors such as Henry Miller, Gertrude Stein, D. H. Lawrence, and James Joyce. While achieving higher sales was a consideration, Lustig believed it was unnecessary to "design down" to the potential buyer.

Lustig's approach developed from an interest in montage as practiced by the European moderns of the 1920s and 1930s. When he introduced this technique to American book publishing in the late 1940s, covers and jackets tended to be painterly, cartoony, or typographic—decorative or literal. Art-based approaches were considered too radical, perhaps even foolhardy, in a marketplace in which hard-sell conventions were rigorously adhered to. Unlike in the recording industry, where managers regarded the abstract record covers developed at about the same time as a potential boost to sales, most mainstream book publishers were reluctant to embrace abstract approaches at the expense of the vulgar visual narratives and type treatment they insisted captured the public's attention.

Lustig rejected the typical literary solution of summarizing a book through a single, usually simplistic image. "His method was to read a text and get the feel of the author's creative drive, then to restate it in his own graphic terms," wrote Laughlin in *PRINT* in October 1956. Although mindful of the fundamental marketing precept that a book jacket must attract and hold the buyer's eye from a distance of as much as ten feet, Lustig entered taboo territory through his use of abstractions and small, discreet titles. His first jacket for Laughlin, a 1941 edition of Henry Miller's *Wisdom of the Heart*, eclipsed previous New Directions titles, which Laughlin described as jacketed in a "conservative, 'booky' way." At the time, Lustig was experimenting with nonrepresentational constructions made from slugs of metal typographic material that reveal the influence of Frank Lloyd Wright, with whom he briefly studied. Though *Wisdom of the Heart* was unconventional for the early 1940s, Laughlin was to dismiss it some years later as "rather stiff and severe. . . . It scarcely hinted at the extraordinary flowering which was to follow."

Laughlin was referring to the New Directions New Classics series, designed by Lustig between 1945 and 1952. With few exceptions, the New Classics titles appear as fresh and inventive today as when they were introduced almost fifty years ago. Lustig had switched from typecase compositions, such as his masterpiece of futuristic typography, *The Ghost in the Underblows* (Ward Ritchie Press, 1940), to drawing distinctive symbolic "marks" which owed more to the renderings of his favorite artists, Paul Klee and Joan Miró, than to any accepted commercial art style. Indeed, Lustig was a sponge who borrowed liberally from painters he admired. He believed that after Abstract Expressionism, painting was dead, and design would emerge as a primary art form—hence his jackets were not only paradigmatic examples of how modern art could successfully be incorporated into commercial art, but showed other designers how the (dying) plastic arts could be harnessed for mass communications. He also believed that the book jacket should become the American equivalent of the glorious European poster tradition, and so used it as a tabula rasa for the expression of new ideas.

Each of Lustig's New Classics jackets is a curious mix of expressionistic and analytical forms which interpret rather than narrate the novels, plays, or poetry contained within. For Franz Kafka's *Amerika*, he used a roughly rendered five-pointed star divided in half by red stripes, out of which emerge childlike squiggles of smoke that represent the author's harsh critique of a mythic America. Compared to an earlier jacket by montagist John Heartfield for the German publisher Malik Verlag, which shows a more literal panorama of New York skyscrapers, Lustig's approach is subtle but not obtuse. For E. M. Forster's *Longest Journey*, Lustig formed a labyrinthian maze from stark black bars; while the jacket does not illustrate the author's romantic setting, the symbolism alludes to the tension that underscores the plot. "In these as in all Lustig's jackets the approach is indirect," wrote C. F. O. Clarke in *Graphis* in 1948, "but through its sincerity and compression [it] has more imaginative power than direct illustration could achieve."

The New Classics designs succeeded where other popular literary series such as the Modern Library and Everyman's Library, with their inconsistent art direction and flawed artwork (including some lesser works by E. McKnight Kauffer for the Modern Library), failed. Although each New Classics jacket has its own character, Lustig maintained unity through strict formal consistency. Yet at no time did the overall style overpower the identity of the individual book.

Lustig was a form-giver, not a novelty-maker. The style he chose for the New Classics was not a conceit but a logical solution to a design problem. This did not become his signature style any more than his earlier typecase compositions: using the marketplace as his laboratory, he varied approaches within the framework of Modernism. "I have heard people speak of the 'Lustig Style,'" wrote Laughlin in *PRINT*, "but no one of them has been able to tell me, in fifty words or five hundred, what it was. Because each time, with each new book, there was a new creation. The only repetitions were those imposed by the physical media."

This creative versatility is best characterized in the jacket for *Lorca: 3 Tragedies*, one of many covers for New Directions that tested the effectiveness of inexpensive black-and-white printing in a genre routinely known for garish color artwork. Another superb jacket in this suite of photographic work is *The Confessions of Zeno* (New Directions, 1947), for which Lustig combined a reticulated self-portrait that resembles a flaming face, with a smaller-scale image of a doll and coffin. The background is cut in half by black and white bands, with an elegant, wedding-script type (reminiscent of the surrealist graphics of the 1930s he admired in arts magazines such as *View*) dropped out of the black portion.

In addition to being unlike any other American jacket of its time (although it looks as though it could have been designed today), *The Confessions of Zeno* pushed back the accepted boundaries of modern design. With this and other photoillustrations (done in collaboration with a photographer with whom he routinely shared credit), Lustig reinterpreted and polished the visual languages of Bauhaus, Dada, and Surrealism and inextricably wedded them to contemporary avant-garde literature. He was not alone: Paul Rand, Lester Beall, and other American moderns also produced art-based book jackets. But Lustig's distinction, as described by Laughlin in *PRINT*, "lay in the intensity and the purity with which he dedicated his genius to his idea vision." While the others were graphic problem-solvers, Lustig was a visual poet whose work was rooted as much in emotion as in form.

Lustig once claimed that he was "born modern" and made an early decision to practice as a "modern" rather than "traditional" designer. Yet he had a conservative upbringing. Born in 1915 in Denver, Colorado, to a family which he described as having "absolutely no pretensions to culture" (*The Collected Writings of Alvin Lustig*, 1955), he moved at age five to Los Angeles, where he found "nothing around me, except music or literature, could give a clue to the grandeur that had been European civilization." He was a poor student who avoided classes by becoming an itinerant magician for various school assemblies. But it was in high school that he was introduced by "an enlightened teacher" to modern art, sculpture, and French posters. "This art hit a fresh eye, unencumbered by any ideas of what art was or should be, and found an immediate sympathetic response," he wrote in 1953 in the *AIGA Journal*. "This ability to 'see' freshly, unencumbered by preconceived verbal, literary, or moral ideas, is the first step in responding to most modern art."

Lustig embraced Modernism and turned his attention to Europe, which further exacerbated his antipathy toward American conventions. "The inability to respond directly to the vitality of forms is a curious phenomenon and one that people of our country suffer from to a surprising degree," he wrote. Since his first exposure was to art that challenged tradition, he was to find that, "For me, when tradition was finally discovered, and understood with more maturity, it was always measured against the vitality of the new forms; and when it was found lacking, it was rejected."

Lustig's introduction to Modernism, his espousal of utopianism, and his passion for making magic converged at an early age. He fervently believed design could change the world and began his design career at age eighteen while a student at Los Angeles City College. At this time (1933–34) he also took a job as art director of *Westways*, the monthly journal of the Automobile Club of Southern California. Next he studied for three months with Frank Lloyd Wright at Taliesen East. In 1936 he became a freelance printer and typographer, doing jobs on a press he kept in the back room of a drugstore. It was here that he began to create purely abstract geometric designs using type ornaments—what Laughlin termed "queer things with type." A year or so later he retired from printing to devote himself exclusively to designing. He became a charter member of the Los Angeles Society for Contemporary Designers—a small and intrepid group of Los Angelenos (including Saul Bass, Rudolph de Harak, John Folis, and Louis Danziger) whose members had adopted the modern canon and were frustrated by the dearth of creative vision exhibited by West Coast businesses.

Lustig was a leader of "the group of young American graphic artists who have made it their aim to set up a new and more confident relationship between art and the general public," wrote C. F. O. Clarke. Yet lack of work forced him to move in 1944 to New York, where he became visual research director of *Look* magazine's design department. While in New York, he took up interior design and began to explore industrial design. In 1946 he returned to Los Angeles, where for five years he ran an office specializing in architecture, furniture, and fabric design, while continuing his book and editorial work. But to hire Lustig, notes former wife Elaine Lustig Cohen, was to get more than a cosmetic makeover. He wanted to be totally involved in every aspect of the design program—from business card to office building. Cohen speculates that this need for total control scared potential clients, so the profitable commissions came in erratically and the couple often lived from hand to mouth. In 1951 they returned to New York.

Lustig is known for his expertise in virtually all the design disciplines (he very much wanted to be an architect, but lacked the training). He designed record albums, magazines, advertisements, and annual reports, as well as office spaces and textiles. He even designed the opening segment for the popular animated cartoon series *Mr. Magoo*. He was passionate about design education, and conceived of design courses and workshops for Black Mountain College in North Carolina, the University of Georgia, and Yale. Yet of all these accomplishments, it is his transformation of both book cover and interior design that lives on today.

While the early moderns vehemently rejected the sanctity of the classical frame and the central axis, Lustig sought to reconcile old and new. He understood that the tradition of fine bookmaking was closely aligned with scholarship and humanism, and yet the primacy of the word, the key principle in classical book design, required reevaluation. "I think we are learning slowly how to come to terms with tradition without forsaking any of our own new basic principles," he wrote, prefiguring certain ideas of post-Modernism. "As we become more mature we will learn to master the interplay between the past and the present and not be so self-conscious of our rejection or acceptance of tradition. We will not make the mistake that both rigid modernists and conservatives make, of confusing the quality of form with the specific forms themselves." A book like Thomas Merton's *Bread in the Wilderness* (New Directions, 1953), which uses both asymmetrical and symmetrical type composition, should not be seen as a rejection of past verities, but as an attempt to build a new tradition, or, in Lustig's words, "the basic esthetic concepts peculiar to our time."

Although Lustig's work appeared revolutionary (and unacceptable) to the guardians of tradition at the AIGA and other book-dominated graphic organizations, he was not the radical his critics feared. His design stressed the formal aspects of a problem, and even his most radical departures should not be considered mere experimentation: "The factors that produce quality are the same in the traditional and contemporary book. Wherein, then, lies difference? Perhaps the single most distinguishing factor in the approach of the contemporary designer is his willingness to let the problem act upon him freely and without preconceived notions of the forms it should take." (*Design Quarterly*, 1954.) Lustig's covers for Noonday Press (Meridian Books) produced between 1953 and 1954 avoid the rigidity of both traditional and modern aesthetics. At the time American designers were obsessed with the new types being produced in Europe—not just the modern sans serifs, but recuts of old gothics and slab serifs—that were unavailable in the United States. Lustig ordered specimen books from England and Germany, which, like many of his colleagues, he would photostat and either piece together or redraw. Rather than being severely modern, these faces became the basis for more eclectic compositions.

At the same time, Lustig also became interested in, and to a certain extent adopted, the systematic Swiss approach, which, perhaps, accounts for the decidedly quieter look of the Noonday line. To distinguish these books—which focused on literary and social criticism, philosophy, and history—from his New Directions fiction covers, he switched from pictorial imagery to pure typography set against flat color backgrounds. While the Noonday covers are not as visually stimulating as the New Directions work, they were unique in their context. At the time, the typical paperback cover was characterized by overly rendered illustrations or thoughtlessly composed type. Lustig's format used the flat color background as a frame (or anchor) against which various eclectic type treatments were offset. The covers were designed to be seen together as a patchwork. Lustig's subtle economy was a counterpoint to the industry's propensity for clutter and confusion.

A study of Lustig's jackets reveals an evolution from total abstraction to symbolic typography. One cannot help but speculate about how he might have continued had he lived past his fortieth year. In 1950 diabetes began to erode his vision and by 1954 he was virtually blind. This did not prevent him from designing: Cohen recalls that he would direct her and his assistants in meticulous detail to produce the work he could no longer see. These strongly geometric designs were "some of his finest pieces," claimed Laughlin, but were not as inventive as his earlier covers and jackets that, in Lustig's words, transformed "personal art into public symbols."

Lustig died in 1955, leaving a number of uncompleted assignments to be finished by his wife, who developed into a significant graphic designer in her own right. He left a unique body of book covers and jackets that not only stand up to the scrutiny of time, but continue to serve as models for how modern form can be effectively applied in the midst of today's aesthetic chaos.

Originally published in EYE, *Fall 1993.*

FORTUNATO DEPERO: CHEERING UP THE UNIVERSE

Steven Heller

The task of redefining the spiritual and material world fell to visionaries, "men of talent and memorable fools,"[1] who led the shock troops of modernism. One of the artists inspired to action by modernist fever was the Italian Fortunato Depero, born in 1892, the son of an Imperial Austrian gendarme. On March 11, 1915, he and Carlo Balla cosigned the "Futurist Reconstruction of the Universe," a manifesto dedicated to world renewal through the overhaul of a sweeping variety of design disciplines from interior decoration and clothing to mass communications and postal art. By this act, Depero became a significant figure in the development of Italian Futurism, the influential European avant-garde movement that profoundly altered the process of production and the role of the artist in society.

Depero, "the dynamic modernist," who immodestly called himself "critic & architect & sculptor & musician & mathematician & physicist & chemist & lecturer & soldier & crazy man; a free complex genius," created an eclectic, modern graphic vocabulary which predates the recent New Wave by many decades. But to appreciate his achievement, one must understand a little about Futurism and its impact.

By the early 1900s, art was no longer a benign and pleasurable endeavor engaged in by idealistic bohemians oblivious of society's turmoil. Art was now a disruptive force, a weapon to agitate and propel society into the future. For the futurists, the creative act was a violent, sometimes irrational, response to those who embraced an idealized past and a rigid concept of the future—the bourgeoisie. Futurism, as proclaimed by its founder, the poet F. T. Marinetti, in the 1909 "Futurist Manifesto," was a call to battle: "United, we must attack! We must create with absolute faith in the imperishable richness of the earth! There's no turning back! Boldly, let us advance! Forward, Faster! Farther! Higher! Let us lyrically renew our joy in being alive!"

Marinetti espoused a permanent artistic and political revolution. He rejected tranquil traditionalism in favor of "the new religion of speed," mythologizing the machine—the automobile and later the airplane—as totems of the modern spirit. Technology, though somewhat primitive in Italy, was the exalted savior of mankind. Wrote Marinetti: "a racing car, whose head is adorned with great pipes . . . is more beautiful than the Victory of Samothrace." Futurist ideas, which were first realized as free-verse orchestrations of sound and image in the renewal of Italian poetry, were soon applied to painting and sculpture by exponents such as Umberto Boccioni, Luigi Russolo, Gino Severini, Giacomo Balla, and

Carlo Carra, all of whom saw the need for an all-out war on romantic Italian art. Their intent was to translate the tenets of free-verse poetics and the language of the machine age into visual terms suggestive of the "whirling world of steel, pride, fever and speed."

Although Futurism was intellectually fueled, as evidenced by the movement's varied and verbose manifestos, it was propagated by a sustained bombardment of cultural agitation. Boisterous publicity campaigns preceded futurist events that were part theater, part political rally, and part rabble-rousing, whereby Marinetti and his "band" would assault the audience with verbal and visual attacks on mind, body, and senses. Marinetti also formed a Futurist political party that embraced the working class, exhorting its members to violence as the means to end bourgeois dominance. The antidote to cultural decay was war—bloody yet heroic. Marinetti anticipated, and then reveled in, the First World War as just such a cleansing ritual.

During 1919, he allied Futurism with Mussolini's emerging Fascist party, going so far as to organize *fasci di combattimento*, or political combat squads. In its early stages, Fascism was perceived as a revolt against stagnation, clericalism, and monarchy. Though some adherents ultimately rejected Fascism, Marinetti continued to be an active supporter until 1944.

Futurism was said to be the avant-garde of the masses, influencing the production of everyday products and commodities. Toward this end, Carlo Balla proposed brightly colored phosphorescent clothes, which would dazzle in the streets, and wrote a manifesto on Futurist menswear. He, moreover, introduced a carnivalesque mythology into futurist poetics and doctrine. This art of theatrics, perhaps more than anything, engaged the imagination of Fortunato Depero.

At an early age, Fortunato (meaning Lucky) moved with his family to the little town of Rovereto, Italy, where he took courses at the Royal Technical and Applied Art School. Suffocating in his provincial surroundings, he applied in 1908 for admission to the Fine Arts Academy in Vienna, but was rejected. Remaining in Rovereto, he worked as an interior decorator, a painter of social realism, and a marble cutter. He mounted some small, uneventful showing of his work, and his creative frustrations grew. He took sojourns to Florence, spending time with the antitraditionalist artists he met there, but longed to move to Rome where, as he wrote in a letter to his wife-to-be, "there's Marinetti who thinks the same way I do." His initial interest in Futurism was sparked in 1913, when he read *Lacerba*, the counterculture magazine in which Marinetti's writings appeared. In 1914, after finally moving to Romek, he met Balla, a kindred spirit, who sponsored Depero's participation in some futurist exhibitions.

At twenty-four, Depero was already artistically formed, with a distinct personal style neither derivative of other Futurists nor of contemporary decorative arts. While he shared Marinetti's belief in "art action," Depero was engaged in considerably more playful pursuits. And, although he followed the movement's political dictates, his personal politics were based on aesthetics. As an example of his futuristic humor, he produced stylized robots that were brightly colored, joyfully mysterious, and resolutely metaphysical. Art historian Giorgio Ruggeri writes, "In Depero one rediscovers applied art, the happening, kinetic art, dadaist provocation, abstract painting: to sum up, a heritage of so many new directions in art."

Accepting the proclamations of the other Futurists about language, art, sound, noise, and smell, Depero and Balla announced in their 1915 "Futurist Reconstruction of the Universe," "We Futurists . . . want to create this total fusion in order to reconstruct the universe, cheering it up: in other words, recreating it integrally. We shall give skeleton and flesh to the universe, to the impalpable, to the imponderable, to the imperceptible. We shall find abstract equivalents of all forms and elements of the universe. Then we shall combine them all together, according to the whim of our inspiration, to form plastic complexes which we shall put into motion." These "plastic complexes" infused everyday objects with all the speed-oriented obsessions held by the futurists. This is really the key to Depero's uniqueness in the futurist movements; for he did not proffer inaccessible theories, but, rather, the means to make art, for adult and child alike, that would, in a pleasurable way, help change the cultural environment.

Depero was an indefatigable laborer when it came to art and the propagation of futurist principles. Accepting Marinetti's view of war, he volunteered in 1915 for army service, but was deemed unfit. Says Ruggeri: "He returned to Rome and threw himself headlong into work." He drew, painted, sculpted, and engraved. He devised "noisy songs and poems," composed collages, made tapestries, cushions, and advertisements. He wrote for newspapers, promoted the art of the futurist book, founded and directed the machine-art magazine *Dinamo,* organized personal exhibitions, and worked in the theater as a scenarist and costume designer. He also invented an "onomalanguage," a "free world, free sounding," expressive verbal rigamarole. But, as Ruggeri says, "It was not enough." In later years, he designed trade-fair pavilions, and participated in various biennial, triennial, and quadrennial exhibitions. He represented the Futurists at the 1925 Paris exposition of modern decorative and industrial art, exhibiting his emblematic, life-sized mechanical men. He produced futurist radio programs. He decorated cabarets, bars, restaurants, game parlors, and dance halls. With his wife, Rosetta, he opened the Casa d'Arte Futurista in Rovereto, Italy, where he made wooden constructions, furniture, and costumes for a mass clientele. He extended futurist poetics into scenic design for the cinema. He followed Balla's lead in the design of futurist clothing, making vests and jackets.

"Futurism, that of the late-teens through the thirties, is unquestionably Fortunato Depero. At once a razzle-dazzle popularization of Futurist and Cubist ideas and an art that borders on the physically disturbing, Depero's work deserves more attention in the English-speaking world," wrote Kenneth E. Silver in a review in *Art in America* of the 1985 Venice exhibition *Futurism & Futurisms.* Depero's acceptance in the English-speaking world is clouded by Futurism's relationship with Fascism, and, moreover, by the fact that he is considered part of the so-called second stage of Futurism (the first stage being more closely akin to the traditions of the Russian and German avant-garde—a term Depero intensely disliked). Indeed, the aesthetic tendencies of the second stage, which began after World War I, were substantively altered by the advent of machine art. The machine, as an abstract concept, adopted by Marinetti as a metaphor for speed and power, was replaced by the actual factory machine as the ultimate production tool. The futurists attempted to reconcile themselves with the real machine, but the results, at first, were sterile and formalized, except in the work of Depero, who both embraced and satirized the machine's function and aesthetics in many artistic forms. For example, he created, in cooperation with Prampolini, costumes for futurist ballets that interpreted the movements and noise of machines.

A particular Depero triumph was in book design and production. During the twenties, the "book-object" was seriously practiced as a futurist art form, the logical confluence of futurist magazine layout and typographical experimentation. For the 1927 Biennale Internazionale delle Arti Decorative in Monza, Italy, Depero designed the Book Pavilion built entirely out of giant block letters. It was decidedly a grand architectural achievement, but not as historically important as his bolted catalog, which, along with Marinetti's famous tin book, is emblematic of futurist applied-arts thinking. Titled *Depero Futurista*, it is a lavish compendium of his own design work (including advertisements for Campari) covering the years 1913 through 1927, reproduced both by letterpress and photographically, and bound, in industrial fashion, by two stainless-steel bolts.

By 1927, Depero was recognized as an innovator. His synthesis of dynamic and expressionistic graphic forms was undeniably original. He reconciled craft, fine, and applied arts, and, believing that product advertising was the means to stimulate a dialogue with the public, he took on such advertising assignments in Italy, including his highly visible series for Campari, as well as smaller jobs for printers and others. But, perhaps to stimulate his own self-dialogue, enhance his reputation, and fulfill a dream, Depero decided in 1927 to move to New York to carve out a new market, promote Futurism, and revel in the mechanocity that fueled the Futurists' predictions of an ideal metropolis.

In the recent book *Depero Futurista & New York: Futurism and the Art of Advertising*, Maurizio Scudiero and David Leiber detail Depero's curious success in New York on the eve of the Depression, when in America modern art was emerging as a dominant force, *Il Duce* was admired by America's industrial giants, and a preference for the decorative prevailed in publishing and advertising centers. For Depero, New York was a theatrical vision, as the city was experiencing an architectural renaissance with the construction of the Chrysler, Chanin, RCA, and, later, Empire State Building—all discernible influences on Depero's subsequent work.

In this tough, but challenging, environment, Depero and Rosetta opened Futurist House in the New York Transit Hotel on West 23rd Street. From these small rooms he hoped to convince patrons of his artistic merits. He was given an exhibition of paintings and tapestries at the Guarino Galleries (for which he produced a catalog that Scudiero lauds as a "masterpiece of typographic art"), and received positive notices in many newspapers, such as the *New York Sun,* which proclaimed, "There can be no doubt that the most emphatic art exhibition of this week is that in the Guarino Galleries by Fortunato Depero . . . Speed in the abstract seems to have endless attraction [for him]. In that, one might almost imagine him an American."

Despite the plaudits, slow sales forced Depero to rely almost exclusively on advertising and theater work to pay the bills. He received commissions from BBD&O (the Venus pencil account), *Vanity Fair, Theater, Sparks,* the *New Yorker,* the *American Printer, Movie Makers, Vogue* (all magazines), the *New York Daily News* (for an atlas), and Macy's.

As Leiber points out, Depero's ideas for these clients were often recycled Italian projects. For the *Vogue* assignments, however, he was forced to adapt to its Deco preoccupation; hence, the *Vogue* work was decidedly weaker. Left to his instincts, however, Depero was predisposed to an "Aztec Deco" sensibility that was informed by New York's set-back skyscrapers. Depero's use of bright colors and collaged colored papers was a startling contrast to the rather conservative realism which then held sway over most American commercial art.

While Depero succeeded at the applied arts, sales of his fine arts and crafts were not progressing so smoothly, partly because the stock market crash limited the funds available for art purchases. Attempting to rectify this, he mailed postcards and announcements to prospective clients, but without positive results. And then an unprecedented idea hit him. Rather than engage in the hard-sell approach, he would invite the cognoscenti, critics, and tycoons to regular Futurist House lunches where Rosetta would (figuratively) seduce them with her incomparable ravioli. It was the Italian version of networking, and it worked. "The ravioli are the keystone of this difficult moment," Depero wrote in his diary, "and they seem to be the secret to overcome the 1929 crisis in New York."

After having absorbed New York's influences to the point of saturation, Depero and Rosetta returned to Italy on October 9, 1930, on the steamship *Roma*. His firsthand urban vision was transcribed as a series of "free-word" plates, a marriage of text and image, including one homage to the underground, entitled "Subway." He also conceived the idea for *New York Film Vissuto*, a "free-word sound-book." New York also apparently solidified Depero's belief that, as Leiber writes in his astute essay on "The Socialization of Art," in *Depero Futurista & New York*, advertising held the key to social engagement with the masses.

In his 1932 manifesto, "The Art of Advertising," Depero announces: "The art of the future will be powerfully advertising art." He also asserts: "All last centuries [*sic*] art was advertising oriented." Meaning, of course, that the paintings of the past were selling devices to exalt war, religion, and even love. Leiber states that while this "may be a facile approach to the history of art, [it] . . . nonetheless illustrates Depero's commitment to advertising." Depero believed that the artist must train his audience in visual matters and proposed that the artist's individuality be harnessed as a selling tool for products, as a means to stimulate artistic dialogue with the public. Thus, Depero would only work for clients (such as Campari) who allowed him free license. And with such assignments he deliberately used the product as the source of his own iconography, inspiring, he believed, "a new pictorial taste for the image."

In 1933, with the coming to power of the Nazi party in Germany, the already ugly face of European Fascism grew even more hideous. To compete with and impress Hitler, Mussolini embarked on a violent expansionist course; this and other government policies had a degrading effect on Italian Futurism. The theory of "aeropainting," which literally embraced the plane as the supreme modern invention, was a politically expedient means of reconciling the impotent avant-garde with *Il Duce*'s ideologies (and showed to the world that modernism was "healthy" in a Fascist country). Although Depero had said early on that "Futurism attracted me and made me better, gave me a new strength, showed me new fields and possibilities," by the late thirties Futurism had become an official style, rather than a progressive force. Assimilation into the popular taste of the period marked the beginning of its demise.

In 1922, Depero said, "I am neither Fascist nor supporter of Monarchy, but

Mussolini's coming is of great importance to us!" Indeed, until the advent of the Second World War, he prospered creatively amid the antibourgeois revolution. However, once the war was in full swing, the Fascist regime required heroic, rather than abstract or experimental, art to sell its policies. Depero continued to work throughout the war, but his cover for *La Rivista* (the magazine supplement of Mussolini's *Il Popolo* newspaper) shown here suggests a profound artistic compromise.

Marinetti's death in 1944 signaled the de facto death of Futurism. After the war, many former Futurists were called to account for their pro-Fascism. In order to explain himself—and more or less apologize—to Rovereto's town council, Depero wrote a sixteen-page, handwritten document, "Report on My Artistic Relationship with Fascism," in which he admits to "those human and justifiable mistakes committed in good faith." He was forgiven and was allowed to continue working. In 1957, the Commune di Rovereto decided to found a Depero Museum and permanent gallery to house and exhibit his collected work.

In 1947, Depero penned an autobiography entitled *So I Think So I Paint: Ideologies of an Italian Self-Made Painter*, a somewhat disjointed (and at times awkwardly translated) but fascinating compilation of his philosophies. Produced originally in English, the book was intended to pave the way for his return trip to New York City. This return, however, was not greeted with the same enthusiasm as his earlier stay. Jobs and commissions were few, if any. He and Rosetta lived briefly in a house on MacDougal Street, in Greenwich Village, and later moved to a benefactor's home in Marryhall, Connecticut. Upon the benefactor's death in 1949, they returned to Italy. Around 1950, true to his progressive stance and in keeping with futurist tradition, he wrote a *Manifesto of Nuclear Plastic Painting*. He died ten years later, on November 29, 1960, in Rovereto.

Depero unquestionably gave vivid life to Futurism and the applied art of his time. But he also has had a discernible effect on contemporary art and design. Whether or not the designers of Memphis, or the exponents of New Wave, post-Modernism, or Swiss Punk are even remotely conscious of Depero, today's prevailing color, form, decoration, and, of course, wit can be directly traced to his dynamic input.

Originally published in PRINT, *March/April 1987.*

Note

1. *Magica Allegria Di Naufragi: Fortunato Depero*, by Giorgio Ruggeri.

seventeen

MAY 1949 · 25 CENTS

ALL YOURS

CIPE PINELES: ARTIST AS ART DIRECTOR
Martha Scotford

In the days when American graphic design seemed the province of European immigrants, the men were joined by a young woman born in Austria. The graphic design career of Cipe Pineles (pronounced SEE-pee pi-NELL-iss) began when she was installed by Condé Nast himself in the office of Dr. M. F. Agha, art director for Condé Nast publications *Vogue, Vanity Fair,* and *House & Garden.* Through the 1930s and early 1940s, Pineles learned editorial art direction from one of the masters of the era, and became (at *Glamour* magazine) the first autonomous woman art director of a mass-market American publication. She is credited with other "firsts" as well: being the first art director to hire fine artists to illustrate mass-market publications; the first woman to be asked to join the all-male Art Directors Club, and later their Hall of Fame. After experimenting on *Glamour,* she later art-directed and put her distinctive mark on *Seventeen* and *Charm* magazines as well. Until her death in 1991, Cipe Pineles continued a design career of almost sixty years through design work for Lincoln Center and others, and teaching and promoting design at the Parsons School of Art and Design.

Pineles had piqued Nast's interest with some shoebox-sized models for store window fabric displays she had developed for Contempora, a design collaborative willing to tackle projects ranging in scale from a coffeepot to a World's Fair. The Condé Nast job was Pineles's first since graduating from Pratt Institute in 1929. It had taken her a year of portfolio reviews to land the position: the too-frequent pattern had been a positive reaction to the work followed by dismay when a woman showed up for the interview.

Working with Agha on the design of *Vogue* and *Vanity Fair,* she learned how to be an editorial designer. "Agha was the most fabulous boss to work for," Pineles reported later. "Nothing you did satisfied him. He was always sending you back to outdo yourself, to go deeper into the subject." He told his staff to visit galleries and museums and bring back new ideas. During the early 1930s Condé Nast publications were innovative in their use of European Modernism in magazine design. Typography was simplified, and typefaces such as Futura became common. Headlines and text could be anywhere on the page. Photography took precedence over fashion illustration and was reproduced large on the page, bleeding off to create "landscapes" or transgressing across the gutter. Space expanded as purely decorative elements disappeared and margins were opened.

Watching and listening to Agha, Pineles also learned how to be an art director: "He spent a lot of time talking with his creative people . . . about problems related to type; pictures and the selection of pictures as satisfying an editorial concept or not." Creative people doing one thing were urged to take on another medium to gain a new perspective. Pineles, in addition to design and spot illustration, was one of his talent scouts for new illustrators and photographers.

Pineles rose to the position Agha had been preparing her for; in early 1942 she was named art director of *Glamour*, becoming the first autonomous woman art director for a mass-market American publication. Ignoring her publisher, who turned out to have little respect for this middle-market fashion audience, Pineles used the best talent of the day, among them photographers Andre Kertesz, Herbert Matter, Cornell Capa, Toni Frissell, and Trude Fleischmann; designer Ladislav Sutnar; and artists S. E. and Richard Lindner and Lucille Corcos.

After a short hiatus during World War II when she worked in Paris on a magazine for servicewomen, Pineles became the art director of the three-year-old *Seventeen* magazine, a radical invention directed toward a hitherto undefined audience: teenage girls. The founder and editor, Helen Valentine, addressed her readers as serious and intelligent young adults, rather than as the silly, only-marriage-minded girls other publishers saw. In support of Valentine's mission to educate teenage girls, Pineles moved *Seventeen* out of the common idealized and sentimental school of illustration to use the best contemporary artists working in America. The reader's visual education would begin with the best artists' work.

Pineles is credited with the innovation of using fine artists to illustrate mass-market publications. Important because it brought fine art and modern art to the attention of the young mainstream public, it also allowed fine artists access to the commercial world. Pineles commissioned such artists as Ben Shahn and his wife, Bernarda Bryson, Richard Lindner, Jacob Lawrence, Reginald Marsh, John Sloan, and Dong Kingman. Some young artists "discovered" by the magazine became well known: Richard Anuszkiewicz and Seymour Chwast. An artist and illustrator herself, Pineles was the perfect art director: she left the artists alone. She asked them to read the whole story and choose what they wanted to illustrate. Her only direction was that the commissioned work be good enough to hang with their other work in a gallery.

Neither was Pineles averse to using her own talents. She had an affinity for food painting and used objects, furniture, and even her own large-scale country house as props and locations for many photographs in the magazine. In one instance, finding potatoes too ugly for photos to go with her story, the food editor turned to Pineles, who recalled: "I thought they were pretty, so I dug out my kitchen tools, bought ten cents' worth of potatoes, painted them on a double-page-size sheet of paper, indicated the type layout and left town. Total time, an hour and a half. Two weeks later, when finished art was needed, I went about the job more seriously. I nursed the potatoes, considered the type more carefully, and then tore the whole thing up. The rough was more fun. Total time, eighteen hours." The potatoes won her an Art Directors Club gold medal.

In Pineles's hands, the design of *Seventeen* followed the more classical tradition of magazine and typographic design. For the fiction, the quiet and bookish typography supported the primacy of the artwork. For editorial and fashion pages, the type was more playful, even showing early tendencies in American figurative typography where objects replaced letters as visual puns. Bear in mind, this was during a golden age of magazine design when art directors had thirty pages of uninterrupted editorial well in which to develop their visual ideas in a more cinematically dynamic way than is possible now. Pineles remained at *Seventeen* for three years, leaving to art-direct *Charm* magazine in 1950.

Twelve years before *Ms.* and twenty-six years before a magazine called *Working Woman*, the cover of *Charm* boldly carried the subtitle: "The magazine for women who work." The audience needed, but did not yet have, a service and fashion magazine that helped them fit together their two jobs. In *Charm* (as in *Seventeen*), surrounded by the advertisements that reflected society's limits on girls and women, the editorial pages showed something different: ways for American females to see themselves involved in the wider world and in possession and control of knowledge, money, and their destinies. Consciously, she turned her professional challenges at *Seventeen* and *Charm* into opportunities; less consciously, she turned them into places where, while addressing women's usual beauty and fashion interests, their values and changing roles also might be addressed and supported.

Charm's presentation of fashion revealed its take on its readers. The clothes for working women were shown in use: at the office, commuting, lunch-hour shopping, and as practical answers for quotidian problems. As Pineles put it, "We tried to make the prosaic attractive without using the tired clichés of false glamour. You might say we tried to convey the attractiveness of reality, as opposed to the glitter of a never-never land . . ." Pineles used modern architecture and modern industrial design as locations and props for the photo shoots. For a repeated series of cover articles called "She Works in [City Name]," Pineles designed entire issues to reflect each city theme. In the Detroit issue, for example, Pineles used the city as a backdrop for the fashion pages, constructing the layouts from photos of buildings and expressways and in other ways reflecting the city's connection to the automotive industry. An extension of the theme included the vernacular typography of the parking garage.

In 1961, briefly following Bradbury Thompson's long tenure as art director at *Mademoiselle*, Pineles became an independent consultant designer and a design teacher. During the mid-1960s, when the Lincoln Center complex was rising, Pineles took on the difficult task of coordinating much of the educational and promotional material. Working for the corporation that managed the fund-raising and public information for an uneasy consortium of arts groups, she established a graphic system for publications, an identifying mark, and attempted to educate management and the arts groups about the value of a unified visual image and organized information distribution. By the late 1960s, Lincoln Center's monetary problems distracted attention from this area, which needed constant political and financial support, and Pineles moved on.

At the same time, Pineles was discovering the intense pleasures of teaching by offering a course in editorial design at Parsons, a course she taught until the mid-1980s. The course required the student to identify a topic and its audience and develop a magazine for that audience: to design the publication from cover to interior spreads, as well as the marketing materials needed to find the audience. Several current art directors are products of this course; one (Melissa Tardiff, art director of *Town and Country* in the 1980s when she spoke) described the Pineles approach in this way: "She didn't teach style—she taught content. She taught you to start with the content of the magazine and then work from there, rather than just think about what design was going to look nice on the page." Pineles later developed a follow-up course in which students developed, designed, and printed a college "yearbook," first redefining what a yearbook could be. The most famous product of that course, the *Parson's Bread Book,* went into a trade edition and was named one of the AIGA's Fifty Books of the Year in 1975.

Pineles was part of Parsons during years of rapid growth when it became part of the New School and expanded to Los Angeles. She became the director of publications for an extensive promotional program. Using students, faculty, and others to supply art and photography, Pineles established a strong, colorful, often amusing, and varied visual identity for the school. The conceit of identifying New York and Los Angeles with apples and oranges was probably the most powerful hit on the public's consciousness, though there were many smaller taps. Though she handed off the promotional design program and production duties a few years before, she continued to teach at Parsons into her mid-seventies.

Until the mid-1950s, when much younger women started making their way into positions of independent responsibility in magazines and graphic design, Cipe Pineles was by herself and a "first" in many respects. She had accumulated innumerable art direction and publication design awards over the years from the Art Directors Club, AIGA, Society of Publication Designers, and others. While there were some other women receiving awards, they were always paired with their hovering (male) art director, while Pineles got single credit. Though she paid her professional dues early and often—awards, juries, panels, presentation, lectures, committees, and boards, including the AIGA—and though Dr. Agha had been proposing her for ten years, the New York Art Directors Club would not offer her a membership. The club did not budge until faced with this dilemma: it offered membership to William Golden, the energetic design director of CBS, who pointed out that the ADC was hardly a professional club if it had ignored his fully qualified wife (he and Pineles had married in 1942). Both became members in 1948; she was the first woman member. Also in 1948, Pineles and Golden became the first couple to win individual Gold Medal awards in the same year. In 1975, she was the first woman inducted into their Hall of Fame.

As a "first" female allowed on some closely protected male professional turf, Pineles was pleased to be included with all her friends. Although these rewards were late in coming, Pineles was of a generation and demeanor that were gracious and patient. She has remained, unfairly and unfortunately, a footnote to American graphic design history, overshadowed by the attention paid to her two husbands, but this is soon to change.

Cipe Pineles was an established designer at Condé Nast when she met William Golden in the late 1930s and helped him get a job with Agha. Golden went on to direct corporate identity for CBS and become a standard bearer for high quality and ethical corporate design. (He was a posthumous AIGA Gold Medalist in 1988.) Golden died at a young age in 1959, leaving Pineles with their young son. Within two years, Pineles married the recently widowed Will Burtin, who, with his wife and daughter, had been very close friends of the Goldens. Burtin, for his part, was a wartime German immigrant who quickly established himself in New York as an art director, corporate designer, teacher, extraordinary exhibition designer, and a founding member of the Aspen Institute conferences. He received the AIGA Gold Medal in 1971. With an AIGA Gold Medal going to Pineles, the three will now be the largest "family" of medalists, each medal bestowed for independent achievement.

Talented, assertive, with charm enhanced by her lingering Austrian accent, and with a fortunate first job, Cipe Pineles became the first independent female American graphic designer. As art director of *Glamour*, *Seventeen*, *Charm*, and *Mademoiselle* for over twenty years, she collaborated with hundreds of artists, illustrators, photographers, and editors. She mentored her assistants, and later formally taught a generation of designers at Parsons. As an art director she provided an encouraging, enthusiastic, and collaborative model; as a professional woman in a predominantly male field, she was a model for the next generation of women in design. As a friend and colleague to legions of creative people across the globe, Cipe Pineles was always ready with good food and lively conversation, as well as advice, a letter of support, a contact, or a commission.

Martha Scotford is professor of graphic design at the School of Design, North Carolina State University. Her book Cipe Pineles: a Life of Design *was published by W.W. Norton in 1999. She is a 2000–2001 Fullbright Fellow in India, teaching in Ahmedabad and Mumbai.*

Originally published in AIGA: Graphic Design USA *(1998).*

LE DIRECTEUR
DE LA TOUR EIFFEL
leur fait les honneurs de la

TOUR EIFFEL

Il leur montre

PARIS

 A VOL D'OISEAU

MASSIN AHEAD OF TIME
John Gall and Steven Brower

It's the end of typography as we know it, and Robert Massin feels fine. Massin, who in the mid-1960s turned conventional design wisdom on its head with his daring graphic translations of Eugène Ionesco's plays *La Cantatrice Chauve* (*The Bald Soprano*)[1] and *Délire à Deux* (*A Frenzy for Two or More*), in unconcerned with recent developments from the design front. *"La mode c'est ce qui se démode* [Fashion is what falls out of fashion]," he says, quoting Jean Cocteau. "I create things to last—the opposite of a trend."

Decades before legibility became a hotly debated topic among designers, or even a consideration, Massin, who lives and works in Paris, was breaking traditional design rules and challenging the ways in which type could be presented and comprehended. Long before buzz words like "vernacular" and "semiotics" became associated with post-Modern design trends, he was busy cataloging historical and contemporary letterforms and their symbolism in his seminal book, *Letter and Image*. But, though his designs for the Ionesco plays are well documented and he is acclaimed in his native France, he is little known in the United States despite a fifty-year career in which he has been not only a designer but also art director, typographer, writer, editor, and publisher.

Massin was born in 1925 in the Eure-et-Loire, a plains region of France, from which one can see clearly the spires of Chartres Cathedral. His mother was a schoolteacher, and his father, a sculptor/engraver who nurtured Massin's artistic skills from an early age. By the time he was four-and-a-half, although he did not yet know how to read or write, Massin was already engraving letters. Displaying what would turn out to be a lifelong fascination with typography, he scrawled illegible letterforms on soft stone supplied by his father. "I had been so attentive to typography," Massin recalls, "that when I later learned to read, I still had in mind the characters of my alphabet primer—their design, their body, everything. Once I knew typography fifteen years later, I was able to say that my alphabet primer had been made up of Bodoni and Bodoni Bold, of English calligraphy, and so forth. About four or five years ago, I happened to drop in on an antique dealer in the provinces and I spotted my alphabet primer. I was not mistaken. They were exactly the characters I had imagined. So I think I had an absolutely perfect eye, just as some musicians have a perfect ear—which I understand is inborn." At seven, Massin was beginning to assemble little books made of folded paper and stitched together with string. Inside, he would list himself as "Photographer, Publisher, and Author."

Massin also developed an early appreciation of literature that was almost too sophisticated for his rural surroundings. "During my childhood, I knew Marcel Proust," he says, "but not *the* Marcel Proust. The one I knew was very stocky, with a thick mustache and a ruddy complexion, and was totally illiterate. He was a shepherd in my village. Later, when I attended high school and my philosophy teacher read me some Proust, I thought, 'But this isn't possible, Marcel Proust can't write!'"

By the time he reached high school, Massin had begun to develop other interests. "I hesitated between literature, theater, the graphic arts, and music," he says. "In those days, you had to choose one or the other. There were no connections between the disciplines as there are now." Eventually, he settled on literature and right after the liberation, he went to Paris, as many young writers did, to start working in journalism. One impressive early assignment was to go to Copenhagen to interview the disgraced writer Louis-Ferdinand Céline, who, imprisoned for his collaboration with the Germans during the occupation, had just been released. Massin was the first journalist to meet with him, and the interview, when it was published, attracted a good deal of attention. However, at that time, newspapers consisted only of one double-page spread or a total of four pages, and competition for the available space was fierce. Despite the success of this article, Massin's career as a journalist never really took off.

In 1948, after a few years of struggling to make a living, Massin had the opportunity to break into publishing when he became an editor at Le Club Français du Livre, a mail-order book club founded in 1947. Massin joined the staff six months after the club was formed. The agenda was to publish four books a month in limited editions of four to five thousand, with jackets and bindings designed especially for the book club edition.

At first, Massin was in charge of editing the club's bulletin, *Liens* (a *lien* is a thread made of leather, used on book bindings). One of his responsibilities was to have the bulletin typeset and printed. With no formal design training, he learned on the job how to do layouts and pasteups. "I was panicked when they sent me to the printer," he recalls. Fortunately for Massin, his father introduced him to an Italian typographer, an anti-Fascist refugee in France, who taught him the trade in only six weeks. Eventually, with the complete works of Arthur Rimbaud as his first assignment, Massin began designing books and book covers. It was also at Le Club Français du Livre that Massin met his mentor, Pierre Faucheux.

Faucheux, who had studied with Le Corbusier and was in his thirties when Massin met him, was already an established designer. Massin credits him with revolutionizing design in France. "France was mired in a typographical tradition that was completely obsolete and ossified," he explains. "With the interruption of World War II, we had lost contacts abroad. We no longer could see American typographical art. We were no longer aware of anything. Faucheux started again from scratch using Surrealist and Dadaist typographic ideas." These ideas had a profound effect on Massin.

Hired by the book club to create a case cover for a work by Baudelaire, Faucheux produced a design featuring Baudelaire's handwriting bleeding across the front and back covers on a white field. Years later, this solution inspired Massin's jacket for *Lettres à L'Amant* by Mireille Sorgue. Because he believed that illustration is "a betrayal" since it always illustrates the text, which is never "the truth," Faucheux often used archival art or pure graphic design to create a "unique atmosphere that was true to the book."

Toward the end of the 1940s, Le Club Français decided to publish special editions, for which particular care would be devoted to the individual character of the book, the originality of the design, and the use of unusual materials. Often these *livre-objets* (books as objects) took on a Dadaist or surrealist aspect. For example, Massin pasted a circular mirror to the binding of *Le Miroir de la Magie* by Kurt Seligmann.

"The interesting thing about these books is that they were completely homogeneous," Massin says, "just like the buildings Gaudí erected in Barcelona. As in Baroque and Rococo, everything was in the same style, down to the chimney or a doorknob. Similarly, with the boards, the typography, the bindings, the flyleaves, there was really a total coherence in the book, but with a constant diversity. It was like music. The principle of variations in general is that you have a theme which is constantly enriched by variations. As Schoenberg said, in variations, it is not the subject that is important, but the countersubject, or the variation."

In 1952, Massin helped create another book club, Club de Meilleur Livre (which he still considers the best of them all), where he continued to produce limited editions that featured experimentation with typography, materials, and color. In 1958, he went to Editions Gallimard as art director. "When I entered Gallimard, there was nothing in the way of graphics," he says. "Everything was done at the printer's. There were no pasteup or layout artists. I invented everything there because at first I was alone. Later, I had a part-time assistant, then a full-time one, then a second and a third one."

The publisher was supportive of Massin's efforts. "I was lucky that Gaston Gallimard believed in what I was doing," he says. "But he didn't have a mind for graphics. He said so himself. He said that although he had known all the Impressionist painters—they had been his friends—he didn't have a head for graphics. He wanted to work in literature. He wanted no part of graphics, drawings, designs, illustrations, and so forth. He was not interested. He had one thing on his mind and that was literature. He was a great man."

In 1961, Massin designed *Cent Mille Milliards* (*100,000,000,000,000 Poems*), by the experimentalist author Raymond Queneau. Although the text actually consists of only ten poems of fourteen lines each, Massin cut each line into strips, so that the type could be mixed and rematched. In 1963, he reinterpreted another Queneau book, the previously published *Exercices de Style*. Surrealist in style, it was, Massin recalls, "neither poetry, nor novel, nor theater, nor an essay, but everything at the same time." Having suggested to Queneau that he illustrate it, he produced a unique black-and-white plaid patterned binding that sported a button and looked like a coat. This innovative idea, along with his futurist/Dadaist–inspired experimental mixing of typefaces and effects, laid the foundation for what was to become his best-known work, his graphic interpretation of Ionesco's play *La Cantatrice Chauve*.

"I was fascinated by the play," Massin explains. "I tried to do a typographical translation of the diction, the voices of the characters, as well as a typographical layout that was a replica of the staging in the theater." A visual tour de force and technical marvel, Massin's *La Cantatrice Chauve* (1964) was an extraordinary achievement and unlike anything else. Just as Ionesco and other writers of the Theater of the Absurd had reinvented the ways in which plays could be presented and understood, Massin redefined the way a book could be perceived. Graphically interpreting the play's attack on conformity, Massin's layout is a no-holds-barred assault on conventional book design.

Printed entirely in black-and-white with no halftones for reasons both economic and graphic, *La Cantatrice Chauve* combines Henry Cohen's high-contrast photographs of the characters with Massin's anarchic type treatments, creating explosive layouts that enhance the irrationality of the play. Type is used not only to present the story but to intensify the dialogue. During a fight scene, lines of dialogue overlap, then fly off the page. Occasionally, words are distorted almost beyond recognition to represent the actors' vocal inflections. The book is not necessarily an easy read, but Massin provides helpful clues. By assigning a different typestyle to each of the eight characters, he identifies the participants of mad conversations. When they speak loudly, he uses large type. When the stage goes black between scenes, there are two black pages. "Massin's aim," explains André Deval, the curator of France's cultural center IMEC (Institut Mémoires de l'Edition Contemporaine), "was to introduce the idea of time and space to the printed page."

Ionesco was somewhat hesitant about this graphic treatment until he realized that Massin was going to expand the meaning of the play. "What really pleased Ionesco the most was the scene we called 'the scene of silences,'" Massin recalls. "It lasts two minutes, which is an eternity in the theater. In the book, which is 192 pages long, this passage takes up 48 pages, a quarter of the book. So, I played with the length, and this is what pleased Ionesco the most. Having his subject exaggerated in translation."

To create these layouts, Massin started with 8-point type, enlarged it through a projector, and made tracings of the final results. He achieved his distorted type effects by printing on a piece of rubber that was then stretched to produce the desired effect and photographed.

In addition to the French edition, there were two English-language versions, one published in England and one in the United States for Grove Press, and because each publisher engaged his own translator, there were two different translations. "Thus I had three different mock-ups," Massin explains. "One for France, one for England, and one for the United States, with three different requirements. For example, in French, 'caiman' becomes 'crocodile,' then becomes 'cayman' once again in the other edition. It was difficult because the words were never the same length." Barney Rosset, publisher and driving force behind Grove Press until 1985, recalls, "I thought this was a tour de force of its time, a new way of doing a play, as good as seeing the play. It was done for Gallimard, and I saw it, and thought it was great. I met Massin and asked him to adapt his design to the American edition. It was a lot of work, but he did it. That was before they had Xeroxes. Today, they can blow everything up automatically."

Not only did Massin have to deal with the daunting task of reproducing these complex layouts in other languages, he also had to assemble different mechanicals in accordance with the trade practices of each country. In Europe, for instance, printers tended to do most of the technical work with the designers supplying trace layouts as guides. In the United States, it was standard practice to supply camera-ready art. Massin had to create all the special effects himself and then paste them into position. The entire process took three months of work, day and night, seven days a week.

As a follow-up to *La Cantatrice Chauve*, Massin took his ideas to further extremes. *Délire à Deux* (1965), another play by Ionesco, was given an even more chaotic treatment. Words, sound effects, and inkblots all collide on the page with reckless abandon. The seemingly random splotches are not gratuitous, however. They are a graphic translation of sound effects, outbursts, and words. Predating punk graphics by a good ten years, *Délire à Deux* is an abrasive and uncompromising work, a cacophony of words on the page.

Rosset thought so highly of Massin's work that he commissioned him to do a typographical homage to Edith Piaf for the *Evergreen Review*. Working once again with high-contrast photographs, this time taken by Emil J. Cadoo, Massin brings Piaf's performance of *La Foule* to stirring life. By distorting type to suggest the way the words were sung, Massin wrenches every bit of emotion from each word. Massin's idea was to make letterforms that echoed Piaf's inflection and the music itself. He achieved this by writing on rubber. First, he tried the kind of rubber used to line baby's cribs but it was too difficult to stretch and control. Finally, he settled on condoms, because they were the thinnest, toughest, most pliant surface he could find. Massin explains that he went through three dozen condoms for this project, and he had to go to the drugstore three times. "They were looking at Massin like maybe he was Superman," says Deval.

Massin's graphic innovations were not only in the service of other authors. In 1970, after years of studying and cataloging typographic forms, he assembled his own book, *Letter and Image*, an illustrated history of the relationship between man and typography. It consists of the twenty-six letters of the alphabet illustrated by a hundred artists from every century. Animals, human beings, silhouettes, monsters, vegetables, instruments, and a whole catalog of natural and man-made objects become part of and extend the alphabet. An entire word is incorporated into one image, and one letterform becomes the image of a whole word. Massin also includes the historical background of typography in general and of these letterforms in particular.

Throughout the next two decades, Massin developed a varied and prestigious clientele. In 1972, he became freelance art director for Folio, a new mass-market library imprint sponsored by Gallimard. The covers of this series of books reflected Massin's modernist sensibility. To the top third of each cover, he applied simple classical typography on a white background. For the remaining space, he commissioned illustrations. Over the course of time, more than two hundred wonderfully diverse images appeared. The illustrators were chosen not so much because they were skilled in rendering the subject matter, but, rather, for their own unique styles. During the late '70s, Massin left Editions Gallimard to join Hachette-Réalités as art director. In 1981, he became an editor at Editions Denoel. In 1989, he designed for the French Ministry of Finance two versions of a logotype made of numbers that form the shape of France. For the cover of his monograph, *Massin*, published by IMEC in 1990, Massin rendered his own name in the same shape.

Today, seventy years old and semiretired, Massin spends his time compiling his work on video disk and doing the occasional design project. He has a steady income from past design jobs. "Everything I get paid is in royalties," he explains. "Whether I write a book, do a cover, or design a poster, I get paid in royalties, not in fees. So this allows me to make a nice living.

"Four years ago, I started with a computer," he continues. "No doubt, my projects are completed faster, but I have many more responsibilities than I had before. Nonetheless, I spend at least ten hours a day in front of that computer. I don't think it produces more talent, which you naturally have. It has to be considered more a means than an end. I'm a man in a hurry. I work faster and faster. Sometimes, when someone asks me for a job, the idea formulates in my mind before I've even said good-bye to the person. Or I might get a job order and five minutes later, walking down the street, the idea pops into my head. If it doesn't work that way, if I have to wait a couple of weeks, what I eventually come up with is much less interesting. On the other hand, sometimes I do happen to accept a job because it is difficult to do. That's exciting. I have done some very difficult jobs, and the difficulty was stimulating. This still happens."

Massin's advice for today's young designers is "not to follow fashions. There are so many different fashions in typography," he says. "Because they are so quickly publicized through the media, things get worn out very quickly. When I was a child, a new fashion took two years to reach the provinces. The Italian Renaissance took a century to reach France and two centuries to reach England. Nowadays, a new fashion or trend is instantly known the world over, just like stock market fluctuations."

Massin notes that his own work hasn't often been copied. "People can't do it because I am always questioning myself, reinventing myself," he says. "Every now and then, because of a lack of time, laziness, or to make the job easier, I do happen to take an old idea and redo it, but more often than not, I try to change things. Anyway, it keeps me young.

"At present, I am creating a logo for the great champagne labels. This particular logo is mainly intended for bottles for foreign markets—Japan or the U.S. It will be a mark of recognition for the 25 great brands, like Veuve Clicquot and Paul Roger. So it will be a label of quality. But I haven't created it yet. I'll drink some champagne first. That will be fun."

The authors would like to thank Valerie Adam and Morris Taub for their help in making this article possible. Their extensive research and interview with Robert Massin are greatly appreciated.

John Gall is the art director for Vintage Press. Steven Brower is the art director of PRINT.

Originally published in PRINT, *July/August 1996.*

Note

1. See "The Bald Soprano," *PRINT* (September/October 1994), pp. 72–79.

VOGUE

ALEXANDER LIBERMAN: ON OVERCOMING AESTHETICS
Véronique Vienne

Alexander Liberman, the legendary editorial director of Condé Nast Publications (CNP), always insisted that magazines had to be readable. Readable? The magazines he supervised during his fifty-plus-year career at CNP—*Vogue, Glamour, House & Garden, Vanity Fair*, and others—had distinctively crowded, messy layouts; page after page incorporated jumbled-up montages of text and images. Forget about curling up quietly to read the articles. Liberman's signature look was much too lively to invite contemplation.

A word to the wise: Liberman, now eighty-six and living in semiretirement, never bothered reading a manuscript before laying out a story. Once, when I was art director of *Self* magazine, he caught me actually reading a piece I was working on. With the authority of a man thirty years my senior, he reprimanded me severely for wasting time on the job. Magazine readers must get a feel for a story before reading it, he explained. It's best if art directors don't get involved with the text. My role, he said, was to communicate ideas—not illustrate words.

He summoned to my office the editor in charge. She scurried in, holding the culprit—a hard copy of the edited manuscript—against her chest. She was asked to put it aside and pitch her story aloud to Liberman. Whether dealing with fashion, beauty, health, food, or travel, CNP articles were scripted to have a dramatic plot line. Always polite and suave, Mr. Liberman, as we called him, rebuked her whenever she looked at her notes. He was not about to be text-driven. With a series of questions, he tried to unveil the reader's emotional relationship with the article. "Are you saying that vitamins are bad for you?" he asked. "If that's so, rewrite the headline."

While listening to the editor, he began to build a new layout from scratch, his hands moving almost magically over the drawing board. "I don't search, I find," he liked to say, paraphrasing Picasso. Headlines, quotes, sidebars, photographs, dummy text, and pieces of colored paper came together in less than three minutes. I had to hold my breath, literally, not to disturb this impromptu collage. As soon as Liberman declared that he was done, he made it clear that my responsibility was to hold the elements in place with tiny bits of transparent tape—and God help me if I straightened anything in the process. David Carson, whom I hired in 1990 as a pasteup assistant, remembers trying to copyfit Liberman's montages with the final text. "It was surreal," he now says. He had to treat Liberman's fragile piles of scrap paper as if they were works of art. He thought it was all pretty silly. "At the time I didn't know who this guy was," says Carson. "Now, looking back, I get the feeling that he has been undervalued and underappreciated as a graphic designer." Although the two never spoke, I can't help but wonder if Carson was not influenced by the old man's serendipitous approach to the page.

And Liberman was right: the magazines he designed were highly "readable." Condé Nast publications are compelling because they trigger in readers an instant sense of identification with what's on the page. A glance is all one needs to grasp the sum total of what the editors are thinking about. These are magazines that one doesn't need to decipher in order to read. "Clarity and strength of communication is what interests me," says Liberman. "I hate white space because white space is an old album tradition. I need to be immersed in the subject matter."

Unfortunately, few of Liberman's collaborators were ever able to read him as effortlessly as readers were able to read his layouts. From 1942, when Liberman, then thirty, was named art director of *Vogue* magazine, replacing the formidable Mehemed Fehmy Agha, to 1994, when he announced that James Truman, the thirty-five-year-old editor of *Details*, would be his successor, he has kept everybody mystified with abrupt decisions and unexpected turnarounds.

"The creative process is a series of destructions," he was fond of saying. For him, the creative process was also a series of dramatic dismissals. Great editors got the ax under Liberman's watch: Diana Vreeland, Grace Mirabella, and Louis Oliver Gropp, to name just a few. And countless great art directors, as well: Priscilla Peck, Lloyd Ziff, Dereck Ungless, Ruth Ansel, and Rip George.

To this day, the mere mention of Liberman's name can set off a heated discussion between designers and editors who have worked with him. People who have been fired by him are sometimes said to break into hives. Others relish the opportunity to tell some particularly amusing story. Because of him, there is an instant sense of community among ex-CNP employees. Commenting on Liberman's "absurdly hip" collage approach, design critic Owen Edwards today says: "When I worked with him, I always thought he was dead wrong—which only shows how dead wrong I was."

Liberman had a knack for astounding and confusing people around him—and his attempts to explain his design philosophy were more alienating than reassuring. "You are not quite vulgar enough, my dear," he once told me before scrapping one of the spreads I had designed for *Self*. Eager to please—no one was ever immune to his old-world charm—the next day I presented a revised, Fleet Street–inspired layout. Such a look of contempt I had never endured. "Simply lurid," he said, before walking out of the room.

Liberman was not a teacher. Although very articulate, he could never find the appropriate words to share his vision with others. Looking back, I believe that his inability to communicate with his design associates was due to the fact that his ideas were so radical, he couldn't begin to describe them. He used an antiquated vocabulary that dated from the days of Gutenberg to introduce a way of thinking that foreshadowed the revolution of the information age. Although Liberman dismissed computers as "too slow," ten years before the introduction of the Macintosh, he was already designing pages as if they were interactive screens, with layered rather than linear narratives.

Liberman was no stranger to revolutions, cultural or otherwise. Born in Kiev, Russia, in 1912, he remembers the first days of the Bolshevik upheaval. His father, a powerful forestry manager, prospered under Lenin's regime. His mother, an out-of-work actress, created a children's theater to keep starving urchins off the street. But in this climate of anarchy and social chaos, young Alex, a sensitive and difficult child, was displaying troubling behavior. His parents were afraid he was turning into a delinquent. In 1921, with Lenin's permission, Liberman was shipped to school in England where he was forced to learn manners. A quick study, he acquired, at age ten, the genteel demeanor and slight British accent that would later become the trademarks of his elegance.

After Lenin's death in 1924, the Libermans left Russia and settled in Paris. Alex was transferred to a chic French private school where he made valuable friends among the sons of the aristocracy. But the turning point for him was visiting the 1925 Paris Arts Décoratifs exhibition. He was just thirteen, but the discovery of Art Deco, then called Moderne art, was "one of the most important events of my life," he said later.

From then on, the concept of modernity became something of an obsession to him: "Alex tried and tried to get everyone to be modern—his idea of modern," notes Lloyd Ziff, who was art director at *House & Garden, Vanity Fair,* and *Traveler* in the 1980s. But he notes that the way Liberman worked, juxtaposing photographic and typographical elements, was more reminiscent of Russian Constructivism than of French Art Deco.

Liberman's early career in design was somewhat erratic. A bleeding ulcer kept interrupting his attempts to find an enjoyable line of work. He studied painting with Andre Lhote, architecture with Auguste Perret, and was briefly employed by Cassandre. In 1933, he got a job at *VU,* a Parisian weekly, and one of the very first news magazines to use reportage photography. There, he befriended Lucien Vogel, the editor, and met photographers who would help him define his taste for photojournalism: André Kertész, Robert Capa, and Brassai.

In the late 1930s, after a brief marriage to Hilda Sturm, a German ski champion, he fell deeply in love with Tatiana du Plessix, niece of Stanislavsky and a striking Russian beauty who was then married to a French aristocrat. Hitler's invasion of France in 1940 forced their fate: Tatiana's husband was killed while trying to join de Gaulle in England. Liberman escaped to New York with Tatiana, soon to be his wife, and her daughter, Francine.

In New York, Liberman was quickly hired by Condé Nast, who was impressed with his experience with photojournalism at *VU.* Back in 1931, Clare Booth Luce had submitted to Nast, her boss at the time, the prototype for a weekly picture magazine called *Life.* He had rejected it. Now *Life* was a raging success, and Nast was sorry he had missed the opportunity to start a breakthrough publication. When Liberman proposed, during his job interview, to inject some reportage into *Vogue,* Nast loved it. From that day on, Alex Liberman thought of himself as a journalist—a super editor with visual understanding. He never liked the title of art director and was relieved when, in 1962, he was appointed editorial director of all Condé Nast magazines.

During his career at CNP, Liberman carried a grudge against art directors. Their title, he felt, was misleading. He didn't want them to be artists, but managers of the image of the magazine. He understood his role, and the role of all editorial designers, to be what we call "brand managers" today. Unfortunately, the notion of brand was still in its infancy, so Liberman never got full use of it. What a pity. He would have loved to wrestle with concepts such as "perceived quality," "brand equity," and "visual territory."

Instead of rewriting the art director's job description, Liberman spent five decades fighting the idea that editorial design was an artistic endeavor. He went out of his way to undermine art directors in front of editors. With remarks like, "This layout is utterly provincial, wouldn't you say," or, "Remember: you are not a scarf designer, you are a journalist," he could reduce some of the most talented designers to tears. In the hallways of Condé Nast, you could easily spot the art directors: they were the walking wounded, the folks wearing neck braces. While at *Self*, I, too, became afflicted with a frozen shoulder, tension migraines, and lower back problems.

Editors who attended the daily public floggings of art directors would look at their shoes in embarrassment—but, internally, they were rubbing their hands. Liberman can be credited with weakening the authority of editorial art directors in the United States. He trained three generations of editors to belittle the opinions of their visually oriented coworkers. Today, every publication in America has at least one editor who once worked at CNP and refers to QuarkXPress and Photoshop users as "my art people."

Liberman didn't consider art direction an art because he was, in his spare time, an amazingly prolific painter and enterprising sculptor—always working on a large scale. He led two distinct lives. Careful to cultivate a Clark Kent, charcoal-gray-suit persona by day, he would become an ambitious abstract expressionist by night. His wife, Tatiana, called him Superman. "Art is the violent expression of resentment against the human condition," he told Barbara Rose, the author of a monograph on his work as an artist. Rose was under the impression that Liberman kept that resentment a private matter. "Alexander Liberman, the artist, is deeply suspicious of taste," she wrote in 1981. "Alexander Liberman, the editorial director of CNP, is, above all, a man of taste."

Rose was misinformed. With each passing year at CNP, Liberman showed less and less patience with issues of taste. He became committed to banishing forever "the vision of loveliness" that he had inherited at the beginning of his tenure at Condé Nast from Josephine Redding, Marie Harrison, Edna Woolman Chase, and Jessica Caves, *Vogue*'s early editors. Diana Vreeland set him free. "Laying out a beautiful picture in a beautiful way is a bloody bore," she once said. Like him, she treated the magazine as a series of collages, wantonly pasting together her models' body parts to get the "perfect whole." Liberman was impressed. "I put legs and arms and heads together," she said. "I never took fewer than two ribs."

When I first encountered Liberman, in the late 1970s, Diana Vreeland had been replaced by Grace Mirabella, and the *Vogue* art department, where I worked as a pasteup assistant, was run by Rochelle Udell. The magazine layouts were deliberately untidy, to differentiate *Vogue* from its competition, *Harper's Bazaar*, the absolute leader in design and visual innovation. Still under the influence of its renowned art director, Alexey Brodovitch, *Harper's Bazaar* was a thorn in Liberman's side. But he did what a good brand manager would do: instead of trying to play catch-up with *Harper's Bazaar*, he carved out a new niche for *Vogue*. As soon as he did, circulation began to rise dramatically. And advertisers loved being associated with a smart fashion publication that embraced the spirit of the Pepsi Generation.

Like David Carson did fifteen years earlier, I spent long hours in the *Vogue* art department, trying to fit type around Liberman's photomontages. Meanwhile, in his studio at home, the "Silver Fox," as some editors now called him, was throwing paint by the bucketful on huge canvasses, working as fast as possible to try to bypass the mental process, which he believed could only produce preconceived and banal solutions.

In 1989, I jumped at the opportunity to work with him again, this time at *Self*. By now, the seventy-seven-year-old Liberman had dropped all pretense of good taste. Although he had retained his suave, David Niven look, I was told that he was fiercer than ever. And indeed, soon after I joined CNP, Anthea Disney, the editor who had hired me, was unceremoniously fired for not following Liberman's directions. In no position to assert myself to the new editor, Alexandra Penney, I decided to look at the situation as a chance to resolve the Liberman mystery once and for all. I galvanized my staff and made it clear to Liberman that my entire art department was at his service. For the next six months, we were on a roll.

As soon as the great man would walk into the room, we were poised in battle formation: one assistant was at my side with scissors, knife, and loupe; another was posted next to the color copier; a third was assigned to the phones, keeping the lines open in case Liberman got a call. I had two "runners" ready to spring into action to either fetch an editor, find a color swatch, or alert the photo department. Helen Maryles, the youngest designer, was on tape duty. I will never forget the sight of her, standing next to Liberman, palms open, fingers extended, with tiny pieces of transparent tape stuck to the ends of all ten digits.

In his biography, *Alex*, written by Dodie Kazanjian and Calvin Tomkins, Liberman says: "If ever I have done what I'd call my own layouts, it's at *Self*." The pages he designed then and there were a debauch of bold type and cut-paper blocks of colors, a look reminiscent of the *papiers découpés* technique Matisse favored at the end of his career. Liberman had met him briefly in 1949, when the painter was in his late seventies—still mentally alert and youthful in spite of age and poor health. Now, Liberman had a chance to emulate his favorite artist. The *Self* layouts were an unmitigated homage to the author of "The Dance."

For the first time ever, Liberman was doing "art" at the office. He did concede to his biographers that at *Self* there was "not much difference in the psychological process between a composition on canvas and arranging material like this on a page." So this was it. In a long career dedicated to overcoming aesthetic considerations, the *Self* experiment represented a brief, but fleeting, moment of reconciliation between Clark Kent and Superman—between the art director and the artist. But it had to happen. The advertisers hated the "new" *Self*. The readers didn't get it, either. The magazine had lost its sacrosanct "readability." I was fired—and rightly so. "Seduction is a trap one has to get beyond," Liberman once said.

Mark my words: beware of artists—they'll get you in trouble.

Originally published in Graphis, *May/June 1998.*

FILTER CIGARETTES

VENI · VIDI · VICI

Marlboro

20 CLASS A CIGARETTES

THE BRAND NAMED WALTER LANDOR: HISTORICAL VIEW
Véronique Vienne

In Japan on a business trip in the early 1960s, Walter Landor and Mim Ryan, his young research analyst, stopped the car on the side of the road to admire a flowering bougainvillea tree. A dapper gentleman with a very European mustache, Landor was an admirer of all things visual, "from beautiful flowers to pretty women," remembers Ryan. "He got out of the car and I saw him bend over toward the fallen blossoms and pick what I thought was a delicate flower petal. But when he came back to the car, he was holding in his hand a discarded candy wrapper he had found on the sidewalk."

Landor was already a well-known packaging designer at the time. From his small waterfront office in San Francisco, "a funny little place," says Ryan, "with a creaking staircase in the middle of the vegetable market," he had redesigned the Benson & Hedges cigarette packs, the Sapporo beer can, and the Kellogg's Corn Flakes' cereal box (the famous one with the spoon and the rooster).

And yet Walter Landor never received the acclaim of other designers like Raymond Loewy, Walter Dorwin Teague, or Donald Deskey. His name is ostensibly kept out of twentieth-century design anthologies. Over the years, I managed to find a few books, journals, and trade publications that mentioned his work, but none that dwelled on his life or personality.

Landor was not a hands-on designer, I discovered, but a creative visionary, the ultimate concept-man. His fascination with design was driven by a youthful curiosity, not an aesthetic. "Products are made in a factory, but brands are created in the mind," he once said. His San Francisco design company, established in 1941, is credited with creating or repositioning some of the world's most ubiquitous consumer brands, including Del Monte (1965), Levi's (1968), Cotton Inc. (1973), Schaefer Beer (1975), Marlboro (1977), Tab (1979), Frito-Lay (1980), Dole (1984), Coke (1985), and Fuji Film (1987). He also single-handedly branded much of the commercial aeronautic field, designing the logos and corporate identities of Alitalia, British Airways, Japan Airlines, Delta Airlines, Cathay Pacific Airways, Varig Airlines, and Thai Airlines.

But one of the most enduring brands Walter Landor created was himself. Though he retired in 1989, the company he founded is still the number one choice for big business. "In our field, the Landor brand is as big as Coca-Cola," says Cheryl Swanson of Wallace Church Associates, one of the firms that often competes with Landor Associates on prestigious Fortune 500 branding jobs. As a marketing expert, she's not prejudiced against commercial artists. "If it wasn't for Walter, none of us would be here today. He's the father of what we now call brand-design packaging."

In contrast, when I told friends in the chauvinistic New York design world that I was researching a story on Landor, they dismissed him as a "regional artist," their attitude a holdover from the days when there was no there west of Chicago. It was only in the late 1970s, when Pentagram Design opened an office in San Francisco, and "The Michaels" (Vanderbyl, Cronan, Mabry, and Manwaring) called attention to the Bay Area, that Landor finally came up as a blip on the east coast establishment's radar.

Clay Timon, Landor Associates' present CEO, believes that what made Walter Landor hard to categorize was his uniqueness. "Part of Walter's brand appeal was that he never did what was expected. He never showed up when you thought he would. He did things his way. And clients adored him." Forty years ago, long before anyone else, Landor sold himself as a brand—not as a package designer with a house style, but as a man with a unique approach to problem-solving. "Landor would be tickled if he came back today," adds Timon. "He would see that, at long last, the corporate culture is catching up with his vision."

Today, on *www.landor.com*, his sepia portrait is featured in a medallion—a benign Dr. Freud lookalike, with the same trimmed white beard and natty British three-piece suit as the celebrated analyst—all subtle visual references to the fact that Landor, born Landauer in Munich, Germany, in 1913, was not a San Francisco native but a refined European émigré. "Like me, Walter came from an assimilated, German Jewish family," says Irina Bosner, a close family friend. "He was the quintessential immigrant, absorbing the culture everywhere he went. Yet never quite belonging anywhere."

In 1931, young Walter was sent to England to pursue his art education. During his first year, he changed the spelling of his name when he happened upon a London street named after Walter Savage Landor, a nineteenth-century English writer. It was the first time, but not the last time, he would fix a name. During his life, he was often called upon by clients to come up with names for products, concepts, and brands. Today, Landor Associates is famous for its "naming" expertise—a skill much in demand in a world in which big corporations must negotiate cultural nuances across international boundaries. Disney's "Touchstone," Delta's "SkyMiles," FedEx's "The World On Time," and AT&T's "Lucent" are some of the carefully scripted words created by Landor Associates.

With his new British name, Landor adopted a well-tempered English manner. Years later, in San Francisco, he would charm everyone with his so-called "distinctive European demeanor," an expression that conveyed the slight confusion his friends, employees, and clients felt when trying to identify the specific ethnic origin of his natural warmth, his quiet urbanity, his low voice, his slight accent, and his impeccable elegance.

In England, where he enrolled at London University's Goldsmith College School of Art, Landor quickly outgrew his Munich design influences—Bauhaus but also Werkbunk, the German equivalent of the Arts and Crafts Movement. A quick study, he became, at age twenty-two, founding partner, with Misha Black and Milner Gray, of Industrial Design Partnership (IDP), the first industrial design consultancy in England. In 1939 he came to the United States as part of the design team for the British Pavilion at the New York World's Fair. He fell in love with San Francisco while traveling across the country to familiarize himself with contemporary American industrial design. Upon learning that there were no designers in northern California, he decided to colonize the region. "My father knew how to make every situation work for him," says his daughter Susan, who worked with him for years. "He realized that he could be successful in this town because he could have it both ways: establish for himself a good life, one that blurs the line between work and play."

Right from the start, Landor drew people to him. Teaching at the California School of Fine Art (now CCAC), he attracted—and partied with—an artsy crowd of colleagues, students, painters, architects, and sculptors, among them his future wife, Josephine, still an artist today, and painters like Mark Rothko and Richard Diebenkorn, then unknown. "It was a struggle at the beginning," remembers Jo Landor. They married in 1940 and at first worked together from an apartment on Russian Hill. The couple had two daughters, Susan and Lynn. Early on, Walter decided that his specialty would be packaging. "He realized that he had a natural talent for designing things that appealed to the masses," recalls Jo.

After the war, between 1945 and 1951, Landor worked from a small rented office at 556 Commercial Street, on the edge of Chinatown, where, according to Phil Durbrow, a close associate of Landor's for decades, "a lot of art teachers had their studios." At the time, the art schools in the Bay Area were abuzz with young World War II veterans eager to get an art education. Durbrow remembers Landor telling him that when prospective clients came to visit, Landor would act as if he owned the premises, taking them up and down to meet the various artists in residence. If he got a job—and most of the time, he did—he farmed out the assignments to these ambitious freelancers.

From the start, Landor thought of himself as a talent broker. Rodney McKnew, who worked with Landor from 1947 to 1988, credits his boss's early successes to what he calls his peripheral vision: "His eye wasn't on the center that held everyone's attention, but off to the side where something far more interesting was going on." Adds Susan Landor: "My father was a master of encounters and meetings. He would sit with the clients and the designers and say nothing at first, listening in to everyone until he figured out the politics, the tensions, the possibilities. He only spoke when he had a clear take on the situation."

In 1951, Landor moved his operation to Bush Street, and, in 1956, to a small waterfront building on Pier Five. Photographs taken at the time show staff members at lunchtime, basking on a deck overlooking the water, the women in their pretty dresses and sunglasses, the men in shirtsleeves, holding fishing rods. "Walter's strategy was to create business by having a good time," says Durbrow, who joined the company in 1972, when the relaxed atmosphere was still a trademark of the Landor working environment. "Around the office, there were always eclectic young people and attractive girls with names like 'Wendy Darling' or 'Nancy Love.' They were part of Walter's cheerful entourage. You would bump into them on the decks, taking in the sun. Clients loved it!"

The move to larger quarters gave Landor a chance to focus his professional practice and establish his leadership in package design. He installed on the premises a mock retail environment to help designers and clients visualize the new packages in the real-life context of grocery shelves. "Back in the early days," Mim Ryan says, "designers did not try to understand consumers or get feedback from them. In the 1960s, eye-tracking and two-way mirrors were new to the marketing field." Hired in 1963 as a research analyst, she helped develop focus groups by creating a full-blown research department, including a large in-house supermarket, complete with two crowded aisles and a freezer case.

In 1964, Landor put the final touch on his brand image by buying an old ferryboat, restoring it, and moving his entire office in it. Anchored along Pier Five, the *Klamath,* as the boat was called, became his proud flagship. It was large enough to accommodate four design departments, a research area for focus groups, a new-and-improved supermarket environment, a photo studio, and a slide library. But just as important, the boat became the setting of the weekly Friday-night floating extravaganzas. Often organized to entertain clients, but just as often to keep the spirit of the place upbeat, the events attracted every celebrity who happened to be in town that night. As soon as the word was out that Tom Wolfe, Andy Warhol, Howard Gossage, the Grateful Dead, or Marshall McLuhan were expected, hundreds of Landor friends, clients, and protégés would show up to meet the impromptu guests of honor.

Landor drew people to him because he was interested in everyone, even critics who didn't necessarily agree with his design philosophy. "Walter wasn't an ego. He didn't need to leave his fingerprint on the work itself," explains Ryan. "He had a great tolerance for other people's eccentricities. He encouraged everyone to forge ahead and explore new ideas. He took the position that the work coming out of his office was a team effort, not a style statement."

Called by his critics "the guy who puts stripes on everything," Landor could layer colors over colors, cartouches over cartouches, and stripes over stripes like no one else. Though he didn't have a house style, what he had was an uncanny instinct for guessing what would appeal to consumers in any given situation. "His approach was humanistic," says John Diefenbach, who went to work for Landor between 1984 and 1989. "Walter was not in love with the Swiss International Style, he preferred warm, colorful designs. He knew what worked. He understood the appetite appeal of a product. After years of focus groups and consumer feedback, his taste was in perfect sync with that of the public at large."

Landor was a maestro. The last to come into a room (he liked to make an entrance by being a little late), he even looked like a conductor. But with everyone depending on his direction, his comments, and his approval, a lot of time was spent anticipating his next appearance—so much so that someone suggested the accounting department issue a job number for "Waiting for Walter."

His loose managerial style, which would eventually be his undoing, was actually a draw during the early years of the company's growth. Landor consistently attracted the best people in the business by creating serendipitous conditions in which everyone had a chance to work on the most interesting projects. "He gave young designers and veterans alike the opportunity to do their best work," says Kay Stout, who was hired in 1974. "Right out of school, you sat down and began to design next to someone twice your age."

Marc Gobé, of Desgrippes Gobé in New York, a leading branding firm, was a young, upstart designer in San Francisco in the 1970s. For the local Art Directors Club, he had organized a show of then-controversial Polish posters. "Walter Landor came to the opening with a dozen young people from his office," he recalls. "A recognized authority in the field, he was still interested in what was new and cutting edge. Right there, I decided to emulate him. I promised to myself to always take the time to mentor members of my staff." Michael Carabetta, now with Chronicle Books in San Francisco, worked for Landor in the late 1970s: "The first Thursday of the month, rain or shine, Landor made the rounds of the art galleries, taking us along, and gathering more people as we went."

But the times were already changing. John Diefenbach can almost pinpoint the exact moment when Landor lost his gumption—and with it control over the company he had created. It was at a meeting in the late 1970s, during which a young designer, freshly hired out of Yale, presented a rather clean and slick-looking design solution—something Landor would have usually rejected. "Walter preferred the fuzzy stuff as a rule," Diefenbach says. Expecting his boss to ask for something more flowery, Diefenbach couldn't believe it when Landor listened to the presentation and made no objections. "He went along with the general consensus that this staid approach was what the client needed. At that moment, the company changed." Instead of being driven by a perception of what consumers wanted, design decisions were now driven by what the client wanted. This was a major shift. Landor Associates was now poised for the 1980s—a decade that turned out to be the most profitable era for the company.

"The first generation of Landor executives were not as good as managers as the second generation," concedes McKnew. "We served Landor well, but we weren't 'suits.' We were emotionally involved. Our intuition was more developed than our proposal-writing skills."

For all his youthful enthusiasm, Landor was showing his age; the generation gap became more evident. In 1980, Phil Durbrow was surprised to discover that the man who had designed countless soft-drink cans and corn-chips bags had no concept of what fast food was all about. "Once we were running behind schedule and had no time for lunch," Durbrow says. "Walter wanted to stop at a good restaurant for a proper meal, as was his habit, but I argued that since we were so late, we'd better pull in front of a McDonald's and get a couple of hamburgers." Confronted with a burger, a Coke, and a straw, Landor had no idea how to proceed. When Durbrow explained to him how to eat the stuff, Landor took the packaging apart, and, with nothing short of glee, said "Brilliant!"

All those years, Landor had been an astute tactician, "but not a good strategist," says Durbrow. "He had never been a good manager and he didn't work as hard as we did." Rodney McKnew explains that while most business types were morning people, Landor was a night person, "working late, when no one was around, only interrupting himself for parties." Clay Timon remembers that Landor would sometimes vanish for two weeks at a time. "Then he would show up in the Paris office before disappearing again on one of his minisabbaticals."

Then there were all those unbillable hours wasted waiting for Walter to show up, the weekly bashes, the lavish presentations to clients. "Before I came to the company," says Diefenbach, "Walter used to propose up to 150 designs of beer bottles or cigarette packs to clients, all finished drawings!" Indeed, Landor seemed to care more about the fun, the designers, and the creative atmosphere than the bottom line. In contrast with Landor's old-world charm, Diefenbach, a charismatic man in his own right, was industrious and aggressive. Under his stewardship, the company became a truly international entity. Though it already had offices in Tokyo, Mexico City, and London, it now expanded to Washington, Chicago, Seattle, Hong Kong, and Paris. Internal reorganization was initiated, with teams working more independently and more efficiently. In what many consider an unnecessary blow to Landor's ego, the offices were moved out of the *Klamath* in 1987, to allow Diefenbach to upgrade the infrastructure and refurbish the interiors to reflect the splashy taste of the Reagan years.

To oppose John Diefenbach's ambitious drive, Landor would act dense during their discussions, as if he didn't get the point. The tug-of-war between them was painful to watch for employees who were loyal to Walter, but had to admire John's leadership qualities. "John was bound to run into problems," says Timon. "You can't take over the role of an icon."

Landor and Diefenbach would come out of their meetings together looking exhausted. Walter, always the gentleman, was trembling with repressed anger. John was cool and determined. Though the older man was still the star, it was clear to everyone that the younger man now ran the company. "We had made earning projections, and exceeded our expectations," explains Durbrow. "As a result of some previous financial arrangements, Walter made a lot more money than what was expected. John, who was getting sizable stock options all along, felt nonetheless that he did not receive the ego gratification he deserved."

In 1989, Diefenbach, by now president, CEO, and the main shareholder of Landor Associates, spearheaded a move to buy out Walter Landor. Later that same year, the company was sold to Young & Rubicam, and, according to Durbrow, "everyone did just fine." Diefenbach and Landor Associates parted ways. The new owners promised Walter Landor that they would complete the renovation on the *Klamath* and move the company back in it. But the reconditioning of the boat was indefinitely postponed. It soon became evident that Landor Associates would be permanently headquartered on Front Street—the silhouette of the ferryboat now only a quaint icon next to the company logo.

"Walter Landor's goal was not to make money but be surrounded with people who were different," notes Durbrow. Susan Landor agrees: "My father was a shrewd businessman, but he was never greedy. He was not impressed by the fact that everyone in the 1980s made buckets of money. He cared more about the future of the company he had created." On his tombstone, she says, he wanted the words: "I could not have had a better time."

Landor died in 1995 after a series of strokes, at the age of eighty-one, but today his brand is still very much alive. The firm he spent fifty-four years nurturing remains in good hands. New clients who come to one of the twelve Landor offices are shown pictures of the ferryboat and told about the man who championed the idea that understanding consumers and getting their feedback was critical to the design process and the branding of products. Apparently, they are even told about "Captain Walter" and the wild parties on the boat. But whether or not this means anything to them is your guess and mine. As the saying goes, you had to be there.

I was there briefly, in the mid-1980s, living in San Francisco. Walter Landor and his boat were part of the local folklore. One rainy Friday night, a friend suggested I meet him on the *Klamath*, with the promise that we would go out for a drink later, after the party.

The boat was rocking and the place was mobbed. In the push, I couldn't find my friend. I didn't bump into anyone I knew and soon became self-conscious. As I was thinking about leaving, an older gent, who had probably noticed my discomfort, came to my rescue. We began to chat, and in the course of the conversation, I asked him how he came to be here. "I am Walter Landor," he said. "I don't know anyone here, and it's too noisy. Let's go out for a drink."

Now, I thought, wait a minute. He was married and I was single, and his reputation as a flirt was as much part of the local lore as his boat and his prestigious clients. But I was young and reckless back then, so I said, why not? We sneaked out of the party and he told me to get in my little Mazda and follow him to a bar he knew. A notoriously bad driver, he headed toward the Golden Gate Bridge at the wheel of his classic Mercedes coupe convertible. With the rain obscuring my windshield, I had trouble keeping up with him. When we crossed into Marin County, he boldly took for the hills.

At long last he pulled in front of what looked like a deserted Irish bar, an unlikely vision in this pristine and bucolic part of the world. Cold, wet, and somewhat peeved, I slunk on a stool next to him at the bar. We settled down, ordered beers, and resumed our chat. He seemed genuinely interested to hear about my work, my life, my daughter, my family. He was a great listener indeed, with a knack for making you feel special. Watching the city twinkle in the distance over his shoulders through the window, I realized that this was one of those moments when life makes sense: you sit in a funky old bar in the rain with a nice little fellow with a bow tie, while somewhere down there, by the bay, the party is still going on.

Véronique Vienne is the author of short essays on culture and lifestyle and has written The Art of Doing Nothing, The Art of Imperfection, *and* The Art of Growing Up, *published by Clarkson Potter in 1998, 1999, and 2000. Also available is a collection of her design essays,* Something to be Desired, *published by* Graphis *in 2001.*

Originally published in Graphis, *May/June 1999.*

ELLE

Les nouvelles lois de l'accord
MODE – BEAUTÉ

Jupes raccourcies : Jambes vedettes

Couleurs, tissus : maquillage

N° 409 - 5 OCTOBRE 1953 - **76 Pages - 50 Frs**
Suisse : 1 fr. s - Canada : 25 cents

HÉLÈNE GORDON-LAZAREFF: THE TSARINA WHO WAS *ELLE*
Véronique Vienne

Hélène Gordon-Lazareff used to say that women who understand how men look at them will spend all their life sipping champagne on sunny terraces. And, indeed, *ELLE*, the smart-looking, weekly fashion magazine she created in Paris in 1945, showed war-weary French readers how to be that fantasy creature—the attractive and sympathetic woman men dream of meeting on the terrace of a chic resort hotel.

To capture this fizzy image on paper, Gordon-Lazareff, whose first name, Hélène, is pronounced "*ELLE*-n" in French, surrounded herself with men who were in love with her—and with female employees who adored her. Frank Horvart, a photographer who calls her "one of the most remarkable personalities in the magazine world," explains that there was almost no difference between *ELLE* and Hélène. "She identified with her readers to the point of never worrying about what they wanted, convinced that what was right for her couldn't be wrong for them."

Russian-born, pert and petite, Gordon-Lazareff was passionate about everything. "You have to love the people you are with," she used to say. "It's the only way to look natural." The "tsarina," as her staff called her affectionately, could only do well what amused her. It worked for her. She had an uncanny instinct for picking—or creating—the next star or the next trend. In 1947, she embraced Dior's then unpopular New Look. In 1950, she launched Brigitte Bardot, still completely unknown, by featuring her on the cover of *ELLE*. In 1952, she hired Françoise Giroud, a dedicated feminist who later founded the French weekly news magazine *L'Express* and became a prominent political figure. In 1958, she promoted Coco Chanel's comeback, even though, at the time, the French press snubbed the famous Mademoiselle. In 1965, she adopted designer Courrèges and his all-white futuristic vision. And week after week, she published articles by controversial female writers such as Colette, Simone de Beauvoir, Marguerite Duras, and Françoise Dolto.

I met Madame Gordon-Lazareff a couple of times in the early 1960s, when, as a high school student, I worked as a summer intern in the *ELLE* art department. I was mesmerized by her presence, much larger than her diminutive size, and by her ability to empower her entourage. The bright journalists, fashion editors, and designers who worked for her were brazenly opinionated (no one was ever fired for disagreeing with her), yet still flexible. On closing day, they almost relished the moment their tiny boss would walk into their office and say, with a glint in her eyes, "I've got a great idea: Let's change everything!" How could you argue with someone who had her finger on the pulse of one million readers?

"We all had a crush on her," says Peter Knapp, the Swiss artist and photographer who was art director of *ELLE* between 1954 and 1966 and who established the magazine's deliberately modern graphic signature. "She was intelligent, in touch with people and events, and a great judge of talent." She hired Knapp at a time when the magazine was a runaway success but needed revamping to keep up with the expectations of both readers and advertisers. "She had a good eye and knew that Swiss graphic design would be the defining style for the magazine," he explains. "She hated everything trivial, cute and fussy—everything *kiki*, *coco*, *cucu* as she used to say in slang." Trained at the famous Zurich art school, in the Bauhaus tradition, Knapp, with Gordon-Lazareff's support, developed for *ELLE* an elegant grid system, a restrained sans-serif typography, and a bold layout approach.

But she had another compelling reason for choosing Knapp as art director. "She could tell that I was a fan of the opposite sex—that I looked at women more than at their clothes," he says. "She wanted me to give her magazine the imprint of a straight man's sensibility." One of Knapp's contributions was to assemble a team of male photographers—David Bailey, Guy Bourdin, Fouli Elia, Robert Frank, Mark Hispart, Frank Horvart, Helmut Newton, Uli Rose, and many more—who extolled femininity as defined by men in love with women. Not surprisingly, the fashion spreads were upbeat, friendly, youthful, and seductive. "In the rarefied fashion context of the time," insists Knapp, "this was a revolution."

This strategy brought the weekly circulation of *ELLE* from six hundred thousand in 1954 to one million in 1960. One French woman out of six was a regular *ELLE* reader. I was one of them. I became dependent on my Monday fix, too—on this appreciative masculine gaze focused on my gender. Knapp's clean delivery made me feel smart, open-minded, and innovative. Seduced as I was by the heterosexual zest displayed on the fashion spreads, I never questioned the magazine's ultimate motives.

Knapp's smart, cutting-edge design, while fostering a perception of avant-gardism, masked the subtle sexist subtext of the editorial message. How to attract and please a man was the driving force behind most of the articles. Keeping house, cooking, sewing, knitting, shopping, and taking care of children were celebrated. And though French people love to argue about politics, the magazine dodged the topic. In 1945, French women voted for the first time, but the magazine's only comment was to tell readers what to wear to the polls. And year after year it alluded to political events by describing in detail the wardrobes of the wives of presidents and heads of state. Under Françoise Giroud's influence, the coverlines and headlines often asked provocative questions, about everything from abortion to adultery—but the answers were always deeply conservative.

ELLE's moniker was "The Magazine for Women Men Admire." (In French, there is a double entendre: *Le journal des femmes que les hommes regardent* also means "The Women's Magazine Men Admire"). Through the years, a growing number of men confessed that they indeed liked to flip through the pages of *ELLE* to "check the fashion." They got hooked, with most of them becoming fashion connoisseurs. To this day, in department stores and boutiques, French men routinely walk right into fitting rooms with their female companions to advise them on the choice of a garment—evidence of how comfortable they are with designer labels, styles, and trends, and how much women welcome their educated opinion. The best-kept fashion secret of French women is the fact that the men in their life, thanks to *ELLE* magazine, feel that they are part of the seduction charade.

Today, there are sixteen international editions of *ELLE* magazine, including Japan, Korea, and China, as well as Australia, Brazil, Italy, USA, and Great Britain. With only a few exceptions, they all have adopted the original French graphic format as defined by Knapp almost fifty years ago. The magazine has become a global brand, with well-defined visual cues, such as bright white paper, cheerful color photography, lavish fashion spreads featuring models who are sexy, though not sexual, and clean, sans-serif typography. And most of the design rules so dear to Gordon-Lazareff are still respected. Namely: Never show a photograph without a caption; never start a story at the bottom of a page; never interfere with the readability of the text; and always use boldface for heads and subheads.

In the history of magazines, few founding editors have had such a lasting influence on their publication. Yet, when you call the public relations department of the New York office of Hachette-Filippachi, the company that acquired *ELLE* in the early 1980s, and ask for press clips on Hélène Gordon-Lazareff, no one knows who you are talking about. In Neuilly, France, where the French branch of *ELLE* is headquartered, you have to spell her name three times over the phone before the head of publicity gets it. And when eventually you obtain permission to sift through old issues of French *ELLE* in the cramped research library, the nice lady at the desk assumes that you are a graduate student working on some obscure Ph.D. thesis.

Why is the "tsarina" so completely forgotten? Why is no one interested in who she was—her persona, her spirit, and her contribution? Could it be that folks who run *ELLE* magazine today are simply jealous? Indeed, when Gordon-Lazareff officially retired from the magazine in 1972, the weekly circulation was still a cool million. By the time she died of Alzheimer's disease in 1988, it had dropped to a mere 370,000. To understand why such a talented woman is today cast as a nonentity, I decided to dig through her personal life in search of an answer for such a willful omission.

• • •

Hélène Gordon was born in 1909 in Rostov, Russia, into a well-to-do Jewish family. Her father, Boris Gordon, a sophisticated man who loved the arts, owned a prosperous tobacco company, a small theater, and a literary newspaper. The rich little girl was raised by a British nanny, who taught her to speak English. Thanks to Miss Woodell, Hélène, years later, living as a refugee in New York during World War II, was able to adapt effortlessly to the American culture, even getting a job as a reporter at the *New York Times*. Though Slavic by birth and temperament, she was forever under the spell of all things Anglo-Saxon.

In 1917, at the onset of the Bolshevik revolution, the Gordons fled to Turkey. Eventually, they ended up in Paris, their wealth somehow intact. Both intelligent and frivolous, Hélène thrived in the White Russian milieu of the French capital. Spoiled by her parents, she manifested early on a pronounced taste for expensive clothes and adoring young men. Naturally self-confident, she felt nothing was impossible. As an adult, she kept this fearless outlook. "She sincerely believed that women were equal, if not superior, to men," remembers Knapp. "That's why she wasn't much of a feminist. She never understood why women wanted to fight for something they already had."

A brilliant student in high school, well-read in French, English, Russian and German, Mademoiselle Gordon entered the Sorbonne after graduation to pursue a degree in ethnography. In the midst of it all, she managed to get married, have a child, get divorced, and go on a mission to Sudan, in Northeast Africa, to study the life of the Dogons, one of the last primitive tribes of the Sahara. According to Denise Dubois-Jallais, a poet who worked at *ELLE* as a journalist, Hélène Gordon perfected in the African desert the observation skills she used later when deciphering the manners and idiosyncrasies of French culture. In *La Tzarine,* the only published biography on Gordon-Lazareff, author Dubois-Jallais writes, "All the elements of her brand of journalism were in place. To listen. To go see for yourself. To note the details . . . To see the big picture . . . To be precise. Not to jump to conclusions . . . To work as a team. Never to take no for an answer. And to be ready to revise your world's view, if need be."

Upon returning from her African expedition in 1936, Hélène Gordon met her soon-to-be husband, Pierre Lazareff, a young and talented journalist who ran *Paris-Soir,* a progressive evening newspaper. Though born and raised in Paris, he was a Russian Jew like her. But more than their origins, what they had in common was a ferocious ambition. It was love at first sight—a love that lasted all their lives, although their sexual intimacy was short-lived. In the French tradition, they stayed devoted to each other in public and private while having affairs—with Hélène flaunting lovers too numerous to be counted.

In 1940, with France defeated by Hitler, Hélène, with her new husband Pierre and her daughter Michèle, then ten years old, escaped to New York. Fluent in English, she quickly found work, first at *Harper's Bazaar*, where she met Diana Vreeland and legendary art director Alexey Brodovitch, and at *Vogue,* where she was exposed to the formidable Carmel Snow. These American editors became her role models, though she liked to tell that she learned her métier and paid her dues as a journalist at the night desk of the *New York Times,* where she was in charge of writing and editing the women's page.

Pierre Lazareff, so articulate in French, never managed to overcome the language barrier in the United States. While his wife was busy absorbing the finer points of fact-checking (a practice still unknown today in France), he frittered time away with other illustrious French refugees, among them Antoine de Saint-Exupéry, author of *The Little Prince.* The painful discrepancy between their careers only deepened the sentimental gulf between them. While Hélène was walking down Broadway, developing in her mind the format of the women's magazine she would launch in France as soon as the war was over, Pierre, on the edge of despair, was considering suicide.

In 1944, as soon as Paris was liberated, Pierre was back in his hometown. In no time he was his old self again, as editor-in-chief of *France-Soir,* the postwar incarnation of the progressive evening paper he had created in 1935. From 1944 to 1972, when he died of cancer, he remained one of the most respected men in French journalism, the big boss of the most popular French daily paper. "The first duty of a journalist is to be read," he used to say. The *France-Soir* office, in the heart of the Paris garment district, at 100 rue de Réaumur, is now a landmark, with the small alley in front of the building named after Pierre Lazareff, a man remembered for using his considerable charm and intelligence to get the story first.

To convince his wife to leave New York and join him in Paris, Lazareff quickly raised money for her to start the magazine of her dreams. He made room for her on the fifth floor of the *France-Soir* building, setting the stage for what would become the most talked-about his-and-her journalistic venture: Pierre and Hélène; the newspaper and the magazine; the couple that literally *made* news.

Before leaving New York, Hélène Gordon-Lazareff arranged to have the first fifteen covers of *ELLE* shot by American photographers, with color film she knew was not available in Europe. "She was the first to master color photography, still unknown in France," said Françoise Giroud. Color photography—with models wearing bright outfits and vibrant accessories—is still the trademark of *ELLE* magazine. As the French saying goes, "When there is color, there is life."

The first cover of *ELLE*, an instant success at the newsstand on Monday, November 21, 1947, featured a sophisticated blond model in a chic, bright red, fitted military jacket, sporting a top hat and an amused smile on her face. In her arms, she is holding a squirming calico cat. Unexpected and charming, the photograph was quintessential *ELLE* style: not a look, but an attitude. More dash than cash. High fashion made accessible to the woman in the streets.

"Hélène never made women feel inferior," says Frank Horvat. "In contrast, most fashion magazines today, including *ELLE*, are too clever. They give readers the impression that they are not good enough—too fat, too old, too uncool, too outmoded, too this, too that."

Antoine Kieffer, who worked with Knapp at *ELLE* in the late 1950s before going to *Marie Claire,* agrees. "The editorial content was people-oriented. Hélène liked to give parties. Her magazine was like her parties: done with flair, with everyone mingling and having a good time."

In France, *ELLE* is still a weekly magazine, "but it looks like a monthly," says Knapp. "It's no longer spontaneous. There is too much second-guessing. It has retained the clean graphic signature of the early days, but the message is not what Hélène would have called 'feminine.'"

Hélène Gordon-Lazareff slipped into oblivion long before the end of her life. In 1968, during the student revolt in Paris, she already showed signs of memory loss. Maybe the unrest in the streets reminded her of how she was forced to flee Russia in the middle of the night in 1917, and how, again, in 1940, she had to escape hastily to save herself and her family. By 1972, she was a mere shadow, wandering aimlessly in the hallways of the magazine she had created as her alter ego. People couldn't help but remember the two-line poem French surrealist poet Philippe Soupault, one of her many talented lovers, had written for her in 1930: "Little me, little smoke/And oblivion in a wool dress . . ."

It would be a sad story indeed if it wasn't for all the women happily sipping champagne on sunny terraces. Take my word for it: there is nothing like it.

Originally published in Graphis, *July/August 1999*

194

A RETROSPECTIVE: HERBERT MATTER

Armin Hofmann

Herbert Matter, born in Engelberg, Switzerland in 1907, studied painting in Geneva, Paris, and under Fernand Lèger. After designing a famous series of posters for the Swiss tourist office, he went to New York in 1936, working there for leading magazines, Knoll and others. He was a professor of photography at Yale University (1952–76), has had major one-man exhibitions in the USA and Europe, was accepted into the Hall of Fame of the Art Directors Club in 1977, and received a Guggenheim Foundation Fellowship in photography in 1980. He lives in New York. —Editor

The personality, work, and career of Herbert Matter might well furnish stimulation and encouragement for a younger generation that is beginning to question the motives, aims, and consequences of design more critically than was formerly the custom; but they would also supply plenty of food for thought.

Born in Engelberg, a Swiss mountain resort, Herbert Matter soon left the confined life of his native village to go to Geneva and study painting at the Ecole des Beaux-Arts. He continued these studies in Paris, where he was lucky enough to meet Fernand Lèger and Amédée Ozenfant. His confrontation with Lèger's work, philosophy, and working methods was no doubt a major event in Matter's life and helped to decide his artistic evolution. Even though he moved gradually away from painting to photography and graphic design, the criteria that he had learned to apply to painting were to retain their validity throughout his later life.

To understand Herbert Matter's espousal of applied art, we must remember that in the thirties graphic design seemed to offer a widening of creative scope rather than any limitation. His meeting with A. M. Cassandre and Le Corbusier may also have led him to see the mastering of problems affecting daily life as the more urgent task. In New York, which soon became his second home, he found the wide field of activity that best suited his temperament and that still keeps him on his toes. As in Paris, he soon established contact with a circle of friends that included the painters of the New York scene in 1960, Jackson Pollock, Willem de Kooning, Franz Kline, Philip Guston, Alexander Calder, and others. Among them he found confirmation of his own intentions and aims, he discussed his work on new projects with them and began to be aware of the great importance of the teaching he had already embarked upon.

Herbert Matter is in many ways—as a graphic designer, a photographer, a filmmaker, a teacher, a critic—an exception to the rule. If the aspect of his work, as presented here, that first surprises the observer is his insistence on clean design, on clarity of utterance, on the original use of lettering and image, it must be added that he also harbors a deep mistrust of everything specious and superficial.

He endeavored from the very first to close the gap that threatened to open between the higher aims of art and the lower standards that to many seemed adequate for the everyday uses of applied design. He was uniquely successful in giving the artistic development of photography a place in his graphic activities and in ensuring its validity in practical life. He sought with a perseverance equalled by very few of his colleagues the narrow and difficult path between the shaping area we tend to think of as fine art and that we have come to connect with the requirements of modern advertising.

Design formulations of such experimental verve as we find in the posters for the Swiss National Tourist Office, in the *Knoll* advertisements, and in the brochures done for a printing house would have been unthinkable if the aim had been merely the maximum economic effect. In the course of his years in New York, a conception based on a humanist philosophy of how modern man should react to word and image took an ever more distinct form in his mind. It was on the strength of this vision of his that he made the very finely conceived Calder film, that he began the preparatory work for the educational film about Buckminster Fuller, and that he compiled the magnificent book on Alberto Giacometti and perfected his photographic work.

Although Herbert Matter left his home country unconditionally in his early youth, it would be quite wrong to interpret this as a flight. On the contrary, it seems as though—just like Giacometti—he was better able in the far-off city to grasp and process the deep impressions the mountain world had left upon his spirit. In his character, his outward appearance, and his behavior Herbert Matter remained a son of the mountains—quiet, modest, thorough, and very critical. These are no doubt the qualities that made him such a success as a professor at Yale University, for apart from his high qualifications as a photographer, he was able to reply to the ever-repeated questions of his students as to which was the right path to take with the example set by his own life. As a teacher he has always been revered and loved; as an artist and photographer he ranks among the pioneers.

Armin Hofmann, an exemplar of "Swiss" design, taught design at the Allegemeine Gewerbeschule in Basel and the School of Art, Yale University, New Haven.

Originally published in Graphis, *May/June 1981.*

MEMORY ENERGY DESIRE BEAUTY FANTASY RISK JOY CHANGE 1989 PASSION IRONY CHAOS

FROM DAN FRIEDMAN 2 FIFTH AVENUE NEW YORK NY 10011

DAN FRIEDMAN: THE DESIGN WORLD'S FAVORITE ENIGMA
Steven Holt

There is no one else quite like Dan Friedman—no body of work like his, and no story quite like his. The diversity of his work invites and deserves close, almost curatorial, attention. Friedman the person requires the same scrutiny, too, because he and his work are inextricably linked in a sense that few, if any, contemporary practitioners are. Like the peoples of earlier, primal cultures who did not separate art out of their daily lives, Friedman attempts to fuse art into every activity; it becomes his way of living, breathing, and doing even the simplest things.

Yet, for all this wonder, Friedman received only peripheral attention in the 1980s. He was invited to conferences, but the feeling there was that no one really knew what to make of him. There was something in his work—and him—that resisted inspection, that somehow deflected our most insistent gaze. I think back to one of our earliest conversations where we had a discussion about the importance of conspiring against our own identities. In 1984, this was a new idea to me, but to Dan, it was history; he had conspired against his identity since the 1970s—the legendary years when he worked as a corporate graphic designer, played the role of the young and gifted professor at Yale, and was married to April Greiman.

Today, Friedman is arguably the most enigmatic man in graphic design.

Back in the 1970s, Friedman was clearly on the high road to Fame, Money, and Power (the late twentieth century's equivalents to Life, Liberty, and the Pursuit of Happiness). He was a star, working at the best places with the best people, and producing much-heralded work. But the Cleveland-born Friedman did something no one expected: he switched lanes, changed direction completely, and turned inward to question the very conditions under which modern graphic design existed. Ultimately, he left it all; he just jumped on the exit ramp and waved good-bye to the convoy of highly logical, award-winning, two-dimensional work he had achieved at the prominent firms of Anspach Grossman Portugal and Pentagram.

That work is gone now, but not entirely forgotten. Along with Friedman's work from the early 1970s, it lives on occasionally in essays, books, and exhibitions, a testament to the growing efficacy of design historians everywhere. It also stands the test of time as a tribute to Friedman's own academy-bound, capital "E" Education: the Carnegie Institute of Technology, followed by stints at two of Modernism's temples, the Hochschule für Gestaltung in Ulm, West Germany, and the Allgemeine Gewerbeschule in Basel,

Switzerland. Friedman himself says, "I consider myself to be an Eternal Modernist, a Radical Modernist. I am too troubled by post-Modernism to be anything else."

Friedman's relationship to Modernism has continued to evolve, particularly over the last twelve years. Since the late 1970s, Friedman has worked in furniture and art-based product design more than graphics, although he has taken the occasional project. Not surprisingly, Friedman has found greater acceptance of this shift in his work in Europe—particularly in France (a WilliWear store, the Neotu gallery), and Italy (he has an established ongoing relationship with Alessandro Mendini as well as the avant-garde Alchimia group)—where the idea of the interdisciplinary designer dates back at least as far as da Vinci.

In working increasingly on furniture and objects, Friedman has very often slipped between the cracks of media coverage. His work was too three-dimensional for graphics publications, too arty for most design publications, not technical enough for the crafts publications, and too functional for the art journals. Friedman criticized the graphics field as well, and many were less than inclined to discuss, let alone publish, his work. Friedman also pursued an approach—a series of questions (akin to the way Robert Venturi and Denise Scott-Brown question notions of architecture and the environment)—rather than a style, a series of answers (akin to the way Phillipe Starck creates buildings, furniture, and objects with a distinctly related wave motif), too. Approaches are concerned with questions and with what lies beneath the surface; styles are the surface.

The key to understanding this changeover from answer-oriented tasks to probing-question-based work was Friedman's decision to pursue projects of personal, rather than professional, meaning. In shifting so, Friedman's life has taken on the dimensions of an experiment rather than a career. A paramount concern for meaning and awareness defines all of Friedman's projects since the late 1970s. While his contemporaries geared up (and lined up) for mega-dollar corporate-identity jobs, Friedman chose a different route. Already familiar with many of New York's artists, creators, and nightclub regulars, he began drawing inspiration from the way that they challenged norms with their almost folk-art-like obsession for fashion, color, coverings, and surfaces of all sorts. In particular, Friedman met Keith Haring, and began a relationship that continued until the artist's death. Haring was Friedman's opposite—intuitive, facile, spontaneous, and unschooled in design—and these qualities struck Friedman's imagination, so much so that Friedman designed the catalog for Haring's historic, first-ever exhibition (held in 1982 at the Tony Shafrazi gallery in SoHo, New York). The irony was delicious, even palpable: Friedman, the perfectionist packager of mainstream corporate identities, created an entire work on an unknown urban graffitist *before the show ever opened*, breaking all the rules. When Haring died in 1989, he and Friedman were at work on a major book of the artist's work in the '80s. Today, Friedman acknowledges Haring's primacy as an artist but also calls him "one of the most interesting graphic designers of the decade."

Friedman encourages others to stretch the rules, too. In lectures, Friedman is known for rebuking designers "who are the janitors of the corporation, [who] clean up after the company's visual messes"; the implicit message being that designers must create the conditions under which they work, not just accept them. Friedman notes that "Modernism forfeited any claim to a moral authority when designers sold it away as corporate style," and he asks us to also question why this is so. As Friedman has come to believe that design is more and more the trusted, well-compensated handmaiden of American industry ("a dangerous idea") and less and less a socially innovative agent of change, he has gravitated toward the art community, "a place where people are dealing with social issues—and having more fun."

This has not made Friedman popular with many designers, but Friedman insists that his work, besides being more fun, "is the logical outcome of a Modern impulse gone wild." Since these words are so loaded, it's easier to view his work as a meeting between competing sensibilities. On the one hand, there is the early Friedman as represented by an industrial (direct-from-the-academy) modern aesthetic, and, on the other hand, there is the later Friedman as represented by an intuitive (straight-from-the-streets) folk tradition. In his best work from the late 1980s, for example, his early pureness meets the later obsessiveness head-on. Projects such as his Deste Foundation catalogs or his screens fairly crackle with the unleashed energy of the illusion between new and unfamiliar.

The difference comes down to this: in the 1970s, solving the problem well was sufficient reward for Friedman; in the 1980s, he discovered he had to *enrich* the problem as well as solve it.

Very often, Friedman enriches the problem by bringing together opposites, anticipating visual richness because "there are always more ideas than space [so] complexity is a necessity." Take Friedman's own fifth-floor, Greenwich Village apartment. It is not so much an apartment in the traditional sense as it is a laboratory of three-dimensional canvases (walls, floors, ceilings, and objects) that he has periodically tinkered with since the late 1970s. Picture, if you will, Friedman, after a long day at The Pentagram Good Design Factory, coming home exhausted, and then slowly, rhythmically, and, later, almost compulsively applying colors, shapes, and street-scavenged forms around his home; the palette is astute and intense; the forms, more often than not, have a two-dimensional quality. It is quite an image.

What could have been an unmitigated visual disaster was brought under control bit by bit as Friedman mixed his found material, new work, and texture palette with selected applications of Modernism's stauncher compositional and balance-based principles. "Good design" was taken to its wildest extremes—exploded from within—and "excess with limited means" became a Friedman *leitmotif*, a way that he could enjoy the production of a new kind of visual coherence. Katherine McCoy visited the apartment in those early years: "I remember a corn plant held in bondage, scattered Basel archetypes," she says. "Clearly, Dan's turn toward other media allowed him to express himself more fully, to move ahead."

Progressive Architecture described the apartment's program as "a continual experiment in imagery and visual effect." What Friedman achieved was not a masterwork of spatial discourse, but a space that was hyperconcerned with surfaces. Friedman excelled at making surfaces nonsuperficial, at giving visual and intellectual depth to the thinnest of layers. While some visitors found the apartment chaotic, Friedman showed, if anything, that the study and practice of such chaos was purposeful and revealing of a higher level of visual order.

Steven Heller of the *New York Times* says of the industrial and folk-inspired apartment, "It is like Simon Rodia's Watts Towers—like living inside of an artistic framework, within pure expression." Friedman, in turn, says, "I created an extreme caricature of the beautiful modern American home in order to bring into question our notion of what a beautiful modern American home is." Precisely at this point, irony—along with optimism—became part of the Friedman equation. It is in this sense that Friedman became a practitioner *critically* exploring the possibilities of image—and object-making.

The reasons that Friedman embraces spontaneous street or folk cultures in his work are myriad, but it is clear that he believes "society has moved way ahead of the designer," and by tapping into what real people are doing, he hopes to reassert the designer as an artistic visionary. This, to him, is what modern design was really about. Like Walter Gropius, Frank Lloyd Wright, and Le Corbusier, who practiced design as a way of affecting culture and lifestyle, Friedman sees his profession "as a service and inspiration to humanity." Now, picturing Friedman, with his shaved head and grinning visage, among the pantheon of design heroes along with Gropius may seem funny as an image, but Friedman is clearly one of this generation's most original thinkers, and his most important work is yet to come. By refusing to accept the status quo and by looking at design in nonelitist terms, Friedman investigates what made Modernism worthy in the first place: its connection of design to real cultural changes.

The painting and "sculpting" of the walls, and the *assemblage* of the apartment used to create the unexpected from familiar elements, led to Friedman's first furniture pieces: folding screens. In retrospect, these were perfect vehicles to begin with, both graphic and three-dimensional. Done first for the Tony Shafrazi gallery in 1982, and then later for New York's Fun Gallery and on an ongoing basis for the Art et Industrie gallery, the screen has been an ongoing project for Friedman for almost a decade, realized by turns in both maximal and minimal ways. With the screen projects, however, the method of enriching a project by bringing together opposites that was first initiated in the apartment began to take on new and unexpected dimensions.

Rick Kaufman, director of Art et Industrie, recalls of Friedman's work: "Dan was the first to use a retro-futuristic, techno-primitive language—specifically, futuristic forms, grass skirts and fetishistic symbols." Again, Friedman brought together these opposites as a way of going beyond mere solutions, and he left this area after pioneering it, a pattern he has repeated numerous times. Friedman notes, "I aimed for clarity. Because I am a graphic designer, even in the furniture projects I am involved with the act of communication, with issues of legibility (which favors conventionality) and readability (which favors unconventionality)."

My favorite Friedman furniture pieces are probably those pieces that are the most graphic, the most language-oriented ones—the immediately readable pieces with words such as the hand-painted "TRUTH" on the front or the cutout wood letters that say "DREAM" on the sides. The words are carefully picked, overscaled, and they loom large on the pieces, filling panels in their all-capital, generic sans-serif type: these qualities make the TRUTH chair a seminal art furniture piece.

One of the best examples of Friedman's concerns for both personal meaning and social issues was the "ART AGAINST AIDS" logotype done for the American Foundation for AIDS Research. Done originally in black, white, and a pinkish flesh tone, the logo has since been seen in a number of manifestations, including rainbow-colored. The same all-capital letters from his furniture pieces are used again, and they stand out starkly, even ominously. Formally, the piece is successful but not revolutionary; the figure-ground relationship is neatly resolved, for example. But personally, Friedman has seen people dear to him contract the disease and die—Haring and Willi Smith among them, giving this project significance. Friedman is increasingly adamant about doing "Work that is true to the actual translation of the words 'pro bono,' work that is not necessarily for free but for the greater good of society."

One of Friedman's recent projects is a book called *Artificial Nature*, done jointly with art consultant Jeffery Deitch and sponsored by the Deste Foundation of Greece. It is a curious, stunning book that accompanies an exhibition of the same name, and it follows the little-known *Cultural Geometry*, a book done in 1988 as a catalog for an exhibition. In both books, found or anonymous images are juxtaposed with contemporary art pieces. Type is dropped into imagistic contexts in a way that is evocative of Barbara Kruger's work, yet distinctly different.

Friedman sees the books as "an expression of other ways to go, a direction based on content and not on form" (again a transcendence of the Basel/Ulm dogma). The reaction that the carefully culled images inure is almost archeological. "Some of the found images are actually more provocative than the art itself," notes Friedman, "so they extend and contrast with the art." This observation is reminiscent of the one made by author Philip Roth, who noted that he and his colleagues had trouble imagining anything as interesting and as bizarre as what was on the front page of the newspaper every day, so they began to use the news as a basis for their fiction.

The boundaries for Roth and Friedman between fiction and fact, normal and abnormal, synthetic and genuine, are ever more blurred. Juxtaposition between two extremes has become a large part of our daily life, and the fact that Friedman visually expresses this cultural fact of life renders his work all the more poignant. Friedman's use of juxtaposition is not only a way of commenting on the state of things, it is fundamentally attuned to how things are now. "We live in a culture which generates all kinds of recipes for how we should look. . . ." notes Friedman. "We are shown that everyone can aspire to various lifestyles, from the look of Ralph Lauren to the look of Guns 'n' Roses." Between the graphics, furniture pieces, and environments that Friedman has designed, certain elements repeat and cross back and forth. For example, elongated circles that assume a teardrop shape appear in elevation on his new limited-edition furniture for Neotu, in plan on his rolling satellitelike lighting piece, and on his postcard for Neotu of 1988. Even more, the circle, the sphere, and a pattern of three circular, often spherical shapes that modulate from big to small show up in almost every piece—as an absolute, as a symbol, as negative space, as a spiritual domain, as a bubble, as a shaved head, as a planet, and, most of all, as a Friedman signature—they appear in a diverse group of projects, including the Paris WilliWear showroom: the Gallimaufry poster; the year-end greeting cards; the three-dimensional, slightly Judy Pfaff-like wall pieces; and the TRUTH chair and other spaceshiplike furniture done for Art et Industrie. Friedman's spheres don't simply exist, they often seem to defy gravity or natural law, to be fixed preternaturally still; they also represent a bastion of order—for example, in the wall pieces, which teeter toward a certain assemblage-based chaos. Friedman is aware of the presence of symbols in his own work. "They are at the core of my visual identity, the basis for most of what I do in graphic design . . . and the core of every corporate identity project I did in the 1970s," he says. The symbolic assumes significance in Friedman's work because, in order to make things new, he must make them strange. Friedman's odyssey as a designer, after training in strict Modernism, has turned toward a more intuitive, symbol-oriented path. "I am trying to instill in contemporary objects what primal cultures always had: a spiritual dimension."

In fact, Friedman went to India on a spiritual journey in 1985 and 1986, and came back very taken by the place. The influence of a drastically different culture not only showed him other ways of expression, but allowed him to understand more clearly the larger condition of being an American at the end of the American century. Friedman has put himself in the position of being a filter for huge amounts of information, and, simultaneously, of being actively involved in sorting it all out. It also goes some way toward explaining Friedman's penchant for "mixing it up" because Friedman approaches his projects as both an artist and as an editor. As Heller said of Friedman, "He's of Renaissance character, without his foot in any one place."

Friedman believes, "Most graphic design now has to do with excessive formal manipulation, with the layering of text and image, and what I am more interested in is radical content, expressions of other ways to go." The irony is that Friedman had much to do with creating the conditions under which this layered, formalistic work—variously called California New Wave (or Pacific Wave), Cranbrook Style, Swiss Punk, and so on—developed as a major focus for graphic designers in the late 1970s and early 1980s. The 1990s are the time for Friedman to bring it all together, for him to create experiences, images, and objects that are fueled by Modernism, but that travel beyond. His investigation into the true radicality of early Modernism is beginning to manifest itself, and his best projects demonstrate an ergonomics that is more cultural than physical. Those who insist on claiming that Friedman's graphics are better than his objects miss the point. Friedman explored, exploded, and exported the canons of modern graphic design for all to see and use.

In so doing, he himself evolved more and more into a mutant, a man searching for meaning who fits in nowhere but has work everywhere. His inner self has followed a path toward personal awareness, heightened self-expression, and a sense of truth, while his outer self has ambitiously attempted what few now dare: to be avant-garde in several creative fields at once. He just finished the design of a book for Rizzoli on Italian design, he has finished a collection of sweater designs in France, his first limited-production furniture is out with Neotu and his next group is just coming out with Italian furniture leader Driade, he is working with Mendini on a project for Alessi, he continues to make art, and he is working toward his next furniture exhibition for Neotu in January. Such are the multiple perspectives enmeshed within Friedman's work that Art et Industrie's Kaufman described him this way: "It is as if a graffitist was sent to the Bauhaus to study primitive work from the vantage point of a spaceship."

Friedman cares passionately about what he does—he burns inside—and how many designers of any persuasion can any of us say that about? Far too many of us see Friedman's appearance, and label him our resident eccentric. But those who do take the easy way out miss the richness of his work and his ideas. Recently, an AIGA representative of a local chapter called Friedman up to ask him to lecture on his artwork; she was unaware that he was a graphic designer. Perhaps all of his conspiring against his image has worked too well. But by looking to the academy for rules that could be creatively managed, and by looking to the street for data that might be selectively interpreted, Friedman has provided us all with an interesting model for late twentieth-century designers. He doesn't fit in, but maybe the best designers of our wild and contradictory era shouldn't.

Steven Skov Holt is director of strategy at frogdesign, where he has been involved with building the company's identity. He is also the chair of the Industrial Design program at California College of Arts and Crafts in San Francisco. He is a former editor of I.D. *magazine.*

Originally published in Graphis, *September/October 1991*

SHOW

THE
MAGAZINE
OF
THE
PERFORMING
ARTS
$1.00
OCTOBER 1961

#1

BRENDAN
BEHAN

ROBERT
BENDINER

AL
CAPP

HAROLD
CLURMAN

BILL
DAVIDSON

LESLIE
FIEDLER

MARTIN
MAYER

JACK
RICHARDSON

ARTHUR
SCHLESINGER JR.

VIRGIL
THOMSON

KENNETH
TYNAN

THE BEST THEATRE

SATURDAY EVE

SEPT
16

A 108

THE VISUAL THINKER HENRY WOLF!
Michael Kaplan

After four decades as a design master, making the transition from Renaissance man to living legend has not been easy for Henry Wolf.

Henry Wolf's studio is an enviable space. Large and loaded with memories, it provides physical and emotional proof of a brilliant career. There's an equipment-laden photo area, drawing tables, and a few framed examples of the work that made him famous. On the walls of this former horse stable on Manhattan's Upper East Side are images of the designer/photographer/illustrator in his heyday: Wolf posing on the fender of his Rolls-Royce, Wolf as the center of a surrealistic self-portrait, Wolf goofing around with a pair of garden shears that seem poised to clip the tip of his nose.

In that last photo, he smiles. Right now, however, sixty-eight-year-old Henry Wolf scowls as he scrutinizes a poster that recently arrived in the mail. It is designed to hype an upcoming graphic design show at an art school in Massachusetts. The exhibit will feature none of Wolf's work, but exclusion is not what raises his ire. Staring at the kinetic design, the clashing text styles, and the overlays of color, he does a slow burn. "Look at this type!" Wolf exclaims at the graphics that run distressingly counter to the clean elegance that he spent his career pioneering. "They call Paul Rand a curmudgeon because he doesn't want to say that computer-generated stuff is good. But compare this to Paul Rand. Here there are lines going through the words, running in, running out, different kinds of type. The designers want to be unique—they don't want to be like anyone else—so this is what they come up with. This is the worst that I've seen."

Design-by-computer is done by people who don't understand the tools. There's no thinking. They can scan in pictures over one another, all different colors. It's like having 420 channels on television, and finding nothing that you want to see.

Wolf places the poster down on his desk, leans back in his chair, and looks tired of fighting an aesthete's uphill battle. "Design-by-computer is done by people who don't understand the tools," he says, allowing a sad laugh. "They sit down like a secretary at the typewriter. There's no thinking, they scan in pictures over one another, all different colors. It's like having 420 channels on television, and flicking the button but finding nothing that you want to see. And when I say this kind of stuff, people think that it's sour grapes. They think it's because I'm not doing it."

Wolf's disgruntled state is understandable. From the 1950s through the 1970s and into the 1980s, he reigned as a grand master of graphic design. He created cleverly stylistic looks for *Esquire, Harper's Bazaar,* and *Show* magazines; he shot and designed lucrative catalogues for Bloomingdale's, Saks Fifth Avenue, and I. Magnin; he produced some one hundred book covers and worked on a wide range of advertising and editorial assignments. Making the transition from Renaissance man to living legend has not been easy for Wolf. "It's difficult to see Henry at this point, feeling betrayed by the world after he's done so much good work," says Milton Glaser, a longtime friend and colleague of Wolf.

Likening the designer's natural sense of proportion to perfect pitch for a vocalist, Glaser adds, "Henry's work is about old values, scale, and refinement. People aren't interested in that any more; the style has changed from classical to confusion. Stay around long enough and it's inevitable that you get out of step. Very few designers remain in the rhythm of the times so long that they die on the job."

Rather than going gently into the night, Henry Wolf sits stolidly in his studio, waiting for the telephone to ring, coiled to spring out against philistines. These days, they tend to be people who aim to lowball him into accepting bargain-basement jobs. Following one such attempt from the editor of a small periodical, Wolf hangs up the phone and says, "They find something in my book and want to use it for free. Instead of paying me, they want to give me credit. F—k credit." Four decades ago, and light-years away from the above scenario, New York's publishing world was a magical place for Henry Wolf. That was when, in 1952, his life took on the quicksilver momentum that's most common in golden-boy players who suddenly find themselves on seemingly endless upward trajectories.

The blastoff happened after the twenty-seven-year-old Viennese-born designer got himself kicked upstairs at *Esquire* magazine, from the promotion department to editorial. Prior to that fateful event, he spent most of his days designing greeting cards and renewal forms (they went out to the magazine's advertisers and readers, respectively), making the best of the numbingly dull routine. One piece that particularly pleased Wolf was a promotional booklet that he had designed for the purpose of generating liquor advertising. It fell into the hands of Arnold Gingrich, the publication's legendary publisher and editor. He glanced at it, recognized something special in the layout, then wondered, "Why can't the magazine look like this damned book?"

Soon it did, as the nascent designer suddenly became *Esquire*'s art director. There Wolf enjoyed a six-year stint, revolutionizing the way the magazine looked and elevating the visual sophistication of its reader. The design became erudite, sexy, and unpredictable; illustrators were assigned to derive artistically challenging concepts from stories rather than to simply paint a picture that literally depicted a key sentence or two. A cover on the Americanization of Paris featured "powdered wine" being dumped into a glass of water—it drew readers to query as to where the metaphorical instant *vin* could be purchased—and stories opened with giant swaths of type.

The magazine resonated not only with Wolf's graphic designs, but with his ideas on style and substance as well. "Every month Arnold gave me four pages with which to do whatever I wanted," he recalls. "I could show Italian labels, French mystery games, magic tricks, *whatever*." He hesitates for a beat and contemplates what differentiated periodicals in the 1950s from those of today. "Magazines didn't cater to the lowest common denominator then," he continues. "Now everybody figures that Michael Jackson is a big deal, so they put him on the cover. Some of our covers had famous people, like Gina Lollobrigida, but for the most part it was to make a point or a joke—it was not just to show a picture that you've seen a hundred times."

The same aesthetic carried over to his art direction of *Harper's Bazaar* in 1958 and the great *Show* magazine (rivaled only by the revived *Vanity Fair* for taste and cutting-edge bravado) that he designed from scratch three years later. A confirmed art star before his fortieth birthday, Wolf began doing much of his own photography at *Show*. "It was just easier than asking somebody else to take pictures," he says modestly. "I'm not a great photographer, but I am a photographer who uses the camera to facilitate his ideas."

Following *Show*'s demise in 1964, Wolf entered into an incredibly productive period. During the next two decades he produced numerous photographs, illustrations, and designs for a diverse group of clients, working long hours and reveling in the creative momentum that begets more creative momentum. One afternoon he might have illustrated an *Esquire* story on the conflicts of being kosher (Wolf made an icy photograph of a Hasidic Jew turning his back to a pork-chop dinner), while the next day would be taken up with a high-concept cover for *New York* or *Holiday* magazine. "It was no big deal," he insists, looking at a photo/illustration effort for the travel publication. "I did that one in three hours. In the office there was a girl who had a nice body. I told her to take her clothes off and stand against the light. I put a salad bowl on her head and shot the photo. Then I drew in colorful Caribbean fruit."

Sitting with Wolf, going through the pages that mark his career like entries in some regal diary, it's easy to lose sight of precisely what it is that riles him up right now. After all, he's had his time, he's enjoyed a good run, and he's able to live comfortably for the rest of his life. Perhaps it is simply inevitable that he must adjust to the fact that his look has gone out of fashion, reckon with his own mortality, and realize that art directors now seek younger, trendier names; Wolf himself half admits to being guilty of that back when he was a hot player.

Milton Glaser puts it this way: "At one point, to paraphrase John Cage, no matter who you are, your work will be taken away from you. I don't think that you can adjust your sensibilities beyond a certain point. You make some accommodations, but the people who are endlessly adaptable are hacks. If you can last thirty or forty years and still have your work looking fresh, well, you're doing very well."

Wolf's designs have been influential enough to win him enduring respect within the graphic world. It is evidenced by the influence he's had on young designers like Fabien Baron, and by the students who flock to classes that he's been teaching at Cooper Union, the School of Visual Arts, and Parsons since the 1950s. Respect, however, is hardly what Wolf wants. "I'd rather be hated than respected," he insists. "If you're hated, then at least you exist. To a lot of designers today, I'm dead."

• • •

Though a talented eye has clearly remained with Henry Wolf—a recent series of nudes lives up to his design dictum of clean precision—his problem seems to be an inability or disinterest toward adjusting himself in less concrete ways. Like a typesetter who refuses to stop kerning, Wolf remains set in his methods—stylistically and technologically. Asked if he could learn to use a computer he replies that of course he could. Then Wolf peevishly adds, "But I don't need one in order to design."

Rather than seeing today as an exciting time of discovery, he seems to focus on the dark residue that stems from a society for which espresso is not only the drink of the moment but also the engine that drives its quick-clipping pop culture. "Design is indicative of society in general," he says. "They always do what sells. If the public wants violence, then you don't get Cary Grant. You get people with knives stuck in their eyes. You get art directors with their own press agents." Wolf shakes his head. "During my days at *Harper's Bazaar*, we didn't care about press—we cared only about doing good design."

When Henry Wolf looks back on his career and the times in which he's worked, he concludes that his own broad-sweeping changes coincided with those that resonated through society as a whole. In other words, the demise of his own positive vision collided head-on with that of the world's. "The Vietnam War marked the end of an era," he says. "The late 1960s was the end of optimism, and the end of believing in good work for its own sake. The end of the funny stuff." He hesitates for a moment. "We had the best days. But now they're gone."

Michael Kaplan is a New York–based journalist. He writes on topics that range from crime to travel to pop-culture to design.

Originally published in Graphis, *September/October 1990*

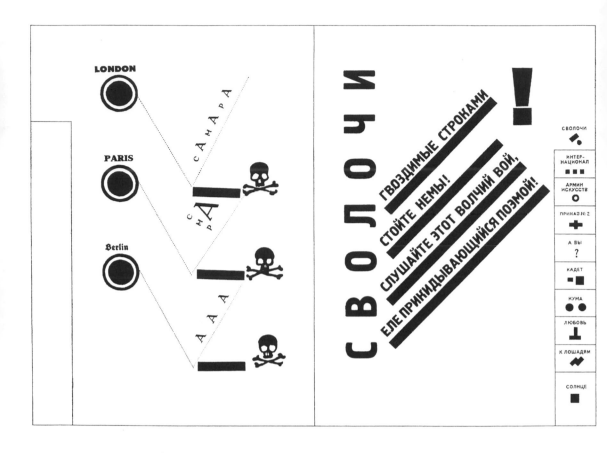

4. Avant-Garde

FOR THE VOICE
Philip B. Meggs

A chance meeting between a Russian poet and a Russian graphic designer in Berlin in the early 1920s led to the creation of a milestone in graphic design history. Late in 1921, the Russian constructivist El Lissitzky had traveled to Berlin in connection with a major exhibition of Russian art to be held there in 1922. Russia had been isolated from Western Europe by the battle lines of World War I and the turbulence of revolution, and this exhibition provided an early opportunity for Western Europeans to see works by Archipenko, Chagall, Lissitzky, Malevich, Rodchenko, and Tatlin. The new Soviet government had not yet turned against radically new art, and asked Lissitzky—whose German education and mastery of the language made him an ideal link between the two cultures—to stay in Germany and design a new trilingual publication called *Vesch* (*Object*) to introduce avant-garde Russian art to the West.

On October 8, 1922, Vladimir Mayakovsky, the leading poet of the Russian Revolution and early Soviet period, arrived in Berlin to join his mistress, Lili Brik. The Berlin office of Gosizdat, the Moscow State Publishing House, had decided to publish a collection of Mayakovsky's poems selected by the poet for reading aloud and titled *For the Voice*. Since Lissitzky was in Berlin, Mayakovsky recommended that he be commissioned to design and illustrate this volume. Their collaboration brought together two major creative forces in avant-garde culture. Both held the same ideas about Constructivism: Art should descend from the ivory tower to play a pivotal role in the restructuring of society; it should become a meaningful part of everyday life in the new socialist state.

Although Lissitzky and Mayakovsky had very different backgrounds, both had been closely associated with Moscow's avant-garde art and literature movements during the 1910s. Mayakovsky had been a teenage activist in the Social Democratic Workers' Party. The czarist regime jailed him repeatedly for subversive activity. While in solitary confinement in 1909, sixteen-year-old Mayakovsky started writing poetry. He was also keenly interested in art, and after his release, he attended the Moscow Art School. There, he joined David Burlyuk and a few others in the Russian futurist group and became its leading spokesman. The form and content of Mayakovsky's poetry became increasingly assertive and rebellious. Wearing greasepaint, a yellow shirt, and a radish in his buttonhole, he frequented cafés where he recited poems written to be deliberately offensive to bourgeois audiences. He sought to "de-poetize poetry" through stunning technical innovations and by adopting the crude language of the common people. His work was declamatory and often written specifically for dramatic public readings before large groups. When the Russian Revolution erupted, Mayakovsky became an ardent supporter of the Bolsheviks, writing stirring poems in support of the Revolution, the workers, and the peasants. After the Revolution, he became an ardent spokesman for the Communist party.

Lissitzky had traveled to Germany in 1909 to study architectural engineering in Darmstadt, then returned to Russia when war broke out in 1914. After working at a Moscow architectural firm, he was appointed, in 1919, to the faculty of the revolutionary art school in Vitebsk by the headmaster, Marc Chagall. The painter Kazimir Malevich, founder of the Suprematist movement, which advocated the supremacy of pure geometric form and color over traditional representation, also taught there. Under Malevich's influence, Lissitzky began to paint geometric abstractions called PROUNS, an acronym for the Russian phrase meaning "project for the establishment of a new art." In 1921, Lissitzky became head of the architectural faculty at the new Vkhutemas art school in Moscow. He combined the nonutilitarian formal language of Malevich with the ethic of the constructivist group, whose proclamations called upon artists "to construct" art and change the world instead of merely depicting it. Constructivist theory embraced applied design: It said, in effect, "Go to the factories, this is the only task for artists." In his work during the 1920s, Lissitzky emerged as a major force in modern graphic design, exerting a powerful influence upon the Dutch De Stijl group, the Hungarian Constructivist László Moholy-Nagy, and the Bauhaus.

For the Voice proved to be one of Lissitzky's most influential designs. Mayakovsky selected thirteen poems, and Lissitzky developed a 19-by-13.5-centimeter (approximately 7^{1}/$_{2}$ by 5^{1}/$_{3}$") format of sixty-four pages. He resolved to "construct" the book working solely with elements found in a letterpress printer's typecase: wood and metal types; rules, bars, and bullets; a few dingbats; and one old engraved image of an imperial eagle. Layouts were developed as a guide for a German typesetter who could not read or write a single word of Russian. The printing firm's staff became fascinated by *For the Voice* and its unique format and asked Lissitzky to translate parts into German so that they could understand it.

As with most graphic forms, the shapes and images Lissitzky used in *For the Voice* have a dual life: They are perceived optical phenomena as well as communicative signs functioning with other signs to form a message. Western designers unable to read Russian have viewed *For the Voice* as a masterly arrangement of forms, apparently unaware that Lissitzky was translating the pure forms from his mentor Kazimir Malevich's suprematist paintings into communicative signs. The broad influence of this book has been based solely on the impact of its visual aspect; Lissitzky's symbolic interpretations of the titles and texts of Mayakovsky's poems have not been comprehended by the reading public.

The cover of *For the Voice* reveals the resonance of the graphic approach used in the book. Mayakovsky's name runs horizontally and intersects the vertical placement of the title on a red bar. A large capital M composed of typographic rules balances the lower right placement of concentric circles.

Lissitzky illustrated the title page with a halftone reproduction of "Announcer," one of ten lithographs published in 1923 as a portfolio titled "Victory over the Sun." The book title and author are superimposed over the lithograph, and at the top left-hand page appear the words, "Constructor of the book El Lissitzky." This attribution was chosen with care, for Lissitzky did not feel that he illustrated or decorated the book in the traditional sense; rather, he saw his role as a designer who "constructed" the totality of the book in an architectural sense.

Mayakovsky dedicated *For the Voice* to Lili Brik. For the dedication page, Lissitzky designed an abstract eye which appears to look toward the viewer as a straight-on image while simultaneously appearing as a cross-sectioned side view. When read clockwise twice, the three Cyrillic letters placed around the eye image read, "I love."

Each poem begins with a double-page spread containing the title and Lissitzky's constructivist interpretation. Since the book was intended for oral presentations before audiences, Lissitzky wanted readers to be able to quickly find the next poem they wished to present without having to look it up in an index in the front of the book; thus, he designed a series of thirteen diecut tabs down the right-hand margin, enabling readers to move their right thumbs down to the title of the poem they wished to read and easily flip the book open to its title page.

The first poem in the book was written in 1918 and is titled "Left March" (Levy Marsh). It is dedicated to the Red Marines. The title appears on the right-hand page opposite an iconographic ship constructed of typographic elements and flying the Soviet flag. With "Left March," Mayakovsky found his tone as a revolutionary poet. Suddenly, his work gained a dynamic boldness with a brilliant series of short, staccato images emphasized by a thundering repetition: "Left! Left! Left!" When Russian sailors march, they chant "Levoi" ("left") over and over as their left feet hit the ground in unison. Mayakovsky used this as an auditory theme in the poem. A segment of the poem demonstrates Mayakovsky's new rousing style:

> Rally the ranks into a march!
> Now's no time to quibble or browse there.
> Silence, you orators!
> You
> have the floor,
> Comrade Mauser.
> Enough of living by laws
> That Adam and Eve have left.
> Hustle history's old horse.
> Left!
> Left!
> Left!

Whenever "Left March" was presented at a public poetry reading, the entire audience would rise to its feet each time the reader arrived at the refrain "Left! Left! Left!" In unison, they would raise their right arms and thrust their fists into the air, changing, "Left! Left! Left!" A kinetic excitement would fill the hall as participation forged a communal bond. The political implications of a call to march to the left were, of course, understood by all.

Lissitzky expressed the auditory theme of the poem graphically in the top left area of the left-hand page. A sequence of three marching legs is constructed from metal rules and printed in red, and "levoi" is set three times in black sans-serif type of descending size.

The second poem in the book is entitled "Our March" (Nash March) and was written by Mayakovsky for the only issue of the Futurists' newspaper, which appeared on March 15, 1918. This homage to those who risked their lives in the early stages of the Revolution begins:

> Beat your drums on the squares of riots!
> Keep your heads higher with the
> second deluge!
> We are going to wash
> the cities of the world.

The poem evokes city squares washed with the blood of martyrs who gave their lives in the struggle against the czarist regime. Lissitsky's large red square is not merely a decorative graphic element but a symbol of martyrdom during public demonstrations. Responding to the A and W in both words of the title, Lissitzky layered these letterforms to create a staccato graphic rhythm evoking the rhythmic beat of drums in the opening line. The typographic configuration below the large red square on the left-hand page demonstrates Lissitzky's delight in typographic play inspired by futurist poetry. By selecting either the top of the bottom vowel, one can read two messages: boy means "fight," and bey means "beat them." The placement of this element creates a lively counterpoint to the diagonal accent on the upper right-hand page.

The title of the third poem, "My May One," is presented as an emblematic typographic configuration, taking advantage of the similarity of the Russian words My and May—they are spelled MON and MAN, respectively—to create a symmetrical design in a circle evoking arm patches and insignia. This poem is a celebratory ode to the May Day holiday, which is very important to Russians for two reasons: It was designated as an International Labor Day by the 1889 International Socialist Congress; and it marks the end of the long, severe Russian winter. Since over 90 percent of the Soviet Union is above the latitude of Montreal, Canada, the arrival of May Day is a real cause for celebration.

The title of the fourth poem, presented vertically on the right-hand page, is a Russian slang word which has been translated as "Rabble," "Swine," or "Scum." This poem is a rabid propaganda attack upon the evil capitalists. The four lines of text set in bold red sans-serif type on the title page read:

> By the nailing of these lines
> Stop mute!
> Listen to this wolf,
> Howling of this weak poem!

On the left-hand page, dotted lines connect large dots, labeled with the names of major "capitalist" European cities, to skull-and-crossbones symbols from the typecase.

Lissitzky used a connotative typeface for each of the cities: a sans serif reminiscent of Edward Johnston's London Underground type; an old-style roman for Paris; and the black letter still being used in Germany for Berlin. (The Bauhaus did not begin its extensive use of sans-serif type and constructivist space until 1923, influenced in large measure by Lissitzky's Berlin work.) These diagonal lines are drawn at a sixty-degree angle to the edges of the page. In contrast, the diagonals on the right-hand page are at forty-five-degree angles—a differential that creates tension between the elements.

On the following page of text, two lines of type are separated from the body of the poem and pushed to the right of the page number. They read:

> You see?
> Behind the naked digit . . .

A large pointing-hand dingbat from the printer's typecase dominates this layout. This is graphic humor on Lissitzky's part, offering a visual pun by permitting both the pointing finger and the page number to function as "the naked digit" of Mayakovsky's poem.

The fifth poem celebrates "The Third International." This was an association of national Communist parties formed in 1919 whose stated purpose was to foment world revolution and transnational class war, and to promote what Lenin called "civil war, not civil peace." Lissitzky used two printer's rules to form a huge letter that becomes the T in the words "Third" and "International." On the left-hand page, an overlapping complex—composed of a hammer, a sickle, and two roman numeral threes—forms an appropriate symbol. The angle of the word "International" echoes and repeats the angle of the hammer handle, and the black roman numeral three is placed at a right angle to it, creating a dynamic yet rigorously stable composition.

A poem to strike fear in every capitalist's heart, it begins:

> We are coming
> like a revolutionary lava,
> above our ranks the red flag is burning,
> our leader leads millions.
> The Third International.
> For older censors
> the Third International is sounding.

The title pages for the 1918 poem, "Orders to the Army of the Arts," are active and informal. The composition on the left, made of three letterforms and overlapping grids and rules, is graphic rather than symbolic. Scale changes and layering create a sense of dynamic movement and depth.

This poem, which first appeared in the periodical *Art of the Commune* (*Iskusstvo Kommuny*), on December 5, 1918, was written at a curious time in the evolution of Soviet culture. For a brief moment, the futurist artists and poets, who had spent the decade of war and revolution calling for a clean sweep of the old order, seemed to be closely aligned with

Bolshevik policy, which was also advocating a "clean sweep" of the past. Mayakovsky and other Futurists were installed as editors of *Art of the Commune* and sought to become the official cultural voice of the new society. Mayakovsky passionately believed that traditional art had no value to the workers, the communes, and the streets, and that all artists should join the Revolution and revise their work to accommodate the new reality of Russian society. This poem calls Mayakovsky's futurist comrades to "the barricades of heart and mind":

> Out with cheap truths.
> Erase the old from hearts.
> Streets are our brushes,
> Squares are our palettes . . .

In this poem, Mayakovsky and the periodical *Art of the Commune* were struggling with a dilemma. Unorthodox and experimental art is difficult to understand and, therefore, by necessity, elitist; yet a proletarian culture requires art on the intellectual level of the masses. This posed a serious issue for Mayakovsky, Lissitzky, and all members of the Russian avant-garde.

In 1921, Mayakovsky wrote a sequel titled "Order No. 2 to the Army of the Arts." He opened each of the first four sections of the poem, addressed to actors, painters, poets, and musicians, with an exclamation to all artists: "This is for you." In his call for art that supports the Revolution, Mayakovsky issues an urgent command:

> I admonish you—
> Before they disperse you with
> rifle-butts:
> Give it up!
> Give it up!
> Forget it!
> Spit
> on rhymes
> and arias
> and the rose bush
> and other such mawkishness
> from the arsenal of the arts.

He closes by urging:

> There are no fools today
> to crowd, open-mouthed, around a
> "master"
> and await his pronouncement.
> Comrades,
> give us a new form of art

an art

that will pull the nation out of the mud.

On the title page, Lissitzky emphasized the No. 2 and illustrated this poem with two pointing hands from the type-case. One points to a red plus sign, while the other points to a black X symbol for crossing out or negating the old art. Each is accompanied by the caption, "This is for you." The two large pointing hands echo the poem's accusatory tone, urging artists to reject or cancel out the old art and adopt new forms appropriate to the new society.

The poem "And You, Could You?" was first published in 1913 when Mayakovsky was a youthful and irreverent Futurist poet and painter. The shortest poem in *For the Voice*, it appears complete on its title spread and reads:

Suddenly I confused the everyday map,

by spilling paint/color from a

drinking glass.

I have shown on a plate of fish aspic

the crooked jaws of an ocean.

On the scales of a tin fish

I have read the calls of new lips.

And you—

could you play a nocturne

on a drainpipe flute?

This poem has been called a "Cubist still life in verse" (Stapanian, p. 69) for its nonlinear meaning and manipulation of imagery. The disjunctive imagery is open to varied interpretations and has been seen as a challenge by the poet (who can see the ribbed pattern of an aspic as a metaphor for the ocean) to the reader. The artist takes the mundane material of everyday reality and transforms it. Are you able to hear music in the clinking noise from downspouts? Lissitzky created a matrix of question marks and combined it with typographic elements from the title, including an inventive arrangement of the two forms of the word Bbl (you).

This is followed by a poem entitled "The Story of Little Red Riding Hood." It expresses a very different view of the Revolution, for Mayakovsky issues a strong allegorical warning to the reader:

There was a cadet

who had a red hat.

Besides that hat,

he had nothing red in him.

If the cadet

hears about the Revolution somewhere,

immediately he puts his hat on his head

and all lived well.
Cadet after cadet
and the father of the cadet
and the grandfather of the cadet.

But after a huge wind destroyed the red hat, the wolves of the Revolution take note. They decide the cadet is not true to the Revolution, so they seize and devour him, cufflinks, trimmings, and all. Mayakovsky closed the poem with a stern warning.

When dealing with politics
my children don't forget
the fairy tale
about the little cadet!

Lissitzky illustrated this poem with a stylized—one might even say cute—little geometric figure with outstretched arms proudly showing off his red hat. This poem can be seen as a forewarning of the persecution of artists and writers during the Stalinist period when they did not adhere to the state's official cultural policies.

The tenth poem is titled "The Story of How a Gossiper About Wrangel Was Engaged Without Any Brains." The small subtitle within a ruled box adds, "Old, but Helpful Story." Written during the height of the civil war, this poem warns against false gossip. In 1920, an organized White force operated in the Crimea under Baron Pyotr N. Wrangel, striking northward at the Red Army, occupying parts of the Ukraine and Kuban, and posing a serious threat to the Bolshevik triumph. The gossiper in the poem told false tales about White Army victories. Eventually, Wrangel's forces were battered by the Red Army, holding out only long enough to evacuate 150,000 soldiers and civilians by sea from the Crimea. This ended the Civil War and assured Bolshevik rule over Russia.

This title page lacks the structural cohesiveness of the others. Lissitzky used a decapitated engraving of a two-headed imperial eagle as a symbol of the opposition. This is an effective symbol, but it is an alien element in the context of the abstract geometric signs used throughout the book.

The eleventh poem, titled "Military Naval Love," is filled with sexual metaphors. Mayakovsky tells an allegorical tale about the romance between a male minesweeper and a female minesweeper. Once again, Lissitzky uses the futurist technique of simultaneity, combining stylized images of an anchor and a heart with typography to make a smiling frontal face.

"Good Treatment Toward Horses" is one of Mayakovsky's masterpieces. The opening verse uses an onomatopoeic device to imitate the sound of a horse's hooves on the pavement. Mayakovsky uses four words containing the basic vowels of the Russian language, each presided over by a guttural *gr* sound and followed by a short *b* sound. The Russian-language sounds of the opening lines are:

Bili kopyta
Peli budto:

—Greeb
Grab
Grob
Grub—
 The English translation reads:
Hooves beat
As though singing:
—Mushroom
Plunder
Coffin
Rude—

Mayakovsky used these four words for their sound, independent of their literal meanings. In combination, they become the rhythm of a horse's hooves. Lissitzky responded with a stunning graphic interpretation, using large black type for each of the three letters common to all four words. Then, four horizontal sequences of marks connect these letters to four different vowels, permitting the reader to decipher and understand the four words. Continuing the theme of shared vowels, Lissitzky uses a big red O as a common letter in the words for "good" and "treatment."

This poem was written in 1918 when war and revolution in Moscow were creating chronic shortages of food and fuel. The horse in the poem collapses onto the street from hunger and fatigue. A crowd gathers, ready to butcher it if it cannot rise. But the horse's owner coaxes it until finally it is able to rise and continue on its way.

The last poem in *For the Voice* is among Mayakovsky's most famous works. Lissitzky constructed one of his finest typographic compositions from the words in the complex title: "An Extraordinary Adventure Which Befell Vladimir Mayakovsky in a Summer Cottage." The subtitle at the bottom documents the location: "Pushkino, Akuslas Mount, Rumyantsev Cottage, 27 Versts on the Yaroslav Railway." (A verst—a Russian unit of distance—is slightly less than 1½ miles.)

In this poem, a desolate Mayakovsky is visited by the sun for tea and conversation in his cottage one hot July afternoon. He discusses his despair with his visitor, then vows to overcome it:

Always to shine,
to shine everywhere
to the very depths of the last days
to shine—
and to hell with everything else!
This is my motto—
and the sun's!

Lissitzky needed only a large red circle on the left-hand page to signify the visiting luminary.

An unending argument in graphic design centers on the relationship of style to content. Designers who have definite stylistic approaches are sometimes accused of forcing their style upon the client's message. Designers without a recognizable or consistent style often assert that they let the solution grow out of the problem. In *For the Voice*, Lissitzky proved that a graphic designer can have a definite style and philosophy and effectively use it to interpret the specific message and content of the assignment at hand. In this and other works from the 1920s, Lissitzky pioneered a new approach to typographic art which became a profound influence upon the evolution of twentieth-century graphic design.

Originally published in PRINT, *September/October 1990.*

Bibliography

Bann, Stephen, ed. *The Tradition of Constructivism.* New York: Viking, 1974.

Barooshian, Vahan D. *Russian Cubo-Futurism: 1910–1930.* The Hague: Mouton, 1974.

Blake, Patricia, ed. *Vladimir Mayakovsky: The Bedbug and Selected Poetry.* Princeton: Princeton University Press, 1975.

Charters, Ann and Samuel. *I Love: The Story of Vladimir Mayakovsky and Lili Brik.* New York: Farrar, Straus & Giroux, 1979.

Cohen, Arthur A., ed. *ExLibris 6: Constructivism & Futurism: Russian and Other.* New York: ExLibris, 1977.

Lissitzky-Kuppers, Sophie, ed. *Lissitzky: Life Letters Texts.* London: Thames and Hudson, 1967.

Markov, Vladimir. *Russian Futurism: A History.* London: MacGibbon & Kee, 1969.

Nisbet, Peter. *El Lissitzky: 1890–1941.* Cambridge: Harvard University Art Museums, 1987.

Stapanian, Juliette R. *Mayakovsky's Cubo-Futurist Vision.* Houston: Rice, 1986.

Woroszylski, Wiktor. *The Life of Mayakovsky.* New York: Orion Press, 1970.

THE BAUHAUS IN DESSAU
Rudolf Arnheim

It is kept apart by the railway tracks from the thicket of dingy, crotchety small-town houses and is thereby isolated even in its location—two glaringly white giant boxes, one upright, the other horizontal, on a grassy plane. A few red balconies and large windows subdivide the surfaces; otherwise, the whole is bald and flat. In no way do these boxes meet the concept of a house. It is rather as though someone tried with a comfortably surveyable exhibition model to demonstrate the size of 32,000 cubic meters of enclosed space—a container model for a definite quantity of people and material. Just as in the workshops of the Bauhaus the smallest utility object is given the simplest geometrical shape, so are these, the biggest of them all. Thus one is made to receive here the sense of a convincing uniformity of all objects made by man regardless of size, from a metal ashtray to a building—as distinguished from nature.

The striving for cleanliness, clarity, and largeness has won a victory. Through the big windows one can watch the people when they are at work and when they rest in their privacy. Every object reveals its construction. Not a screw is hidden, and no embellishment conceals the raw material that has been used. One is tempted to value this honesty even in its ethical sense.

A building of pure utility. The procedure is "constructive," not as in the past to obtain the visual impression of the maximal individual abundance. And yet, this constructive approach results in something visually satisfying. Quite in general, it shows more clearly than ever that the practically useful is at the same time the beautiful. Even from the viewpoint of aesthetic composition it feels good to see how railings, chair legs, door handles, or teapots can be made of the same metal tubes. The old "unity in the complexity," which up to now could be applied only to architecture, statues, or pictures, acquires here a new meaning. One can now comprehend a building, which contains a thousand different objects, as an organized whole.

The result is all the more important since in the production the aesthetic aspects were considered quite secondary. Even the colors are used for a purpose; they serve to subdivide and to provide orientation: different colors help to distinguish a building's stories or a desk's drawers or the direction in which a door opens.

Even so, much must be solved by feel, because it is not directly dictated by the purpose. Which color should be chosen? Where on a door should the room number be placed?

Because the tasks known to everybody from his own home, when he wants to hang a picture on the right spot, are of course enormously multiplied when a room and all the household stuff in it have such simple, surveyable proportions that it matters everywhere how an object relates to the next. In a room cluttered by big draperies and in which a couch is placed at an angle and ten encumbered little tables stand around randomly, how should one decide where to place a new lamp? In a Bauhaus room the placement of every object determines itself almost by inherent law. Soon we shall learn to understand even theoretically that here we are not dealing with matters of subjective taste, but that this kind of feel is a very definite psychological phenomenon of general validity. It makes different people come to rather similar results. Therefore, even this kind of task permits us to speak of its solutions as demanded by the facts.

To be sure the Bauhaus is not yet prepared today to supply industry with definitive norm patterns. And surely it is not quite immune to affectations and mannerisms. But the idea of freeing ourselves of tradition and of starting again from the two basic motives, the practical requirements of life and the conditions deriving from the raw materials, is so good that nothing else matters for the time being.

Rudolf Arnheim is Professor Emeritus of the Psychology of Art at Harvard University. A student of the original Gestalt psychologists, he has published more than a dozen books on art, architecture, and film.

Originally published in PRINT, *November/December 1997. Translated by the author from "Das Bauhaus in Dessau," first published in the German newspaper* Die Weltbuhne, *1927.*

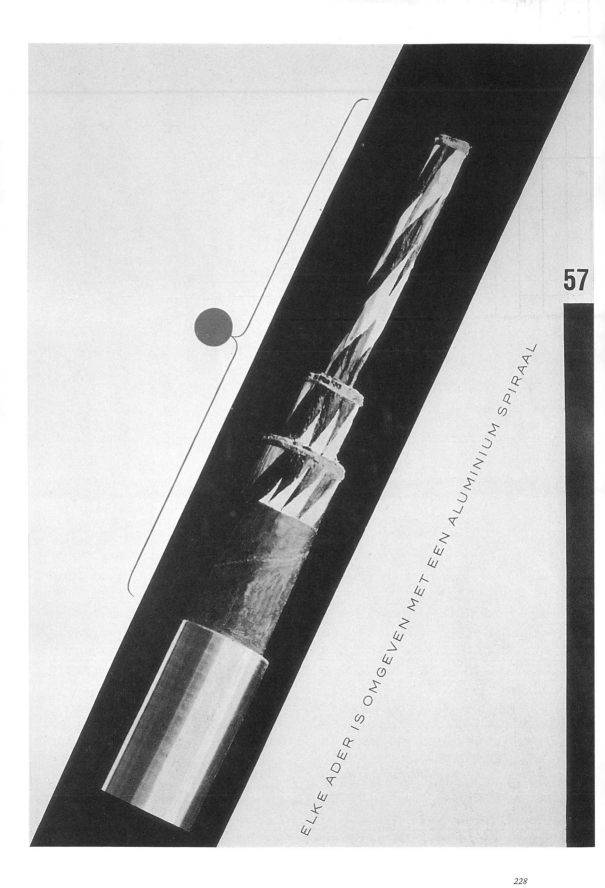

ELKE ADER IS OMGEVEN MET EEN ALUMINIUM SPIRAAL

57

PIET ZWART'S NKF CATALOG
Philip B. Meggs

Writing to a friend in 1926 about his current activities, designer Piet Zwart said, "I also have much advertising work. I do this for relaxation. I have achieved quite something in this, especially for the Nederlandsche Kabelfabriek [Dutch Cable Factory] in Delft. Although these designs appear to be very simple things without much pretension, I find this work very important as a sign of our times. . . . [I]t relates to my total perception of the mind and the tasks of this time period. It is a very multi-sided work. I am now working on a foreign catalogue for the NKF in which I am creating some very strange things."[1]

In a letter to his wife, Nel, Zwart added, "There will be some significant things in [the catalog], and I am trying various experiments which, I think, have never been used in advertising."[2]

Zwart was part of an international movement after World War I to "give a new form to typography. The common goal of every endeavor was not so much to improve typography as to reform a branch of art which had lost all distinction. An endlessly swelling flood of printed matter, a gray boundless sea of uniformity, was crying out for some kind of revolution."[3]

Innovation and experimentation often seem raw and extreme when they first appear; only later, after the forms and spatial arrangements have filtered into the mainstream of mass communications, are they accepted and incorporated into the design vocabulary. Today, the NKF catalog appears as functional—even classic—Modernism; but in the 1920s, it was a radical application of a new design vocabulary to a large industrial firm's publicity material. The NKF management was willing to risk the use of designs not yet proven in the realm of business competition. This evinces a rare managerial trait: a capacity to lead rather than follow.

This eighty-page, perfect-bound volume was issued in 1926 and 1928 editions.[4] Red, yellow, blue, and black inks were printed by letterpress on a glossy white coated stock. The European DIN format A4 was used, with pages approximately twenty-one centimeters (8½") wide by twenty-nine centimeters (11½") tall. In addition to the Dutch-language version, an English-language edition was published.

Traditional hierarchy and structure of page layout were rejected by Zwart, whose asymmetrical page layouts are vigorous and open. He created a cinematic visual flow from spread to spread; elements echo earlier elements, and the placement of the focal point in the spreads keeps changing unexpectedly. Razor-sharp photographs of cables and cable cross-sections move in syncopated rhythms with diagonal bars and lines of text. Zwart often wrote his own copy, so form and message are merged into a dynamic unity. White space became an important design element, ebbing and flowing as photographs and type expand and contract through the book.

The NKF catalog was innovative in its form and space, but this inventiveness was designed to effectively present factual catalog information through lucid words and images. Zwart's Modernism was not about style or visual effects; rather, it was about innovating ways to engage the reader and effectively communicate messages.

The cover displays the NKF initials and logo—a circular cross-section of a three-strand cable—printed on yellow cover-weight paper. The opening spread provides Zwart's first visual jolt. A large black logo thrusts downward on the yellow left-hand page, while the initials NKF are printed in overlapping red and blue at the top of the right-hand page. A vertical black bar bleeds down from the top on the left-hand page, and another bleeds up from the bottom on the right hand page. These bars become a structural theme throughout the book. Zwart created two imaginary horizontal lines moving across the space and aligning with the ends of these bars, and a third one runs between these two. Elements are aligned with these three positions on many spreads, creating a visual flow. Page numbers are consistently placed at the ends of the bars. Zwart said the black bars protect the paper from being marred when the book is handled.

The next spread reverses the movement. The left-hand circle becomes yellow and rises upward, while overprinted blue and red slabs on the lower right present an aerial photograph of the factory. The area of the blue halftone overprinted by red becomes purple, thereby separating the NKF factory from other buildings in the photograph. These have a dynamic downward thrust, balanced by the upward thrust of the company name.

The content is presented in three sections. The opening section is eight pages long and introduces the reader to NKF through interior and exterior photographs of the factory, accompanied by a descriptive statement about the company and its philosophy. As the reader turns to pages 4 and 5, he goes from the exterior to the massive interior of the factory. Pages 10 and 11 have a caption on the left: "From wirebar to thread on the roller works. We provide other sections besides round as well." Diagrams at the bottom of the page identify round, flat, and square wire configurations. The title on the right-hand page identifies the section of the pull works where brass wire is worked. The yellow circle from page 2 reappears, relating back to the earlier page. Zwart delighted in repeating forms with size and color changes, such as the two circles here.

Photography was becoming increasingly important in Zwart's work during this period. He retained a photographer to make the close-up photographs of cutaway cable specimens and cross-sections. He also began to make photographs and photograms himself. Pages 12 and 13 display "square and flat filaments for electric machines." In this superb page composition, every form makes a statement. The yellow square and rectangle on the left signifies square and flat filaments; the sequence of yellow rectangles on the right symbolizes the variety of sizes; and the photogram of filaments demonstrates flexibility. The relationship between the two vertical lines creates unity. Zwart learned relational composition from painters, especially artists of the Dutch De Stijl movement. Pages 18 and 19 have six paper swatches tipped in onto a ruled grid structure that becomes part of the composition.

An innovative layout appears on pages 26 and 27. The left-hand page has a montage relating to the generation, transmission, and use of electrical power. A red arrow zooms from a caption, "The certain foundation of modern industry," to a cross-section of an NKF cable. The dynamic typography on the right translates, "Knock out breakdown! You use NKF CABLE and forget that word BREAKDOWN."

Pages 28 and 29 present two views of the electrified modern city: a diagrammatic map, and a photomontage of high-rise buildings.

In the book's large central section, NKF's product line of electrical and telephone cables is illustrated and described. Descriptive data and photography combine to give viewers an immediate understanding of the various cables. Silhouetted cable photographs are arrowlike shapes slashing across the page. Diagonal cable photographs are composed against horizontal and vertical typography and rules on some spreads; others have vertical photographs in spatial opposition to diagonal type. Cross-section and profile photographs provide immediate understanding of the structure of each wire. The page designs make information immediately accessible. Pages 30 and 31 present one-strand 600-volt prescription number 217: Three versions are clearly identified as: (1) with massive conductor wire; (2) with forged conductor wire; and (3) with forged conductor wire and support grade. The note on the right-hand page translates to "big stuff." On the next spread, Zwart placed type and images on the diagonal. The copy reads, "Multi-strand 500 volt light construction Dutch prescription Number 219." The captions identify two-, three-, and four-segment cables.

Zwart introduces new forms, such as the blue rectangle containing a photograph of a "six-segment strong-current cable with 10,000-volt protection applied to the split conductor system." Bold type overprinting the image proclaims, "Split conductor of the future." On the opposite page, a black-and-white photograph of a "three section high-tension cable for 30,000 volts with an isolation zone" overprints the yellow circle seen on earlier spreads.

Pages 46 and 47 feature a high-tension cable with patented metallic-treated paper around the strands. The cross-section of this three segment paper inspired the NKF trademark. Faced with page after page of cable photographs and product information, Zwart innovated page-design variations. Pages 48 and 49 depict 50,000-volt single-strand ground (left) and water (right) cables with a 50-kilovolt three-phase system and special armament for minimum loss. Pages 48 and 49 are almost identical, but the left halftone is printed in red, the right one in blue. Black type and a yellow bar overprint the photographs. Zwart establishes repetition, then breaks it by shifting the position of the yellow bars and cross-section photographs.

On pages 50 and 51, Zwart shows his brilliance at taking simple type matter and using size, weight, color, and position to enliven the ordinary. An advertising slogan on page 50 loosely translates, "We will not have a single discontented customer, we will foster enthusiasm." Page 51 opens the section showing telephone cables.

The section on telephone cables makes extensive use of enlarged detail photographs to show the cable construction. On pages 56 and 57, the left photograph is identified as 30-segment telephone cable; the detail at right has a caption, "every strand encircles an aluminum spiral." Red dots are used to signify the relative scale of the two images. On pages 60 and 61, a different device, a red dot overprinting a blue halftone, is used to identify the segment enlarged as a circular photograph. The left caption identifies strong current combination telephone cable; the right states that joint or common telephone call transmissions are encompassed with aluminum bands.

The opening spread for the section on signal and control cables opens with a photomontage showing a control panel and film strips of a railroad switch and locomotive. A lively rhythm of diagonals is punctuated by the blue silhouetted control panel moving back in space on the left.

A miscellaneous product, a fill-mass material, is presented on pages 66 and 67 through a full-page photograph and a smaller diagram. Page 68 illustrates a telephone cable with a high self-induction system. This is the final illustrated page, for page 69 opens a ten-page section of technical specifications and engineering data.

An ordinary, even pedestrian, line of industrial products is presented in a book that has been hailed as a breakthrough achievement in early twentieth-century graphic design. The designer's vision transcended subject matter, even as it focused on the applied design problem of presenting this subject matter to readers. Zwart's background, philosophy, and influences clarify how and why this happened.

Zwart began his career as an interior and furniture designer and arrived at graphic design by a circuitous route. He was born on May 28, 1885, in Zaandijk, Holland, and educated at Amsterdam's School of Arts and Crafts from 1902 to 1907. While there, Zwart embraced strong beliefs including humanitarian, pacifist, theosophical, and socialist doctrines. He became a vegetarian and adopted a philosophy espousing a simple approach to life.

From 1908 until 1913, Zwart taught art history and drawing courses at the Girl's School of Domestic Sciences in Leeuwarden. During this period, he produced interior, fabric, and furniture designs.

Decorative and floral motifs characterize much of Zwart's work before 1919, when he first had contact with De Stijl—the Dutch movement founded in 1917 by Piet Mondrian, Theo van Doesburg, and others. Although Zwart was deeply influenced by De Stijl's reduction of art and design to elemental geometric structures and pure primary colors, he never became a member of the group.

From 1919 to 1921, Zwart worked in the office of architect Jan Wils, who belonged to De Stijl from the very beginning, and collaborated on furniture designs with De Stijl member Vilmos Huszar. For Zwart, De Stijl's strict vocabulary of horizontals and verticals and primary colors was too limiting; he was unwilling to banish other elements, such as churning diagonal thrusts and the color green, from his work.

While working in H. P. Berlage's architectural office in The Hague in 1921, Zwart executed his first typographic designs: a logo and stationery for Wils, and printed matter for Vickershouse, a manufacturer of flooring. In his earliest works, after making a rough sketch, Zwart ordered proofs of type, rules, and symbols from the printers. At his drafting table, these typographic materials became collage elements, moved around by Zwart as he searched for a dynamic and functional spatial arrangement. He approached page layout as a searching process and kept an open mind, unfettered by preconceived notions or typographic conventions.

The following year, Zwart met the Russian constructivist El Lissitzky and found that they were exploring similar typographic designs. This encounter reinforced Zwart's direction, as did his meetings with the German collagist Kurt Schwitters. The Dada movement was an important resource, for its emphasis upon chance, process, and a playful manipulation of elements inspired Zwart's keen sense of experimentation.

About design's social role, Zwart said, "Design is not a matter of taste but an expression of our attitude toward life, dictated by the meta cosmos. Design and use of material are not matters of individual whim, but responsible factors in the community."[5] A profound concern for the reader characterized Zwart's graphic designs. He believed the fast pace of twentieth-century life robbed people of adequate time to read and absorb vast amounts of gray text. Innovative ways to present messages were clearly needed. White space, diagonal movements, and contrast of scale and weight were used to engage readers and propel them forward into the material. Static symmetrical balance was rejected; space was made active and fused into a dynamic whole. Copy was stripped to its essence.

In 1925, Berlage introduced forty-year-old Zwart to one of his relatives, who was a director of the Nederlandsche Kabelfabriek in Delft. Soon Zwart was designing their publicity, and graphic design began to consume almost all of his time. The ads, brochures, and catalogs he designed for NKF number in the hundreds.

Zwart became active as a photographer in 1926, and this influenced his graphic design. While the NKF catalog is widely regarded as Zwart's masterpiece, his work continued unabated after this remarkable accomplishment. In 1928, he began a twelve-year association with PTT, the Netherlands' postal, telephone, and telegraph agency. Commissions from PTT included the design of postage stamps and postal indicia, advertising and publicity, and exhibitions. The Bruynzeel firm, a manufacturer of wood products, was an important client for whom Zwart designed new product lines, notably modular kitchen components in 1937. This project had a tremendous impact on kitchen design.

During 1943–44, Zwart was under Nazi detention and kept apart from his wife and four children. After the war, he resumed his collaboration with Bruynzeel and produced new stamps for the PTT. Zwart died in Leidschendam on September 24, 1977, at age ninety-two. His legacy is a profound influence on graphic design that spans the globe.

In 1937, Zwart explained his approach to typographic design: "The task of functional typography is to create a form of typographical design in harmony with the present age, a form free of traditional conventions and as animated as possible; it is to find a clear, well-ordered means of visual expression which shall be decided by modern typographical problems and modern methods (e.g., phototype, techniques such as machine setting, typewriter script and photographic setting); it is to break with the spirit of handwork."[6] His designs for NKF, including the catalog, achieved a remarkable functional vitality and are an historically important expression of a dynamic age of change. About the NKF catalog, Zwart said, "What is the beauty of this kind of work? That it is a slice of life, and that it also is your whole life?"[7] Seldom has the viewpoint of designer as artist been so eloquently expressed.

Originally published in PRINT, *March/April 1996.*

Notes

1. Broos, Kees. *Piet Zwart* (The Hague: Gemeentemuseum, 1973), p. 46.
2. Cohen, Arthur A. *Herbert Bayer and Piet Zwart: Masters of Design* (New York: Ex Libris, undated), p. 14.
3. Jaffé, Dr. Hans L.C. "Piet Zwart: A Pioneer of Functional Typography." *Neue Grafik*, No. 10 (Zurich, 1961), p. 6.
4. Various sources cite 1926 and 1928–29 as the publication date. One says it was originally printed in 1926 and reissued in 1928.
5. Zwart, Piet. *Keywords* (The Hague: Staatsdrukkerij Den Haggen, 1966), p. 6.
6. Jaffé, op. cit., p. 9.
7. Broos, op. cit., p. 46.

Bibliography

Broos, Kees. *Piet Zwart*. The Hague: Gemeentemuseum, 1973.

———— and Hefting, Paul. *Dutch Graphic Design: A Century*. Cambridge: MIT Press, 1993.

Cohen, Arthur A. *Herbert Bayer and Piet Zwart: Masters of Design*. New York: Ex Libris, undated.

————. *Piet Zwart: Typotekt*. New York: Ex Libris, 1980.

Friedman, Mildred, ed. *De Stijl 1917–1931: Visions of Utopia*. New York: Abbeville, 1982.

Jaffé, Dr. Hans L. C. "Piet Zwart: A Pioneer of Functional Typography." *Neue Grafik*, No. 10. Zurich, 1961.

Muller, Fridolin. *Piet Zwart*. New York: Hastings House, 1966.

Purvis, Alston. *Dutch Graphic Design: 1918–1945*. New York: Van Nostrand Reinhold, 1992.

Spencer, Herbert. *Pioneers of Modern Typography*. New York: Hastings House, 1969.

Zwart, Piet. *Keywords*. The Hague: Staatsdrukkerij Den Haggen, 1966.

ah ! oh ! oh ! oh !
laissez-moi grincer des dents
allons
caïman
Ulysse
je m'en vais habiter ma
cagna dans mes cacaoyers
donnent du cacao !
les cacaoyers des cacaoyères donnent pas des cacahuètes
les cacaoyers des cacaoyères donnent pas des cacahuètes donnent du cacao !

THE BALD SOPRANO
Philip B. Meggs

In 1964, Ionesco's revolutionary play was reinvented on the printed page by means of graphic experiments far ahead of their time.

In 1948, Eugène Ionesco decided to learn English by copying sentences from a conversational manual. The Rumanian playwright, who was working in Paris as a proofreader, became fascinated by the stilted, commonplace phrases of the characterless characters in the *Assimil Manual* who dutifully told one another that the floor is below, the ceiling is above, and there are seven days in the week. Although Ionesco had always hated theatrical plays because he felt embarrassed for the actors, this dialogue prompted him to write a one-act "antiplay," *The Bald Soprano*. Two proper middle-class English couples, Mr. and Mrs. Smith and their visitors Mr. and Mrs. Martin, are joined by a maid named Mary and a Fire Chief in an encounter defying time and logic. These characters chat, argue, and restate the obvious until it becomes inane, exposing the inadequacies of verbal communication. The puns and nonsense of vaudeville humor bob along the surface of a deeply serious message about the dilemmas of contemporary life. In a decade scarred by World War II, the Holocaust, atomic weapons, and the Cold War, Ionesco realized, "One can speak without thinking; for this we have clichés, automatic expressions."[1]

As he contemplated the deep mysteries of the universe and of life, he concluded that "science is not knowledge, rhetoric and philosophy are nothing but words, sets of words, strings of words. . . . When we have learnt everything, or if we could learn everything, we should still know nothing."[2]

After *The Bald Soprano* was first performed, in 1950, it inspired a revolution in dramatic techniques and helped inaugurate the Theater of the Absurd. This theatrical direction of the 1950s and '60s was based on a belief that the human condition made no sense, and that European and American dramatists were presenting a vain struggle to find meaning in life. The naturalistic conventions of the theater that were used to tell stories and offer social messages were supplanted by surreal, nonrepresentational techniques representing human powerlessness. Plot was eliminated; the traditional ending or summation was replaced by a wandering, often circular movement in time.

The French text for *La Cantatrice Chauve* was first published in 1954, and the English translation, entitled *The Bald Soprano*, appeared in 1956. Characters shouting and talking simultaneously, actors facing away from the audience, and other expressive aspects of Ionesco's drama were lost when his play script was printed in monotonous lines of type on gray pages. This breakthrough play needed the intervention of a graphic designer capable of reinventing Ionesco's dramatic techniques on the printed page.

In 1964, Robert Massin, the art director of Editions Gallimard, took on the project. Acting as "a sort of stage director," Massin translated "the atmosphere, the movement, the speeches, and the silences in the play, trying at the same time to convey an idea of duration of time and space on the stage by the simple device of the interplay of image and text."[3] The unprecedented brilliance of Massin's design can be fully appreciated only when one looks at it in relation to the play's meaning and content. Graphic invention was not an end in itself but grew out of a serious effort to understand and interpret the play.

Massin's design called upon the techniques of the comic strip and cinema to express time and sequence. The actual faces of the actors in Cohen's photographs "acquired the importance of an ideogram"[4] by becoming symbols identifying the speaker. High-contrast photography reduced the actors to black shapes on the white page. This technique robbed the characters of their individuality, turning them into stereotypes—cliché-people living in a cliché-world, filling time with cliché-ridden conversation.

The covers, shown here from the 1965 English-language edition, are illustrated with front and back views of the cast. Opening the book, the reader encounters the cast staring out from what would normally be the half-title page. The tight cropping of the photograph and the actors' posture, leaning forward toward the viewer, create a feeling of confrontation. Rather than invite the reader into the book, this image becomes a barrier to entry. The title page follows, jolting the reader with its large-scale, crude type. Massin achieved a rough, tattered typographic image by extreme enlargement of metal type, which had not yet been replaced by phototype in the early 1960s.

The next two spreads introduce the actors through full-figure photographs that serve as a legend for the reader, since photographs will identify the speakers throughout the book. Each actor and actress has a unique characteristic—Mr. Smith has a mustache; Mrs. Smith, a turtleneck sweater; Mrs. Martin, a hat; Mary, a hairbun; the Fire Chief, a hat— enabling the reader to quickly identify the speaker. Massin selected a different typeface for the words spoken by each character. Stage directions and explanations, set in an 8-point light, slab-serif font, are clearly delineated from the other typography.

As the play opens, Mr. and Mrs. Smith are in their suburban London sitting room. Mrs. Smith prattles on about food and setting a good example for the children, while Mr. Smith reads his newspaper, paying no attention. Her conversation is filled with blatant contradictions; for example, the soup had too many leeks and not enough onions. The Smiths leave to dress when their guests, Mr. and Mrs. Martin, arrive for dinner.

In the play's most famous scene, the Martins chat while they wait for the Smiths to return. Mrs. Martin tells her husband that she believes she has met him somewhere before. Mrs. Martin's dialogue is layered over her image on the left-hand page, opposite her husband's dialogue and image on the right. As the conversation unfolds, they discover coincidence after coincidence: They're both from Manchester, took the same train to London, reside at 19 Bromfield Street, and have a two-year-old daughter with one red eye and one white eye. They suddenly realize they must be a husband and wife named Donald and Elizabeth; they embrace and fall asleep entwined on a chair.

Mary, the maid, enters quietly and addresses the audience in a soliloquy taking the shape of her body. She devastates Donald and Elizabeth's carefully constructed logic used to prove their relationship by telling the audience Donald's daughter has a white right eye and a red left eye, while Elizabeth's child has a red right eye and white left eye; therefore, their daughters can't be the same child. She concludes by announcing that her real name is Sherlock Holmes and leaves the room.

After Mr. and Mrs. Smith join the Martins, the two couples sit stiffly, looking out toward the audience. A long silence ensues, periodically broken as the actors utter interjections and clichés totally disconnected from earlier statements. To illustrate the passage of time, Massin showed the four actors seated in their chairs over and over for twenty-two consecutive spreads. One actor utters a sound and phrase on each spread.

The couples begin to share stories of extraordinary things they have seen—a man tying his shoelace; a man quietly sitting on his seat in the Underground reading a newspaper—when their conversation is interrupted by the doorbell. It rings twice, and each time Mrs. Smith goes to the door, only to find no one there. The repetition of this incident is conveyed through a dynamic layout. Each page is dominated by a full-length image of Mrs. Smith standing before the other three characters, who are seated in the background, as she tells them that no one is at the door. An argument begins over whether the doorbell ringing means someone is there, or whether recent experience teaches that no one is there.

This time, the Fire Chief is at the door, wearing his uniform and shiny helmet. An extraordinary layout records the dialogue as the Fire Chief tells Mrs. Smith that she looks angry and the group explains to him over Mrs. Smith's protestations that she is miffed over losing the argument. To achieve the warped lines of type, Massin had metal type set and proofed on sheets of rubber. These were stretched and bent into the configurations shown here and photocopied using high-contrast film. Although this graphic technique is simple to achieve with contemporary computer software capable of stretching, bending, and skewing type, it was truly innovative in the early 1960s, when typesetting was still locked in the straitjacket of the metal letterpress.

The small pictures and open spaces of this spread are followed by large images of the Fire Chief and Mrs. Smith—then the senseless argument about the meaning of a doorbell's ring resumes on the right-hand page, in a format used for numerous pages in *The Bald Soprano*. By replacing the speaker's name set in type with small photographs of the actors, Massin enlivens the page. A different indentation is used for each actor, imposing a random yet rhythmic downward movement into the space. White space, contrast, and scale change were important design considerations in the pacing of the book.

After helping resolve the dispute, the Fire Chief informs the Smiths and Martins that he has come to see if they have any fires to put out, lamenting that business is bad. While there, he begins to tell them stories—nonsensical fairy tales and fables—each set in a contrasting typeface. The storytelling culminates in a tale, "The Headcold," in which the Fire Chief delineates a long series of relationships ("My brother-in-law had on the paternal side a first cousin whose maternal uncle had a father-in-law whose maternal grandfather had married. . . ."). Four dozen relationships into the story, the Fire Chief concludes with "an old woman who was the niece of a priest whose grandmother, occasionally in the winter, like everyone else, caught a cold." The playgoer or reader becomes hopelessly confused by this convoluted mockery of gossip and people's fascination with relationships. Massin set this tale in all-capital condensed sans-serif type to express its incoherence. The typography also introduces a dense textural contrast into the visual flow of the book. Jamming the lines of justified type together by squeezing all leading from between them further intensifies their verbal confusion and visual tension.

The storytelling ends when Mary, the maid, interrupts, calling "Madam" and "Sir" in a loud voice. Mr. and Mrs. Smith reply, "Why have you come here?" and "What do you want?" By positioning Mary's image across the center of the spread, Massin causes a visual interruption, suggesting a break or shift in the play. Discussion begins about the maid's behavior and her desire to tell the group a story.

After Mary recites a poem, the Fire Chief goes to the door, turns to the group, and exclaims, "Speaking of that, the bald soprano?" Massin conveys the Fire Chief's impending departure by cropping his image on the far right of the spread. This device also signals another shift in the tone of the play.

On the following spread, Mrs. Smith remarks that the bald soprano "always wears her hair in the same style." The Fire Chief exits, and a nine-page sequence begins with four or five images of the actors on each page. Their unconnected proclamations, placed above their heads at a diagonal, include lines from the language manual, clichés, and nonsensical proverbs. This reaches a summation when Mr. Smith rises and shouts, "To hell with polishing!"

Following this proclamation, the actors fall silent for a tense moment. The script directions tell us that a new series of speeches begins in a "glacial, hostile tone. The hostility and the nervousness increase. At the end of this scene, the four characters must be standing very close to each other, screaming their speeches, raising their fists, ready to throw themselves upon each other."

Over the next fourteen spreads, Massin gives visual articulation to this steadily intensifying confrontation by increasing the scale of the type and disintegrating the lucid graphic order present in even the most dynamic of the earlier spreads. Each spread provides a new opportunity to increase the level of chaos. The first seven spreads have typography and photographs of the actors, with a dynamic structure created by lively diagonals and careful use of white space. Overlapping words can still be deciphered by the reader. The eighth spread dispenses with the images, using only typography to suggest the actors' increasingly incoherent shouting.

The graphic entropy moves toward a crescendo as Mr. Smith shouts the vowels *a, e, i, o, u* over and over; Mrs. Martin responds with the consonants *b, c, d, f, g* . . . ; and Mrs. Smith repeats the sound of a puffing train, *"teuff, teuff, teuf* . . ." Massin creates a series of typographic abstractions to express this chaos.

Suddenly, the actors become completely infuriated and begin shouting in unison into each other's ears, "It's not that way, it's over here."

The stage lights are extinguished, and from the darkness the actors continue chanting, "It's not that way, it's over here," in increasingly rapid rhythms. Massin illustrates this by reversing the field and layering white type on the black void; the chant becomes bigger and overlaps more as it moves down the page.

The next spread expresses this auditory frenzy with even bigger type, followed by a spread decomposed into an abstract pattern formed by details of the letters.

The words cease abruptly, and the lights come on again. Mr. and Mrs. Martin are seated like the Smiths were at the beginning of the play. They begin to recite the same lines spoken in the opening scene as the curtain softly falls.

This marked the end of the play in the original version, but in the 1964 edition Ionesco offered three alternative endings. The first has Mary return and lead the actors off for dinner, and the stage remains empty for a long time. The annoyed audience begins to boo and whistle, and a dozen actors planted in the audience storm the stage, only to be machine-gunned by policemen in the dark corners of the stage. The director, author, and police commissioner appear on the stage. The director tells the audience, "Let this be a lesson to you . . . We'll defend [the theater] against the public by keeping it away." He then tells the policemen who gunned down the people who stormed the stage to kick the audience out, and they clear the theater.

Another version has Mary return to the stage and introduce the author, who is praised by a shill in the audience. The author then shakes his fist at the audience and proclaims, "Bunch of idiots, I'll kill you!" as the curtain falls.

Ionesco's third alternative ending, illustrated by Massin, has the actors literally explode or collapse like their language, with heads detaching from their bodies and arms and legs flying to pieces. Ionesco commented wryly that this ending could be possible only in a film version.

When Ionesco's plays were first performed, many critics derided them. Jean Jacques Gautier, influential reviewer for *Le Figaro*, wrote that Ionesco was "a fraud whose activities could best be summed up by the following telegram: 'Fake surrealism not defunct. Stop. Ionesco follows.'"[5] Others understood Ionesco's message. Jacques Lemarchand "was won over by *The Bald Soprano* when he observed with amusement the audience's puzzlement and rage."[6] He wrote, "Within its walls, the theater holds a stock of dynamite which might blow sky high every other theater in Paris."[7]

Ionesco was a visionary who believed "the renewal of language could bring about a fresh vision of the world";[8] Massin is a graphic designer "whose primary concern has been to give visual reality to the literary content."[9] To achieve a genuine expression of the absurd, Ionesco had to invent his "own language and create forms that are not those of rational discourse."[10] Massin was able to reinvent his graphic-design language to create an appropriate vehicle for Ionesco's imagination.

Originally published in PRINT, *September/October 1994*

Art Center College

Notes

1. Eugène Ionesco, *Fragment of a Journal* (New York: Grove Press, 1968), p. 30.
2. Ibid., p. 32.
3. Robert Massin, *Letter and Image* (New York: Van Nostrand Reinhold, 1970), p. 226.
4. Ibid.
5. Rosette C. Lamont, *Ionesco's Imperatives: The Politics of Culture* (Ann Arbor: University of Michigan, 1993), p. 245.
6. Ibid., p. 246.
7. Ibid.
8. Ibid., p. 260.
9. Nancy House, "Robert Massin," in *Contemporary Designers* (Chicago and London: St. James Press, 1990), p. 375.
10. J. S. Doubrovsky, "Ionesco and the Comic Absurdity." Reprinted in Rosette C. Lamont, ed. *Ionesco: A Collection of Critical Essays* (Englewood Cliffs: Prentice Hall, 1973), p. 12.

Bibliography

Hayman, Ronald. *Eugène Ionesco*. New York: Ungar, 1976.

Ionesco, Eugène. *Fragment of a Journal*. New York: Grove Press, 1968.

———. *La Cantatrice Chauve*. Paris: Editions Gallimard, 1964.

———. *Present Past/Past Present*. New York: Grove Press, 1965.

———. *The Bald Soprano*. New York: Grove Press, 1965.

Lamont, Rosette C., ed. *Ionesco: A Collection of Critical Essays*. Englewood Cliffs: Prentice Hall, 1973

———. *Ionesco's Imperatives: The Politics of Culture*. Ann Arbor: University of Michigan, 1993.

Massin, Robert. *Letter and Image*. New York: Van Nostrand Reinhold, 1970.

Woods, Gerald, Philip Thompson, and John Williams, eds. *Art without Boundaries*. New York: Prager, 1974.

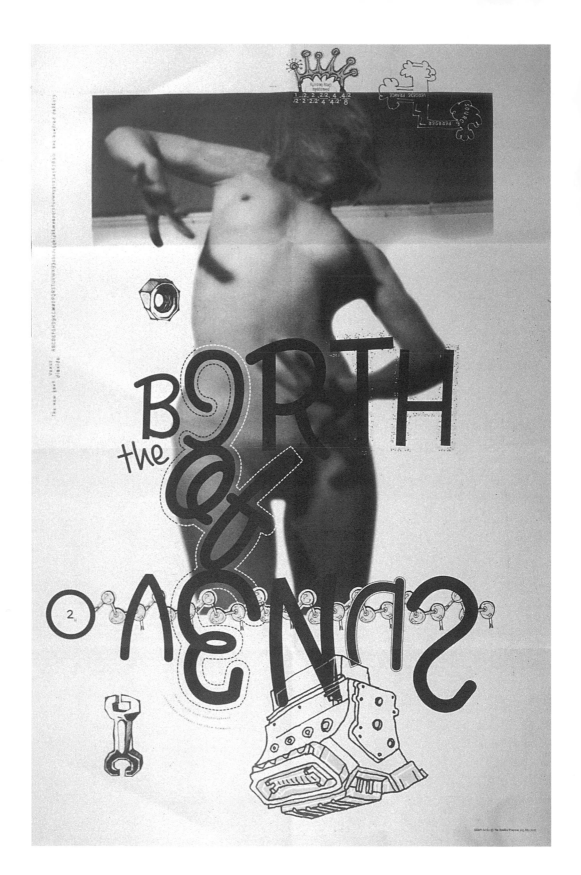

the B**I**RTH of SENAS

A BRAVE NEW WORLD: UNDERSTANDING DECONSTRUCTION
Chuck Byrne and Martha Witte

When it comes to aesthetic theory, designers today perceive themselves as originators, not followers, and most are loath to admit that they are influenced by much of anything other than their own inner creative resources.

To suggest that there is a link between new directions in design and ideas or developments taking place in contemporary society ought not to give offense to this ideal of creative individualism. Believing it does is a relatively new phenomenon and one that many respected figures in the history of graphic design would probably find puzzling, for the seeds of many a historic movement in graphic design are found in contemporaneous literature, painting, philosophy, politics, and technology.

In a January/February 1960 *PRINT* article, "The Bauhaus and Modern Typography: The 'Masters' Liberate the Typographic Image," Sibyl Moholy-Nagy discusses the relationship of the designer to culture and technology. She points out that one of the most significant reasons for the success of the Bauhaus was its artists' abilities to make creative use of the inventions of the time. Under the aegis of a fundamental group philosophy, Bauhaus designers were able to capitalize on new, and seemingly alien, construction procedures and materials, exploiting them for their production and aesthetic advantages. They did not resist change, but embraced it and engaged in meaningful discourse about it.

Today, the technological changes taking place in typography have been brought about by the personal computer. Relatively inexpensive and easy-to-use desktop publishing equipment and software have given those designers choosing to take advantage of them direct control over typographic arrangements which were previously dependent upon expensive typesetting techniques or laborious handwork.

The ability of the computer to allow variations at low cost gives the designer the freedom to experiment until the page seems "right," whereas previously, tried-and-true formulas were necessary in order to predict the outcome more certainly, and avoid undue expense at the typesetter. Today's seemingly boundless freedom precludes the need for many typographic conventions and even brings into question the need for that most sacrosanct of mid-twentieth-century graphic design devices—the grid.

Grids are but one means of organizing visual material—a means to an end, not an end in themselves. Ostensibly, the best grids are based on a general evaluation of content and reflect the particular character and presentational requirements of that content. Besides being useful to designers from the Middle Ages to the present as visual organizers, they are useful to those designers who, because of the expense involved, are unable to visualize or mock-up accurately more than a small amount of the total material that will be controlled by the grid. Based on this sampling, the designer using the subsequent grid, with its inherent regimentation, can predict the visual outcome of the entire body of the material. At the same time, however, general assumptions about all or portions of that material are made that may not be specifically responsive to the content, nor in its best interpretive interests.

The computer permits the designer to view all the material that needs to be organized at one time. It does this by allowing the designer to place into the machine, and then maneuver and accurately view, the actual copy and images before even the most rudimentary of design decisions are made. This versatility includes the particulars of the page itself, the style, size, character, and position of type, as well as the size, shape, position, and other features of all kinds of imagery. Just as important, the designer is able to experiment freely with the relationship of these elements one to another—left to right, top to bottom, and even front to back. These capabilities allow the designer to organize empirically, that is, from within the actual environment of the material, thus permitting the development of a more responsive grid, or the exploration of other means of visually organizing materials, or quite possibly eliminating the need for any kind of restrictive structure. The grid may be dead, and if so, the computer will have been the culprit.

But while the computer provides the technical ability to accomplish a seemingly new look in typographic design, it is certainly not the only inducement to aesthetic innovation.

The evolutionary temperament of general culture is capable of producing an atmosphere that stimulates a variety of creative disciplines to respond simultaneously, sometimes similarly, sometimes dissimilarly. And designers often find concepts and images generated by disciplines remote from design seductive and worthy of appropriation.

Sibyl Moholy-Nagy writes that two of the most dynamic revolutions in twentieth-century typography, Futurism and the Bauhaus, were fueled by the excitement of ideas generated by such seemingly unrelated developments as the automobile, Einstein's Theory of Relativity, and Freud's theories of the self. According to Moholy-Nagy, the inventive quality in all of these ideas had to do with motion, and so typography, "in its age old function of filtering the great artistic movements down to a residue of simple communication, then took upon itself this restlessly evolutionary trend. . . ."

Within the last few years, typography and design in general have been influenced, either directly or indirectly, knowingly or unknowingly, by the concept of "deconstruction."

Most designers moving in deconstructionist directions vehemently deny any knowledge of deconstruction, much less admit to being influenced by this encroaching concept from critical thought and philosophy. But design does fall under its influence, if for no other reason than because designers live in the culture that gave birth to deconstruction. We live in a deconstructed world, a world agitated by more and more complexity, where the attention span diminishes hourly (turning us into a society of information grazers), and values appear to change weekly. It is inevitable that heretofore clear and supposedly resolved notions about what design does and the way it does it will begin to blur and ultimately reshape themselves.

Deconstruction, which began as an avenue of literary criticism, involves the examination of texts in terms of the language and ideas of which they are composed. Evolutionarily, deconstruction (also referred to as post-Structuralism) grew out of—but later disputed—an earlier movement called Structuralism, which, led by the linguist Ferdinand de Saussure, sought to establish language study as a science in and of itself. Deconstructionist ideas were first introduced in the United States by the French philosopher and critic Jacques Derrida, who, in 1966, was invited to speak at Johns Hopkins University. Beginning in the late '60s, Derrida's writings, including *Of Grammatology, Writing and Difference,* and *Dissemination,* became available in English and are now widely read, albeit with some difficulty.

As the word itself suggests, "deconstruction" refers to the breaking down of something (an idea, a precept, a word, a value) in order to "decode" its parts in such a way that these act as "informers" on the thing, or on any assumptions or convictions we have regarding it. Its intention, revolutionary insofar as critical thinking is concerned, is to activate the discussion of ideas by demonstrating how their interpretation is influenced less by their actual meaning than by the amount of play in the fabric that holds them together.

For example, think about deconstructing the word "whole." We think of a whole as one complete thing, but in actuality we never understand any one thing except in terms of its parts, and at the same time our understanding of the details is conditional, or informed by an idea of how they are a part of and make up a totality. In concept, therefore, "wholeness" is inherently incomplete. Its meaning depends on the multileveled, mental play of the parts that hold it together. This kind of deconstructive thinking has moved philosophy away from meaning-centered discourse and into a sort of flirtatious game-playing around meaning, or with multimeaning.

One deconstructs something for a variety of reasons, which may be political, artistic, philosophical, or otherwise expressive. Political/cultural positions such as feminism and Marxism work deconstructively when they uncover aspects of our society which, while appearing to be universally humanistic, actually suppress the needs of one social group while serving those of another.

While several branches of art and design, most notably the practice of architecture, have been heavily influenced by deconstructionist ideas, typographic design is probably the most logical visual extension of deconstruction because of its basis in words and text. Deconstructionist writings are linked with the visual world, in that their authors often utilize graphic nuances in order to illustrate difficult concepts or subtle contradictions in meanings. Derrida, in the essay "Différance," demonstrates in print the concept of something being present and absent at the same time, by cleverly inserting a "rogue" vowel to replace one of the correct characters in the French word "différence." The new word reads "différance," in which the "a" is a misspelling—in French, this change is visible (present) but inaudible (absent). Thus, the distance between two seemingly contradictory concepts, presence and absence, is remarkably abbreviated, collapsed into one typographic solution.

Similarly, deconstructionist Jacques Lacan, a French psychoanalyst and structuralist, uses an illustration of two side-by-side, identical lavatory doors, over one of which is the sign "ladies," and over the other, the sign "gentlemen." With this simple picture, he attempts to show the impossibility of there being only one point of reference or "meaning" for any one word or concept. The difference again is graphic: The lavatory doors look the same, but the designation over them—and each viewer's reference point to either sign—is different.

The deconstructionist view asks that a reader comprehend and account for complex differences in signification, at one level meaning one thing and at another level meaning its possible opposite—to point out that "meaning" is an elusive business. For designers, using different layers to create a sort of comparative visual vocabulary in order to present the evolution of a particular idea has become a fairly common, and sometimes arbitrary, practice. But when the deconstructionist approach is applied to design, each layer, through the use of language and image, is an intentional performer in a deliberately playful game wherein the viewer can discover and experience the hidden complexities of language. While this approach is effective when the purpose of the game is to extend or enhance the message being conveyed, it can be a communications paradox when merely used for stylistic purposes.

The intricacy of this kind of work virtually requires the designer to participate in the writing process, if not actually be the writer, something more and more designers seem willing, able, and even anxious to do.

Some graphic designers may be inclined to think of a process like deconstruction that is so deeply involved in theory as absurd and remote. But the very essence of contemporary typography-driven design lies in the process of determining the characteristics and arrangement of type relative to the interpretation or presentation of the text or words in order to enhance communication or expression. With this in mind, it is easy to realize the susceptibility of typographic design to this kind of deconstructionist visual discourse.

The modernist movement advocated simplicity, and so it is understandable that many of today's designers view the visual complexity found in much deconstructionist design as extraneous and alien. Far from being the mere application of style, however, deconstructionist design potentially clarifies or extends certain aspects of communication that the uniform treatment of elements inherent in Modernism has a tendency to obscure. Some signposts of deconstructionist design are: empirical page design and juxtaposition of elements based on context rather than traditional presuppositions (for example, the entire character of a particular page being determined by the subject of that page alone); typographic coding and modulation arising from content and language rather than convention (for example, articulating the content/context of significant words in the text by visual or literary punning); and/or meaningful layering and contrast to create discourse rather than adornment (for example, superimposing selected portions of text directly over the appropriate area of a related photograph, in order to comment on or emphasize aspects of their association).

Throughout the history of graphic design, there have been reinterpretations of the contextual assumptions concerning the typographic page, and it is possible to find isolated examples of fascinating deviations from the norm that rival in typographic intricacy anything being done today. But for the most part, until the revolutionary explosions of the early twentieth century, and much later the work of Wolfgang Weingart in the late '60s and the '70s, changes have been evolutionary rather than revolutionary.

The way was prepared for the introduction of deconstruction to graphic design by the reissuing in 1982 of *Pioneers of Modern Typography,* first published in 1969, and the publication of *The Liberated Page* in 1987, both by Herbert Spencer. These books made it possible for designers to see a substantial collection of the work of those twentieth-century innovators, the Dadaists, Futurists, De Stijl artists, and Constructivists through examples by designers such as Filippo Marinetti, El Lissitzky, Piet Zwart (who often wrote his own copy), Kurt Schwitters, Herbert Bayer, László Moholy-Nagy, Jan Tschichold, and Theo van Doesburg.

Spencer points out that the visual interpretation of the meaning of words to provide emphasis, and even the portrayal of the sounds of words, was of interest to both Dadaist and futurist typographers. The futurist Marinetti proposed a revolution against formulaic design, and began by refuting the uniform integrity of the text block: "My revolution is aimed at the so-called typographical harmony of the page, which is contrary to the flux and reflux, the leaps and bursts of style that run through the page. On the same page, therefore, we will use three or four colors of ink, or even twenty different typefaces if necessary."

Regardless of whether Marinetti might reconsider the idea of using twenty different faces on a page upon seeing the progeny of the average "desktop publisher," his work and ideas as well as those of his contemporaries have had a direct impact on work from the studios of Rick Valicenti, Neville Brody, Ross Carron, Katherine McCoy, Nancy Skolos, Gordon Salchow, Rudy VanderLans, Tom Bonauro, Stephen Doyle, Lucille Tenazas, Tibor Kalman, and others. Some of these designers also reflect the influence of the turn-of-the-century French poet Guillaume Apollinaire and the American concrete poets of the '60s, writers who understood the importance of the visual presentation of words and chose to make typography an extension of poetry by taking direct personal control of it. The work and ideas of these designers is in strong contrast to the aloof minimalist typography generally seen in the fifties, sixties, and seventies.

Deconstructionist design continues to collapse traditional typographical harmony even further than Marinetti's claim. The visual coding accomplished by style, size, weight, and position of each typographic element on a page, from initial caps, text, and headlines to captions, has begun to disintegrate. Evidence of this can be seen in the new work of Joel Katz, Michael Mabry, David Carson, and Joe Miller, where what are still obviously initial caps are distorted or appear in unexpected places, or the contrast, in weight, of a portion of the text causes the eye to begin reading in a nontraditional location.

In graphic design as a whole, formulaic structures seem to be blurring in favor of a kind of empirical context for the page that serves to create a new relationship between form and content specific to an individual piece of work. Although pages from different issues of *Emigre* bear a family resemblance to one another, for example, the resemblance does not spring from traditional graphic structure. John Weber's work exploits these methods not only in traditional print graphics, but also in type animations that take place on a computer screen, or in video, where the relationships between typographic elements constantly change.

At the MIT Visible Language Workshop, designers are experimenting with the very nature of the perception of typographic information. Their work goes so far as to tamper with presumptions about the eye moving from the top to the bottom of a body of information. Here, powerful computers allow the viewer to control interactively the sequence or movement through information, rather than over it. Moving a pressure-sensitive pen up or down, left or right, and in or out causes text and images on the screen to be moved or selected, indicating to the computer the interests of the viewer. The computer reacts with the new information in the form of new type and visuals on the screen.

Deconstruction brings into question and reshapes the entire typographic vocabulary, the orientation of the page, whether there should be a page, and whether type itself should do more than perform its basic historical function of being readable. Discussing legibility, both Rudy VanderLans, designer and publisher of *Emigre,* and Tibor Kalman of M&Co are quick to point out that there are many ways to approach reading and that type and text can have a purpose other than to be read.

While saying so might seem heretical to some, type can have purposes which are illustrative, atmospheric, interruptive, and expressive in addition to, or beyond, mere legibility—what Sibyl Moholy-Nagy refers to as "the non-communicative function of type." Designer Paula Scher, who occasionally uses typography executed by hand, maintains, "The legibility of type is dependent upon the goal: If it's supposed to be legible, it should be. If it's not supposed to be, it shouldn't be." With this observation, she clearly points to the need for the designer to understand the reason for a particular approach rather than merely engaging in meaningless stylistic mimicry.

If the computer has been an important influence on typographic design, it promises to challenge equally the traditional use of photography in design. With the newfound ability to capture images, manipulate, crop, and mask them on a screen, designers are beginning to rediscover the power of the photographic image. Photography is being used less and less to isolate rectangles of "reality," and is instead becoming more fully integrated in the "reality" of the entire page—a circumstance that quite naturally serves deconstructionist ideas about the discourse and play between language and image achieved through positioning and layering. The visual expression of these ideas can be seen in the work of April Greiman, Lorraine Wild, Chuck Byrne, Katherine McCoy, Rudy VanderLans, Ross Carron, Lucille Tenazas, Elliot Earls, Edward Fella, and Jeffery Keedy.

Sibyl Moholy-Nagy states that her husband's special contribution to his era was the integration of photography with typography. He would surely have recognized and appreciated the significance of the introduction of the computer into the two, and the potential for that relationship to be more synergistic. Doubtless, László Moholy-Nagy and his contemporaries would have embraced the computer with a passion.

The most extreme deconstructionist reassessments of design precepts tend to distinguish themselves clearly from other forms of reinterpretation, such as those of the early twentieth century. A recent issue of *Emigre,* titled "heritage," is devoted to the state of Swiss design today. In it, Richard Feurer, a founder of the studio Eclat, states the goals of his work in a discussion with other young designers. "To me, it's neither a question of bringing across a significant message, nor of being 'understood.' I don't expect to be understood in the way that I myself understand my visual message. . . . My task is to generate an effect. You can't define what exactly, or how, the viewer will take in your visual message. There are an endless number of possible ways of looking at it. The only thing I can do as designer is to animate the person through my message. He himself should act, should analyze, and reproduce the visual message for himself."

These designers, as do most, grouse at the suggestion that what they are doing involves deconstruction. But the new thinking behind their work stands in strong contrast to modernist concepts of visual clarity and reduction of complexity and reflects the introduction of deconstructive ideas, directly or indirectly, into graphic design.

While some critics feel that these ideas are a moral transgression of the designer's commitment to clear visual communication, it can't be denied that reading and the perception of visual information is a learned skill, the practice of which can be altered. Interestingly, many designers who find great fault with the legibility of this kind of typography tend to forget the hue and cry that was raised concerning readability when the use of small-size, unjustified, sans-serif type was introduced in the early 1960s—the model held up today as the ideal of readability! The pages of *Emigre,* and many of its mainstream visual imitators, are not only widely admired, they are even read—suggesting that human perception, or at least young human perception, is more flexible than it seems.

Some designers are more closely tuned than others to the world of ideas outside design, and the educators and writers among them are beginning to disseminate these ideas in the classrooms and various design publications. But these designers, too, respond cautiously when it is suggested that deconstructionist characteristics originating in fields such as literary theory, semiotics, linguistics, and philosophy are apparent in their work.

Hans Allemann, an instructor at the University of the Arts in Philadelphia, finds that training in semiotics is a useful "tool" for graphic designers, but warns against the complexity of "signs" brought from the vernacular environment distorting communications on the printed page. Allemann argues that, for the most part, it is still a designer's responsibility to communicate clearly, regardless of his or her facility with complex language. In discussing the influence of literary theory and criticism on graphic design, Katherine McCoy at Cranbrook is similarly cautious. "Some of these ideas," she says, "fit the role of art better than design, since designers have an implicit agreement to accept the client's message as their primary content."

The ultimate effect on graphic design of deconstruction and computers can't be known. What is apparent is that even though they tend to isolate themselves from its philosophical origins, many designers today are engaged in deconstructive design. That they should wish to isolate themselves from the origins of a philosophy so intertwined with the visual is unfortunate, as it seems to be the source for a significant change in graphic design. They should instead follow the example of the early pioneers of twentieth-century design: seek to understand these sources and engage them.

Chuck Byrne is a member of the Graphic Design Faculty at the San Jose State University School of Art and Design. From 1988 until 2000 he was a Contributing Editor to PRINT *magazine. Martha Witte is a designer and writer living in Philadelphia. She served on the executive board of the American Institute of Graphic Arts Philadelphia Chapter from 1997 to 1999.*

Originally published in PRINT, *November/December 1990*

5. Mass Communication

THE ADVERTISING OF MAGRITTE/THE MAGRITTE IN ADVERTISING
Georges Roque

An exhibit which appeared not long ago in Paris's Museum of Advertising—*Magritte and Advertising*—brought out an aspect of the Belgian painter's work that was hitherto relatively unknown. Several times during his life, Magritte, in order to survive, worked in advertising—at the start of his career during the years 1918 to 1920; during the years of his discovery of Surrealism (1926–27); in a systematic fashion between 1931 and 1936; and finally more sporadically during and after World War II.

Magritte's earliest known advertising work consists of posters he did when he was twenty and still living with his father. Though he was painting at the time, he designed these posters to earn pocket money. He may even have considered earning a living in this manner, if only temporarily. The very first advertising works, which date from 1918–19, were done before the young artist had discovered his own style and are marked by the Art Nouveau style still prevalent at the time. Subsequent designs, however, dating from 1923–1925, can be described as "Cubo-Futuristic" and are similar in some respects to Art Deco. It was also during this period that Magritte worked for Norine, the most important Belgian fashion house of the day, where he created posters, ads, and brochures.

The fairly radical change which appears in his style of painting in 1926 heralds his passage into Surrealism and brings with it a like change in his advertising work, which also became surrealistic. From this period comes a surprising series of twelve ads (for a restaurant, a jeweler, a bookstore, a milliner, a wine merchant, and other small businesses), which appeared in a small Belgian avant-garde magazine called *Le Centaure*. These ads reduce the elements of advertisements to the strictest minimum required for them to work as ads. The object is reduced to its simplest form, mounted on a pedestal or dais, and accompanied by the name of the product or sponsor.

The most astonishing of Magritte's advertising work from that period, however, is the brochure done in 1927, which presented the winter fur coat collection of the furrier, Samuel. In it are twenty reproductions of designs in ink and pencil, highlighted with watercolor and combined with such found elements as photographs, prints, and scraps of paper, which were glued to the brochure. Most of the designs were freely inspired by the paintings Magritte was doing at the time, and the poetic texts accompanying them are attributed to Magritte's friend, Paul Nougé. This was doubtless one of the first attempts to "divert" advertising to a more poetic purpose.

The bulk of Magritte's advertising work was done in the context of the thirties. By that time, it was no longer a question of his designing ads for low-circulation, avant-garde magazines, or even for fur brochures directed at a wealthy and supposedly cultivated clientele, but rather of engaging in a professional activity whose product was destined for a much larger audience.

In 1931, Magritte went into business with his brother Paul, founding the Dongo Studio (so named in homage to the Stendhalian hero, Fabrice del Dongo, whom Magritte greatly admired). Most of the work uncovered from this period (1931–36) consists of small cardboard posters made for wholesalers, which were meant to be left at retail stores, tobacco shops, pharmacies, and bars. These ads for various brands of cigarettes, pharmaceutical products, and aperitifs were obviously created in a different context and addressed a different audience from that of the earlier, surrealist advertising. They are dominated by a desire for efficiency, legibility, and a restraint that excluded all humor.

Magritte was again obliged to design advertisements near the end of World War II. "Business is slow, much too slow," he complains in a letter from this period. The inspiration for the work of that time—particularly for Provence and Mem perfumes—was taken from the heart of his painting. These ads, consisting of disconcerting scenes rich with color, are often very successful. A special niche, however, should be reserved for the last and best-known of Magritte's contributions to advertising—the ad for Sabena, the Belgian airline. In this case, it was not Magritte the advertising designer who was asked to create the ad—that aspect of his work had remained pretty much unknown—but Magritte the surrealist painter of international fame. Magritte was hired by Sabena simply for reasons of prestige.

Curiously, the influence of Magritte's painting today appears less in the work of fine artists than in the work of graphic designers, illustrators, and art directors. To fine artists, or at least to many of them, Magritte is a figure from the past, however glorious and regardless of the admiration they may have for him. But to graphic designers, illustrators, and their ilk, he remains a great contemporary!

If one judges the importance of an artist not by his followers—though Magritte has a great many, especially in northern Europe—but by the new ideas his work continues to generate, then it is incontestably in the field of graphic design that one should look for the intellectual descendants of René Magritte. The *Magritte and Advertising* exhibit made it possible to show more than a hundred examples of Magritte's influence in this area.

There is a tempting explanation for the popularity of Magritte's imagery in advertising and other forms of graphic design. Since Magritte himself had been a designer of numerous ads and posters, what could be more natural than for advertising to turn around and seize upon these works of Magritte for inspiration? But this explanation is inadequate for two reasons: Advertising designers and other graphic artists have not been influenced by his ads and posters (until recently, they were unaware of their existence), but by his paintings; and second, Magritte hated advertising—an attitude he reaffirmed on several occasions. In fact, Magritte took the mechanisms of representation that he used to make his advertisements work and forced himself to question and thwart them in his paintings. The relationship between images and words is an especially good example of just such a mechanism. In general terms, one may say that all advertising tries to *associate* the image of a product with a name; yet Magritte spent his life trying to *dissociate* words from images—paintings from their titles. How can one explain, then, how work which is as antiadvertising as possible, and which actually seeks to undermine the mechanisms of representation used in advertising, can be exploited to such a great extent by advertising designers?

In the enlightening texts that he left us on the subject of his art, Magritte states more than once that he was satisfied with a painting only when it escaped as much as possible all explanation and interpretation. Magritte forced himself—and this is a problem he constantly addressed in his writing from the thirties on—to evoke *mystery*. This word should not be taken in a mystical or esoteric sense, but in the sense that his canvases resist the explanation one is tempted to give them. In other words, they attempt to deliver a "naked" image about which one must interrogate oneself. These images are always very readable in that one can immediately recognize what is being depicted—an apple, a pipe, or a hat—but one is also incapable of explaining the "meaning" of the image because familiar objects are presented in disconcerting contexts—contexts in which they appear with other objects with which they are not commonly associated. This mystery further complicates the issue: How can paintings created with the specific goal of resisting interpretation be used to such an extent by the advertising media—to the point where Magritte is the contemporary painter whose work is most copied by those media?

Asking the question in that way, paradoxically, gives one the answer: By removing semantics from his paintings, Magritte created images which certainly evoke mystery and make one think; but in so doing he paid the price of extreme ambiguity. That is to say, since his images are not linked to a single explanation or interpretation, all explanations and interpretations become possible. And simply by substituting a suitable slogan for the title of a painting, one can create an excellent advertisement.

We understand better now the essential role the titles play in Magritte's paintings. It was his work in advertising that accustomed him to associating images and words. He therefore learned to be wary of words; he knew how easy it is to use words to orient the meaning of a picture and give it an interpretation. That's why he often used words against the grain, as it were, as a sort of guardrail. Far from giving an explanation or meaning to a painting, they create more mystery, further intriguing the viewer.

In dissociating the image from its title, Magritte made the work for illustrators and graphic designers easier in spite of himself. An illustrator can easily reproduce one of Magritte's paintings for a book cover, and in so doing, channel or focus the original multiple meanings of the image. This may explain why one sees so many of Magritte's paintings on the covers of books which have nothing to do with Surrealism.

These images, which are universally recognizable and whose disconcerting character attracts attention without being aggressive (on the contrary, they encourage the imagination to wander), are extraordinarily flexible for illustrating articles, book covers, and, of course, record album covers. It is not surprising, therefore, that Magritte's images are found in book and record stores everywhere in the world.

Illustration is only one aspect of the use of Magrittesque imagery. If advertising (television as well as print) uses Magritte's images—or the ideas they contain—very often intact or by adapting them to its needs, this is also due to the special way Magritte treats the object in his paintings.

The Surrealists' interest in the object is well-known—indeed, "Glory to the object!" was their slogan. It was by means of a clever setting, particularly one that isolates it, that Magritte rendered the object glorious. Isolated from its normal context, the most banal object suddenly acquires a kind of nobility and aura which lend it brilliance. A mysterious presence seems to emanate from an object which, before, might have been completely ignored. This is something which could obviously be useful to advertising designers. They, too, deal with banal objects: chiefly consumer goods from which they seek to evoke some charm in order to sell them. The Magrittesque settings allow them to play up products which, of themselves, offer little interest.

In a remarkable text, written about forty years ago but still astonishingly current, Paul Nougé was the first to call attention to the Magrittesque isolation of the object in art. And with remarkable insight, he tied this isolation of the object to the trademarks on stalls of fairs—thus bringing one back to advertising.

"The perfect painting," Magritte once wrote, "produces an intense effect in a very short time." This statement may surprise painters, who generally place great importance on the contemplation of a painting. Their wish is to have the spectator absorb himself slowly in the painting and be attentive to every detail—even the paint and canvas. On the other hand, it would make advertising artists rejoice, because it states exactly what is required of a good ad: that it leave an impression in the brief instant one's glance rests upon it. Magritte and advertising designers also agree on the practice of putting everyday objects in the forefront—in order to accentuate their mystery, in the case of Magritte, and to increase their sales, in the case of advertising designers.

But the plundering of the works of Magritte can be analyzed in still a different way. Magritte's isolation of a particular object is only one aspect of his work; most of his paintings present diverse elements, combined, mixed, and metamorphosed according to a carefully planned scheme of composition. The term "object" is thus too restrictive. Magritte spoke of "familiar figures of the visible"—the sky, people, trees, mountains, furniture, stars, etc. He endowed the object with a cosmological dimension (or better, cosmological dimension, since it is a question of a world in perpetual change), with elements mixing and unmixing in an unusual way. These elements of nature are themselves elements from which myths have always derived their raw materials. Magritte's art is that much more fascinating in that he instinctively used images from the collective unconscious which have a universal resonance.

Moreover, these many combinations of cosmic elements to which Magritte, the painter-creator, abandoned himself were not made at random. With incessant research, he created a store of archetypal imagery which has not yet become commonplace in visual thought and perception. From this comes the paintings' double interest: They touch the imagination with their improbability, and as archetypes they can be used to prop up different types of arguments—commercial as well as political.

The arguments used by advertisements are always being modified, and to reinforce their messages, they frequently call upon paradoxical and unreal imagery. Unconscious logic, which ignores contradictions, will always be more effective than rational or conscious logic, which, however, can be supported by such imagery. It is for this reason that today one sees so many ads and posters which resort to surrealistic and fantastic imagery (though this imagery is not always—far from it—Magrittesque).

It is not surprising, then, to find insurance companies among the advertisers who borrow from Magritte. The unusual and improbable characteristics of the paintings—which were created to make one think and to evoke a sense of mystery—are now presented only to be clarified by a company slogan: "We help you to expect the unexpected. You must prepare for the unforeseeable."

George Roque is an art historian of French and Belgian citizenship. He was curator of Margritte et les Publicitaires *(Margritte and Advertising), the exhibit shown in Paris during the summer of 1983 and which subsequently toured Japan. He is also the author of* Ceci n'est pas un Margritte *(This is Not a Margritte), published in France in 1983 by Flammarion. M. Roque's article was translated from the French by Linda Silver.*

Originally published in PRINT, *March/April 1985*

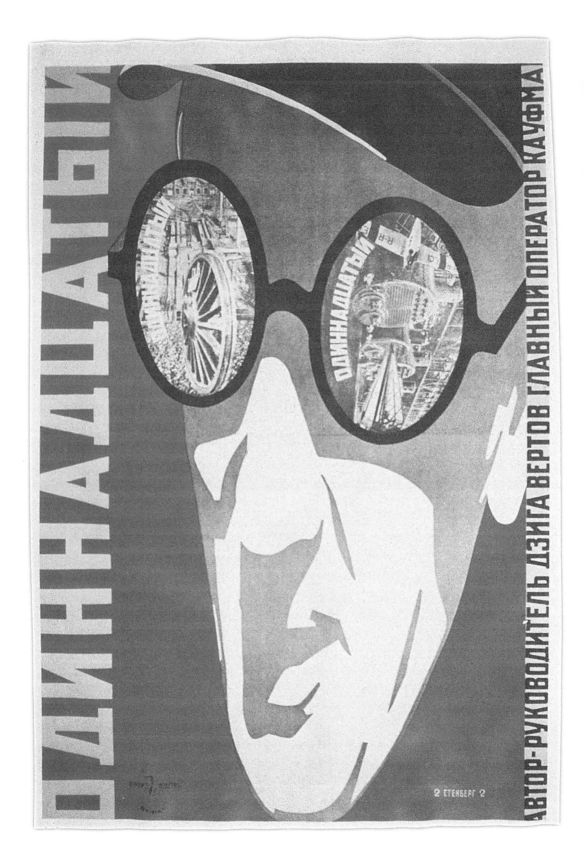

FILM POSTERS BY MOSCOW'S STENBERG BROTHERS, 1923–33
Christopher Mount

"Ours are eye-catching posters which, one might say, are designed to shock. We deal with the material in a free manner . . . disregarding actual proportions . . . Turning figures upside-down; in short, we employ everything that can make a busy passerby stop in their tracks."

—Vladimir Stenberg (1928)

From the 1917 Bolshevik Revolution to the onset of the Stalinist purges in 1934, the Soviet Union underwent not only social and economic upheaval but also a revolution in the arts. A new breed of "artist engineer" emerged with a conspicuous role in building the new society. Chief among this new breed were two brothers: Vladimir and Georgii Stenberg. The Stenbergs gained their first renown as constructivist sculptors. Later they worked as successful theater designers, architects, and draftsmen. Their design commissions ranged from railway cars to women's shoes, but their most significant achievements were advertising posters of Soviet Russia's newly burgeoning cinema.

The film posters of the Stenberg brothers, produced from 1923 until Georgii's untimely death in 1933, are radical-looking even today; yet they are not the consequence of some brief flame of eccentric artistic creativity. Rather, they evolved out of the brothers' knowledge of contemporary film theory, suprematist painting, Constructivism, and avant-garde theater, as well as their skill in the graphic arts. This eclectic experience (combined with new artistic inventions) resulted in posters that should not have been produced in any other era.

Born in Moscow to a Swedish father and a Russian mother—Vladimir Augustovich in 1899, and Georgii Augustovich in 1900—the Stenberg brothers shared from an early age an unusually strong bond. They were inseparable both in work and in life. "[In] the second grade I was kept back because I was sick a lot," recalled Vladimir in 1981. "And when my brother entered school we sat together at the same desk. It was that way until the end." While designing film posters, they worked on the same piece simultaneously, quickly alternating turns in the rush to complete it. After 1923, they began signing their work "2 Stenberg 2," deliberately fostering the impression that the objects had been produced by a collective rather than individuals. The equality of this partnership reflected not only a fraternal attachment, but also the idealism of the "new society" proposed by the Bolsheviks.

Teens at the outbreak of revolution, the Stenbergs were inspired by the sense of extraordinary possibility. They experimented freely, embracing the change that had occurred in the relationship between fine and applied arts. It was believed that for this new society to succeed, art must be integrated into everyday life and serve the needs of the proletariat. Avant-gardists such as the Stenbergs rejected representational painting as old-fashioned and bourgeois. For these young artists, the value of art now lay in its usefulness to the community. Movie posters were a revolutionary art form that merged two of the most important agitational tools of the new Communist regime. In a country that was overwhelmingly illiterate, film helped convert the masses to the new social order, while graphic design, especially when featured on political placards, became a direct, economical means to elicit support.

Between 1917 and 1922 the Stenbergs attended the Stroganov School of Art (later renamed The State Free Art Workshops). They took classes in military engineering, specializing in bridge and railroad construction. They also became members of The Society of Young Artists and participated in all of the group's exhibitions. In 1921, along with Alexei Gan, Varvara Stepanova, Alexander Rodchenko, and Carl Ioganson, the brothers formed a faction within the Institute of Artistic Culture called the First Working Group of Constructivists. A year later, in conjunction with an exhibition of their spatial paintings and constructions, they helped to write a manifesto titled "The Constructivists Address the World."

During the same period, the Stenbergs began to work for several of the local theaters, designing display posters, stage sets, and costumes. As with film and graphic design, the Soviet state clearly understood the powers of theater as agitprop. Stage productions were reconceived as a conceptual union of décor, costumes, music, and text, to which actors' individual performances were subordinated. The Stenbergs immediately translated to the theater many of their ideas about "structuring" space.

The 1920s and early 1930s were a revolutionary period for the graphic arts throughout Europe. Not only did the formal vocabulary of graphic design change; so did the designer's perception of self. The concept of the designer as "constructor"—or, as the Dadaist Raoul Hausmann preferred, "monteur" (mechanic or engineer)—marked a shift within the field from an essentially illustrative approach to one of assemblage and nonlinear narration. This new idea of assembling preexisting images, primarily photographs, into something new freed design from its previous dependence on realism. The subsequent use of collage—a defining element of modern graphic design—enabled the graphic arts to become increasingly nonobjective.

By 1923, when the Stenbergs created their first film poster, *The Eyes of Love*, film was already a significant new art form. The following year, all private film production was centralized under the government agency Sovkino. With increasing support from the state, production soared. Alfred H. Barr, Jr., soon to be appointed the first director of New York's Museum of Modern Art, wrote of the new Soviet cinema while traveling in Russia in 1928, ". . . at least the revolution has produced great art even when more or less infected with propaganda. Here at last is a popular art; why, one wonders, does the Soviet bother with painters?"

The first step the Stenbergs took with this new format was to revise the notion of how a movie should be advertised. Heretofore the most common method was to illustrate a dramatic scene, preferably one featuring the star. (This method is still common today.) In contrast, the Stenbergs tried to capture the overall mood of a film, and rarely depicted specific moments. They often worked quickly after viewing, producing a finished design overnight. Through montage they emphasized a simultaneity of events, recreating their immediate impressions of the film from distilled bits and pieces. A Stenberg poster is about implication, an allegory composed of small separate signs. The formal devices they used vary depending on the film's genre. In the poster for *A Commonplace Story*, a 1927 melodrama about a young mother driven into prostitution after the death of her son, the device is a simple one: a close-up of the woman's torso, her terrified face turned toward a phalanx of shadowy male figures, suggesting imminent danger and the impossibility of escape.

To achieve this effect, the Stenbergs varied the technique of photomontage. Photomontage—the joining of discrete photographic images to create a composite—became popular with many leftist avant-garde movements of the period. Its use in the graphic arts is analogous to that of metaphor in a poem. (It is not coincidental that Alexander Rodchenko's photomontages published in 1923 for Vladimir Mayakovsky's "Pro Eto," a love poem, are among the earliest known uses of the technique in Russia.) As a visual poem, a work of photomontage is more than the sum of its parts; it is a unique entity whose meaning relies on an associative reading of its disparate elements.

The Stenbergs used the technique but not the materials of photomontage—at least not directly. Rather than composed of photographic images, the designs for their posters were made up of drawings *after* photographs—a neat subversion of photomontage that simulates the "magical realism" of photography. The printing processes then available were inadequate to the reproduction of black-and-white photographs in the size and number demanded of an advertising print run. In many respects, this technical limitation was liberating. The modification of photographic realism through the addition of linear abstract forms allowed a vast array of possibilities—for example, the outlines used to suggest the force of a blow in *The Pounded Cutlet*. Here, as in many of the posters, the effect is one of movement, implying the cinematic passage of time.

Some abstracted shapes are not narrative but appear primarily for reasons of composition and structure. Influenced by the suprematist works of Kazimir Malevich and Vassily Kandinsky, the Stenbergs often used a diagonal format or a geometric configuration that made little sense for storytelling purposes. It is ironic to observe elements of nonobjective art used as formal devices in a fundamentally *objective* art form such as the movie poster, whose purpose is to illustrate a specific film.

To achieve this new "magical realism" the Stenberg brothers created their own projection device. As described by Vladimir in a 1975 interview, "To make it possible for us to freely manipulate projected images we invented a special [film] projector which was capable of not only enlarging and reducing, but also distorting the projected image; we could distort a vertically organized image, for example, to make it look like a diagonally organized image. Also, when we had to insert a face of a well-known actor into a poster, we used the principle of photography to copy an image from the film frame exactly onto a poster. All kinds of techniques were possible. But rather than being scared of them, we motivated ourselves to integrate these new technologies for our own benefits."

This sophisticated tool (an invention made more extraordinary when one considers the shortages of basic materials in the postrevolutionary 1920s) freed the Stenbergs from conventional compositional organization and permitted the unrestricted manipulation of images and typography. With it, the Stenbergs constructed a new, entirely modern perspective, in which each image remains true to its own perspectival rules yet has little connection to other images in the picture. The variety and juxtaposition of scales, and the frequent subversion of spatial relationships, are extraordinary. For example, in their poster for the film adaptation of the "Miss Mend" detective stories, there is no discernible connection between the size of the figures and their relation to the picture plane. Only because the images are drawn, and not made from photographs of dissimilar quality and tone, does the work hold together as a unified conceit.

The Stenbergs' use of the projector reflects their early constructivist infatuation with mechanical reproduction and preoccupation with the relationship between the process of design, labor, and the final product.

The materials used in the design of these posters—strips of celluloid and a light projector—are the basic materials of the cinema: the posters' manner of construction is faithful to the conception of their design. Rather than being divorced from the final object, the process forms an integral part of the work.

A stylistic innovation pioneered by the Stenbergs is the extreme close-up—later a hallmark of twentieth-century advertising design. The repeated illustration of an enlarged face had little precedent (as did few of the Stenbergs' experiments) in Western graphic arts. Clearly, this dramatic device was borrowed from the cinema, where it appeared even before it was used in still photography. Often, the faces appear split in two horizontally, suggesting a sequence of film frames. At times, the division simplifies different aspects of a character's personality, as in the androgynous portrait in the poster for *The Three Millions Case*.

One of the Stenbergs' most vigorous designs was for Dziga Vertov's *The Man with the Movie Camera*, a film recording the events of a single day in Moscow. This poster, a disjunctive image even for the Stenbergs, features a woman's body represented by a movie camera and tripod. The substitution of the camera for half of the woman's face and the lens in place of an eye reflects the Bolsheviks' idealization of the machine—their desire to realize a utopian society through technology. Vertov once stated that the camera could be used to "create a man more perfect than Adam . . . From one person I take the hands, the strongest and most dexterous; from another I take the legs." It is not coincidental that one of the rare appearances of actual photographic elements in a Stenberg poster occurs in the second of two advertisements for Vertov's *The Eleventh*. Here, eyeglass lenses have been replaced by photographs depicting the mass industrialization of the new Soviet Union.

As an extension of their interest in film and montage, the Stenbergs introduced a new sense of movement into graphic design. Their attempt to "agitate" the static form of the poster had a number of precedents; indeed, the implication of motion, and its corollary, progress, was seen as an appropriate goal for artwork produced during a period of profound social change. Examples include the Russian cubo-futurist works of Malevich, Mikhail Larionov, and Natalia Goncharova; the kinetic sculptures of Vladimir Tatlin; and, most obviously, the "moving image"—the cinema—as well as the Stenbergs' own early sculptures and stage designs. In the Stenbergs' posters, figures are rarely at rest; they fall or spiral through space, sometimes in and out of the picture plane. Abstract elements or type twist and spin around them, suggesting invisible forces at play. Furthermore, the ingenious, rhythmic repetition of images within one poster—as in *The Three Millions Case* and *SEP*—becomes a metaphor for movement and the structure of film. By manipulating the image during the printing process, the Stenbergs were able to suggest a gradation from light to dark in the tone of the repeated figure, which comes more sharply into focus as it "approaches" the foreground, enhancing the temporal quality of the image.

To further underscore the animate qualities of the posters, the Stenbergs used color in a new, more expressive manner. The severe artificiality of the tones is exceptional for this or any era, the colors chosen not as a reflection of nature, as had been the norm, but to elicit an emotional response. It must be remembered that the films the posters advertised were shot in black and white, and consequently the Stenbergs had no existing model from which to work. Their entire oeuvre, which consists of more than 300 posters, illustrates a rare fearlessness of color exploited through the astute manipulation of the lithographic printing process. The "simultaneous contrast" of reds, blues, oranges, and greens causes an optical vibration that heightens the surrealism of the works; natural elements, particularly faces, often take on monstrous tones of green, yellow, or blue.

The brothers were also innovative in their use of black ink, particularly as a background. These posters are very dark, with sharply contrasting areas of light, evoking the experience of viewing a film in a darkened theater. Often, a futurist-like shadowing at the edges of forms indicates volume. At other times, figures are mere silhouettes in surrounding areas of highlights, suggesting film's translucency. Again, this effect is both an apparent attempt to replicate the experience of the cinema and a consequence of using projected film in the creative process.

Keenly aware of technology's importance to the development of a strong Soviet state, the Stenbergs used the machine and the modern skyscraper as recurring motifs. In fact, there is little appearance of the natural world in any of the posters. Although the Stenbergs apparently never saw a skyscraper, tall buildings in the international functionalist style appear in many of their works like a benign fantasy of the future. In several, the skyscraper is abstracted as a background geometric grid that suggests modernity. Other appearances of these cement-and-glass structures seem to have more negative connotations, isolating the characters and suggesting the anonymity of the big city—and, perhaps, the moral bankruptcy of the capitalist West, as well.

The typography in the film posters is almost exclusively blocky, sans serif, and mechanical in appearance, but far from dull. Words or sentences become structural elements, as in *General*, where the name of Buster Keaton, the film's director and star, is repeated to form the elaborate fabric of a suit.

Evident in all of the Stenbergs' posters are a sense of playfulness and an openness to experimentation. Humorous, sexy, and psychologically complex, they display a confident autonomy from the dictates of studio clients, as well as from what would soon be a totalitarian regime. What is significant is not the posters' range of themes, dictated by movies from Hollywood slapstick to Soviet propaganda, but the diversity of graphic solutions. These reveal a high degree of personal expression and genuine affection for the films themselves.

The Stenbergs clearly enjoyed their involvement with the cinema, and were offered jobs as cameramen and even roles in some of the Russian productions. They were free spirits, "rogues" who enjoyed drinking and riding their motorcycles fast. Although it was a time of tremendous economic uncertainty and severe privation, they acquired enough work to be financially secure. As the sons of a Swedish émigré they remained, to a certain extent, foreigners in their own homeland. Both refused to become naturalized citizens during Georgii's lifetime, and although they did much propaganda work for the state, neither became a member of the Party. This status as expatriates may ultimately have hastened the end of their collaboration.

On October 15, 1933, while riding his motorcycle in Moscow, Georgii Stenberg was killed when a truck collided with the front of his bike; his wife, seated next to him, survived. Vladimir maintained until his own death in 1982 that this was not an accident but murder, a conspiracy involving the KGB. Regardless of these suspicions, Vladimir continued to receive commissions from the state following Georgii's death, and was shortly afterward appointed chief of design for Red Square, a post he occupied intermittently until 1964. He also completed various projects, including film posters, in collaboration with his sister Lydia and son Sten, but these graphic works lack much of the vitality of the earlier collaborations with Georgii.

It would be wrong, however, to conclude from Vladimir's late work that Georgii possessed the bulk of the Stenbergs' talent and ideas. It must be remembered that in 1934, Josef Stalin proclaimed the end of experimental art and anointed Socialist Realism the new official style. These years marked the end of not only the Stenbergs' collaboration but also the careers of many in the avant-garde.

Though the period of their making was relatively brief, the early posters left an indelible mark on design history. The Stenbergs' numerous innovations—rethinking the content of the film poster, introducing implied movement, using expressive typography and color, distorting scale and perspective—were investigated and extended by later designers and movements. Many of the Stenbergs' experiments with letterforms can be seen as precursors to the phototypographic advertisements of the 1960s. And their facile manipulations of pictorial space seem prescient in light of the infinite mutability of the photographic image made possible by the desktop computer only in the last ten years.

Most important, the Stenbergs understood the function of the poster, and their remarkable innovations were clearly means to an end: the creation of a visually compelling work. The purpose of any poster is to attract the eye in the briefest of intervals. It is in this deceptively simple ambition that these complex works so excel.

Christopher Mount was assitant curator in the Museum of Modern Art's department of architecture and design. He directed the 1977 MoMA exhibition Stenberg Brothers: Constructing a Revolution in Soviet Design, *from whose catalog this essay was adapted.*

SOULS ON FIRE
Michele Y. Washington

> If white people are pleased we are glad. If they are not, it doesn't matter. . . . If
> colored people are pleased we are glad. If they are not, their displeasure doesn't
> matter, either. We build our temples for tomorrow; strong as we know how, and
> we stand on top of the mountain, free within ourselves.
> —*Langston Hughes*, The Negro Artist and the Racial Mountain *(1926)*

At the turn of the twentieth century, the words, visual images, and musical expression of
black Americans began to be celebrated in American popular culture as never before. A new
consciousness had emerged from the black intelligentsia of the 1890s, articulated by W. E.
B. DuBois, a cofounder of the National Association for the Advancement of Colored People
(NAACP) and editor of its magazine, *The Crisis*, and activist Marcus Garvey, whose Universal
Negro Improvement Association (UNIA) manifesto promoted black self-esteem and racial
pride. For twenty-five years, DuBois and Garvey primed the growth and blossoming of the
New Negro Arts Movement. This Black Renaissance (more popularly known as the Harlem
Renaissance) characterized the social and cultural activity of a community only a few
decades removed from slavery and Reconstruction, which sought to invest the American
consciousness with positive images of its own making.

In the 1890s, the black intelligentsia, literati, and artists began to produce a recognizable body of work. They sought a realistic portrayal of black life to replace the exaggerated and derogatory images of black-faced minstrel singers and other coon-like popular
figures. Characters then used to promote products in the commercial market—the Gold
Dust Twins, Aunt Jemima, Uncle Ben—drew on the iconography of servitude and slavery,
domesticating images of the black savage and the beast. In dignified opposition to this sensibility was the literature created by playwright, folklorist, and novelist Zora Neale Hurston;
poets Countee Cullen and Langston Hughes; novelists Claude McKay and Wallace
Thurman; and many other luminaries. Visual artists also influenced by Marcus Garvey's
UNIA and by the rhetoric of Alain Locke, the black cultural critic and proponent of a new
black aesthetic, served these writers with a complementary visual language. Collectively, they
worked to define a new cultural identity reflecting their African roots. The Negro came into
vogue, offering unprecedented visibility to black people in twentieth-century America.

By the 1920s and through the 1930s, the flourishing Black Renaissance produced a distinctive literary language, combining the folklore of Africa and southern black America, whose population was relocating in a long, migratory stream to the urban centers of the North. Masses of black people from the post-Reconstruction South, oppressed by its Jim Crow segregation laws, moved to New York, Philadelphia, Detroit, and Chicago, hoping to find better work, living, and educational opportunities. With this great migration came a group of educated black men and women, whom W. E. B. DuBois, in his 1903 book, *The Souls of Black Folks*, called "the Talented Tenth."

The artists who came into prominence during these years included Aaron Douglas, widely known as the "father of Negro art," as well as Richard Bruce Nugent, E. Simms Campbell, Marcellus Hawkins, Charles Dawson, Gwen Bennett, Laura Wheeler Waring, Robert Pious, Miguel Covarrubias, and James Lessene Wells. Exchanging ideas and inspiration with black literary lights, they produced works that were experimental, political, and racial, resonant with both anger and joy.

Alain Locke, a professor of philosophy at Howard University in Washington, D.C., and the first black Rhodes scholar, instigated the flurry of cultural activity. He was well-versed in the arts, literature, and music. (Howard set up the first art department for black students in 1920, at a time when only a handful of institutions truly welcomed African Americans.) Locke challenged younger artists to seize their pens and brushes and give birth to a black aesthetic.

Offered the chance in 1925 to guest-edit a special issue of the popular social science journal *Survey Graphic*, titled "Harlem, Mecca of the New Negro," Locke announced to white America that the black literati had "arrived." Its culture could now be made visible to an audience that knew little of its interests or endeavors. Black and white writers were featured together, a first in any major white publication. This issue had two print runs and became the highest-selling number in the magazine's history.

"Harlem, Mecca of the New Negro" laid the groundwork for the 1926 anthology *The New Negro*, a collection of essays and short stories edited by Locke. Although some date the beginning of the Harlem Renaissance to the publication of this volume, the seeds had been planted long before. In *Black Art and Culture in the 20th Century* (1997), Richard Powell defines "New Negro" as an enlightened, politically astute African-American sprung from the turn-of-the-century progressive race rhetoric of educator Booker T. Washington and of black women's rights advocate Fannie Barrier Williams. The "New Negro" was defined not only in terms of political influence, but through a black aesthetic evolved in literature, music, film, theater, and the visual arts. In his introduction, however, Locke redefined the "New Negro" in cultural terms, almost ignoring the political emphasis of a decade earlier.

Locke's writing discussed African art's influence on modernism, the shift from the stiff traditional forms of European sculpture and painting to the kinetics inspired by African sculpture. Egypt was more than a source of motifs popular in Art Deco; for some black artists, it was the birthplace of the Negro race. Borrowing Egyptian design elements proudly signaled a line of descent.

The dynamism of African art unshackled the modern artist. Blacks were crucial to the development of modernism, writes art historian Leslie King-Hammond. "After all,

Picasso's cubism is about the discovery of the 'other,' the African. His co-opting of this information is a historical legacy that rightfully belongs to Afro-Americans." Without the encouragement to explore the abstract form, Picasso, Matisse, Braque, Modigliani, Brancusi, Epstein, and other modern masters would not have reached their pinnacle.

Harlem, a small section of uptown Manhattan, emerged as a new black metropolis, with the largest concentration of blacks in any urban center. It was the place to be for black intellectuals. It was also the place for anyone in the arts to rub shoulders, though notable art also was being produced in Philadelphia, Chicago, Detroit, and Washington, D.C.—cities King-Hammond refers to as "The Little Harlems of America." According to art historian Mary Schmidt Campbell, American culture in the Black Renaissance experienced "an infusion of Black creativity unknown since the birth of artistic genius in the homeland of Black Africa prior to European colonization."

In the years before and after World War I, whites invaded the cultural life of Harlem—especially its nightlife—and white benefactors were sought after to sponsor some of the Black Renaissance's artists and writers. Among those benefactors was the philanthropist William E. Harmon, founder of the Harmon Foundation, whose exhibitions showcased black artists. Writer Carl Van Vechten befriended many Harlem artists and writers and found mainstream publishing outlets for some of their work. Nancy Cunard, the British heiress, artist, and political radical, compiled black literature and art for her 1934 *Negro Anthology*.

Visual artists also found outlets in the many publications that sprang up during the era. W. E. B. DuBois fostered his ideology of enlightened black culture by hiring many of the new visual artists to illustrate for his NAACP magazine, *The Crisis*. The National Urban League magazine, *Opportunity*, also provided design and illustration work. A. Philip Randolph's Brotherhood of Sleeping Car Porters produced *The Messenger*, and Marcus Garvey's UNIA published its own magazine. Multifaceted visual artists mastered the skills of designing, illustrating, and hand-lettering type. With vigor and passion, they turned out dust jackets, illustrations for book interiors, covers of race journals, and posters for film and theater.

The Messenger, The Crisis, and *Opportunity* also helped launch the careers of two women in the Renaissance: Laura Wheeler Waring and Gwen Bennett. Their entry into the male-dominated world came through editor Jessie Redmond Fauset, an assistant to DuBois and an accomplished writer herself.

Music gave the new Negro visual art its rhythm, and dance its sequential motion. While the swing bands blew their horns in New York, the funk of jazz came sweeping in from the South Side of Chicago, stimulating these artists to equate syncopated rhythms with the offbeat of abstract modernism.

One of the most provocative journals to burst onto the scene, in 1926, was *FIRE!!*—named after a spiritual written by Langston Hughes with music by Hall Johnson. The powerful title was suited to the new publication's agenda. Conceived by writer and editor Wallace Thurman, with seven young colleagues, *FIRE!!* went against the grain of *The Crisis* and *Opportunity,* whose editorial, Thurman felt, catered too much to whites and the black bourgeoisie.

Although *FIRE!!* lasted only one issue, the well-traveled, culturally astute artists behind it came to represent a bohemian group intent on speaking to the masses in their own voice. Thurman ironically dubbed this group the Niggerati, a nickname that both celebrated and mocked its black and literary roots. The rooming house where Thurman lived, a popular meeting place for the group, was called Niggerati Manor.

The Niggerati included novelist Zora Neale Hurston and poet Langston Hughes. Artist Richard Bruce Nugent served as associate editor of *FIRE!!* and Jonathan Davis as business manager. Illustrations were by Gwen Bennett and Aaron Douglas.

What made this group unique was its sense of comfort with its own diversity in gender, background, and skin tone. This was a time when the black bourgeoisie played out the skin-color games. Homophobia and sexism were common. The Niggerati rejected such attitudes.

According to Nugent's biographer, Thomas Wirth, *FIRE!!* was clever and cultured, and perhaps a bit pretentious, but its creators were urbane enough to find their own pretenses amusing. Although the magazine couldn't find the funding to survive, it provoked controversy in its short life. A cry of outrage arose from the black bourgeoisie, who wanted to forget the abuses of slavery and not to be identified in any way as African. Ignoring this backlash, Thurman convened the Niggerati a year later to produce another magazine, *Harlem*, which also lasted only a single issue.

During the Depression of the 1930s, FDR's New Deal set up the Works Progress Administration (WPA), which eventually put many artists to work on the government payroll. Playwrights wrote plays, actors starred in performances, visual artists created theater posters, printmakers formed workshops, and poets and biographers recorded oral histories—all supported by Uncle Sam. Many Americans, especially black artists, were employed in areas where they normally would have been denied work, and the Black Renaissance flowed on, gaining greater public exposure.

Thanks to WPA support, for example, artist Robert Savon Pious produced a collection of posters for the military. One of Pious's most visually striking posters garnered him a $100 prize in 1940 from the American Negro Exposition in Chicago, which exhibited the works of many popular black artists. Pious also illustrated the cover of the exposition program. His four-color poster style displays some of the same Egyptian influences seen in the work of Aaron Douglas.

The WPA also fostered the print workshops of Dox Thrash in Philadelphia and the Harlem Arts Center, originally directed by sculptor Augusta Savage in New York. Even after government support of the arts ended with World War II, the Renaissance endured, and continues to renew itself with each new generation of artists, writers, musicians, and intellectuals. For such scholars, "renaissance" is a word defined by white culture only when it chooses to take notice of black influences that have existed all along. Today, one can still sense the evolution of the architects of the Renaissance. The collective of skilled visual artists left an abundant body of work for the contemporary community to draw upon—a vast visual language created at a time in popular black culture when younger artists were truly steeped in the spirit and passion of the moment.

Author's note: The following people or institutions loaned or assisted with reproduction of art for this article. Thanks to the Archie Givens Senior Collection of African-American Literature at the University of Minnesota, Minneapolis; Schomburg Center for Black Research, The New York Public Library, New York City; Paul Coates and the Black Classic Press; Art Institute of Chicago, Imaging and Reproductions divisions; and Thomas Wirth and the estate of Richard Bruce Nugent. Additional thanks are due to the E. Simms Campbell Collection, Boston University Library; Tuliza Fleming, University of Maryland; and A'Lelia Bundles, The Walker Collection.

Michele Y. Washington is principal of Washington Design and currently a visiting instructor at Pratt Institute, in New York, where she teaches graphic design. Her articles have appeared in CHICAIGA, AIGA's Journal on New Media, *also* International Review of African American Art, Designing Pioneers, *and* PRINT *magazine.*

Originally published in PRINT, *May/June 1998*

POLEMICS AND POLITICS, AMERICAN STYLE
Steven Heller

Neither art nor graphic design can appreciably change the world. Only those persons who wield political (and military) power have the capacity to alter events and history. But just think what could happen if a political leader was also an artist or designer. Adolf Hitler was both: a poster artist and watercolorist who, though denied admission to the Vienna School of Applied Arts, presided over the most effective and venal national identity program the world has ever known. On a more positive note, our own Founding Father, Benjamin Franklin, can rightfully be called America's first graphic designer. In 1754, as publisher, editor, and cartoonist for the *Pennsylvania Gazette,* he created the "Join, or Die" emblem, showing a snake divided into eight parts that symbolized the need for the feuding American colonies to unite in the face of war with France and her Indian allies. As merely a designer, Franklin may not have had much impact, but his ability to champion republicanism *and* to design its arresting emblem greatly enhanced his influence.

Ronald Reagan's doodles aside, most political leaders do not practice art or design while in office, but rely on others to visualize their ideas and make them accessible. Even the most charismatic leaders must be buttressed by persuasive graphic statements and symbols. Though artists alone cannot implement even the slightest political turnabout, they can support change (for good or ill). The political image—as cartoon, painting, illustration, or typography—can caution, affirm, stimulate, persuade, and satirize. It can be benign or dangerous.

Native political imagery began with a few charged symbols. The Pine Tree Shilling Stamp issued in Massachusetts in 1652 was the earliest colonial emblem. It represented the tree of life—"ever green, ever blooming, ever bearing"—but soon it became the Tree of Liberty, which Thomas Jefferson said "must be refreshed from time to time with the blood of patriots and tyrants." This was not the only symbol adopted by the early colonists. That "noble savage" the American Indian symbolized the strength and promise of the New World settler—who was sometimes the Indian's ally, but more often was his enemy.

When the Indian fell victim to America's Manifest Destiny and became, in the early nineteenth century, an object of scorn, the political imagists turned to the white-clad, full-breasted female figure with flowing hair, alternately referred to as Columbia, Liberty, and America. She became the national ideal that Jefferson called the "Fine Female Figure," and represented the classical traditions of Greek democracy, which the Founding Fathers sought to emulate. Columbia was emblazoned in the American consciousness by her appearance on coins, stamps, and monuments. Two other images from antiquity also came to represent America: the liberty cap, which signified men freed from the bonds of slavery, and the eagle, a symbol of power and majesty adopted by Congress in 1782 as one element of the Great Seal. These emblems were integral parts of early patriotic iconography, appearing on everything from military insignia to tavern signs to elixir bottles.

An even more dynamic symbol was George Washington himself—a real-life hero imbued with mythic qualities, who, after his death in 1799, was virtually deified by his countrymen. His visage was synonymous with America's noblest ideals and was seen on canvasses, banners, and countless ephemeral items. Other presidents and statesmen also found their way into the hierarchy of American icons. But curiously, the most enduring American symbol is the likeness of a meat wholesaler from Troy, New York, named Samuel Wilson, who by happenstance was used as the original model for Uncle Sam.

Significant differences exist between these enduring symbols and the transitory political image. Though Columbia and Uncle Sam have been altered over time (to conform to improved printing methods or to a particular artist's style), their meaning has not changed. Icons are enduring, but they are not inviolate. Political image-makers use and distort them for their own "patriotic" purposes.

Early American polemical imagery as distinguished from patriotic painting and naïve art was ostensibly left to the cartoonist. Its pioneers were printers, like Franklin, who had their own presses, and silversmiths, like Paul Revere, who were proficient with the engraver's burin. Of more consequence than Revere's famous night ride were his pictures depicting the 1770 Boston Massacre, when British soldiers shot down five American colonists. William Bradford's October 31, 1765 edition of the *Pennsylvania Journal* was a seminal example of design as protest. The front page resembling a tombstone was a mordant response to the notorious Stamp Act that excessively taxed the colonists and ultimately was a cause of revolution.

Despite occasional memorable images, the American cartoon before the Civil War was, in the words of Charles Dana Gibson, "hardly worthy of the name." Influenced by the British style, it nevertheless lacked the asthetic and conceptual brilliance of Hogarth, Gilray, and Rowlandson. Not until Andrew Jackson's presidency (1829–37) did a school of distinctly American cartooning emerge, including lithographs inspired by presidential campaigns and assorted political scandals. The Mexican War of 1846–48 provided the impetus for images that developed into the archetype label-laden political cartoon, similar to the still featured on today's editorial pages. In the 1850s cartoonists found a cause célèbre in the slavery issue. Even if their draftsmanship was faulty, the passions they ignited on both sides of this debate demonstrated the persuasive power of the cartoon.

Before the Civil War, the lithographic print and a few crudely produced magazines were the primary vehicles for polemical imagery. Between 1831 and 1849, Henry R. Robinson of New York was the most prolific publisher of political prints. In 1835, Nathaniel Currier opened what became the most successful lithographic publishing house in America, which, around 1852, when he went into partnership with his bookkeeper, James Merritt Ives, became known as Currier and Ives. Though attempting to emulate the style of the superior

English magazine *Punch*, America's antebellum humor and satire journals were usually sophomoric and stiffly illustrated. Periodicals like *Yankee Doodle, The John Donkey*, and *The Lantern* were interesting, if only for their marriage of text and illustration. More efficient printing methods ultimately allowed for finer reproduction and greater pressruns. The general-interest magazine *Harper's Weekly*, begun in 1850, was the most influential (and longest-running) journal. And in 1855 its leading competitor, *Frank Leslie's Illustrated Newspaper*, made its debut. While design was of secondary importance, subject to the constraints of letterpress technology, illustration and caricature excited the readers of these publications. Although a truly effective mix of writing and political cartoons did not occur until after the Civil War, *Harper's* and *Leslie's* created an environment for fine visual journalism by providing an outlet for America's leading political caricaturists: Thomas Nast and Joseph Keppler.

Working originally for *Leslie's*, then for *Mrs. Grundy* (his own short-lived periodical), and ultimately for *Harper's*, the Bavarian-born Thomas Nast developed a classical linear style that defined a genre of American cartooning. At *Harper's*, Nast invented some of America's most memorable symbols, including the Republican elephant (inspired by the elephantine size of the Republican vote in the 1874 presidential election), the Democratic donkey, and Santa Claus. In 1871, Nast's lethal caricatures of New York's corrupt political czar William "Boss" Tweed helped accelerate his downfall. A furious Tweed was reported to have said, "Stop them damn pictures. I don't care so much what the papers write about me. My constituents can't read. But, damn it, they can see pictures." After being toppled, Tweed fled to Spain, where he was identified on the strength of Nast's images and was arrested.

Joseph Keppler, a Viennese immigrant, originally went to work for *Leslie's* as a cartoonist, then failed at publishing his own humor magazines. In 1876, he tried again with a German-language satiric weekly called *Puck*, to which he added an English edition the following year. *Puck's* art epitomized the American Victorian graphic style, enhanced by lavish chromolithography that made the exquisite beaux-arts caricatures strikingly appealing. *Puck* had a Democratic bias, while *Judge*, its leading rival, took the Republican side. Each wielded Rabelaisian visual humor with rapier vigor against the enemies of its party. With the verisimilitude of photographs, their caricaturists ridiculed leading politicians by presenting them as unwed mothers, circus clowns, jesters, and animals, among other insulting guises. Racial stereotypes, at once humorous convention and malicious distortion, were among the most frequently used metaphors. Recurrent use as political symbols of savage redskins, black-faced minstrels, lazy plantation hands, coolie Chinamen, and simian-faced Irishmen reinforced the racism prevalent in America at the time. Even the liberal-minded Nast engaged in harmful racial stereotyping as in illustrations that depicted childlike Indians in his rendition of the poem "Yankee Doodle." Despite their insensitive use of these conventions, and their frequent attacks on open-door immigration policies, *Puck* and *Judge* often championed the rights of minorities, as well as causes like women's suffrage.

During the late nineteenth century, a seductive commercial culture increased the need for periodicals and other printed matter. As the number of magazines and newspapers grew, exposés of rampant political and social scandals proved potent draws. Despite a few constraining Victorian attitudes, the more dirt the better. The mix of politics and entertainment (or politics *as* entertainment) in *Puck* and *Judge* fostered many imitators. One such publication was *The Wasp* in San Francisco, which covered many of the same national issues, but fanned the flames of regional controversy as well, such as how to handle unwanted Chinese immigrants. *The Wasp*'s cartoonists saw the Chinese as a threat to the status quo, and often rendered the stereotyped "Joe Chinaman" as human debris. The editors of *Life* (which before it became Henry Luce's picture magazine in the 1930s was America's oldest published humor weekly) encouraged its writers and cartoonists to take stands on social issues. Charles Dana Gibson (who edited the old *Life* in its final years) not only created the idealized Gibson Girl for the magazine, but also joined, among others, James Montgomery Flagg and W. A. Rogers in making sometimes liberal, but often jingoistic, graphic political commentary. Unflagging patriotism was still the rule.

At the turn of the century, when American cartoons and comic strips were the primary means of visual political commentary, graphic design (with the exception of some prettified covers) was merely something added by the printer. In Europe, however, graphic artists were involved in a total union of text and image. This occurred first in the French and British commercial posters that spawned Art Nouveau. A new typography was devised to conform to fresh methods of drawing. Satirical magazines like *Simplicissimus* and *Jugend* in Germany and *L'Assiette au Beurre* in France wed the curvilinear forms of the "youth" style to their acerbic drawings. Designers involved in the American art poster movement during this period, such as Will Bradley and Edward Penfield, were more interested in aesthetics than politics, and their adoption of this European styling opened the door to a wider design consciousness.

The turn of the century was also a critical period in U.S. political history. Along with America's rise as an industrial and imperial power came social factionalization and stratification. A manufactured war with Spain in 1898 fostered some interesting visual critiques of foreign policy. Also at this time, European radical movements—anarchism, syndicalism, and communism—took hold in America, particularly among immigrant workers, resulting in a plethora of printed matter publicizing such philosophies. One of the earliest leftist periodicals was *The Verdict,* which had an essentially socialist viewpoint. Its format was similar to *Puck*'s, and its cartoonist railed against government shenanigans. Yet, by the early twentieth century, all these voices of dissent became, according to the writer Alexander King, "arrogant, conservative, and stuffy, [losing] complete sight of their prime functions as humorous weeklies."

The Masses, which published from 1911 to 1917, was a veritable wellspring of oppositional and confrontational writing and graphics. A forum for anarchist and socialist rhetoric, this Greenwich Village–based magazine was also an outlet for some of the most acerbic graphic commentators. With John Sloan (one of five "Ash Can School" painters who regularly contributed drawings) as its first art editor and designer of its format, *The Masses* was an inviting environment for the political message. Its graphics were a blend of popular Art Nouveau motifs and the gritty crayon drawing popularized by the French cartoonists. Although *The Masses'* circulation was only about 12,000 its artists had a profound influence on the style and tone of mainstream American cartooning. The magazine assumed a belligerent antiwar stance, which led to its suppression by the U.S. government when cartoonist Art Young and other editors were brought to trial under the Espionage Act. Although two trials ended in hung juries, by 1917, when American troops were committed to the European war, *The Masses* had folded, superseded in 1918 by the equally contentious *Liberator*.

During the war, a few of *The Masses*'s artists who had vociferously criticized the government became devoutly nationalistic and patriotic. Indeed, *many* artists and designers contributed their talents to the war effort. Working with limited funds, George Creel, a midwestern journalist and advertising man who had been asked by President Wilson to set up the Committee on Public Information, formed a coalition of some 250 illustrators and cartoonists. Under Creel's supervision, Charles Dana Gibson became the art director of a massive poster assault on the citizenry, the goal being to raise both money and morale. James Montgomery Flagg painted his compelling "I Want You" and "Tell That to the Marines" posters. Creel's so-called strategy of "agitation propaganda"—exemplified by the aerial release of hundreds of thousands of diecut leaflets in the shape of handbombs declaring "How Many Bonds Would You Buy If These Were Bombs Dropping on Your Home?"—was overwhelmingly successful in raising funds and recruiting soldiers.

The war's end saw Europe in shambles; attention now turned to the Continent's reconstruction, as well as to insuring that the horror would not reoccur. In Europe, a groundswell of peace activism ensued (often under the banners of socialist and communist organizations) and in the United States, advocacy groups, such as World Peaceways, mounted cautionary campaigns in the national media. From 1919 to around 1938, ads by leading cartoonists, including Abe Birnbaum, Rube Goldberg, and Boardman Robinson, were run frequently in general magazines, often next to cereal and soap ads, warning that the next war could be the last. "Never again" was the watchword of a generation and the rubric under which poster artists would do battle against militarism.

The war against war was undertaken in a climate of political upheaval throughout Europe, which pitted the left against the right. The Bolshevik Revolution of 1917 provided the impetus for kindred movements to seek their own utopias. In the United States, the left, which before World War I had been a loose amalgam of disparate ideological and labor groups, consolidated under a more rigid communist banner. While some artists and designers were influenced by the graphic experiments advanced by Soviet Constructivists and Productivists, the overall style of American polemics was more conservative. Periodicals like *The New Masses* were kept in tight rein by dogmatic editors. On the whole, its art was less imaginative than that of the old *Masses,* and some of its artists eventually embraced Stalin's Socialist Realism as the true means to communicate with the people. The graphic style of the thirties, the period of the Great Depression, was developed by politically-conscious artists employed by the Works Progress Administration (WPA), whose prints, crayon drawings, and murals defined a distinctly American *social* realism. This style, a distinctive combination of Ash Can School grittiness, a certain heroicism, and editorial cartoon fluidity was emblematic of the left. One leading liberal cartoonist of the era who had worked in this way, upon being called to testify before the House Committee on Un-American Activities in the early fifties about his presumed communist affiliations, was asked by his interrogator how long he had been a communist. Denying that he had ever been a party member, the witness asked in turn, "What ever gave the committee that idea?" To which the Kafkaesque reply was, "You must be a communist; you draw with crayon, don't you?"

Left-wing graphic commentary supported labor over management, criticized police brutality, championed civil rights, and railed against the specter of European Fascism. Inspired by the political art produced in Europe during the early thirties, stinging anti-Fascist images began to appear in American publications, such as *Ken* magazine. Some of these were general indictments against Hitler, while others proffered support for comrades in peril, notably the Spanish Republicans who were engaged in a bloody civil war. Paul Rand's pro bono covers for the anti-Fascist *Direction* magazine from 1939 to 1942 were heartfelt statements in a distinctive modernist idiom. By the time America entered World War II, many graphic artists were already seasoned veterans of propaganda warfare. They consequently were asked to serve the graphics department of the Division of Information (later known as the Office of War Information) of the Office of Emergency Management.

"A war poster is not a picture to sell pills, but to save civilization . . . Posters, however clever, are a waste of paper unless they kill Germans," wrote J. B. Nicholas, chairman of London's Advertising Service Guild. His admonition was heeded by the U.S. Division of Information, which was responsible for the issuance of all war-related press releases and propaganda and for the ultimate selling of the war. With George Creel's World War I accomplishments in mind, the agency used posters as its primary information medium. In 1941, poster and pictorial publicity was placed under the direction of Horton William Phillips, who had been in charge of graphic publicity for the Tennessee Valley Authority. Unlike Creel's shoestring operation, Phillips's agency had large sums of money at its disposal to build an art department that could facilitate the production of defense posters. As chief art director, Charles Tudor, a former assistant art director of *Life* and art editor of the newspaper *PM,* hired several expert advertising men as consultants, including Charles T. Coiner, art director of N. W. Ayer & Sons; Nelson Gruppo, a designer with Charles Cooper, Inc., and Jean Carlu, who, as art director of the French Ministry of Information, had come to New York to oversee the French exhibit at the 1939 New York World's Fair and remained in the United States when war broke out in Europe. Carlu's dramatic "Production" poster is one of the best known and most effective icons of the war.

Unlike the antiwar images of the thirties, which were often steeped in strident emotionalism, the government-sponsored messages of the forties were rationally composed and systematically produced. In the early months of the war, however, disorganization marked the process for creating effective propaganda; as Frances Brennan, chief of the Graphics Division of the Office of War Information (OWI), wrote in an open letter to *Arts* magazine in 1942: "It must be admitted that, thus far, the Government has fumbled the ball (first, because it had no central organization . . . second, because there was a split point of view on how the war graphics job was to be done." Brennan and other critics argued that the traditional advertising methods were ineffectual, meaning that saturation bombardment of images merely made the citizenry poster-drunk, and, so, oblivious to the messages being conveyed. One critic argued in early 1942 that "not only are the posters too many, too soft and too full of technical errors, but many of the issues have been ill-timed . . ." By not adequately differentiating the prewar calls for defense from the selling of a war that had arrived, America's poster art was not yet truly battle-ready. The creation of a more centralized graphics division in 1942 provided a means to effectively transform commercial into wartime advertising.

Some observers argued that Soviet war propaganda was the best model on which to base an American style. Stalin, who had long before the war prohibited the experimental graphics of the Russian avant-garde, insisted on an unambiguous, literal graphic vocabulary. Nevertheless, Americans were receptive to modernist ideas, which influenced their work and resulted in stylistic diversity. Their output ran the gamut from conventional painted realism and conservative typography to experimental approaches involving photomontage and asymmetrical layout. Indeed, many of the designers hired to create wartime advertising based their methodologies on the prevailing New Typography and trends in dynamic layout; among them were Bradbury Thompson (who designed publications for OWI), Leo Lionni (who was employed to do posters through N. W. Ayer & Sons), Robert Osborn (who illustrated survival manuals for the Office of Navy Information), Herbert Bayer, Lester Beall, and E. McKnight Kauffer. Though graphic style was important to the success of a message, even more important was a compelling slogan (such as "Keep 'Em Rolling," "Remember Pearl Harbor," and "Loose Lips Sink Ships"). Often, a visually appealing modernist design would not adequately underscore the slogan or convey the message, forcing those designers at odds with tradition to find a compromise between the polemic and aesthetics—a compromise that influenced the look of graphic design after the war.

The atomic destruction of Hiroshima in 1945 ended the war but ushered in an age of anxiety. Only six months after V.J. Day, Robert Osborn, who had created scores of survival manuals for the Navy, responded to this anxiety by publishing a book of drawings which, he explained, "is an attempt to show some of the miseries that make war no damn good." The vivid, horrifying images recalled from wartime service provided the basis for a visual testament to the "frustration, waste, and agony in war." The cautionary image that concluded his expressionistic memoir (which was appropriately titled *War Is No Damn Good*) was of a mushroom cloud emblazoned with a human skull—the first time this icon of the nuclear era was used. Subsequently, many other artists and designers contributed antinuclear emblems, including Herblock's sinister Mr. Bomb in the *Washington Post,* and Ben Shahn's haunting H-bomb specter for his memorable SANE poster.

Stalin's geopolitical machinations in Eastern Europe and a fresh conflict in Korea ignited the next round of international enmity. Sadly, petitions for peace, during the fifties, were often overwhelmed by the saber rattlers of the Cold War. Though artists and designers did not mobilize into a patriotic group to produce Cold War propaganda, a fair amount of banal graphic materials was produced that supported the myth of an internal Red Menace. General-interest publications, such as *Life* and *Collier's,* ran profusely illustrated articles that prophesied an inevitable war with Russia, and thus heightened the common fear of annihilation, or even worse, Red occupation.

The Cold War ethos gave justification to repression in the form of the House Committee on Un-American Activities and Senator Joseph McCarthy's anticommunist witch-hunts. Only a handful of graphic-arts dissenters dared defy the cold warriors, notably (but not exclusively) such veterans as Osborn, Herblock, Shahn, Walt Kelly (the father of

Pogo), and the neophyte Jules Feiffer (whose first comic strip, "Sick, Sick, Sick," in the *Village Voice*, altered the look and content of polemical cartooning). These artists influenced a subsequent group of illustrators and designers in the early sixties, including David Levine, Edward Sorel, Paul Davis, Robert Grossman, Seymour Chwast, R. O. Blechman, Milton Glaser, and Tomi Ungerer, who contributed graphic commentary to satiric magazines like the "underground" *Realist* and *Monocle* that, in the tradition of *The Masses*, criticized with caustic wit political, social, and cultural folly. During the Camelot years of John F. Kennedy, constituencies for these periodicals were small, but the artists, nevertheless, influenced the subsequent generation of artists and designers who were motivated to action by the convergence of the Vietnam War and the civil rights movement.

In the late sixties an unprecedented coalition of varied special interests—antiwar, civil rights, black liberation, gay rights, women's rights, free speech, and old and new left activists—triggered a movement with the aim of changing American attitudes toward the nation itself and the world at large. The banner of the epoch was raised by a youth culture which found expression in music, art, comics, pop culture, sex, and drugs, and created outlets for expression in the media. With this torrent of meaningful issues came a great need for communication; artists and designers were as necessary to the flow of information and ideas as they were during the World Wars. Yet the result was not the systematic or dictated dispersion of didactic propaganda, but, rather, a veritable orgy of emblematic visual expression for which the basic tenets of design were irrelevant. The amateur designers of the "underground" newspapers expressed the immediacy of their respective concerns with slapdown layouts and ad hoc graphics that were made without any thought of a grid. In contrast to the formal qualities of the Russian revolutionary avant-garde, the frivolity, gaiety, and informal qualities of the new "revolutionary" design at first suggests an irresponsible, perhaps detached, attitude. But the means of communication were consistent with the audience's ability to receive and understand messages, and were intensely meaningful to their makers and viewers. Buttons played an important role as conveyors of protest. "They were," writes historian David Kunzle, "like an amulet or tattoo, identifying the new political tribe; or a form of self-grafitto." Some of the famous button phrases are as powerful as the World War II slogans: "Make Love Not War," "Draft Beer Not Students," "War Is Good Business, Invest Your Sons."

Sixties political design was concerned with content, not decoration for its own sake. But professionals used various stylistic conceits to convey meaning. Herb Lubalin's elegant design for the magazines *Fact* and *Avant Garde* appealed to a slightly older, more sophisticated constituency, as did *Esquire*—specifically, George Lois's mordant, posterlike covers. Appealing to both new and old Left, Dugald Stermer's format for *Ramparts* was handsome and low-key, an inviting environment for the provocative journalistic revelations that were the magazine's usual fare. Similarly, *Evergreen Review* was designed by Ken Deardorf as a reader's magazine, but employed some of the acerbic Monocle illustrators. *Evergreen*'s most controversial cover was an iconic portrait of the Cuban revolutionary Che Guevara, who, after he was killed in Bolivia, became a martyr to the Left. Paul Davis's saintlike depiction so enflamed the anti-Castro Cubans in New York that they bombed the offices of the magazine.

Lack of space prevents the chronicling here of even a fraction of the arts achievements of the sixties and early seventies. It was a time of great fervor in which some memorable—and much banal—imagery was produced. But the level of passion should not be underestimated. This was a period of American history in which the media—graphics, film, and television—were at their most vociferous and persuasive. The convergence of images—moving and static, real and imagined—was powerful enough to help end a war and topple a president.

The late seventies and the eighties—perhaps out of exhaustion, perhaps out of disillusionment—saw a retreat from activism. Though political imagery is still produced, it is no longer in vogue. It would be unfair to reduce all the achievements of the activist years as merely a response to fashion, but the truth is that the swell of popular receptivity then toward radical issues made political consciousness acceptable and political imagery welcome in the mainstream. With the disintegration of the broad-based antiwar coalition, artists and designers concerned with social issues affiliated themselves with pet areas—AIDS, nuclear disarmament, Central America, human rights, South Africa, etc. Despite the plethora of issues needing the attention of graphic artists, the number of printed protests and critiques have actually dwindled in recent years. The reason, in part, is the absence of a national clearinghouse for this material. More significant, however, is the lack of national unity among disparate interest groups. An underground no longer exists, and youth-oriented media are more concerned with culture and fashion than politics. The nature of mainstream periodicals has changed so as not to allow space for provocative graphic commentaries.

Today, the ranks of young graphic commentators are thin. Many who choose to engage in political commentary do so through their own self-made outlets, such as the irregularly issued comics magazine *World War III*, or else do pro bono work for political groups. But the lack of contemporary role models often means that the young political commentator is forced, so to speak, to reinvent the wheel, often making platitudinous and naïve imagery that is easily dismissible.

Political imagery is an essential component of the ongoing democratic debate. The act of making the polemical image, "whether vehement, caustic and sometimes unpleasantly sharp," is almost a constitutional duty. If the eighties is not a golden period of such work, maybe the next decade will be. One may trust that this vital art form is threatened merely by apathy, not extinction.

Originally published in PRINT, *March/April 1988*

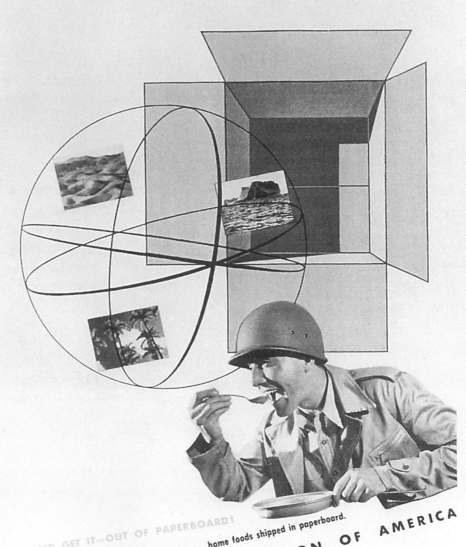

COME AND GET IT—OUT OF PAPERBOARD!

Around the world, U. S. troops are eating American...home foods shipped in paperboard.

CONTAINER CORPORATION OF AMERICA

The Rise and Fall of Design at a Great Corporation
Philip B. Meggs

A scenario occurs periodically in corporate America: An entrepreneur with a vision starts a company and it grows into a major corporation. The value of design to the corporation is recognized on several levels: as a means to communicate effectively with customers, stockholders, and employees; as a means to produce and market superior products; and as a means to help define the corporation not just as a business, but as a progressive force in society. A reputation for design leadership emerges. But then, after the entrepreneur passes from the scene, the commitment to design gradually diminishes and eventually disappears altogether. The saga of Container Corporation of America (CCA) is a vivid example of this persistent pattern in America's corporate history, and provides clues about how and why this process occurs.

CCA began in 1926 after Walter Paepcke, at age twenty-eight, inherited the Chicago Mill and Lumber Company from his father. Paepcke combined its paperboard and container fabrication facilities with additional plants he acquired, then named his new creation Container Corporation of America. Early-twentieth-century American industry was region-based, and CCA was among the first concerns to acquire other regional companies and build a national corporation. (Another was National Biscuit Company, or Nabisco.)

Paepcke was not an ivory-tower idealist but a practical businessman committed to corporate growth and technological progress. He ran a tautly organized, efficient company. But from the start, a sense of values and quality separated CCA from the typical corporation. "Paepcke expected excellence as well as hard work from people," recalls John Massey, who joined CCA as a staff designer in 1956 and became design director in 1964. "Commitment was assumed to be the norm."

Paepcke realized that his major products, such as brown corrugated shipping boxes, were pedestrian. He consciously sought a way to enhance the image of CCA as a corporation apart from the ordinary. Design was important in Paepcke's personal life; he believed it should also be important in employees' and customers' lives, while providing a way to differentiate CCA from its competitors. A commitment to design excellence was just one component of an overall corporate attitude, for product development, quality control, and technological innovation were stressed as well.

There is abundant evidence of the importance accorded design at CCA. When corporate heads and foreign visitors toured Container's headquarters, Massey remembers that

Paepcke always included the design department on their agenda and would emphasize the role of design in the company's total effort. Jeff Barnes, a CCA designer from 1976 to 1981, recalls making a presentation about CCA design to a visiting group of top executives from major Japanese corporations such as Nissan and Minolta. Barnes says he was awed when he interviewed with CCA and found the design department sharing the fifty-fourth floor of the First National Bank Building in Chicago with the legal department, one floor below the president and chairman. Hired as a senior designer, Barnes was given a private office with an "incredible view."

How did this young businessman, Walter Paepcke, acquire his understanding of art and design? Apparently, his aesthetic education intensified when he married Elizabeth Nitze, an artist who had majored in painting and design at the Art Institute of Chicago. Their union produced one of the most important corporate art patronages in history, with Elizabeth as Walter's guide. She once told Wilburn Bonnell, CCA's graphic design manager from 1971 to 1977, about buying a Paul Klee painting for about $250 early in their marriage. She was so afraid of Walter's possible reaction that she hung it in a dark hallway where he wouldn't see it. As time passed, however, his understanding and enthusiasm for art and design burgeoned.

Elizabeth still lives in Chicago. In a telephone interview, she unhesitatingly declared why her husband hired what was perhaps the first corporate design director in America. "I forced Walter into it," she said. Upset over the poor quality of design used by both the Chicago Mill and Lumber Company and CCA, she "argued and argued" until, finally, Paepcke asked Elizabeth herself to oversee CCA's design activities. She insisted that a more experienced professional was needed, whereupon Paepcke asked R. R. Donnelley of the Chicago printing firm that bore his name (he and Paepcke had been classmates at Yale) to suggest qualified persons capable of directing Container's design efforts. High on the list of recommendations was Egbert Jacobson, a nationally prominent art director and color authority. After a protracted interview process, Jacobson was hired in 1936 as CCA's first design director. He immediately set about designing a new logo to suggest CCA's national character, and a unified design program was subsequently applied to all aspects of company life.

The program developed by Jacobson has been called the first fully integrated corporate identity program in America. Additionally, Jacobson oversaw CCA's architecture and interior design, which were also produced on the highest possible level, with special attention given to the use of color and space in manufacturing facilities.

The structural experiments with paper in a Bauhaus foundation course had held a great fascination for Paepcke, and he became a major supporter of Bauhaus masters Ludwig Mies van der Rohe and László Moholy-Nagy, who had emigrated to Chicago from Germany after Hitler came to power. When Moholy-Nagy's "New Bauhaus" school faltered in Chicago during the late 1930s because promised financial support had not been forthcoming, Paepcke personally provided financing critical to its reincarnation as the Institute of Design, predecessor of the design school that continues today at the Illinois Institute of Technology.

Paepcke realized that paper boxes and packaging products did not easily lend themselves to significant differentiation among competitive products, but that distinctiveness could be achieved through design. In 1937, when the renowned French designer A. M. Cassandre came to America, he was retained by Container to create its advertisements. Cassandre's efforts contrasted dramatically with prevailing American advertising, which typically centered an illustration over a headline and rectangle of body text. Cassandre practiced the European approach influenced by modern art: Words and images were composed in a dynamic, asymmetrically balanced composition. Throughout its history, CCA and its designers made no distinction between advertising and other forms of design, bringing the same level of excellence to both advertising and corporate communications.

With the outbreak of World War II, CCA launched its highly successful "Paperboard Goes to War" institutional campaign. Ads were commissioned from émigré European designers who had fled the continent's turmoil, including Swiss photographer/designer Herbert Matter, former master of the Bauhaus typography workshop Herbert Bayer, and French poster artist Jean Carlu. These designers found American clients to be generally conservative and unsophisticated, with CCA being one of the few American companies willing to commission the Europeans' "total design" approach. A number of young American designers, including Paul Nonnast, a twenty-five-year-old Philadelphian, were also retained to design "Paperboard Goes to War" ads.

Using telegraphic copy and symbolic imagery to promote the importance of paperboard packaging in the war effort, the campaign was designed to improve the competitive position of paperboard in the postwar market by touting its strength and durability, features that made it an alternative to the wooden barrels and crates then in use for most shipping.

From 1944 to 1946, Container ran an institutional campaign saluting the nations involved in the struggle against the Axis Powers. This campaign introduced fine art into advertising, with paintings commissioned from artists who were native to each of twenty-seven countries honored with an institutional ad (9-11). A committee selected the artists who were asked to interpret their country of origin. N. W. Ayer and Sons, CCA's advertising agency, and its art directors, including Charles Coiner and Leo Lionni, worked closely with the artists. The series began with Russia in March 1944 and ran until May 1946, when A. M. Cassandre closed the campaign. Called the "Allied Nations" campaign at its inception, it later became known as the "United Nations" campaign. The commissioned paintings became part of the CCA corporate art collection and were widely exhibited.

During the 1940s, CCA became active in creating package designs to address its clients' marketing needs. Albert Kner became the first director of CCA's design laboratory (later renamed the design and market research laboratory), which pioneered packaging techniques for consumer marketing. Kner, a Hungarian designer known to Moholy-Nagy and Bayer in Europe, took package design into uncharted territory. Psychological testing was incorporated into the design evaluation process. A device was invented to monitor the path the observer's eye traveled as he or she scanned a package. The function of color in packaging was explored. A mock-up of a store interior was used to measure client packages against their competition. But for all the emphasis on marketing and sales, Kner maintained a concern for the aesthetic dimension of packaging. He is remembered as a sensitive, empathetic man, deeply committed to quality and open to exploring even screwball ideas, which often led to breakthrough innovations.

The "Allied Nations" campaign was remarkably successful in building CCA's reputation. After the supply of countries was exhausted, an institutional ad campaign honoring the forty-eight states was launched. An artist native to each state was selected to create a painting interpreting his or her home state. The interpretations ranged from realistic to the most avant-garde expressions of the time. From 1946 to 1949, CCA ran one of these ads each month until all forty-eight states were presented. The campaign was an institutional triumph.

In 1946, Herbert Bayer became a consultant to CCA. He played an important role not only in the evolution of CCA design, but also in Paepcke's development of Aspen, Colorado. Paepcke led the transformation of Aspen from a sleepy little backwater into a major resort and cultural center, and Bayer enhanced the locale's new significance by moving his home and studio there. In 1948, Bayer began work as editor/designer of CCA's *World Geo-Graphic Atlas,* a stunning presentation of the postwar world. His innovative information design used the language of graphic design to present the earth's environment and resources. Each country and state was presented through cartography and graphic statistics. Five years and $400,000 (1950 dollars!) were invested in this masterwork of bookmaking, which was published in 1953. Weighing six pounds, the 368-page atlas was distributed free to libraries and Container's customers.

With the supply of states exhausted, Paepcke sought a new institutional campaign, and in 1950, CCA launched the most famous institutional advertising campaign in history, "Great Ideas of Western Man." This series grew out of a "Great Books" discussion group at the University of Chicago, conducted by professors Robert M. Hutchins and Mortimer Adler, in which Walter and Elizabeth Paepcke were participants. Adler selected the quotations for the ads, and a committee initially composed of Adler, the Paepckes, Bayer, and Jacobson selected the artists and designers. James Miho, an N. W. Ayer art director assigned to the CCA account during the 1950s, recalls that agency hard-sell types simply could not comprehend this campaign, which combined excellent art with profound quotations. From inception to conclusion, the series numbered over 200 separate ads. Some of the art, including distinguished works by Lou Danziger, Saul Bass, Herbert Bayer, and John Massey, has been widely reproduced. The ads reproduced here were selected to show the range of approaches in the series and include several examples that aren't as well-known.

The "Great Ideas" campaign opened with a very high frequency, running every month during the early 1950s, and enjoyed astounding ratings in readership surveys. Massey, who was in charge of "Great Ideas" during its final two decades, says the campaign was, in a sense, a victim of its own success. The readership studies showed that people thought it appeared more often than it did and claimed to have seen it in magazines where it never appeared. During the 1960s and 1970s, management reduced its frequency, reasoning that the potency of the campaign could be maintained with fewer and fewer insertions.

In discussing the rationale for the campaign, Paepcke wrote, "It worries us that politicians' appeal for votes seldom hold more than the cynical promise of higher living standards, as if man were a creature who lives by bread alone." For employees, customers, and the general public, the "Great Ideas" series built an image of a company deeply concerned with ideas and the broader issues of civilization. CCA personnel director Connie Steele used the campaign to help recruit the best graduates from top colleges and universities. She also conducted seminars for the sales force to help them understand how they could use the campaign to build Container's image with customers.

In 1938, advertising executive David Ogilvy had denigrated CCA advertising as "an exercise in amateurish pretension" and predicted that "it would soon be consigned to oblivion." Thirty-eight years later, he declared it to be "the best . . . corporate advertising that has ever appeared in print." Ogilvy changed his mind because he came to realize that CCA advertising had been unique, had built admiration for the company, and had successfully differentiated CCA from its competitors.

The CCA corporate culture was an extension of Paepcke himself. Massey remembers lunches with Paepcke sitting at the head of the table in CCA's corporate dining room, leading discussions about international and national events, as well as the cultural scene and civic affairs in Chicago. "You really had to be on your toes to keep up with him," Massey recalls. "He was well-read and very knowledgeable."

Egbert Jacobson retired in 1956. Herbert Bayer, whom Massey remembers as meeting with the design staff about every month, was named chairman of the design department with responsibility for coordinating and overseeing all aspects of design, while Ralph Eckerstrom, one of the most dynamic people ever to work at CCA, was named design director. Described as "charismatic" and "a blond Adonis" by people who knew him in the 1950s, Eckerstrom was a young executive clearly on the move. Prior to coming to CCA, he had been art director of the University of Illinois Press, which had received much favorable recognition for its book design and typography. Under Eckerstrom, the press had received grants from the federal government to research design and color as factors in communications, and to study the influence of type style and size on readability and comprehension. These activities paralleled the interest Paepcke, Bayer, and Kner had in the Bauhaus's search for rational performance criteria for design, as well as their conviction about the value of design for the ordinary person. After an extensive series of interviews with Paepcke and Bayer, Eckerstrom was selected for the position and promptly hired his young assistant at the University of Illinois Press, John Massey, to join CCA as well. Eckerstrom recalls his relationship with Massey as "a complementary one." They worked well together and enjoyed tremendous mutual respect.

Eckerstrom cites his major achievements at CCA as being his work on the "Great Ideas" campaign, development of a new logo, and CCA's identity program. The old logo, he says, had problems. Container had become international in scope, and the U.S. map on the logo didn't play well abroad. Variations for the logo had been used superimposing the box and initials over maps of other countries and continents where CCA was operating. Eckerstrom eliminated the maps altogether. The old logo, moreover, was in brown, a color selected because of its association with corrugated boxes. But the folding-carton division fabricated and printed consumer packaging on white board. The blue color Eckerstrom chose was a hue referred to as "Bayer blue" at CCA, for Bayer loved this particular shade and used it frequently in his work.

Getting the new logo approved was a time-consuming task. The general conviction that Jacobson's twenty-year-old mark needed updating was offset by Paepcke's love for the old mark and his reluctance to throw it out just as Jacobson was retiring. Eckerstrom states that Bayer, who was a close personal friend of the Paepckes, championed the new logo design and "personally talked to Walter about it." Jacobson didn't care for it, but didn't interfere with its adoption.

A year before Paepcke died, Eckerstrom's position was expanded to include responsibility for graphic design, advertising, public relations, architecture, and interior design. After his death in April 1960, the corporate culture Paepcke created continued for a time because leadership passed to a generation of executives who had worked closely with him. The new president, Leo H. Schoenhofen, expressed a strong determination to carry Paepcke's design intent forward.

A significant change in CCA design managers took place in 1964, when Albert Kner announced his retirement as director of the design and market research laboratory. There are conflicting reports of the series of events that subsequently transpired, but after the dust had settled, Kner's associate director, Lony Ruhmann, originally codirector with art director Tom Schorer, emerged as sole director, and Ralph Eckerstrom was no longer with the company. In an interview with Eckerstrom, he told me that he and Schoenhofen had never gotten along very well and that he was fired and given a substantial severance settlement by the management committee because Schoenhofen believed design and Eckerstrom were occupying far too much of the management committee's time. In Wilburn Bonnell's version of events, Eckerstrom had asked Schoenhofen to add the design and market research laboratory to his area of responsibility and wanted a promotion to vice president. When Schoenhofen sought Ruhmann's opinion about Eckerstrom's request, Ruhmann—who himself aspired to Kner's position—was supportive of neither Eckerstrom's bid nor of the role he played in the company. Whatever his reasons, Schoenhofen determined that Eckerstrom had to go. After leaving CCA, Eckerstrom went on to become one of the founders of Unimark, the design firm (1965–71) that was largely responsible for the "Helveticazation of America" with its grids-and-Helvetica-Medium identity systems for clients ranging from Ford Motor Company to JC Penney.

On the day Eckerstrom was fired, John Massey was out of town working with N. W. Ayer on the "Great Ideas" campaign. He was pulled from a meeting to answer a telephone call from Schoenhofen, who informed Massey that Eckerstrom was leaving the company and that he wanted Massey to replace him as CCA's third design director. Schoenhofen, while lacking Paepcke's innate interest in design, recognized its importance to the company and, moreover, possessed great confidence in Massey, telling him, "You do it, John. Just keep me informed."

While the first two decades of the CCA design legacy belong to Walter Paepcke and the corporate culture of excellence he created, the last two decades bear the imprint of John Massey. His ability to maintain CCA design standards for a period of some twenty years is a testament to his commitment, presentation skills, and advocacy of design's contribution to a corporation.

Massey realized that if he was going to create strong unified graphic standards across a far-flung corporate structure, he would have to maintain control over the communications budgets. He persuaded Schoenhofen to centralize all publications, advertising, and promotional budgets in the communications department. When the personnel department wanted a brochure to recruit employees, or a plant manager in Pennsylvania wanted to place an ad in the local newspaper's special issue commemorating the town centennial, they had to go to the communications department, which designed the material for them.

Massey's design philosophy is based on a belief in geometric patterns and volumes as they relate to a kind of universal order. For a quarter of a century, Massey made CCA communication a paradigm of order and consistency, providing American graphic design with a model of corporate design excellence. He updated the corporate identity program in 1968, placing the company signature diagonally in Helvetica Medium against a blue background. Eckerstrom's symbol was retained, and Massey developed a system of grids for all corporate communications. Under his guidance, the "Great Ideas" campaign held to its standard, achieving unity within diversity.

When Massey took the helm, one problem had to be resolved: With the full knowledge of CCA, Massey had maintained a flourishing freelance design office with several employees located in an office building a few blocks from CCA's headquarters. This was permitted for a staff designer, but it seemed inappropriate for a top manager. Schoenhofen resolved this problem rather efficiently by converting the Massey design office into an independent CCA department, transferring Massey's employees to the CCA payroll, and telling Massey to bill CCA for the design office's assets, such as furniture and equipment. Schoenhofen asked only two things of Massey; first, that the design office generate sufficient billing, not to produce a profit, which it wasn't required to do, but to cover its operating costs; and second, that it not do anything that would reflect poorly on CCA and its reputation.

A name for Massey's new department was readily available, for a proposal had been in the works to create a design research center where CCA designers and designers working for CCA clients could have access to resource materials, foreign design publications, and so forth. The title "Center for Advanced Research in Design" had been suggested for this facility, and now Massey's design office was so designated. Thus was one of the more outstanding design offices of the 1960s and 1970s launched. The Center for Advanced Research in Design (CARD) took on a wide range of projects, including large-scale corporate identity programs, such as the one for ARCO, a major oil company formed by the merger of Atlantic and Richfield Oil Companies. CARD also embraced a civic mission: A Chicago poster series included posters honoring the symphony orchestra, the public library, the observatory, and the city's role as a convention center.

The Federal Design Improvement Program of the 1970s, which initiated visual identity systems and graphic standards manuals for federal agencies and departments, turned to Massey and CARD for its first identity program, which was implemented by the U.S. Department of Labor.

Outstanding young design talent flocked to CCA throughout the 1960s and 1970s. Some sixty graphic designers worked for CCA during the Massey era, although at any given time the staffs of both the corporate design office and CARD were fairly small. When I suggested to Massey that the adage "excellence attracts excellence" described those years, he retorted that the process worked both ways: While CCA's corporate culture and design reputation attracted outstanding talent, the company in turn benefited from the quality of its applicants.

CCA's publications ranked with the best editorial design of the period. No corporate communication was too small for thoughtful design treatment. Posters that went no further than the employee bulletin boards were superbly designed, as were trade ads and low-budget black-and-white newspaper ads running in towns where CCA had facilities. One of the objectives of the "Great Ideas" ad campaign was to create a sense of corporate values and standards, not only among present employees, but also in the eyes of prospective employees, enabling CCA to make the most of its recruitment efforts. This emphasis on recruiting the finest possible employees, from production workers to highly trained professionals, was reflected in the high level of graphics for CCA's personnel departments.

In 1970, responding to the first wave of American environmental concern, Container developed a major recycling program. The company sponsored a national competition to design the recycling symbol, which was won by a California college student, Gary Anderson.

After "New Wave" typography arrived from Basel in the 1970s, CCA designers such as Wilburn Bonnell, who became graphic design manager in 1971, and Jeff Barnes, who supplemented Massey's rigorous horizontals and verticals with slashing diagonal movements of his own, began to loosen the grids. They state that Massey was supportive of their work and encouraged his staff to experiment while maintaining the thrust of the corporate image. (One former CCA designer recalled that Massey rejected a design using serif typefaces because it was inconsistent with the corporate look.) Bonnell organized the first American exhibition of "New Wave" typography at the Ryder Gallery in Chicago, an event that spurred interest in the movement away from classical "Swiss" design, or the International Typographic Style, toward a more energized use of space.

As might be expected of a company that manufactured packaging, CCA's three-dimensional work, such as trade show exhibitions, was always superlative, projecting a lively sculptural dynamic. The annual CCA calendar and graphic ephemera such as matchbooks demonstrate how modest utilitarian materials become works of art in the hands of sensitive graphic designers.

It soon became apparent that a schism existed at CCA between Ruhmann's design and market research laboratory and Massey's corporate communications. Philosophically, Massey and Ruhmann were poles apart. A former CCA designer told me that the design and market research laboratory "did work at the opposite end of the spectrum from our stuff," while another contended that Ruhmann did not fully comprehend the CCA philosophy and purpose and was "a real adversary and antagonist toward corporate communications." At the time, Ruhmann had defended his approach as being oriented toward client service, consumer preferences, and marketing research.

"We don't talk about it, it's a dirty little secret," a CCA communications designer confided to me. He was referring to departments within the company that created packaging and displays for clients in the 1970s. And what he meant was that while CCA's design efforts for itself were always at the highest possible level, the thousands of packages designed by the design lab and its regional design departments were always market-driven; that is, they perfectly reflected the design standards of the cereal or frozen-cherry-pie manufacturer whose products were packaged in CCA boxes and shipped to America's grocery stores.

In 1968, fearing a hostile takeover, CCA merged with Montgomery Ward to form a holding company, Marcor, which was believed to be too large to be consumed by a predator. John Massey designed the Marcor logo and visual identity system. Mobil Oil, flush with windfall profits from gasoline prices, which approached $2 a gallon at the pump during the 1970s oil embargo, controlled 54 percent of Marcor shares by 1974, then completed its takeover in 1976. That year was also CCA's fiftieth anniversary, so the 11"-by-14" anniversary book became, in a sense, an obituary for CCA's half-century of autonomy. Container's unique corporate culture began to change as it was "Mobilized," as CCA employees liked to say; but in the early years of Mobil's dominance, its top management respected the importance of design and CCA's program continued. Mobil, however, was a commodity company and its management viewed CCA as a similar type of business. This was a misconception. Packages are not just commodities; they are communications.

Each month, CCA's manager had to make a sales report to Mobil, and along with the other divisions of the company, the Center for Advanced Research in Design was listed as a CCA "profit center." Of course, its sales and profits were minuscule compared to those of the other divisions. At one corporate meeting, someone from Mobil reportedly asked, "What is this CARD thing, and why are we wasting our time on it?" A decision was made by Mobil management simply to shut CARD down, apparently without any understanding of its reputation or contribution to CCA's mission and image. Mobil's idea of corporate communications was opinion/editorial advertisements placed in consumer publications that took up topics of concern to Mobil management, such as government regulation of the energy industry. This wasn't "Great Ideas of Western Man."

By 1980, CCA employees began to feel that the match between Mobil and Container Corporation was something of a mistake. Some of them suspected that Mobil realized it had miscalculated and was preparing CCA for sale, either as a total entity or piecemeal. Jeff Barnes recalls "lots of cost-cutting"; for example, CCA had been using an outside vendor with Genigraphics equipment for producing 35mm presentation slides. Now, they were being produced internally on a typewriter.

Over a 2½-hour period on Valentine's Day, 1983, John Massey and the vice-presidents for acquisitions and development, domestic operations, and international operations—the four people most involved in CCA's philosophy and mission—were called one by one into the office of Mobil-appointed CCA president Bob Swanson and fired. When Massey entered the office, he found a solitary chair in the center of the room, facing Swanson, who was seated ten feet away on a sofa, with personnel director Claude Smith seated about twenty feet away in the background. Perhaps that day, inevitably called "The St. Valentine's Day Massacre" by CCA employees, marks the death knell of CCA's corporate culture as it had been defined by Paepcke.

In a cost-cutting move, the corporate design department in Chicago was eliminated and all design operations were consolidated under design and market research laboratory director Lony Ruhmann, who was promoted to vice president and moved into Massey's former office. A total victory over the Paepcke design legacy had been achieved. Ironically, this occurred just as the American Institute of Graphic Arts notified CCA that it had been named the recipient of the AIGA Design Leadership award. (I have heard some designers refer to this citation as the "kiss of death" award, since a number of corporations, including CCA and CBS, have undergone profound changes in their design philosophies after receiving it.)

Hired to replace Massey as manager of the corporate graphics department was Joe Hutchcroft, who reported to Ruhmann. From that point on, the level of corporate design activity declined, with necessary printed matter produced as quickly and economically as possible. Hutchcroft, despite the adverse circumstances, ranks as one of CCA's finest designers. Sadly, he died of cancer in 1990.

In 1986, Mobil sold CCA to Jefferson Smurfit, a St. Louis–based conglomerate heavily involved in paper, packaging, and timber. Jefferson-Smurfit is known for buying and streamlining undervalued companies. In an organization sense, Smurfit decapitated CCA by closing its headquarters at the First National Bank Building in Chicago. CCA's corporate art collection, including the original artwork commissioned for the "Paperboard Goes to War," "United Nations," "States," and "Great Ideas" campaigns, was donated to the Smithsonian Institution as a tax write-off. Currently, CCA's manufacturing facilities report to Smurfit's St. Louis headquarters and are operated as Smurfit divisions. The CCA initials and identity have been merged with the Smurfit logo. Rick House, manager of structural design at the CCA folding carton plant in Carol Stream, a Chicago suburb, states that many CCA employees believe Smurfit understands their business better than Mobil did. When Smurfit acquired CCA, its management made clear that they valued CCA's employees and creative reputation. Smurfit did not engage in wholesale layoffs, as often happens after leveraged buyouts; rather, it carefully evaluated each employee and position. Vice president Lony Ruhmann was not retained.

House sees greater emphasis placed on working capital and "the bottom line." Operations are more diffuse than they were during the highly centralized Mobil years, and Smurfit has made an aggressive commitment to computerization. From all reports, Smurfit is a well-managed company whose corporate culture is quite different from that of the old CCA. One might say that CCA has ceased to exist as an entity, even though its manufacturing plants are still in operation; many of its workers are doing the same jobs as Smurfit employees, and the CCA name is still used.

The corporate culture and legacy of Walter Paepcke today survive only in a paper trail of yellowing graphics that provides a remarkable record of a company and its founder. Paepcke was a man who cared about the human condition and the corporation's role in society. He believed in design as an invaluable tool for addressing meaningful goals. His attitude about design shaped CCA's communications for a half century and was a public manifestation of a broader philosophy concerning excellence, quality, and responsibility.

Regrettably, for persons such as myself who believed in CCA as a paradigm of design commitment and admired its work from afar, its departure went unheralded; for a long time, I didn't realize it was gone.

Originally published in PRINT, *May/June 1992*

ADVERTISING: THE MOTHER OF GRAPHIC DESIGN
Steven Heller

The word "advertising," like "commercial art," makes graphic designers cringe. It signifies all that sophisticated contemporary graphic design, or, rather, visual communications, is not supposed to be. Advertising is the tool of capitalism, a con that persuades an unwitting public to consume and consume again. Graphic design, by contrast, is an aesthetic and philosophical pursuit that communicates ideas. Advertising is cultural exploitation that transforms creative expression into crass propaganda. Graphic design is a cultural force that incorporates parallel worldviews. Advertising is hypnotically invasive. Graphic design makes no such claim.

Though graphic design as we know it originated in the late nineteenth century as a tool of advertising, any association today with marketing, advertising, or capitalism deeply undermines the graphic designer's self-image. Graphic design history is an integral part of advertising history, yet in most accounts of graphic design's origins advertising is virtually denied, or hidden behind more benign words such as "publicity" and "promotion." This omission not only limits the discourse, but misrepresents the facts. It is time for graphic design historians, and designers generally, to remove the elitist prejudices that have perpetuated a biased history.

In *Layout in Advertising* (Harper Brothers, 1928) William Addison Dwiggins, who coined the term "graphic designer" in 1922 to define his own diverse practices of book, type, lettering, and advertising design, wrote that, "for purposes of argument 'advertising' means every conceivable printed means for selling anything." This suggests that advertising is the mother of almost all graphic design endeavors, except for books and certain journals. In fact, the majority of commercial artists from the turn of the century until fairly recently—from anonymous "sho card" renderers to celebrated affichistes—were engaged in the service of advertising of one kind or another. Despite the common assertion that graphic design began with seventeenth-century Italian printing, modern graphic design is the result of the transition in the late nineteenth century from a product to a consumer culture. The move from producing (or bartering for) goods to buying mass-produced consumables created a need for printed advertising that quickly developed into a huge, dedicated industry.

Dwiggins's manual is not the only one to assert that graphic design was invented to put "an advertising project into graphic form." Jan Tschichold's *Die neue Typographie*, also published in 1928, was a seminal handbook for the practitioners of *Gebrauchsgraphik*, or advertising art. This book and Tschichold's subsequent *Typographische Gestaltung* (1935), which became the basis of the modern canon, were focused not on some idealistic notion of visual communications in an aesthetic vacuum, but on dynamic new possibilities for advertising composition in an archaic and cluttered print environment. In *The Art Director at Work* (Hastings House, 1960), Arthur Hawkins, Jr., describes how such ideas influenced American advertising design: "As competitive pressure squeezed the innocence out of advertising, [art directors] became rougher and tougher. They were usually paste-up boys . . . who had picked up a certain facility with a 6B pencil. Somehow, they discovered *Gerbrauchsgraphik* magazine and the Bauhaus School. Their future was paved with Futura."

By the 1920s graphic design was synonymous with advertising design. In Germany, France, and Italy, agencies and consortia extolled the virtues of the well-designed advertising image. Lucian Bernhard and others associated with the Berliner Plakat group, under the management of printing salesman and advertising agent Ernst Growald, invented artful ways to identify and announce new products. Even the cultural avant-gardes—Futurism, Dada, Surrealism—created design forms for advertising that expressed their particular visions and ideologies. Russian Constructivism's most notable graphic achievements were advertisements for films and products. The "Productivists" Alexander Rodchenko and Lasar El Lissitzky developed ways of composing typecase design elements on an advertising page that eventually influenced layout trends in capitalist nations. In Germany, the Ring, a close-knit association of radically modern designers including Kurt Schwitters, Willi Baumeister, and Piet Zwart, attempted to sell to an expanding industrial clientele a "new advertising" based on the New Typography.

For the avant-garde, producing advertising for technologically progressive corporations, which, incidentally, often sponsored artistic innovation, was such a modern idea that they proudly referred to themselves as "artists for industry" or "advertising engineers." Since advertising was at once the medium of progressive graphic expression and a growing industry, many of the most influential graphic design trade journals of the late 1920s and 1930s had names with advertising in their titles: *De Reclame* (the Netherlands and Germany), *Werbung* (Germany), *Publicité* (France), *Pubblicità d'Italia* (Italy), and *Advertising Arts* (United States). Even those trade magazines that focused on printing and other aspects of commercial art featured many articles on advertising.

Icons of Progress

"Today it is difficult to recapture the intoxicating feeling of aesthetic possibility that once surrounded national advertising," writes Jackson Lears about the American experience of the 1920s (*Fables of Abundance,* Basic Books, 1995). "But for a while, especially during the early years of the courtship, it seemed to many artists as if advertising embodied exhilarating energy, rather than merely impoverishment of spirit." As the modern movements sought to redefine the place of art and the role of the artist in society, advertising was seen not only as a medium ripe for reform, but as a platform on which the graphic symbols of reform could be paraded along with the product being sold. Within this scenario, layout (or craft) was replaced by graphic design as an artistic endeavor, the engine of *style*. Lears points out that during this period, advertising art "became detached from the product to which it referred. 'Advertising design' became a value in and of itself, without reference to the sales that design was intended to generate." Design still served, but was no longer a slave to copy-driven campaigns.

American advertising agencies gradually shifted their preference from "capitalist realism," or unambiguous if mythic representation, to surrealistic imagery which imbued the commodity with a fantastic aura. Refrigerators floating in space signified the abstract notion of progress as well as the fantasy of an ethereal, modern home. Industry became the totem of the American century and advertising extolled its monumentality through modern and moderne graphic forms. As in the Soviet idealization of the industrial state, factories, smokestacks, and gigantic bearings and gears were heroicized as icons of progress. Advertising not only sold, it told a tale about America's aspirations.

American advertising had traditionally been dominated by hard-sell copy, and the shift in emphasis from words to art and design did not occur overnight. But it did change precipitously thanks to Earnest Elmo Calkins, founder of the Calkins & Holden advertising agency in New York. Calkins became interested in design reform in about 1908 and instituted his new ideas by engaging some of the most widely admired magazine illustrators, including James Montgomery Flagg and J. C. Lyendecker, to render ads for common products. Later he led the field in the introduction of modern art (Cubism and Futurism) into advertising. He wrote profusely in trade journals and design and poster annuals and was a frequent contributor to London's *Commercial Art* annual. In articles in general magazines, such as one titled "Beauty the New Business Tool" (*Atlantic Monthly,* August 1927), Calkins expounded on the need for dynamic new design to help communicate the marketing innovation which became known as programmed or forced obsolescence.

Calkins, whom Jackson Lears calls the "apostle of taste" and "corporate connoisseur of artifice," introduced the consumerist idea that all products—from coffee tins to automobiles—should regularly shed their surface style as an inducement to consumers to toss out the old and purchase the new. This pseudoscience of style engineering—a kind of design-based behavior modification—forced American industrial design to shift from its quaint Victorian ornamentalism to machine-age Modernism, and so encouraged the retooling of American industry. As Terry Smith states in *Making the Modern: Industry, Art, and Design in America* (University of Chicago Press, 1994), "Advertising's parentage of U.S.-type industrial design is traceable not only to their common economic purposes but to the histories of the individuals who shaped the design profession. Most . . . spent the 1920s as advertising artist-illustrators. Joseph Sinel, John Vassos, Raymond Loewy, and Walter Dorwin Teague are the outstanding examples."

These pioneering practitioners are rarely cited in graphic design histories. Likewise Calkins, who is arguably the single most important figure in early twentieth-century American graphic design, makes no more than a few cameo appearances in such significant accounts as Philip B. Meggs's *History of Graphic Design*, Richard Hollis's *Graphic Design: A Concise History,* and R. Roger Remington and Barbara J. Hodik's *Nine Pioneers in American Graphic Design.* Yet thanks to Calkins's promotion of European modern and modernistic design, along with his invention of the creative team of copywriter and designer, graphic design grew by leaps and bounds as a service to advertising in the late 1920s prior to the Great Depression. During the 1930s it developed into a field with its own integrity, canon, and luminaries. Though Calkins did not invent contemporary design standards, he codified them and urged their adoption. Advertising design influenced modes of editorial and institutional design until the Second World War; afterward, editorial design surpassed advertising in originality.

Graphic Design as Art

The 1950s saw the beginnings of a schism between graphic and advertising design. Modern graphic design veered from mass advertising toward corporate and institutional communications and evolved into a rarefied practice decidedly more sophisticated than advertising design of the same period. Some advertising artist/designers were celebrated for individual achievement, but as Terry Smith writes, "advertising designed primarily by an individual artist was becoming rare enough in the United States to be remarkable, exceptional, and expensive." Over time such advertising luminaries as did exist—E. McKnight Kauffer and A. M. Cassandre being the prime examples—were detached from the history of advertising and made into heroes of graphic design.

A kind of sociocultural stratification began to distinguish the advertising designer from the graphic designer. Today, a common view among advertising people is that graphic designers simply "do letterheads," while graphic designers scorn their advertising counterparts for being ignorant about type. Job or class distinctions have driven a wedge between graphic designers and advertising designers and graphic design history has perpetuated the schism. While cultural scholars, consumer theorists, and media critics have done considerable work on the social, political, and psychological role of advertising in American culture, their writings are rarely cited in graphic design literature, as if issues of consumerism and marketing have no bearing on the "art" of graphic design. This omission can be traced back to formal prejudices.

The Formalist Lens

If advertising is the function, then graphic design is the form. As Dwiggins pointed out in *Layout in Advertising*, "The advertising piece is not an end-product; it is an intermediate step in a process. The end-product of advertising is not [design]—it is sales." Yet selling is an ignored aspect of the story contemporary graphic design historians choose to tell—after all, graphic designers are not salespeople but form-givers, which is perceived as a more culturally significant activity than being a mere advertising huckster. The problem is that an advertisement must be analyzed as a collaborative endeavor involving considerably more than just its graphics. So to avoid having to admit that graphic design has a subordinate role, the historical discourse has built up around graphic design as a formal endeavor. As if in art history, graphic designs are removed from their contexts, placed on pedestals, and examined under the formalist lens. Like the annual design WYSIWYG competitions in which work is judged entirely on how it looks, graphic design history more often than not focuses attention on style, manner, and structure rather than on the success or failure of a piece of work in the marketplace. The audience, which is rarely considered in formalist critiques of fine art, is likewise ignored in favor of aesthetic and sometimes philosophical or ideological considerations. This not only denies the public's role, but the client's as well.

In the first important historical text published in America, *A History of Graphic Design* (Van Nostrand Reinhold, second ed., 1992), Philip B. Meggs skirts the role of advertising. In his discussion of graphic languages in a chapter entitled "A New Language of Form," he writes: "A spirit of innovation was present in all the visual arts, ideas were in the air, and by the end of World War I, graphic designers, architects, and product designers were energetically challenging prevailing notions about form and function." Where in this litany does the advertising designer fit? In the chapter entitled "The Modern Movement in America," which should focus on the advertising designer. Meggs asserts, "graphic design in America during the 1920s and 1930s was dominated by traditional illustration. However, the modern approach slowly gained ground on several fronts: book design, editorial design for fashion and business magazines catering to the affluent, and promotional and corporate graphics." By subsuming advertising under the term "promotional graphics," Meggs presents an inaccurate picture of the forces that brought about Modernism's ascendancy. In the chapter "The New York School," he further snubs advertising when introducing New York City, the advertising and publishing capital of America: "New York City assumed [the role of Paris] during the middle twentieth century. It may have been that these cultural incubators nurtured creativity because the prevailing climate enabled individuals to realize their potential. Or, the existing climate may have been a magnet that attracted individuals of great talent." In Meggs's otherwise painstaking historical account, advertising is portrayed not as the mother of graphic design, but as a midwife. While scant attention is given to the economic forces that forged the practice, certain key individuals who were nurtured by advertising are highlighted. Thus discussion of advertising is used merely to push the great master narrative along until the individual emerges from the birth canal as a graphic designer.

The problem is not that advertising cannot be read from a formalist viewpoint, but that history demands that its function and outcome be equally scrutinized. This turns the focus away from graphic design, and in order to refocus attention on their discipline graphic design historians tend to treat advertising simply as a matter of surface. For instance, when one of Alexey Brodovitch's advertisements for the New York department store Saks Fifth Avenue is put under the historical/critical microscope, we learn about the typeface, lettering, and illustration, but not about how it functioned as a piece of advertising in a newspaper. Does consideration of its function diminish its artistic—or graphic design—value? By referring to it as "advertising," does the work shrink in stature from a paradigmatic piece of graphics to kitsch?

In *Nine Pioneers in American Graphic Design* (MIT Press, 1989), R. Roger Remington and Barbara J. Hodik marginalize Brodovitch's early advertising design when they write that he "increasingly specialized in poster design between 1925 and 1930 and devoted himself to experimentation with new techniques with the goal of producing intelligible images through good graphics." The fact that the posters under discussion were advertisements is overshadowed by formalistic concerns in such statements as: "He learned how to simplify the subject through analysis of the Purist painters. His posters for Martini, now in the Museum of Modern Art in New York, are among the major products of this fruitful period." Nowhere do the authors acknowledge this work as advertising, even when they report that Brodovitch was invited to create a program in advertising design at the Philadelphia School of Industrial Design. With rare exceptions, when advertising is included in graphic design history, it is as an incidental part of the consideration of individuals and artifacts. In my own *Graphic Style: From Victorian to Post-modern* (Harry N. Abrams, 1988), the advertising artifact is treated merely as a vessel for style, not as a model from which to examine functional attributes.

Remington and Hodik do, however, take a step toward integrating advertising and graphic design in their selection of Charles Coiner, art director of the Philadelphia-based ad agency N. W. Ayer, as one of their pioneers. Coiner brought modernity to America's oldest advertising agency, introducing fine art to the repertoire and hiring some of America's leading graphic designers, such as Leo Lionni and Alexey Brodovitch, to conceive and style print ads. The authors give him full credit for his contribution to his firm's success: "Ayer clients received forty-one awards during the first nineteen years of exhibitions by art directors . . . Ayer pioneered the production of 'beautiful' ads through campaigns for Cannon Mills, Caterpillar Tractor, Climax Molybdenum, French Line, Marcus Jewelers, DeBeers Diamonds, and Capehart." Yet their text—the only contemporary study of this significant advertising pioneer (a profile appeared in *Portfolio* in 1950)—reads more as a list of achievements than an analysis of advertising's, and by extension Coiner's, role in the larger culture. Advertising is used as a backdrop to his endeavor rather than a lens through which consumer culture can be explored. Despite Coiner's inclusion, advertising remains marginalized.

Yet *Nine Pioneers* provides a key insight into how graphic design began to break from advertising during the war and how advertising designers emerged as creative forces afterward. "During the war, very few goods were available for consumer purchase. Advertising had nothing to sell. When the war ended, the scene changed dramatically to a buyer's market. Designers finally had the opportunity to express their ideas in the spheres of advertising and communications." That wartime austerity offered other creative challenges to the advertising industry that were consequential to graphic design is conveniently overlooked.

Of the histories discussed here, only Richard Hollis's *Graphic Design: A Concise History* (Thames and Hudson, 1994) openly addressed the role of advertising. "In the 1930s, it had been art directors who had established graphic design, mainly in advertising and magazine layouts." Hollis concisely argues the importance of the "New Advertising"—the integrated design—and concept-driven campaigns of the late 1950s and 1960s. He focuses on the key art directors—Paul Rand and Gene Federico—and campaigns such as Doyle Dane Bernbach's for Volkswagen, explaining this work as important because it made the spectator active, not passive. But Hollis's brief discussion avoids the broader implications of advertising, focusing instead on iconoclasts who are soon positioned in his narrative as graphic design exemplars.

This is the inevitable paradox of graphic design history. Since advertising is marginalized, the few acknowledged advertising design leaders must somehow be presented as graphic design leaders. For instance, the majority of work by Lou Dorfsman, the former art director of CBS Radio and Television, is institutional and trade advertising, through which he not only set new typographic standards, but increased business. Though the success of his ads is sometimes cited anecdotally in references to his career, Dorfsman is usually presented as either a typographer or an art director, rarely as an advertising man. Likewise Herb Lubalin, the art director of Suddler & Hennesy before branching out into editorial and type design, is routinely discussed as a typographic pioneer who, incidentally, broke new ground in pharmaceutical advertising. Analyzing such figures' design as a milestone in the marriage of typo and image avoids the stigma of it being advertising. Gene Federico and George Lois, both of whom owned ad agencies, are presented as creative forces who transcended the advertising field. Federico was a great typographer, Lois a brilliant art director, and for the purposes of design history they achieved their status in spite of their profession.

Unheroic Artifacts

Graphic designers have distanced themselves from advertising in the same way that children put as much space as possible between themselves and their parents. And, indeed, graphic design did develop its own characteristics. American advertising was originally copy-based and unresponsive to design, and though reformers like Calkins (and later Bill Bernbach) encouraged the seamless integration of works, pictures, and design, the copy, slogan, and jingle have been the driving forces. From the turn of the century, would-be journalists and novelists were recruited as copywriters, giving the field a certain *faux* literary cast. Eventually, advertising developed its own stereotypical professionals, who even today are distinct from graphic design professionals.

The tilting of the scales toward the copy-driven "big idea" is one reason why advertising histories veer away from extensive analysis of graphic design. Another issue is quality as defined by the two fields—a great advertising campaign may not be exceptional graphic design, while a superb piece of graphic design may mask a poor advertising campaign. The history of advertising is more interested in how Marlboro cigarettes tested a variety of trade characters before stumbling on the Marlboro Man as a symbol of manliness. While graphic design appears negligible in the cultural analysis of this campaign, understanding the relationship of this symbol (which is graphic design in the broadest sense) to the larger mythology provides insight into how the American myth was perpetuated.

As important as this long-running campaign is (and not just as an example of politically incorrect thinking), it has never been analyzed in graphic design history for its symbolic connotations. Though the Lucky Strike package designed by Raymond Loewy and the Eve Cigarette package designed by Herb Lubalin and Ernie Smith are featured as design artifacts, the advertising campaigns that sold the designs have been ignored. Graphic design historians are prudishly selective in what they discuss. They base decisions on ideal formal attributes—what is inherently interesting from a design perspective. They write as though consumerism is wicked—us (the canon) versus them (the mass) underscores graphic design history. Yet by eliminating advertising, design history loses rich insights into visual culture.

One of the touchstones of inclusion in graphic design histories is whether or not a work broke the stranglehold of commercial convention. Paul Rand's advertisements for Orbachs, for instance, have become part of the canon not because they were effective advertising, but because they assaulted antiquity. But this criterion is not the only way to read advertising design. Like some of the European Modernists before him, Rand introduced principles of modern art into advertising, bringing the rarefied avant-garde to ordinary citizens. In *Advertising the American Dream: Making Way for Modernity, 1920–1940* (University of California, 1985), Roland Marchand describes the mainstreaming of the avant-garde as a significant marketing ploy that both introduced and made it frivolous. This important aspect of graphic design history can only be told if certain unheroic artifacts are included in the narrative. To refer to or reproduce only billboards, posters, and other aesthetically acceptable tokens of advertising is not enough.

In the 1930s the distinction between advertising art and graphic design was virtually nonexistent. While typography was often written about as a separate aesthetic field, it was also addressed in terms of its function in advertising. Moreover, whether discussing a book jacket, record sleeve, poster, brochure, magazine, or any other form of graphic endeavor, the word "advertising" was not regarded as derisive.

Today, advertising is not totally ignored—many trade magazines cover it—but it is rarely integrated into the broader analysis of graphic design. While certain aspects of advertising—marketing, demographics, and other pseudosciences—are less important to graphic design history, considerably more consumerist theory, media criticism, and even perceptual psychology would be useful in understanding the form and function of graphic design through the advertising lens. Likewise, aesthetic theories can be applied through the lens of design to put a visually bereft advertising history into clearer focus.

During the past decade there have been calls to develop new narratives and to readdress graphic design history through feminist, ethnic, racial, post-structuralist, and numerous other politically correct perspectives. There are many ways to slice a pie, but before unveiling too many subtexts, it is perhaps first useful to reconcile a mother and her child.

Advertising and graphic design have more in common than the postmodern trend for vernacularism (or the aestheticization of timeworn artifacts) reveals. Advertising and graphic design are equally concerned with selling, communication, and entertaining. To appreciate one, the other is imperative. But more important, if graphic design history does not expand to include advertising and other related studies, it will ultimately succumb to the dead-end thinking that will be the inevitable consequence of being arrested in a state of continual adolescence.

Originally published in EYE, *Summer 1995*

Lemon.

This Volkswagen missed the boat.

The chrome strip on the glove compartment is blemished and must be replaced. Chances are you wouldn't have noticed it; Inspector Kurt Kroner did.

There are 3,389 men at our Wolfsburg factory with only one job: to inspect Volkswagens at each stage of production. (3000 Volkswagens are produced daily; there are more inspectors than cars.)

Every shock absorber is tested (spot checking won't do), every windshield is scanned. VWs have been rejected for surface scratches barely visible to the eye.

Final inspection is really something! VW inspectors run each car off the line onto the Funktionsprüfstand (car test stand), tote up 189 check points, gun ahead to the automatic brake stand, and say "no" to one VW out of fifty.

This preoccupation with detail means the VW lasts longer and requires less maintenance, by and large, than other cars. (It also means a used VW depreciates less than any other car.)

We pluck the lemons; you get the plums.

AD CAMPAIGN OF THE CENTURY
Eve M. Kahn

The advertising industry has changed so drastically since the 1960s, when Doyle Dan Bernbach introduced its Volkswagen Beetle campaign, that "You'd almost be showing a lack of sophistication to talk about the ads; it would be like bringing up simple Bible parables in a Joycean literature class." So says Bertrand Garbassi, a thirty-five-year-old creative director at Castle Underwood, who worked at DDB Needham in the late '80s on distant descendants of Beetle ads. But for all their retreat into history, Garbassi goes on, no one can deny that the Beetle ads set off "a shot heard round the world." No previous campaign and few subsequent ones have given inanimate objects such personality and almost single-handedly built a market for a product, as Beetle ads did in the United States for imported cars. Few campaigns have ever stood out so starkly upon first appearance and then lasted long enough to sum up a moment in popular and advertising culture. And few campaigns now seem more poignant, given their muddled and ineffectual offspring.

Andy Berlin of Berlin Cameron Doyle declared to the *New Yorker* late in 1993 that his motto for a VW ad renaissance—he'd just left DDB Needham to form his own spin-off agency and he'd taken VW with him—would be: "Volkswagen. For people who aren't full of shit." But VW fired Berlin Cameron Doyle last December and had not chosen a new agency at press time, partly because there was nothing new in Berlin's swaggering goal.

Even DDB's earliest Beetle ads describe the target audience as daring, thrifty souls willing to drive a silly-shaped car and feel pride in small victories when "the guy at the gas station doesn't ask where the gas goes." Nor did Berlin *et al.* figure out a new way to convey an old message. To restore Volkswagen's lost popularity (some hundred thousand cars sold in the United States last year, more than the fifty-thousand-odd of recent years but an embarrassing drop from the circa-1970 six-hundred-thousand peak), Berlin's print ads featured unsurprising black-and-white scenes of cars weaving through landscapes. Down a white column at far left, stories told in the second person were loosely typeset: a tale of road love ("The road knocks on your door and asks you to come out and play"), or the graphic cliché of two interwoven tales—one in black type of encroaching middle age ("You start a carpool"), the other of persistent youth in red ("You want to go to lunch and never come back"). Has any ad campaign in history but the Beetle's put forth so clear and timely a statement that, like the sons of great kings, no successors ever seem worthy?

The original Beetle ad concept arose in the late 1950s out of what Roy Grace, one of the campaign's early art directors, calls "a confluence of happy coincidences." Concentration of talent helped: Grace is but one Beetle alumnus who went on to renown, along with copywriters Julian Koenig and Bob Levenson and art directors George Lois and Helmut Krone. DDB was ten years old then and becoming the Tiffany agency. Bernbach, a scholarly but unpretentious tailor's son, born in the Bronx, was one of the first ad agency executives to believe that advertising qualified as an art form. After stints with Paul Rand at the William H. Weintraub Agency and at Grey Advertising, he founded his own agency with Ned Doyle, a Grey account executive, and Maxwell Dane, a shrewd businessman then running his own tiny Madison Avenue ad shop. Len Sirowitz, Beetle art director between Drone and Grace, recalls, "We all felt part of an elite group. There was friendly competition, with people really rooting for each other. It was a great feeling—as if nobody could touch us." This was, of course, an era when one agency could still stay preeminent for years at a stretch; "Everything is so much more fluid, more frantic now," says Garbassi.

DDB was making its name with innovative campaigns for Levy's Real Jewish Rye ("You don't have to be Jewish to love Levy's") and Avis ("We're No. 2. We try harder"). The agency was defying all time-tested industry shibboleths, like bans against poking fun at the product or mentioning something so disagreeable as a second-place ranking: "Rules are what the artist breaks" was one of Bill Bernbach's many mottoes. DDB was likewise progressive in including ethnic faces in ads, such as the campaign for Levy's, and a nebbishy, self-deprecating tone that contrasted with the conventional ad posture of seriousness and self-importance. An unprecedented number of staff members of assorted ethnicities worked at the agency, too, a trend that spread and helped reinvigorate the WASP-dominated industry. "The problem wasn't that there were so many WASPs in the business then—a WASP is all right. It's that they were dumb WASPs," growls one DDB alum of Greek extraction.

Car ads, above all, spoke of banal WASPdom in pre-Beetle days. Headlines came half in smarmy italics and half in "Ben Hur" chiseled serif faces over illustrations of larger-than-life automobiles with sunlight sparkling on the chrome trim and huge logos fluttering overhead. Backgrounds contained "broads, mansions, surf, mountains, sunsets, and chiseled chins—everything but the facts," as one art director of the time stated in journalist Frank Rowsome, Jr.'s 1970 study, *Think Small: The Story of Those Volkswagen Ads*. Justified bars of bland copy vaguely emphasized the superiority of the current car model over its ancestors and often ended no more cleverly than by reiterating headlines—"The Incomparable Imperial"—or reminding docile future buyers, "See your Nash dealer and learn how easily your golden dreams can come true."

Volkswagen's management did not consider advertising until the late 1950s. By that point, the company was exporting more than a hundred thousand cars annually to the United States. It had started selling abroad shortly after World War II but in tiny quantities for years, due to limited factory capacity and little publicity. VW's slow growth in popularity had a fortunate side effect: It kept the car's profile low until its Nazi stigma could fade. Hitler had commissioned the car in the 1930s from Czech inventor Ferdinand Porsche, hoping to offer the German masses an inexpensive vehicle that would be called the "Strength Through Joy" car. In 1938, the Nazis started constructing a factory and village in northern Germany called the Town of the Strength Through Joy Car and developing brochures that glamorized the Beetle with Alpine settings or backdrops of Third Reich eagles.

Only a few hundred Beetles were produced for high-level Nazis. The area was heavily bombed during the war and the town was renamed Wolfsburg afterward. Heinz Nordhoff, a determined and ascetic Opel executive, took over the ruins as the war ended and rebuilt both the company and the surrounding company town. But Beetles remained such unusual sights on U.S. roads until 1960, and amid all the tailfins and sprawling front grilles seemed such weird throwbacks to tense parabolic Art Moderne motifs, that VW drivers were prone to honk horns and wave at one another for mutual support. Owners also liked to paste jokey bumper stickers on Beetles (remember, this is around the time that the sitcom "Hogan's Heroes" sentimentalized Nazis as lovable incompetents). One classic slogan: "Made in der Black Forest by der Elves."

Volkswagen started contemplating advertising because it felt its niche and chances for expansion were being threatened. Detroit had sensed a slight national boredom with tailfin excess—the Edsel, despite a multimillion-dollar ad campaign, had just bombed—and was introducing smaller cars like the Falcon and Valiant. Volkswagen sought campaign proposals and, according to a Volkswagen executive quoted by Rowsome, most agencies worked up reams of uninformed spec ads that looked "exactly like every other ad . . . The only difference was that, where the tube of toothpaste had been, they'd placed a Volkswagen." DDB was at first tempted, Rowsome writes, "to out-Detroit Detroit" for VW with "prettier girls than Chevrolet, or higher mountains than Ford." Instead, Bill Bernbach won the $800,000 contract with his penchant for honesty. "The magic is in the product" was another of his favorite mottoes. He proposed to emphasize the qualities that set VWs apart from cars manufactured in Detroit: bizarre looks, interchangeable parts because no frivolous changes were imposed from year to year, hyper-careful manufacturing, and inspection processes that could turn a Beetle with a blemished glove compartment into a "Lemon."

The ads, in Rowsome's words, were "an immediate crazy success." Research showed that readers read them twice as much as other car ads, often more thoroughly than a magazine's lead feature, and VW owners considered them "truthful, excellent, witty, to the point, effective, sophisticated, informative, unique, and cute." The basic format of spare image over centered headline and three shallow columns of easygoing colloquial copy turned out to accommodate infinite variations for Beetle and Bus: "Mass transit" for a billboard under an image of nuns piling into a Bus; Wilt Chamberlain testifying to the economical joys and spatial discomforts of Beetles; even a two-page spread headed "How to do a Volkswagen ad" over a blank sheet with outlines for a photo and three columns of your own copy. TV ads were likewise minimal and wry: the VW that earns a thrifty nephew a $100-billion inheritance, the VW that takes the snowplow driver to his snowplow.

By 1963, as *Sports Illustrated* noted, the campaign was "talked about at cocktail parties, read aloud at the office water cooler, analyzed and dissected in college term papers." Why? Above all, because DDB had foreseen the counterculture's concerns. Ethnic faces in ads spoke to a market that increasingly resented WASP domination of government and society. Honest noncondescending images that admitted that doors could be dented or tires flattened were welcomed as relief from hype. The hazards of suburban conformism were becoming obvious, analyzed in popular sociology books like John Keats's 1956 *Crack in the Picture Window*, and possibly curable by Volkswagen ownership. One ad that now seems quite un-P.C. advised 1960s husbands to buy a Bus only if their wives were Bohemian enough to worry about the Bomb, to allow their daughters to keep pet snakes, to name a cat Rover, and to "let you give up your job with a smile . . . And mean it." VW's high mile-per-gallon ratio and planned non-obsolescence also appealed to the growing environmental and preservation movements, given further impetus by books like Jane Jacobs's 1961 *Death and Life of Great American Cities*. There must have been a sense, in 1960, that of all the cheap, mass-produced, good-looking designs whose form followed function ever promised by the modernists and postwar businessmen in gray flannel suits, the VW was one of the few that materialized, and maybe the only one with any sense of humor or soul.

VW ads were even beloved for their layout minutiae—"Execution becomes content in a work of genius," goes another Bernbach motto. "It was all so pure, so utterly pure," recalls Helmut Krone. The ads were not only functionalist—"We never put in anything that wasn't totally necessary"—they were born in loose brainstorming sessions without thoughts of competitors' ads or market research: "It's important to be innocent of what you're doing, to just go ahead," Krone says. Beetles and Buses appeared in ads unglorified by sunbursts or even by much of a paint gloss; often they were reproduced in black and white, and almost always against a white background.

"We used black-and-white mainly because we couldn't afford much color," Krone explains. "We didn't realize how shocking it would be until we saw it in magazines." He always placed a period at the end of headlines (Futura Demibold and, rarely, Bold), to keep them flatly declaratory, and he manipulated the metal text type carefully. "You can tell the ones I did," he says, by the perfection of the leading, balanced to the weight of the ragged-right body type (Futura Light, in columns about forty-five characters wide) and column length: "You aim for a certain urgent look when setting body copy. It should say, 'I need to be read.'" He asked Levenson to provide plenty of paragraph breaks, "many more than was typical of that time," sometimes reducing paragraphs in Gertrude Stein fashion to one or two words. He also asked Levenson to rework the text everywhere necessary "to keep the texture uniform," with no loosely or tightly spaced lines.

Levenson trained himself for the task by setting the office typewriter margins at forty-five characters and got so accustomed to writing copy packages of two-hundred-odd words that "it took me a long time to write longer or shorter than that," he recalls. "And every art director who succeeded Helmut had the good sense to not screw around with the layout. . . . It was a heady time. But we weren't always aware of how heady it was. We knew we were onto something, but the real problem was getting out the next ad. That it would turn out as big as it got, that you'd be calling me about it thirty years later, who knew?"

By the end of the '60s, however, the campaign was doomed. To paraphrase Roy Grace, VW and DDB faced a confluence of *un*happy coincidences. Harping on the Beetle's ugliness didn't work anymore. The ads had succeeded too well. The cars had become cult objects, customized with psychedelic paint, fake bandages over dents, or Rolls-Royce fronts. But the company was no longer committed to the Beetle, especially after Heinz Nordhoff died in 1968. The German mark was revalued for the first time since World War II and VW's prices rose over those of comparable models from the newly competitive Japanese manufacturers. Other European carmakers and Detroit (which had only toyed with and then abandoned smaller cars around 1960) were waking up to the appeal of smaller cars marketed with a light touch. By the early '70s, ads were touting Novas and Volvos as cars that were small and gas-thrifty, like Beetles, but not cramped, noisy, or scary to drive on highways. Headlines came in Futura or a sans-serif relative, copy was ragged, and photos were populated by ethnic types and were typically background-free, wry, and low-budget. Typical was a generic sedan painted as a dog with the headline, "Do you sometimes get the feeling they named your car after the wrong animal?"

Even Hollywood managed to co-opt the Beetle: Disney's *Love Bug* was a huge hit in 1969, ruining any charm the Beetle might have still held for members of the counterculture. Ralph Nader wiped out the rest of VW's underdog image with a circa-1971 study called *Small—on Safety*, revealing grievous engineering defects like handling instability in high winds, and shells that collapsed too readily in crashes. A less beloved car, with less of a reputation for candor, could have survived such disclosures, but VW owners and fans felt deeply betrayed to learn that VW was as disingenuous as every other car manufacturer. The company stopped selling Beetles in the United States (they're now sold mainly in countries lacking strict car safety regulations, like Mexico) and remodeled the Bus beyond recognition but never figured out what else to sell here or how.

Passats, Polos, Jettas, Golfs, Rabbits, Sciroccos, EuroVans, and Vanagons have filed past, some of them with mechanical problems, few of their ads memorable. Some ads have wallowed in Beetle nostalgia with headlines like "Think fast" and "Think ahead." Many have featured the sunsets and the broads that Bernbach had the wisdom to avoid in the 1960s. The theme "German engineering" lasted a few years, an attempt to catch the coattails of increasingly popular German cars like BMW and Mercedes with ads depicting VWs swerving around chairs occupied by impassive white-coated engineers. Then came the disastrous "Fahrvergnügen" experiment, defined as "joy in driving" and sung on TV by a goofy Abba-like chorus, perhaps in an attempt to capitalize on the old "Made in der Black Forest" humor. Fahrvergnügen had such a short lifespan, just a few seasons, that it looks more ridiculous in retrospect than it might otherwise. More recently, the tag line "the most loved cars in the world" was inspired less by the Beetle's legacy than by the fact that VWs do sell well outside the United States. The condescending implication, so different from the attitude expressed in the early Beetle ads, is that these cars would be popular in the United States, too, if only Americans knew better.

With every year of VW's floundering and DDB's transformation into a stale unit of the Omnicom Group, the 1960s campaign looks more and more like a fluke: the near impossible intersection of a hot but stable agency and a patient and focused client somehow attuned to a society in transition. Its creators do not seem to miss it much: Levenson muses, "What a terrible world it would be if Volkswagen ads were still the hottest things in town," and Krone adds, "Yes, Volkswagen became like every other account in the world, every year something new, but if you're looking for immortality in advertising, you're in the wrong business."

And yet, self-mocking Beetle influence oozes from the more distinctive car ads of our time, like Chiat/Day's 1994–95 campaign for Nissan that looks like deadpan '50s textbooks. Also, by 2000, VW may introduce a Beetlelike arched-roof car called, for now, the Concept 1. VW spokesperson Tony Fouladpour, 33, who has a vivid childhood memory of the 1969 VW ad with the lunar lander and headline "It's ugly but it gets you there," describes the Concept 1 as "a completely new updated vehicle." At first, Fouladpour says he doubts strongly that its ads will speak in Beetle tones. Upon reflection, however, he changes his mind. The old campaign, he says, "Did last a long time, didn't it? . . . There certainly could be some play on it; that would be a neat idea. It would be fun."

Eve M. Kahn is a design and architecture writer based in New York.

Originally published in PRINT, *January/February 1995*

A CERTAIN COMMITMENT: ART AND DESIGN AT THE ROYAL PTT
Paul H. Hefting

The concern shown for design at the Netherlands Postal and Telecommunications Service (PTT) from about 1920 on was the result of both the cultural climate of the period and the vision and initiative of one man: Jean François van Royen (1878–1942). Appointed general secretary to the board of the PTT in 1919, the erudite Van Royen took full advantage of this position to put into practice his advanced ideas about contemporary design.

These ideas had been nurtured in a cultural atmosphere which, because of Holland's geographic location, was open to a variety of European influences. Beginning in the late nineteenth century, the Arts and Crafts movement in England, Art Nouveau in France, and the Wiener Werkstätte in Austria had made an impact in the Netherlands, giving rise to a similar movement in Dutch architecture and design, known as "Nieuwe Kunst""(literally, new art or Art Nouveau), which in turn led to the Amsterdam School and other movements in the decorative arts. In the visual arts, movements such as Symbolism, Expressionism, and a number of variations of Cubism were also represented in the Netherlands during this same period. Yet another group of artists, among them Theo van Doesburg, founded the periodical *De Stijl* in 1917, and maintained close contact with the Russian Constructivists and the Bauhaus. Three years later, in 1922, Van Doesburg began to experiment with Dadaist poetry and typography and to issue Dadaist manifestoes.

It was against this background that, as early as 1900, a few forward-looking private companies began adapting contemporary design styles originating in the applied arts to their products and advertising material. Thanks to Van Royen, the PPT began appropriating this "new esthetic"—still largely based on Nieuwe Kunst and its progeny—in about 1920. It was remarkable that such a bureaucratic organization was able to abandon a design style whose conservative look had long characterized State communications, in favor of an altogether fresh approach.

Van Royen himself championed the ideals of William Morris and children's book illustrator Walter Crane, who sought to restore to artists the recognition they deserved and to integrate their craft into mainstream society. He also thought it was important to develop the aesthetic sensibilities of the community by acting as a mediator between artists and the general public. He regarded this charge as a moral duty; the moral and the aesthetic, in his view of the world, were closely linked. He believed that good design and an aesthetically satisfying environment would not only improve society but would also raise the individual to a higher plane. All Van Royen's work at the PTT (and elsewhere) was informed by this idea, which had an impact on the administration and the general organization of the company as well as on its use of language, its typography, and its approach to every aspect of design. It was Van Royen's conviction that the State should set an example in this sphere. His criticism, written in 1912, of the design of State publications is well-known in the Netherlands: ". . . ugly, ugly, ugly, three times ugly: ugly in typeface, ugly in composition, and ugly in paper—the three main elements which determine the attractiveness of printed matter . . ."

His particular concern with graphic design arose from his love of books and his passion for typesetting and printing them in limited editions on his own private press, a pursuit inspired by the Arts and Crafts movement in England. He was in close contact with English type designers, including Lucien Pissarro, C. H. St. John Hornby, and Gobden Sanderson.

In addition to this hobby and his work for the PTT, Van Royen was also very involved in the arts in the Netherlands, and took a particular interest in improving the position of the artist in society. One of his most important posts in this regard was as chairman of VANK (the Association for Applied Arts and Crafts), established in 1904, an organization which sought to create a "harmonious relationship between the craft of the artist and machine processing" and which aimed to improve the social function of art and design.

The PTT benefited considerably from Van Royen's connections with artists and designers, whom he contracted to design stamps, furniture, advertising material, and other visual material such as printed forms and signs on buildings and vehicles—though not without some resistance from within the organization. He also concerned himself with works of art displayed in post offices and both inside and outside the PTT's office buildings. He felt that in devoting attention to every aspect of its visual presentation, the PTT would reveal its concern for the quality of its services and would thus gain the confidence of the public. With this policy, Van Royen pioneered the twin concepts of corporate identity and public image.

Van Royen's first success with regard to PTT aesthetics came in 1913 with the issue of a series of stamps to commemorate the centenary of Dutch independence. The previous year, Van Royen, then still a relatively junior employee, had invited the architect K. C. De Bazel to design the stamps. Like many architects of his day, De Bazel designed not only buildings, but also furniture and graphic communications. His designs for the centenary issue were very modern in comparison with previous Dutch stamps, which had adhered to neoclassical or neo-Baroque decorative styles. His designs introduced a contemporary look to PTT graphics for the first time. Van Royen was also closely associated with the subsequent new issue of stamps which, because of World War I, did not appear until 1923. From then on, Dutch stamps maintained their allegiance to the new aesthetics.

This change of style was not confined to stamps. It was also apparent in all the printed matter issued by the PTT, as well as in the architecture of its buildings, in the works of art associated with or displayed in them, in furniture, and in postboxes. All such designs echoed motifs popular in contemporary applied arts—most notably certain stylized decorative elements. In about 1928, Van Royen introduced Functionalism and New Realism to the PTT in the telephone kiosk designed by the architect Van der Vlugt (well known for the

Van Nelle factory in Rotterdam, which he designed in collaboration with Brinkman), and in brochures, advertising material, and stamps designed by Piet Zwart, Gerard Kiljan, and Paul Schuitema in 1931–32.

Subsequently, it seems that Van Royen wished stamp designs to reflect his own strict views about typography and decoration; functionalism disappeared from all PTT design, as indeed it was also increasingly overshadowed on the international scene in the 1930s by a trend toward decoration and illustration. *The PTT Book,* designed by Piet Zwart, which was intended for schoolchildren and was published in 1939, shows that Zwart himself had abandoned the strict functionalist principles which had inspired his constructivist work during the 1920s.

Van Royen died in a concentration camp in 1942. Beginning in 1946, his work was continued by the aesthetic design department at the PTT under a succession of Aesthetic Advisers beginning with F. S. Spanjaar, who was appointed in 1945. This department had been set up specifically for the purpose of producing "all work commissioned or undertaken by the company that involves presenting the company to the public. The design and execution of such work should be carried out in consultation with the Esthetic Adviser . . ." The corporate policy unit for art and design, as the aesthetic design department was renamed when the PTT was privatized on January 1, 1989, is responsible for procurement of works of art for display both in employees' offices and in areas frequented by visitors. This department is also responsible for art which is incorporated into the structure of the PTT's buildings and for all graphic and industrial design work undertaken on behalf of the PTT.

After Van Royen's death, the department had to reestablish its position within the organization—not least because it no longer had the benefit of his authority and mandate as a member of the board. However, its repositioning as a unit which reported directly to the director-general of the PTT gave it a status and authority of its own. The department's role as an intermediary between the PTT (which officially and formally commissions projects) and the world of art and design has always been somewhat unusual. Its staff acts as advisers, who must bear equally in mind the interests of the company and the concerns of the artists and their work. There is ample scope for a conflict of interest here, particularly at a time like the present when commercial considerations are becoming increasingly important.

Although the department is only responsible for the company's image in a general and indirect way and is not in charge of the PTT's marketing or advertising, it has recently been asked to adopt a more commercial approach. Reconciling advertising with aesthetics remains a difficult task.

Up to now, the department's focus has been the comprehensive, detailed supervision of all PTT design projects. When considering a new PTT building, for example, the staff is not only concerned with the architectural design, but also bears responsibility for the lettering on the outside and inside of the building, and for procuring works of art for the interior. They may also influence decisions about furnishings or the design of areas open to visitors. Whatever the project, they must always consider its overall effect, a charge which at all times requires them to understand and be sensitive to a variety of disciplines.

When the department was repositioned within the company in 1946, art and design at the PTT were characterized by the illustrative and decorative styles which had been fashionable before the war. These remained in vogue until well into the 1950s, and indeed into the 1960s, when they sometimes alternated with a more abstract use of space, form, and color, which derived from the influence of Swiss design. At that time, the outlook of the staff was relatively conservative, as was the design world in general, a state of affairs that was reflected both in the stamp designs and in the works of art commissioned for PTT buildings. In 1966, however, there was a change in the institution's aesthetic direction, and the PTT began to extend practical recognition to a number of new movements in art and design—a step which provoked considerable discussion within the organization.

During this period, the PTT was rapidly growing, renovating buildings in both the postal and telecommunications sectors, and constructing new ones, too—activities which provided opportunities for major art projects to be commissioned on the recommendation of the art and design department. This was the case, for example, at all twelve of PTT post's mail interchange centers, which were built after 1970 to accommodate a reorganization of the postal service and its infrastructure.

The PTT's art collection has grown steadily, and although it can never be viewed as a whole, since it is displayed in and outside of PTT buildings all over the country, it represents virtually every movement in Dutch art. Since 1989, work has also been commissioned from a number of foreign artists—for example, from the Danish artist Per Kirkeby, who created a large sculpture for PTT Nederlands's corporate headquarters in Groningen, which opened in June 1990.

In the 1970s and '80s, many industrial design projects were initiated, too. New postboxes, post office counters, and postal delivery vans were designed. The telephone kiosk was redesigned, and the PTT cooperated with Delft University of Technology in designing new telephones and the first videophones.

In creating graphic design for the PTT—stamps, annual reports, diaries, and calendars, for example—the art and design department has always aimed at diversity. Every art movement has been reflected in PTT products, for this sector and some of the annual reports by Sandberg and Walter Nikkels (who commissioned the American artist Lawrence Weiner to do the illustrations) are now regarded as outstanding examples of Dutch design.

In the late 1960s, under the direction of Esthetic Adviser H. van Haaren, the first steps were taken toward developing a distinctive house style for the PTT. Other major Dutch companies such as KLM and Dutch Railways had already moved in this direction before the PTT decided in 1969 that it should do likewise. Visual identity had not previously been regarded as an essential component of corporate strategy, and design of corporate communications had generally been considered a mere embellishment. The rapid expansion of PTT business—and the growing complexity of the company—meant that design activity increasingly went unchecked and uncoordinated. This situation needed to be corrected, and because of the PTT's traditional respect for design, the conditions were right for an integrated approach to all aspects of design within the organization. As a service company providing communications services on a massive scale, the PTT needed an overall corporate identity, which would inspire confidence and which would express the PTT's "attitude."

Commenting on the company's position with regard to design, Van Haaren observed in 1976, "At the PTT, a situation has been established which encourages discussion about the significance of the shape of a letter, about a typeface or typography as significant form (with the printed word as its content), about the appearance of functional objects, and about the quality of the working environment as elements of corporate policy. This state of affairs is based on the understanding that processes of change in our culture both spring from and affect our society, and that they should find visible expression there and not just in museums."

In 1970, the PTT drew some initial conclusions from a survey designed to ascertain just what the staff and the public at large thought the actual company image was. The general criteria and a design brief for the new house style were based on these findings, which indicated that changes in visual presentation would have to accompany changes in the range of services and the way in which they were provided. The new image would have to evoke associations of "versatility, vigor, generosity, and courtesy," while at the same time retaining the existing image of honesty and reliability. The PTT had to be seen as a unique, modern, socially and technologically progressive company, responsive to the needs and wishes of every member of Dutch society.

In order to translate these abstract ideas about corporate identity into a house style, the PTT enlisted the services of two leading firms of design consultants who already had extensive experience in this field. One was Total Design, based in Amsterdam, which submitted an initial report on all aspects of a house style for the PTT, taking into consideration both the character of the company at the time and the ways in which it was expected to develop in the future. The PTT also approached Tel Design in The Hague, but subsequently transferred the contract to Studio Dumbar. Working independently, the two consultants presented proposals in 1972, but it was not until 1978—under the direction of R. D. E. Oxenaar, who was appointed Esthetic Adviser in 1976 and continues in that position today—that these led to a final joint concept.

Every conceivable aspect of the project was carefully researched—the readability of forms, the impact of the logo, the colors that should be used, and the typography, as well as all the various elements which were to be given a new look. In 1981, the house style was officially launched.

At the same time, an extensive house style manual was produced, containing detailed guidelines—especially for the typography on stationery, forms, and similar printed materials.

Strict adherence to the house style was more or less ruled out for certain specific items with which the public was bound to come into contact: The house style did not extend to stamps, for example—which had traditionally been designed by distinguished designers—nor did it apply to telephone directories, office diaries, annual reports, uniforms, or the interiors of old post offices, some of which are landmark buildings.

In other words, although a PTT house style had been developed, it was not to be applied dogmatically and unimaginatively; exceptions were permitted, provided that the design of the items in question met the highest professional standards. Quality remained the prime objective: It was important that the individual components—details of which were themselves designed with great care—added up to a cohesive whole. This concern with quality remains an important aspect of the company image.

This same flexibility has been observed in connection with the design of the most recent PTT house style, which was introduced on January 1, 1989, when the PTT was privatized. The PTT's new status as a private company called for a new corporate image, although since the executive board felt that the "old" house style had lost none of its original clarity, force, or character, it was intended that the new identity should resemble the old one in many respects. The old image simply needed adjusting to suggest that the newly privatized company was a different entity from the old PTT. In fact, the new house style drew on the previous one for a number of its basic elements. It was also decided that the house style should be applied consistently throughout the PTT and that adherence to it should be monitored more carefully than had previously been the case. This consistency is important because the PTT has lost its monopoly in some areas. Continual growth in all areas of society and increasingly keen competition make it necessary for the privatized PTT to be immediately recognizable as a service company, to operate faster, and to respond better to the needs of the market.

Good design in such situations usually gives way to the demands of marketing and advertising. But for a company seeking to win customers by establishing its identity as a quality organization, it is essential for all aspects of its operations to be characterized by quality design. What's more, since such a company must keep up with a changing society, the house style should be flexible within the confines of its basic rules.

In 1988, Studio Dumbar was chosen for the mammoth task of redesigning the house style. Substantial progress had been made by early 1989, and the house style has now been fully introduced.

As art and design are held in high esteem in the international business world, primarily as a means of promoting a corporate image, the PTT's art and design department takes the view that the house style represents the company's corporate identity. Both its graphics and its works of art must be of the highest quality, for that very quality expresses the character of the company. In the policies which it pursues through its art and design department, the PTT is continuing a tradition, adjusted to meet the requirements of the present time, which has long been of great importance to the company. Moreover, in paying such close attention to art and design, the PTT continues to make a contribution to contemporary culture in the Netherlands.

Paul Hendrik Hefting is an art historian. From 1963–1966 he was assistant professor at Technical University Delft (Architecture), from 1966–1981 he served as curator Kröller-Müller Museum, Otterlo, and from 1981–1994 he was a staff member at PTT Art & Design, Holland.

Originally published in PRINT, *November/December 1991*

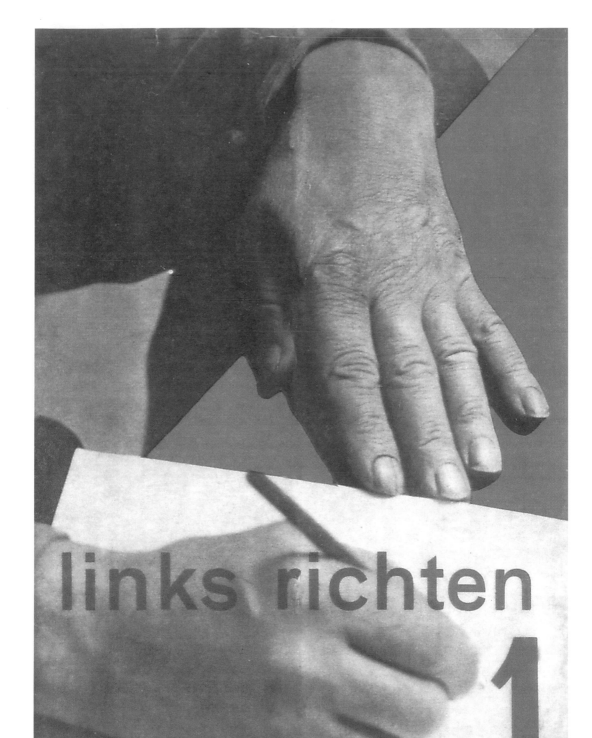

links richten

no. 1

maandblad uitgegeven door het arbeiders
schrijvers collectief „links richten"

Renewal and Upheaval: Dutch Design Between the Wars
Alston W. Purvis

In 1917, the Amsterdam Stedelijk Museum held an exhibition of advertising art that sparked a debate between the artist and poster designer R. N. Roland Holst and the socialist political cartoonist Albert Hahn regarding the artist's role in advertising. Roland Holst maintained that an advertisement could be either straightforward information or a "shout," and since truth did not have to be overstated, the "shout" was both undesirable and unnecessary. Albert Hahn, however, took the opposite position. He maintained that advertising was a true popular "street" art and influenced people who would never think of entering a museum or gallery. He found the "shout" quite appropriate and observed furthermore that an artist could successfully use this approach as well. The dispute kept to these two points of view with no truce in sight.

The Netherlands had remained neutral during World War I, but the country by no means avoided its effects. However, as the war drew to a close, life there, compared to that in most of Europe, was still economically and culturally stable. The security of this atmosphere allowed for discussion of such issues, which, in a more troubled society, might have seemed frivolous. By the end of 1917, there were already signals that a transition to new frontiers had begun and that forces were in position for a twentieth-century renaissance in Dutch graphic design. The end of World War I would serve as a catalyst to this renewal.

Noticeable changes began taking place as industry started using the services of contemporary graphic designers. Also, the organization VANK, the Vereniging voor Ambachts-Nijverheidskunst (Association for Crafts and Industrial Design) played an increasingly vigorous role in this alliance. Since its inception in 1904, VANK had exerted considerable influence and as a professional organization, it was unique in its embrace of practitioners in a wide variety of professions ranging from graphic design to architecture. It lasted until it was disbanded by the Nazi occupiers in 1942. Essentially, VANK had three objectives: to support issues relating to the various professions of its members; to promote the development of the arts and crafts within the industrial sector; and to inform the public about its activities.

During this period between the wars, five reformist forces would emerge in the Netherlands: the traditional but innovative approach of Jan van Krimpen and S. H. de Roos; De Stijl, presided over by Theo van Doesburg; the Wendingen style of the architect H. Th. Wijdeveld; the Constructivism of Piet Zwart and Paul Schuitema; and the very personal approach of H. N. Werkman.

In 1917, Van Doesburg launched the De Stijl movement together with the architect J. J. P. Oud, the writer, poet, and music critic Antonie Kok, and the painters Vilmos Huszár, Bart van der Leck, and Piet Mondrian. The first issue of their journal *De Stijl* (they had considered calling it *The Straight Line*) appeared in October of the same year.

Van Doesburg was an inventive, unyielding, and often belligerent artist who worked in many sectors with passionate energy and was active as a lecturer, writer, painter, architect, poet, sculptor, furniture and industrial designer, and typographer. His own eclecticism reflected the multifarious nature of the De Stijl movement itself and its objective to encompass all aspects of life.

De Stijl was one of many cultural reactions to the devastation of World War I, and the basic goal of its practitioners was to free art from various nonessentials such as subject matter, illusion, ambiguity, and subjectivity. Abjuring all kinds of emotion outright, they attempted in this way to dilute the possibility for another, similar tragedy. They renounced what they considered to be the overdecorative and decadent art of the nineteenth and early twentieth centuries, and looking at the future, they wanted to clear the way for a new art form for an industrial society and believed in a social and artistic revolution where art and daily life would be inseparable. The Arts and Crafts movement and Art Nouveau were both rejected as decadent and sentimental. Visually, De Stijl was based upon functional harmony and elementary rectangular forms and its palette was restricted to black, white, shades of gray, and the primary colors.

Two of the most prominent members of the De Stijl movement were architects Gerrit Rietveld and J. J. P. Oud. Rietveld, the son of a furniture maker, produced his first De Stijl furniture in 1919, and the prototype for his famous "lean chair" was finished in 1918. This was originally made of natural wood, but it was later painted in the primary colors. Oud was a social activist and for all practical purposes the official architect of Rotterdam. In 1925, he designed the Café Unie in Rotterdam, a building which could be described as the architectural embodiment of De Stijl principles.

Van Doesburg had an early empathy for Dadaism. In the third issue of *De Stijl*, he published a series of poems titled "X-Beelden" (X Images) under one of his pseudonyms, I. K. Bonset. This was an attempt to give sound a typographic form, and the meanings of the texts were amplified through arrangement and variations in the type sizes to emphasize individual words, an approach reminiscent of the "Calligrammes" of the French poet Guillaume Apollinaire. A year later, Van Doesburg published the first of four issues of *Mécano,* a journal primarily Dada in its outlook, which even satirized De Stijl.

When Walter Gropius invited Van Doesburg to spend a week at the Bauhaus in Weimar in April of 1921, he decided to extend his stay and began conducting De Stijl courses in the studio of one of the Bauhaus students. Eventually, his activities there created so much hostility that windows of the studio were shattered by rocks thrown by Gropius's followers, and even by gunshots. Gropius disagreed fundamentally with Van Doesburg's total rejection of individualism—a position which contrasted with the Bauhaus approach. Also, Van Doesburg's exclusion had much to do with often uncompromising and contentious manner. His dogmatism is evident in a letter he wrote to Kok in January 1921 about the Bauhaus period: "In Weimar, I have radically turned everything upside-down. This is the acclaimed academy with the most modern teachers! Every evening I have spoken to the students and have spread the toxin of the new spirit. De Stijl will soon rematerialize in an even more radical shape. I have mountains of strength and now know that our ideas will prevail over everything and everybody."

The October/November 1922 issue of *De Stijl* was devoted to a Dutch version of El Lissitzky's constructivist fairy tale, *Of Two Squares*, which had recently been published in Germany. It had a significant impact in the Netherlands, and for Piet Zwart in particular it revealed the immeasurable potential for using words and images on a page.

The Hungarian-born Vilmos Huszar, one of the less-known practitioners of De Stijl, remained associated with the movement until 1923. He designed the wood block logo and masthead for *De Stijl* in 1917 and decisively influenced its initial typographic approach. Like Van Doesburg, Huszar was a versatile artist who was active in painting as well as in interior, furniture, fabric, and industrial design. His graphic design work included new logos for cigarettes made by the Vittoria Egyptian Cigarette Company. They were used both in color and black and white for stationery, cards, billboards, and advertising wagons.

With Van Doesburg's untimely death in 1931, De Stijl lost its driving force. A truly indigenous Dutch movement, De Stijl exerted an international influence lasting far beyond its thirteen years of existence.

In 1918, a year after the De Stijl movement had begun to take shape, the architect T. H. Wijdeveld launched *Wendingen*, a monthly magazine devoted to architecture, construction, and ornamentation. Wijdeveld served as its designer and, until his resignation in 1927, chief editor as well. The vertical and horizontal asymmetrical framework of the layout was soon referred to as the "Amsterdam School," the "Linear School," or the "Wendingen" and "Wijdeveld" styles. Besides Wijdeveld, others who designed covers for *Wendingen* included El Lissitzky and Huszar.

Wendingen delivered the decorative gospel while De Stijl went in the opposite direction. Wijdeveld's style has often been referred to as a progeny of Art Nouveau, but instead of undulating lines and flourishes, Wijdeveld used solid, heavy borders constructed from right angles and built elaborate compositions out of typographic elements.

The Wendingen style generated both followers and strong opponents. Traditional typographers found it appalling: others were captivated by what appeared to be its latent possibilities. The Amsterdam graphic designer Fré Cohen managed to astutely adapt it to government printing. She remained a faithful devotee of Wijdeveld until her tragic suicide in 1943 after she was arrested by the Nazis.

During his long career, Piet Zwart, one of the primary forces behind Dutch constructivism, worked in many spheres including graphic design, architecture, architectural criticism, furniture design, industrial design, painting, writing, photography, and design education. He liked to call himself a "typotekt," a combination of the two words typographer and architect.

In 1918, Zwart met Huszar and the architect Jan Wils, both of whom had been among the founders of De Stijl. Although this association generated a dramatic change in his outlook, Zwart never joined De Stijl and became irate if someone even suggested that he had. Zwart worked as a draftsman for Wils from 1919 until 1921 when he was hired by the architect H. P. Berlage, an association which would last until the beginning of 1927. Also, in 1921 Zwart did his first typographic work for the Dutch representative of the importer Vickers House.

In 1923, Zwart designed his first advertisements for the Nederlandsche Kabel Fabriek (Dutch Cable Works). This commission began an extraordinary client-designer relationship which would continue until 1933 and which generated some of the most original, venturesome, and provocative work in the Netherlands during this period. In 1938, Zwart referred to this style as "functional" typography.

Zwart brought to his work an imaginative use of language and acted as his own copywriter. He amplified phrases with basic typographic elements, and the text serves as a catalyst to his creativity, with words and their interpretations merging into single entities, each reinforcing the other.

As the printing of photographic reproductions became increasingly feasible, Zwart began to use them in his compositions, and in 1926, this "photo-typography" became part of his visual inventory.

Zwart's poster for the International Tentoonstelling op Filmgebied (International Film Exhibition) at The Hague again reflected his adroit versatility as a designer. His 1931 catalog for The Hague printer Trio is also an exceptional piece. The page presenting their type collection is printed in black, red, blue, and yellow and contains over one hundred different typefaces ranging from large wooden display letters to text sizes. Even within this typographic cloudburst, he managed to realize a superb sense of unity and balance. Zwart's covers for ten monographs on the film arts for the Rotterdam publisher W.L. & J. Brusse, also produced in 1931, rank among his finest work, and represent a visual culmination of the earlier experiments.

In 1929, Zwart executed his first commission for the PTT (the Dutch postal, telephone, and telegraph service). In addition to stamps, his assignments included brochures, posters, forms, and displays. *Het boek van PTT* (*The PTT Book*) is an interesting publication because it reflects so many of the new design trends of the 1930s. Typographically, it differs radically from Zwart's earlier work and essentially concluded his major contribution to Dutch graphic design.

Zwart's fellow constructivist Paul Schuitema pioneered the use of photography as an important design element. For both men, montage provided a means both for contrasting large and small images, and for merging incongruous elements and situations into a single, unified message.

Schuitema's important clients were the P. van Berkel meat company, the Mij. van Berkel patent scale and cutting machine factory, and the printer C. Chevalier. His designs for the Rotterdam companies would rank with the most innovative graphic design of the period, and in his hands, what would have otherwise been pedestrian advertising assignments were elevated to dynamic heights.

At the end of 1928, Schuitema published an article called "Advertising" in the progressive magazine *i 10* in which he presented his view of the current state of graphic design. He wrote, "Yesterday was 'artistic, decorative, symbolic, fantastic, anti-social, lyrical, passive, romantic, esthetic, theoretical, craftsmanship-like,' in other words, 'art.' 'Today' means: 'real, direct, photographic, succinct, competitive, argumentative, active, actual, appropriate, practical, technical,' in other words, 'reality.'" Both postures were illustrated with representational images, two of them his own.

As the avant-garde was approaching new typographic frontiers, there was another faction which, though it remained committed to the classical style, nevertheless sought new vitality with no less tenacity. Leading this vanguard was Jan van Krimpen, followed by S. H. de Roos, J. F. Van Royen, and the two printer/publishers from Maastricht, Charles Nypels and A. A. M. Stols.

Van Krimpen, although initially influenced by De Roos, soon forged his own direction and became the most distinguished book and type designer in the Netherlands. An intellectual with an aristocratic outlook, he produced work that was more refined than that of De Roos. Van Krimpen's objective was to present texts that could be comfortably and quickly read by cultivated people. His style was not intended to express feelings, and he felt that the reader should never even be conscious of typography. In Van Krimpen's world, moreover, typography existed only for books. He overtly despised advertising as well as the people and jargon connected with it. De Roos was more artistically inclined and did not share Van Krimpen's unequivocal reverence for text.

For De Roos, however, the revival of Dutch book design was a solitary commitment. Wijdeveld was no less than an all-out adversary who was, he felt, spreading a form of typographic disease, and Zwart was, in his opinion, yet another architect "meddling" with typography. He contemptuously referred to him as "Piet Blok," alluding to Zwart's signature, a *P* next to a black square.

Of the traditional designers, Nypels took the most chances, and in breaking many of the rules, he often visually enriched his design. In 1930, he produced a book in collaboration with Paul Schuitema, one of the rare occasions when the constructivist and classically oriented design factions joined forces. This was *Balans* (*Balance*), an annual publication on Dutch art which featured on its cover a photomontage by Schuitema.

Visually, A. M. M. Stols (1900–73) is the least remarkable of the traditional designers, but the best of his publications are superb, both in design and production. Like Van Krimpen, his doctrine was simplicity and maximum legibility.

J. F. Van Royen (1878–1942), a book designer and private publisher, in 1910 joined the bibliophile publishing concern De Zilverdistal (The Silver Thistle), and by 1913 had taken over the production and design responsibilities. In 1923, Van Royen started another private press, De Kunerapers (The Kunera Press), which continued until his death in 1942. Van Royen's principal contribution to graphic design in the Netherlands, however, came through his work at the Dutch PTT. A born organizer and idealist, he had an innate ability for leadership and an indefatigable appetite for accomplishment.

In 1920, he became general secretary of the PTT and assumed the task of reforming the dismal state of official design. Earlier, in 1912, while serving as a legal aide to the PTT, he had denounced in an article the horrendous state of official printing. "Three words suffice," he wrote: "governmental printing is ugly, ugly, ugly, thrice ugly in form, composition, and paper, the three main elements which comprise the character of printing."

Van Royen made a distinction between his own traditional approach to typography and the contemporary look of the work for the PTT, and he encouraged innovative design by giving assignments to young, forward-looking designers. His post at the PTT gave him a unique forum in which to work for the improvement of design standards on an official level, and he continued in this position until his death at the German concentration camp in Amersfoort in 1942.

In contrast, the "maverick" Hendrik Nicolaas Werkman (1882–1945) represented the unbridled force of Dutch graphic design. By 1904, he had managed to set up his own small printing establishment in Groningen, but for a number of reasons, mainly his total lack of interest in business affairs, it floundered by 1923. (Willem Sandberg described Werkman as someone for whom anything utilitarian was beyond comprehension.) He then moved what was left of the operation to an attic workshop in a warehouse and managed to earn a modest living from jobs such as wedding and birth announcements, invitations, brochures, stationery, and posters.

The first issue of Werkman's avant-garde publication *The Next Call* came out in September 1923. At the same time, Werkman was also producing many larger works using methods similar to those he had used in *The Next Call*, labeling them *Druksels*, a derivative of the Dutch word *Drukken*, meaning "to print." Werkman combined traditional printing with a method he would eventually call "hot printing." In this process, the paper was placed faceup on the bed of the handpress, which allowed him to freely arrange previously inked design elements. The procedure could be repeated indefinitely with an unlimited number of shapes and colors.

One objective of *The Next Call* was to warn Werkman's fellow members of the Groningen art circle De Ploeg against the risks of complacency, but it also served three additional purposes: It was an outlet for Werkman's various manifestoes regarding a new art; it provided a forum in which he could explore and exhibit his experimental typography; and it served as a means of communication with the international avant-garde.

Although Werkman's approach to typography was in most respects "nonfunctional," there is a similarity between his work and that of Zwart. Both used type as collage, and by emphasizing the innate qualities of printing elements, Werkman came close to the constructivist ideal that art should reflect the properties of its material.

In the 1930s, Werkman produced calendars which followed the principles illustrated in his other experimental typography. Also notable were the Ex Libris designs that he made between 1923 and 1934.

During World War II, Werkman designed and printed the forty-two publications of "De Blauwe Schuit" (The Blue Barge), clandestine booklets in various formats ranging in size from four to fifty pages and intended to bolster the morale of the Dutch people during the occupation. The most notable of these publications were the "Turkish Calendar," which appeared between Christmas and the new year, 1942, and the two portfolios of "Hassidic Legends" published in 1942 and 1943.

Werkman was arrested by the Nazis on March 13, 1945, and executed on April 10, two days before the liberation of Groningen.

The political upheavals of the 1930s had an interesting effect on graphic design. Excessive decoration began to reemerge, and traditional illustration regained the ground it had lost to photography. Of the Dutch designers who gained recognition during the 1930s, the most prominent were Willem Sandberg, Gerard Kiljan, Wim Brusse, Nicolaas de Koo, Henny Cahn, and Dick Elffers. There were many talented but unknown designers as well, especially at the advertising agencies. At that time, however, advertising was not considered worth collecting, and only a fraction of their work survives.

Sandberg's major contribution to Dutch graphic design would not come until after World War II, but during the 1930s he was already active as a designer and museum curator. In the winter of 1938–39, he became acquainted with the work of Werkman, who, from that moment on, was his major influence. Because of his underground activities, Sandberg was forced to go into hiding in 1943. This gave him an opportunity for reflection, and between December 1943 and April 1945 he produced his "experimenta typographica," nineteen booklets containing illustrations and handwritten typographic interpretations of quotations and thoughts.

At the Koninklijke Academie van Beeldende Kunsten (Royal Academy of Fine Arts) at The Hague, Kiljan established in 1930 the first official design program in the Netherlands based on principles of functionalism. Schuitema joined him there as a teacher in 1931. Brusse and Cahn both studied at the academy, and although they clearly exhibited the influence of their instructors, they never became disciples of Constructivism.

N. P. de Koo was the least known of the Dutch graphic designers who were active between the two world wars. In the 1930s, he worked as a freelance designer for the PTT and was largely responsible for their visual identity during this period.

Elffers was another practitioner active in various design arenas. A crucial influence in his development was his teacher at the Rotterdam Academy, Jacques Jongert. Among Jongert's better-known clients was the Van Nelle food company, for which he created a corporate identity. He was an outspoken advocate of the subjectivity of design, and maintained that the designer's individuality was essential for any real creativity. During his last year at the academy, Elffers began working as an assistant in the studio of Schuitema, who, unlike Jongert, represented the functional viewpoint. Elffers, however, profited from the ideas of both factions; one of his stronger traits was a capacity to accommodate disparate points of view.

After 1930, when the social climate in Russia and Germany had clearly changed for the worse, there was an influx of refugee intellectuals and artists who came to the Netherlands with new ideas that greatly enriched Dutch typography. Germans such as Henri Friedlaender, Susan Heynemann, Helmut Salden, and Otto Treumann brought with them a fresh spirit and outlook.

The twenty-two years between the end of World War I and the beginning of World War II was a rich and multifaceted period—the source for much contemporary Dutch graphic design. However, this period drew to a close with the same inconclusive ideological battles over design issues that had been raging in 1917. Ironically, it would take another war to resolve them.

Originally published in PRINT, *November/December 1991*

6. Epilogue

Interview with Louis Danziger
Steven Heller

Lou Danziger was one of the first historian-cum-practitioners to introduce a class in graphic design history. In this interview he talks about the practice of design history and shares his continually evolving syllabus.

Where did your interest in graphic design history come from?

I started reading design books and journals including *Gebrauchsgraphik* as far back as 1934 or '35, and belonged to MOMA from 1938. The Bauhaus had closed only shortly before I started my interest in "commercial art." My interest in design history was nurtured while much of the material was current, not yet history. From my earliest days of teaching in 1952 I made reference to the various modern art movements and to the pioneer designers and artists that were part of this history. I encouraged my students to read and research and to be aware of art, architecture, film, etc. It was simply part of the way I teach.

When did you begin teaching graphic design history? Had there been a course of this kind before, that you are aware of?

I began teaching a course called the History of Graphic Design at CalArts, in 1972 or '73. It was a course begun by Keith Godard a year earlier and it was to my knowledge the only course of its kind at the time. It all began because Keith and I who were colleagues at CalArts would often commiserate about how difficult it was to teach students who had no knowledge of the design pioneers. Keith thought we should do something about it, and put the thought into action. As far as I know Keith should be given the credit of teaching the first course in graphic design history that was listed in a school's catalog; it was an official part of the curriculum. He put a lot of work into the course and it was very effective. When he left CalArts for New York City, I picked up and greatly elaborated the course over the next twenty-five years, teaching it in one form or another at other schools as well as doing synopsis lectures at a variety of universities and institutions. I taught it at Harvard almost every summer from 1978 to 1988 where many graphic designers and design teachers were exposed to this material. A number of people who are currently teaching graphic design history took that summer class as a stimulus for their own subsequent efforts.

Other than the obvious value of understanding the past, what additional benefits do students derive from having an historical grounding?

One thing that I have observed is that the students develop a greater commitment to their work, which they now see as part of a continuum. They see themselves as part of something, perhaps the next contributors to this history. They also begin to understand the connections between industrial and social change and how these changes play a role in the shaping of designers' work. The connection between their work and the milieu from which it springs.

How do you teach history? Are you linear? Episodic? Anecdotal? Theoretical?

The course is structured both episodically and in a somewhat linear way and is largely anecdotal. Document 1 is an introduction, which describes the course fully and sets the stage for the lectures. It should provide the greatest understanding of what I am up to. Document 2 is an outline of the course and makes the structure clear as well as indicating the points made and the thrust of the course. Document 3 is a partial list of the people mentioned during these lectures as my course focuses quite a bit on the individuals that played their role in this history. Although I believe in the importance of contexts and historical imperatives, I think that, particularly in design history, the idiosyncratic personality is of prime importance. Different people, a different history! I don't know whether he ever talked to you about it, but Paul Rand was greatly impressed with my history course; here's a direct quote from a letter to me: "Your history is very impressive. I perspire at the mere thought of the hours you put into producing the stupendous outline. And what's more, it is extremely well done." He did think that I included some people like Stephen Dohanos and other illustrators that needed to be edited out. He dismissed them as "cornballs." I had them in there to make a point about the difference in the way illustrators dealt with problems and the way that graphic designers deal with the same problem. The difference having to do with showing the fish or the fishness. He also felt that there were some important people left out but he never said who. He then asked me if I would do a synopsis history lecture at Yale, which I did.

What would you describe as the ideal way to impart history? And should it be integrated, somehow, into practice?

I'm not quite sure how to answer this. My own experiences vis-à-vis graphic design history are quite unique in several ways. For one thing, I am always talking to designers or future designers; for another, unlike most people that I know of who are teaching the subject, I have gained my knowledge incrementally over a very long period of time and through direct experience. So many people who are teaching the subject today gained their knowledge through extensive and concentrated research over a relatively short span of time. That's very different, and leads to different kinds of understanding and thinking. Furthermore, so many of the trade journals used to research, particularly American design, are full of inaccuracies, as they were not of very high caliber. I know what is wrong, as I was there, so to speak; the fairly recent comers to the subject would have no way of knowing. There is a real dearth of reputable material on design history. As a result, my own teaching can't be extrapolated as a model of how to do it. I think each person teaching the subject tries to find ways to optimize their pedagogic capabilities. I don't know if there is an ideal way. There are simply too many variables to speculate about that. As for integration into practice, I believe that is inevitable. Even if you do not intentionally make the effort, such as assigning history assignments in studio classes, the consciousness of design history, the practitioners, and the concepts will have a direct impact on the students' work.

How do you determine what is, in fact, historically important? Conversely, what do you ignore or reject?

I deal primarily with the modern movement, as I believe the ideas fundamental to good design are there (remember, I am directing my teaching to designers in an effort to enhance their performance). It is also the area in which I feel I have the most to offer. I use my own judgment to select material that they need to know about, material that elucidates particular concepts, or demonstrates something of value. I often select things not necessarily because they are important historically but rather because they make a point. I sometimes select material because I find it amusing or interesting for whatever reason; one doesn't want to lull the students to sleep.

I'm sure you are interested in the growth of design history as a discipline. What do you feel is wrong with how it is taught, and what do you feel is right?

A discipline which conducts research, asks questions, gathers credible information, and leads to greater understanding of a subject is of value for general cultural and intellectual reasons irrespective of whom that material is addressed to or to what specific purpose that research is directed. Having said that, I think that in graphic design history particularly, the distinction between the academic historian and the practitioner-cum-historian presents problems. I believe they look at the same material with different eyes. This is inherently problematic. Ideally, I think the research, writing, and teaching would be collaborative. On very rare occasions there are people like Ellen Lupton, for example (there are others), who I think do good objective history and can also see. One can write a chapter on what it means to see. An educated eye is like an educated palate. You don't get it from eating, you have to cook. Seeing, too, has to do not only with looking but with making.

If you had it to do all over again, how would you structure a history course?

My own course was evolved over a period of more than twenty-five years. I continued to modify it as I taught and as opportunity presented itself (finding new material or some new insight). I honed and polished it as I went. I often made modifications based on suggestions from students. One thing that I found to be particularly interesting was the fact that when I first started the course in the early seventies, most of the students had direct experience with the '60s. The lecture on the graphics of the counterculture was one of the most popular lectures. The students loved it! It was like a high school reunion for them, pure nostalgia. I didn't have to tell them anything about the '60s. It was their home turf. As the years went on apace, that all changed. The students now were not yet born in the '60s. Now one has to set the stage, one has to do a lot of explaining. And of course it is impossible, no matter what one shows or talks about, for the students of the beginning new millennium to understand emotionally how truly revolutionary and nation-transforming the '60s were. At the moment I am no longer teaching the course, but were I to do it again tomorrow, I would do it the same way. Based on continuous feedback, it worked well, had a positive impact on the students, and kept me continuously learning and examining my thoughts about what designers do and have done and, even more importantly, what I think they should be doing.

A Danziger Syllabus

Document One: Opening Discussion

1. Not a conventional academic course. Not scholarly. BEWARE! It is full of individual bias and opinion. It is essentially a designer talking to other designers in order to enhance their performance as designers. No practitioner is a good historian. His experience inevitably introduces biases, he cannot be objective. On the other hand, the way the historian perceives and deals with design history, often has little relevance for the practitioner. This course is not only biased but it is also very individual in that it is often anecdotal. I personally know many of the people who have played important roles in this history and I will probably make reference to personal experiences. Perhaps the course should not be called a History of Graphic Design but Lou Danziger's History of Graphic Design. In defense of my biased view you should know that I have played a small role in this history of design and I have sufficient reputation as a designer to reassure you that my views though not infallible, are not without value.

2. There will be exposure to a wealth of visual material. I will show you much more than is necessary to deal with the underlying ideas. It may be visual overload but I have acquired a great deal of material, much of it you will probably not ever see otherwise. (some of it has never been reproduced and much of it is from old sources which are very difficult to find) I have spent over twenty thousand hours working on this course and I want to share this visual feast.

3. I am hoping that this course will stimulate your interest in this rich subject. It is addictive. The more you know the more interesting it becomes. It is a history full of fascinating, idiosyncratic figures and it becomes an increasingly interesting subject when you find out more about them and their work. Knowledge of design history will not only make your work better but it will connect you to your work in ways that will make work the more meaningful and your life richer. Being a graphic designer is more than a 9-to-5 job!

4. It would be best to do this course with multiple-projectors and screens. It would show concurrence of movements and events and their various connections. This unfortunately is not possible. You will have to carry a lot in your head. We do the course in a linear fashion, i.e., Futurism then Dada. then Constructivism, etc. but in

truth these were all happening simultaneously and interactively. You will have to try to remember those connections. The more you read and engage this subject the more clear it becomes and the more it fascinates. Keep in mind that Europe is small, the pioneers traveled and contacted one another. They corresponded and read each other's journals. Marinetti traveled to Paris and Russia, El Lissitzky to Germany and Holland, van Doesburg to Germany, etc.

5. There are four main lines in Graphic Design History: (a.) Posters, (b.) Typography and Books, (c.) Printed Ephemera, and (d.) Advertising.

6. It is useful to know Art and Architecture history. Visual breakthroughs were often made by painters, typographic breakthroughs by poets, much of the philosophy of the modern movement from architects.

7. Participate, interrupt, ask questions, make observations.

8. Think about this course. Make connections to yourself and your work. The value of the course is in the connections you make. Using the course as a visual database is missing its true value.

Document Two: Course Outline

1. Intro: About the course. Why study the history? Tools and their effect.

2. Reaction to Industrialization: Gothic Revival-Arts and Crafts: Social role of design.

3. Reaction to Industrialization: Art Nouveau: Romanticism, anti historicism, natural and organic, the "artful life," expressive rather than descriptive.

4. The development of the large pictorial poster: The emergence of the designer.

5. French: Cheret, Lautrec etc. British: Beggarstaffs etc. Other: Europeans, American, Japanese, etc.

6. German Poster Masters: Bernhard, Hohlwein, etc. and their influence, Swiss, etc.

7. World War I Posters: Psychology of propaganda, basic themes.

8. Futurism: Rejection of the past, adulation of modernity, speed, the machine. The liberation of typography (type as expressive element).

9. Dada: Rejection of bourgeois values, incorporation of intuition and accident. The combined use of type and photo.

10. Russians: Suprematism and Constructivism: Malevich, pure form, (non-objective) spiritualism. El Lissitzky, development of most of the basic tenets of modernism, social purpose of design.

11. De Stijl: Purity, geometry, objectivity, universality. Spiritual. Idealistic.

12. Polish Constructivism: Amalgam of east and west, Cubism-Futurism-Constructivism, etc.

13. Bauhaus: The crucible, synthesis, dissemination.

14. Pioneers of the 1920s and 1930s: Tschichold, Schwitters etc, the refinement of modernism.

15. Pictorial 1920s and 1930s: Pictorial work (modernism and abstraction enters the visual vocabulary)

16. Dutch Pioneers: Werkmann, Schuitema, Zwart

17. Art deco, Cassandre: Decorative popularization of modernism.

18. Thirties: Part One and Two: Refinement and dispersion of modernism. Expatriates, comics etc.

19. World War II Posters and early 1940s: Emphasis on Rand, Beall, Thompson, etc.

20. Fifties: Part One and Two: Growing influence of American designers, the west coast etc.

21. Swiss and Polish Comparisons: The influence of cultural values.

22. Conceptual Advertising: Particularly the influence of Doyle Dane Bernbach.

23. Sixties: Part One and Two: Growth of international style (Swiss), poetic photography, etc. Growing skill and sophistication.

24. Psychedelics: The seeds of graphic design change. The end of reductivism. Increased interaction with process. A shift away from clear communication to a more ambiguous expressivity.

25. Japanese: Unique oriental cultural characteristics particularly the work of Tadanori Yokoo. Setting the stage for computer graphics—the link: Moscoso >Yokoo > Computer Graphics.

Document Three

Arts and Crafts and Art Nouveau
Augustus Welby Pugin
Joseph Paxton
John Ruskin
William Morris
Edward Bourne-Jones
Walter Crane
Arthur Mackmurdo
William Blake
Aubrey Beardsley
Charles Ricketts
Laurence Houseman
George de Feure
Hector Guimard
Alfons Mucha
Manuel Orazi
Victor Horta
George Lemman
Henry van de Velde
Charles Rennie
   Mackintosh
Francis Macdonald
Margaret Macdonald
Herbert MacNair
Talwin Morris
Jugendstil Magazine
Otto Eckmann
Thomas Theodore Heine
Peter Behrens
Walter Tiemann
Vienna Secession
Ver Sacrum (magazine)
Alfred Roller
Josef Auchentaler
Josef Hoffmann
Koloman Moser
Alfred Bohm
Otto Wagner

Jan Toorop
Gerrit Willem Dijsselhof
Carel Lion-Cachet
S. H. de Roos
Jan Bukowski
Edward Okun
J. C. Leyendecker
Will Bradley

Posters 1
Eduard Manet
Jules Cheret
Lucien LeFevre
Eugene Samuel Grasset
Henri Toulouse-Lautrec
Theo Alexandre Steinlen
Alfons Mucha
Jean de Paleologue (Pal)
Leonetto Cappiello
George de Feure
Manuel Orazi
Pierre Bonnard
Dudley Hardy
Beggarstaffs (James Pryde
   and William Nicholson)
John Hassel
Giovanni Mataloni
Adolpho Hohenstein
Leopoldo Metlicovitz
Marcello Dudovich
Henri Meunier
Privat-Livemont
Will Bradley
Edward Penfield
Louis Rhead
Maxfield Parrish
Will Carqueville
J. J.Gould, Jr.
J. C.Leyendecker

Ethel Reed
Alice Glenny
Robert Wildhack

Posters 2
Thomas Theodore Heine
Fritz Helmut Ehmcke
Lucien Bernhard
Jules Klinger
Carl Moos
Hans Rudi Erdt
Peter Behrens
Ludwig Hohlwein
Jules Gipkens
Paul Scheurich
Ernst Deutsch
Anne Koken
Grete Gross
Dore Monkmeyer-Corty
Paul Glass
Max Schwarzer
Louis Oppenheim
Hugo Franke
Carlo Egler
Ferdy Horrmeyer
Wilhelm Schnarrenberg
Adolf Uzarski
Curt Winters
Valentin Zietara
Robert Hardemeier
Emil Cardinaux
Walter Koch
Burkhard Mangold
Otto Baumberger
Ottokar Stafl
Michael Biro
Jensen Boglund

World War I
Alfred Leete
James Montgomery Flagg
Howard Chandler Christy
J. C. Leyendecker
Robert Baden Powell
Saville Lumley
Lucien Bernhard
Ludwig Hohlwein

Futurism
Fillipo Tomaso Marinetti
Umberto Boccioni
Giacomo Balla
Carlo Carra
Gino Severini
Luigi Russolo
Ardengo Soffici
Francesco Cangiullo
Guillaume Apollinaire
Angelo Rognoni
Gino Soggetti
Fortunato Depero
Tullio D'Albisola
Antonio Giulio Bragaglia

Dada
Caberet Voltaire
Hugo Ball
Emmy Hennings
Richard Hulsenbeck
Tristan Tzara
Marcel Janco
Hans Arp
Francis Picabia
Marcel Duchamp
Man Ray
Raoul Hausmann
John Heartfield

George Grosz
Hannah Hoch
Max Ernst
Johannes Baargeld
Johannes Baader
I. K. Bonset (van
   Doesburg)
Theo van Doesburg
Kurt Schwitters

Russians
Kasimir Malevich
El Lissitzky
(others in later lectures)

De Stijl
Piet Mondrian
Bart van der Leck
Theo van Doesburg
Vilmos Huszar
George Vantongerloo
J. J. P. Oud
Gerrit Reitveld

Bauhaus
Walter Gropius
Johannes Itten
Lyonel Feininger
Wassily Kandinsky
Gerhard Marcks
Paul Klee
Oskar Schlemmer
Herbert Bayer
Marcel Breuer
Joost Schmidt
Laszlo Moholy-Nagy
Josef Albers
Hannes Mayer
Ludwig Mies van der Rohe

Modernists
Alexander Rodchenko
Gustav Klucis
Stenberg Brothers
Liubov Popova
Vera Ermalov
Varvara Steponova
Olga Rozanova
Juryi Roshkov
Ilya Zdanevitch
Solomon Telingator
Ladislaw Sutnar
Karel Tiege
Lajos Kassak
Johannes Mohlzahn
Walter Dexel
Kurt Schwitters
John Heartfield
Jan Tschichold
Max Burchartz
Johannes Canis
Anton Stankowski

Polish Modernists
Tytus Czyzewski
Wladislaw Strzeminski
Henryk Berlewi
Mieczyslaw Szczuka
Teresa Zarnower
Kasimir Podsadecki
Henryk Stazewski

Katarzyna Kobro
Mieczyslaw Berman

Various / 1920s
Josef Binder
Otto Neurath (Isotype)
E. McKnight Kauffer
Jean Carlu
Alexy Brodovitch
Paul Colin
Charles Loupot
Otto Arpke
Fred Neumann
Curt Winters
Eduard Kasper
Wilhelm Deffke
Emil Pretorius
Ilse Schroeder
Karl Schulpig
Jupp Wiertz
Marcello Nizzoli
Erberto Carboni
George and David
   Stenberg
Otto Baumberger
Otto Morach
Niklaus Stoeklin

Dutch Pioneers
Hendrick Nicholas
   Werkmann
Piet Zwart
Paul Schuitema

Art Deco and Cassandre
Walter Kampmann
Sonja Delauney
Jean Carlu
Hans Schleger (zero)
Gustav Jensen
Eduardo Benito
A M Cassandre (Adolfe
   Mouron)

The Thirties
Joseph Binder
Ludwig Hohlwein
Sasha Stone
Laszlo Moholy-Nagy
Albert Fuss
Franz Siewert
Kurt Schwitters
George Trump
Max Burchartz
Herbert Bayer
Jan Tschichold
Anton Stankowski
Max Bill
Ernst Keller
Herbert Matter
Richard Lohse
Gustav Klucis
Solomon Telingator
Ladislaw Sutnar
Zdenek Rossman
Karel Tiege
Munjei Satomi
Hiromu Hara
Fortunato Depero
Erberto Carboni
Bruno Munari

Xanti Schawinski
Leo Lionni
Eduardo Perisco
Luigi Veronesi
Giovanni Pintori
Tadeusz Trepkowski
E. McKnight Kauffer
Tom Purvis
Austin Cooper
Dick Elffers
H. N. Werkman
Piet Zwart
G. Kiljan
Henny Cahn
Willem Sandberg
Jean Carlu
Charles Loupot
Paul Colin
John Heartfield
Lucien Bernhard
Alexy Brodovitch
Gyorgy Kepes
Herbert Bayer
Herbert Matter
Will Burtin
Otis Shepard
Lester Beall
Paul Rand

World War II / 1940s
Abram Games
Ben Shahn
Charles Coiner
Howard Willard
Matthew Liebowitz
Bradbury Thompson
Alvin Lustig
Raymond Savignac
Henryk Tomaszewski
Studio Boggeri
Max Huber
Albe Steiner
Walter Ballmer
Enzo Bonini
Ettore Sottsas
Carlo Vivarelli
Giovanni Pintori
Kurt Wirth

The Fifties
Saul Bass
Leo Lionni
Gene Federico
Armin Hofmann
Otl Aicher
Milton Glaser
George Tscherney
Henry Wolf
Andre Francois
Herbert Leupin
Josef Müller-Brockmann
Aldo Calabrese
Franco Grignani
Willem Sandberg

Swiss and Polish
Hans Neuberg
Karl Gerstner
Siegfried Odermatt
Tadeusz Trepkowski
Jan Lenica

Roman Cieslewicz
Waldemar Swierzy
Wojiech Fangor
Henryk Tomaszewski
Josef Mroszczak
Wiktor Gorka
Maciej Urbaniec

Conceptual Advertising
Doyle,Dane,Bernbach
   Agency
Bill Bernbach
Helmut Krone
Julian Koenig
William Taubin
Len Sirowitz
Phyllis Robinson
Mary Welles
Robert Gage
Bert Stern
Ogilvy, Benson, Mather
   Agency
Arnold Varga
Roy Kuhlman
Young and Rubicam
   Agency
Robert Wheeler
Carl Ally Agency
Papert, Koenig and Lois
   Agency
George Lois

The Sixties
Seymour Chwast
Milton Glaser
Robert Brownjohn
Ivan Chermayeff
Tom Geismar
John Massey
Tomoko Miho
Herb Lubalin
Bob Gill
Pino Tovaglia
Bruno Munari
Ettore Sottsas
Franco Grignani
Massimo Vignelli
Hans Hillman
Heinz Edelman

Psychedelics
Peter Max
Wes Wilson
Stanley Mouse
Alton Kelly
Victor Moscoso
Rick Griffen
Robert Fried

Japanese
Yoshio Hayakawa
Yusaku Kamekura
Kasumasa Nagai
Shigeo Fukuda
Ikko Tanaka
Makato Wada
Tsunehisa Kimura
Gan Hosaya
Tadanori Yokoo

Index

Books from Allworth Press

Graphic Design Time Line *by Steven Heller* (softcover, 6³/₄ × 9⁷/₈, 272 pages, $19.95)

Text on Type: Critical Writings on Typography
edited by Steven Heller and Philip B. Meggs (softcover, 6³/₄ × 9⁷/₈, 288 pages, $19.95)

Graphic Design and Reading: Explorations of an Uneasy Relationship
edited by Gunnar Swanson (softcover, 6³/₄ × 9⁷/₈, 240 pages, $19.95)

Design Literacy (continued): Understanding Graphic Design
by Steven Heller (softcover, 6³/₄ × 9⁷/₈, 296 pages, $19.95)

Design Literacy: Understanding Graphic Design
by Steven Heller and Karen Pomeroy (softcover, 6³/₄ × 9⁷/₈, 288 pages, $19.95)

Design Culture:An Anthology of Writing from the AIGA Journal of Graphic Design
edited by Steven Heller and Marie Finamore (softcover, 6¹/₂ × 10, 320 pages, $19.95)

Looking Closer 3: Classic Writings on Graphic Design
edited by Michael Bierut, Jessica Helfand, Steven Heller, and Rick Poynor
(softcover, 6³/₄ × 9⁷/₈, 304 pages, $18.95)

Looking Closer 2: Critical Writings on Graphic Design
edited by Michael Bierut, William Drenttel, Steven Heller, and DK Holland
(softcover, 6³/₄ × 9⁷/₈, 288 pages, $18.95)

Looking Closer: Critical Writings on Graphic Design
edited by Michael Bierut, William Drenttel, Steven Heller, and DK Holland
(softcover, 6¹/₂ × 10, 256 pages, $18.95)

Design Dialogues *by Steven Heller and Elinor Pettit* (softcover, 6¹/₂ × 10, 272 pages, $18.95)

The Swastika: Symbol Beyond Redemption?
by Steven Heller (hardcover, 6³/₄ × 9⁷/₈, 176 pages, $21.95)

Sex Appeal: The Art of Allure in Graphic and Advertising Design
by Steven Heller (softcover, 6³/₄ × 9⁷/₈, 288 pages, $18.95)

AIGA Professional Practices in Graphic Design
The American Institute of Graphic Arts, edited by Tad Crawford
(softcover, 6³/₄ × 9⁷/₈, 320 pages, $24.95)

Business and Legal Forms for Graphic Designers
by Tad Crawford and Eva Doman Bruck
(softcover, 8¹/₂ × 11, 240 pages, includes CD-ROM, $24.95)